EGYPT REVISITED

This painting from the tomb of Ramses 111 (1200 BC) shows that the Egyptians saw themselves as Blacks, and painted themselves as such without possible confusion with the Indo-Europeans [Caucasoids] or the Semites. It is a representation of the races in their most minute differences, which insures the accuracy of the colors. Throughout their entire history, the Egyptians never entertained the fantasy of portraying themselves by types B or D.

A) The Egyptian seen by himself, black type
B) The "Indo-European"
C) The other Blacks in Africa
D) The Semite

(From K.R. Lepsius: Denkmaler aus Aegypten und Aethiopien, Erganzungsband, plate 48)

EGYPT REVISITED

JOURNAL OF AFRICAN CIVILIZATIONS

Edited by

Ivan Van Sertima

ISBN: 9780878559701

Cover design by Jacqueline Patten-Van Sertima

Contents

ACKNOWLEDGEMENTS

I would like to thank the following individuals and publishers for illustrations, translations, donations and reprint permissions.

1. The Unesco Press, for permission to reprint "Origin of the Ancient Egyptians" by Cheikh Anta Diop, which appeared as Chapter 1 in Vol 2 of General History of Africa, 1981.

2. The Institute of Race Relations in London for permission to reprint Basil Davidson's review "The Ancient World and Africa: Whose Roots?" published in Race and Class, 29, No. 2 (1987)

3. The Archeological Institute of America for permission to reprint "The Lost Pharoahs of Nibia" by Bruce Williams, which appeared in Archeology Magazine, Vol. 33, No. 5, 1980.

4. The University Press and Mr Phaon Goldman (Tarharka) for an excerpt from his book Black Manhood: The Building of Civilization by the Black Man of the Nile (1979) which appears in this book as "The Nubian Renaissance".

5. Ms. Sylvia Bakos for the drawing of the Egyptian hieroglyphs in Diop's essay.

6. Elizabeth Clement and Irene D'Almeida, for their excellent translation of the selected sections of Theophile Obenga's manuscript.

7. James Lucas of Washington and William Coston of Philadelphia for their generous donations.

Ivan Van Sertima
Editor and Publisher
Journal of African Civilizations

Editor's note to the Librarians and Annual Subscribers:
While this issue incorporates five essays published earlier in a 1982 Journal issue titled *Egypt Revisited* (Vol 4, No. 2) it is to be regarded as a new work. This new edition—Vol 10 in the series of works published by the journal—offers more than 300 pages of essays and photographs not included in the 1982 volume bearing that title.

RACE AND ORIGIN OF THE EGYPTIANS

Map of KMT (ANCIENT EGYPT)

RACE AND ORIGIN OF THE EGYPTIANS

Introduced by Ivan Van Sertima

Egypt has created the greatest and most enduring of all ancient civilizations. Its remarkable achievements in the arts and sciences, its influence upon the philosophy of both Europe and Asia, is seldom denied. Few studies, however, admit the significant, indeed predominant, role of Africans in the building of this civilization. Migrants and invaders from the north and east, who made very little real impact upon the classical culture of the Egyptian until late in the day, are given all the credit for this most illustrious chapter in the history of civilization. This book and its successor (to be published in the summer of 1990) are designed to restore Egypt to the fountainhead of African civilization, even as Greece has been placed at the fountainhead of European civilization studies.

The most persuasive arguments marshalled to date in favor of the African claim to Egyptian civilization are those made by Africa's leading cultural historian, the late Cheikh Anta Diop. I shall try to summarize a few of his arguments briefly and lucidly in the preface to this first section.

I take this opportunity also to make note a of a few he had not mentioned since he was not aware of these when he spoke to the Unesco conference in Cairo in 1974. Ta-Seti, for example, the pharaonic dynasty in Nubia that preceded the first Egyptian dynasty by 200 years, had already been discovered by American archeologists but not yet announced. Diop was later to speak of this as "the missing link". Tentative work had been done on the domestication of plants in Sudanic Africa, indicating that cultivated plants from that agricultural complex had moved up north into Egypt with the massive migration of Africans during the pre-dynastic and early dynastic era. The bottle-gourd, the tamarind fruit, the watermelon, cultivated Sudanic cotton and the oil-palm fruit. Not a single comparable cultigen from the Mediterranean or Asia had entered early Egypt, which in itself should suggest that no influence of cultural consequence had accompanied the minor trickle of nomadic tribes from the north or east.

It is important to understand from the outset that ancient Egypt was not a sudden and miraculous flower of the African genius. It was not an oasis. It was not an isolate. As we have shown in previous journals, the fragmentation and devastation of Africa over the centuries, our belated knowledge of other African centers of sophisticated culture and technology, have led to the assumption that, if indeed it were African, it were a solitary rose among the thorns. Egypt was the node and center of a vast web linking the strands of Africa's main cultures and languages. The light that crystallized at the center of this early world had been energized by the cultural electricity streaming from the heartland of Africa.

The African claim to Egyptian civilization rests upon a vast body of evidence. Some are cultural (ritual practices of the ancient Egyptian can be traced to the African—his totemism, circumcision, form of the divine kingship are distinct from that of the Asian) some are linguistic (Diop demonstrated convincingly at the Unesco debate in 1974 that the Egyptian belonged beyond question to the family of African languages) some indicate a shared techno-complex (the forerunners of mummification and pyramid-building are found south of Egypt in pre-dynastic times). Most important, however, are the physical evidences. The Greeks saw the Egyptians and described them. Herodotus, after a long sojourn in Egypt, described the typical Egyptian circa 500 B.C. as dark-skinned with wooly hair. Studies in ancient Egyptian crania by Falkenburger tried to prove that only one-third of the Egyptians were of the classical negroid type and that most of them were Euro-African, or, to use the term invented by Sergi "the brown Mediterannean race" Diop showed that, using the same craniometric measurements, many of the unmixed races of inner Africa would fall into the false "Mediterranean" classification. Chatterjee and Kumar in a 1965 study (cited by Chandler in this issue) analyzed crania from pre-dynastic Egypt and compared them with skulls of the Old Kingdom as well as the much later Middle Kingdom (12th and 13th dynasties) and found that all these skulls in respect to "long head, broad face, low orbit and broad nasal aperture have the same characteristic features of the Negroid type".

Certain peoples of West and Central Africa were said by early craniologists to be the most typically "Negroid" of the African stocks or the Black variety of mankind and when features peculiar to these "true" African types were not present in some Africans north of the Sahara, it was deemed to be due to intermixture with "Caucasoid" types or to the fact that such people were dark-skinned Caucasoids. The early Europeans who actually saw the Egyptians did not share in these follies but sometime after the first quarter of the 19th century there was a systematic attempt to move Egypt out of Black Africa. A brown race was created that was said to be indigenous to Africa and Asia, that was European in origin and in no way affiliated with other sub-Saharan or "black" peoples.

A graduate student in anthropology at Rutgers University, Ms. Dana Reynolds, has done an excellent study of this problem in a paper entitled "The Myth of the Mediterranean Race", which I hope to publish in the next issue on Egypt. I quote from her conclusions:

"The new interpretations in regard to biological evolution on the Nile dispel the myth of the "Mediterranean" as a type affiliated with Europeans. They are in accord with the theory of a direct evolution of the ancient Egyptian and other African "Mediterraneans" spoken of by Sergi, Krogman and Coon, from the robust Mechtoid types who possessed the prognathism and broad-nosed traits characteristically assigned to the Negroid type of humanity. These conclusions are based mainly on two developments that have taken place in study of biological and cultural evolution along the Nile.

"First, the detailed analyses of physical anthropologists including Greene, Carlson, Armelagos, Ucko and others, who have done work on discrete discontinuous cranial and dental traits, have pointed to a remarkable homogeneity of the Egyptian population until the period directly preceding the Ptolemies, as well as a noticeable connection with the more robust Nilotes further south from earlier and contemporary periods. Secondly, the new discoveries of archaeologists increasingly confirm the long suggested theory that the Egyptian cultural elements emerged from and were directly linked to cultures of the desert areas directly west, south and east of Egypt.

"The so-called "Mediterranean" type, depending on where and when he lived, often retained the traits of the Mechtoid, e.g. the Natufian, Tasian, Badarian, man of the early El Obeid culture and ancient Mohenjo Daro "Mediterraneans". The incidence and degree of the so-called Negroid features varied then, just as they do now among modern Ethiopians and Nilotes. But the perceived lack of "Negroid" attributes does not nullify the fact that the type designated "Mediterranean", "brown Mediterranean" or "Eurafrican", since the time of Sergi, was in no way allied to, nor descended from, the type now designated "Europoid" or "Caucasoid".

"On the contrary, it is today incontestable that Mediterranean man—the first farmers of Europe, the Middle East and Southwest Asia—were direct genetical and cultural descendants of Mechta-man—the Upper Paleolithic hunter of the Nile. We can say with equal certainty that the latter's lesser modified descendants further to the south and west, who gave rise to the Khartoum variant and Saharan-Sudanese traditions between the 9th and 4th millenium B.C. were those that were to make up the greater part of what are considered to be the Negro populations of Africa."

* * *

In his review of Martin Bernal's Black Athena, the famous historian Basil Davidson outlines for us the racist climate in which Egypt was eventually removed from consideration as an African civilization, even as a physical part of Africa. "The land of ancient Egypt appears to have detached itself from the delta of the Nile, some five and a half thousand years ago, and sailed off into the Mediterranean on a course veering broadly towards the coast of Syria. And there it apparently remained, floating somewhere in the seas of the Levant . . ."

The Davidson review, although largely repeating the thesis of Bernal, showing how the intellectual climate of nineteenth century Europe accounted for the de-Africanizing of Pharaonic Egypt, is important reading for laymen and students. Martin Bernal is a scholar's scholar, virtually inaccessible to the general run of American college students. His Black Athena, to quote Basil Davidson, is "a profoundly liberating work because it sheers through the murk of racism" and is "a major attempt to help old history back upon its feet again" but it needs the lucid, vivid touch of a popular writer to bring its major insights into general circulation.

It must be pointed out, however, contrary to popular opinion, that there is not always a popular way in which a serious scholar can bring about a fundamental re-thinking in his field. He is turning his guns, after all, against a formidable army of intellectual giants (from Hegel down to Trevor-Roper) men with impeccable qualifications, whose respected racist follies still beshadow our narrow world. Fond thus to think he may pierce through the battlement of centuries with a quick spectacular charge and fire of rhetoric. As he himself has so brilliantly pointed out, any attempt to summarize "the complications of this vast and extraordinarily ramified theme can best be described by the Chinese expression "looking at flowers from horseback".

That the ancient Egyptians were African is a belief which was not denied in Europe until about 1830. The Greeks had made this clear and they had also emphasized the primacy of Egyptian civilization. Greek heritage, of course, was also Indo-European and Bernal makes full allowance for this in his revision of what he calls "The Ancient Model". That model, erected by the Greeks, illuminates the enormous debt European civilization owes to African elements. There is no question about this in any objective reading of the ancient documents. But racist scholarship in the late eighteenth century started a shift away from the way the early Greeks saw themselves, a shift that was completed in the early nineteenth century. What Bernal has done is to analyze the shifts in the emotional and intellectual climate in Europe that made scholars reject the earlier and more authentic vision of Greek origins (the Ancient Model) in favor of a completely Caucasoid base for this civilization (the Aryan Model).

This shift in intellectual climate, which Basil Davidson calls "the new racism" belongs to the rise of modern European imperialism. It is, according to him, "specifically and even frantically an anti-black racism, which went together with and was consistently nourished by that imperialism".

* * *

James Brunson, in his study of the symbolic use of black and red and yellow in Egyptian paintings of humans clears up some of the confusions which led to the myth of the Egyptian being a "red race". Red is generally used in the portrayal of Egyptian men on wall and papyrus paintings but this is used in a symbolic context. Red ochre, an oxide of iron, was mixed with a vegetable gum binder to create this color. It was extracted from iron ore called hematite. When Africans entered Europe during the Aurignacian phase of that continent (circa 40,000 B.C.) they initiated burial rituals in which the dead were sprinkled or painted with red ochre. Brunson cites Soviet historians to show that the Africans carried this habit even into the East where a Neolithic painting indicates the use of red ochre on the men (as a symbol of vitality) and yellow ochre on the women (as a symbol of fertility).

Brunson's brief note on the use of red and yellow symbolism in art is followed by a detailed discussion of the use of Black as the color of divinity. Black is also used to depict the non-Egyptian Black (like the Nubian) who, though ethnically related, does not always fall under the same artistic canon (see the Nubian princes in the Tomb of Huy). This has led to great confusion, whereas, as Brunson points out, the red-ochre artistic convention was simply a symbol of male vitality, transmitted from African antiquity to the painters of the Egyptian male.

Black, however, is used for both the Nubian and the Egyptian when other races are in the same painting and literal distinctions between the skin-color of the diverse groupings need to be drawn. This is best demonstrated by Diop in his reference to the painting in the tomb of Ramses 111 (1200 B.C.) when the Egyptian (at A) is painted in his natural Black hue as is the Nubian (at C) to distinguish them from the pale-hued Indo-European (at B) and the Semite (at D). *See frontispiece*.

Figure 1
Ancient Egyptian Wigs

Figure 2
Ancient Egyptian Wigs

These are from a small selection of wigs with Africoid hair used by royal and religious personages in ancient Egypt. These were photographed by Jacqueline Van Sertima in the Cairo Museum in August, 1988.

ORIGIN OF THE ANCIENT EGYPTIANS

by Cheikh Anta Diop

The general acceptance, as a sequel to the work of Professor Leakey, of the hypothesis of mankind's monogenetic and African origin, makes it possible to pose the question of the peopling of Egypt and even of the world in completely new terms. More than 150,000 years ago, beings morphologically identical with the man of today were living in the region of the great lakes at the sources of the Nile and nowhere else. This notion, and others which it would take too long to recapitulate here, form the substance of the last report presented by the late Dr. Leakey at the Seventh Pan-African Congress of Pre-History in Addis Ababa in 1971.[1] It means that the whole human race had its origin, just as the ancients had guessed, at the foot of the Mountains of the Moon. Against all expectations and in defiance of recent hypotheses it was from *this place* that men moved out to people the rest of the world. From this two facts of capital importance result:

(*a*) of necessity the earliest men were ethnically homogeneous and negroid. Gloger's law, which would also appear to be applicable to human beings, lays it down that warm-blooded animals evolving in a warm humid climate will secrete a black pigment (eumelanin).[2] Hence if mankind originated in the tropics around the latitude of the great lakes, he was bound to have brown pigmentation from the start and it was by differentiation in other climates that the original stock later split into different races;

(*b*) there were only two routes available by which these early men could move out to people the other continents, namely, the Sahara and the Nile valley. It is the latter region which will be discussed here.

From the Upper Palaeolithic to the dynastic epoch, the whole of the river's basin was taken over progressively by these negroid peoples.

Evidence of Physical Anthropology on the Race of the Ancient Egyptians

It might have been thought that, working on physiological evidence, the findings of the anthropologists would dissipate all doubts by providing reliable and definitive truths. This is by no means so: the arbitrary nature of the criteria used, to go no farther, as well as abolishing any notion of a conclusion acceptable without qualification, introduces so much scientific hair-splitting that there are times when one wonders whether the solution of the problem would not have been nearer if we had not had the ill luck to approach it from this angle.

Nevertheless, although the conclusions of these anthropological studies stop short of the full truth, they still speak unanimously of the existence of a negro race from the most distant ages of prehistory down to the dynastic period. It is not possible in this paper to cite all these conclusions: they will be found summarized in Chapter X of Dr. Emile Massoulard's *Histoire et protohistoire d'Egypte* (Institut d'Ethnologie, Paris, 1949). We shall quote selected items only.

> Miss Fawcett considers that the Negadah skulls form a sufficiently homogeneous collection to warrant the assumption of a Negadah race. In the total height of the skull, the auricular height, the length and breadth of the face, nasal length, cephalic index and facial index this race would seem to approximate to the negro; in nasal breadth, height of orbit, length of palate and nasal index it would seem closer to the Germanic peoples; accordingly the Pre-Dynastic Negadians are likely to have resembled the negroes in certain of their characterics and the white races in others. (pp. 402-3)

It is worth noting that the nasal indices of Ethiopians and Dravidians would seem to approximate them to the Germanic peoples, though both are black races.

These measurements, which would leave an open choice between the two extremes represented by the negro and the Germanic races, give an idea of the elasticity of the criteria employed. A sample follows:

> An attempt was made by Thomson and Randall MacIver to determine more precisely the importance of the negroid element in the series of skulls from El'Amrah, Abydos and Hou. They divided them into three groups: (1) negroid skulls (those with a facial index below 54 and a nasal index above 50, i.e. short broad face and broad nose); (2) non-negroid skulls (facial index above 54 and nasal index below 50, long narrow face and narrow nose); (3) intermediate skulls (assignable to one of the two previous groups on the basis of either the facial index or on the evidence of the nasal index, plus individuals marginal to either group). The proportion of negroids would seem to have been 24% of men and 19% of women in the early Pre-Dynastic and 25% and 28% respectively in the late Pre-Dynastic.
>
> Kieth has disputed the value of the criterion selected by Thomson and Randall MacIver to distinguish the negroid from the non-negroid skulls. His opinion is that if the same criteria were applied to the study of any series of contemporary English skulls, the sample would be found to contain approximately 30% of negroid types. (pp. 420-1)

The converse of Kieth's proposition could also be asserted, namely, that if the criterion were applied to the 140 million negroes now alive in black Africa a minimum of 100 million negroes woudl emerge whitewashed.

It may also be remarked that the distinction between negroid, non-negroid and intermediary is unclear: the fact is that 'non-negroid' does not mean of white race and 'intermediary' still less so.

'Falkenburger reopened the anthropological study of the Egyptian population in a recent work in which he discusses 1,787 male skulls varying in date from the old Pre-Dynastic to our own day. He distinguishes four main groups' (p. 421). The sorting of the predynastic skulls into these four groups gives the following results for the whole predynastic period: '36% negroid, 33% Mediterranean, 11% Cro-Magnoid and 20% of individuals not falling in any of these groups but approximating either to the Cro-Magnoid or to the negroid'. The proportion of negroids is definitely higher than that suggested by Thomson and Randall MacIver, though Kieth considers the latter too high.

'Do Falkenburger's figures reflect the reality? It is not our task to decide this. If they are accurate, the Pre-Dynastic population far from representing a pure bred race, as Elliot-Smith has said, comprised at least three distinct racial elements—over a third of negroids, a third of Mediterraneans, a tenth of Cro-Magnoids and a fifth of individuals crossbred—to varying degrees' (p. 422).

The point about all these conclusions is that despite their discrepancies the degree to which they converge proves that the basis of the Egyptian population was negro in the Pre-Dynastic epoch. Thus they are all incompatible with the theories that the negro element only infiltrated into Egypt at a late stage. Far otherwise, the facts prove that it was preponderant from the beginning to the end of Egyptian history, particularly when we note once more that 'Mediterranean' is not a synonym for 'white', Elliot-Smith's 'brown or Mediterranean race being nearer the mark'. 'Elliot-Smith classes these Proto-Egyptians as a branch of what he calls the brown race, which is the same as Sergi's "Mediterranean or Eurafrican race".' The term 'brown' in this context refers to skin colour and is simply a euphemism for negro.[3] it is thus clear that it was the whole of the Egyptian population which was negro, barring an infiltration of white nomads in the proto-dynastic epoch.

In Petrie's study of the Egyptian race we are introduced to a possible classification element in great abundance which cannot fail to surprise the reader.

> Petrie . . . published a study of the races of Egypt in the Pre-Dynastic and Proto-Dynastic periods working only on portrayals of them. Apart from the steatopygian race, he distinguishes six separate types: an aquiline type representative of a white-skinned Libyan race; a 'plaited-beard' type belonging to an invading race coming perhaps from the shores of the Red Sea; a 'sharp-nosed' type almost certainly from the Arabian Desert; a 'tilted nose' type from Middle Egypt; a 'jutting beard' type from Lower Egypt; and a 'narrow-nosed' type from Upper Egypt. Going on the images, there would thus have been seven different racial types in Egypt during the epochs we are considering. In the pages which follow we shall see that study of the skeletons seems to provide little authority for these conclusions. (p. 391)

The above mode of classification gives an idea of the arbitrary nature of the criteria used to define the Egyptian races. Be that as it may, it is clear that anthropology is far from having established the existence of a white Egyptian race and would indeed tend rather to suggest the opposite.

Nevertheless, in current textbooks the question is suppressed: in most cases it is simply and flatly asserted that the Egyptians were white and the honest layman is left with the impression that any such assertion must necessarily have a prior basis of solid research. But there is no such basis, as this chapter has shown. And so generation after generation has been misled. Many authorities skate around the difficulty today by speaking of red-skinned and black-skinned whites without their sense of common logic being in the least upset. 'The Greeks call Africa "Libya", a misnomer ab initio since Africa contains many other peoples besides the so-called Libyans, who belong among the whites of the northern or Mediterranean periphery and hence are many steps removed from the brown (or red) skinned whites (Egyptians).'[4]

In a textbook intended for the middle secondary school we find the following sentence: 'A Black is distinguished less by the colour of his skin (for there are black-skinned "whites") than by his features: thick lips, flattened nose . . .'[5] It is only through these twistings of the basic definitions that it has been possible to bleach the Egyptian race.

It is worthwhile calling to mind the exaggerations of the theorists of anthroposociology in the last century and the beginnings of the present one whose minute physiognomical analyses discovered racial stratifications even in Europe, and particularly in France, when in fact there was really a single and by now practically homogeneous people.[6] Today Occidentals who value their national cohesion are careful to avoid examining their own societies on so divisive a hypothesis, but continue unthinkingly to apply the old methods to the non-European societies.

Human Images of the Protohistoric Period: Their Anthropological Value

The study of human images made by Flinders Petrie on another plane shows that the ethnic type was black: according to Petrie these people were the Anu whose name, known to us since the protohistoric epoch, is always 'written' with three pillars on the few inscriptions extant from the end of the fourth millennium before our era. The natives of the country are always represented with unmistakable chiefly emblems for which one looks in vain among the infrequent portrayals of other races, who are all shown as servile foreign elements having reached the valley by infiltration (cf. Tera Neter[7] and the Scorpion king whom Petrie groups together: 'The Scorpion King . . . belonged to the preceding race of Anu, moreover he worshipped Min and Set.').[8]

As we shall see later Min, like the chief gods of Egypt, was called by the tradition of Egypt itself 'the great negro'.

After a glance at the various foreign types of humanity who disputed the valley with the indigenous blacks, Petrie describes the latter, the Anu, in the following terms:

> Besides these types, belonging to the North and East, there is the aboriginal race of the Anu, or Annu, people (written with three pillars) who became a part of the historic inhabitants. The subject ramifies too doubtfully if we include all single pillar names, but looking for the Annu written, with the three pillars, we find that they occupied southern Egypt and Nubia, and the name is also applied in Sinai and Libya. As to the southern Egyptians, we have the most essential document, one portrait of a chief, Tera Neter, roughly modelled in relief in green glazed faïence, found in the early temple at Abydos. Preceding his name, his address is given on this earliest of visiting cards, 'Palace of the Anu in Hemen city, Tera Neter'. Hemen was the name of the god of Tuphium. Erment, opposite to it, was the palace of Annu of the south, Annu Menti. The next place in the south is Aunti (Gefeleyn), and beyond that Aunyt-Seni (Esneh).[9]
>
> Amélineau lists in geographical order the fortified towns built along the length of the Nile valley by the Annu blacks.

 }=Ant=(Esneh)

 }=An =the southern 'On' (now Hermonthis)

 }=Denderah, the traditional birthplace of Isis

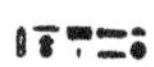 }=A town also called 'On' in the name of Tinis

 }=The town called the northern 'On', the renowned city of Heliopolis

The common ancestor of the Annu settled along the Nile was Ani or An, a name determined by the word (khet) and which, dating from the earliest versions of the 'Book of the Dead' onwards, is given to the god Osiris.

The wife of  the god Ani is the goddess Anet 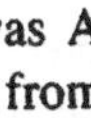 who is also his sister, just as Isis is the sister of Osiris.

The identity of the god An with Osiris has been demonstrated by Pleyte;[10] we should, indeed, recall that Osiris is also surnamed by (?) the Anou: 'Osiris Ani'. The god Anu is represented alternatively by the symbol  and the symbol . Are the Aunak tribes now inhabiting the upper Nile related to the ancient Annu? Future research will provide the answer to this question.

Petrie thinks it possible to make a distinction between the predynastic people represented by Tera Neter and the Scorpion King (who is himself a Pharaoh even at that date as his head-dress shows) and a dynastic people worshipping the falcon and probably represented by the Pharaohs Narmer,[11] Khasekhem, Sanekhei and Zoser.[12] By reference to the faces reproduced in the figure it is easily perceived that there is no ethnic difference between the two lots, and both belong to the black race.

The mural in tomb SD 63 (Sequence Date 63) of Hierakonpolis shows the native-born blacks subjugating the foreign intruders into the valley if we accept Petrie's interpretation: 'Below is the black ship at Hierakonpolis belonging to the black men who are shown as conquering the red men.'[13]

The Gebel-el-Arak knife haft shows similar battle scenes: 'There are also combats of black men overcoming red men.'[13] However, the archaeological value of this object, which was not found *in situ* but in the possession of a merchant, is less than that of the preceding items.

What the above shows is that the images of men of the protohistoric and even of the dynastic period in no way square with the idea of the Egyptian race popular with Western anthropologists. Wherever the autochthonous racial type is represented with any degree of clearness, it is evidently negroid. Nowhere are the Indo-European and Semitic elements shown even as ordinary freemen serving a local chief, but invariably as conquered foreigners. The rare portrayals found are always shown with the distinctive marks of captitivy, hands tied behind the back or strained over the shoulders.[14] A protodynastic figurine represents an Indo-European prisoner with a long plait on his knees, with his hands bound tight to his body. The characteristics of the object itself show that it was intended as the foot of a piece of furniture and represented a conquered race.[15] Often the portrayal is deliberately grotesque as with other proto-dynastic figures showing individuals with their hair plaited in what Petrie calls pigtails.[16]

In the tomb of king Ka (first dynasty) at Abydos, Petrie found a plaque showing an Indo-European captive in chains with his hands behind his back.[17] Elliot-Smith considers that the individual represented is a Semite. The dynastic epoch has also yielded the documents illustrated in Pls 1.9 and 1.14 showing Indo-European and Semitic prisoners. In contrast, the typically negroid features of the Pharaohs (Narmer, first dynasty, the actual founder of the Pharaonic line; Zoser, third dynasty, by whose time all the technological elements of the Egyptian civilization were already in evidence; Cheops, the builder of the Great Pyramid, a Cameroon type;[18] Menthuhotep, founder of the eleventh dynasty, very black;[19] Sesostris I; Queen Ahmosis Nefertari; and Amenhophis I) show that all classes of Egyptian society belong to the same black race.

Pls 1.15 and 1.16, showing the Indo-European and Semitic types, have been included deliberately to contrast them with the quite dissimilar physiognomies of the black Pharaohs and to demonstrate clearly that there is no trace of either of the first two types in the whole line of Pharaohs if we exclude the foreign Libyan and Ptolemaic dynasties.

It is usual to contrast the negresses on the tomb of Horemheb with the Egyptian type also shown. This contrast is surely a false one: it is social and not ethnic and there is as much difference between an aristocratic Senegalese lady from Dakar and those antique African peasant women with their horny hands and splay feet as between the latter and an Egyptian lady of the cities of antiquity.

There are two variants of the black race: (a) straight-haired, represented in Asia by the Dravidians and in Africa by the Nubians and the Tubbou or Tedda, all three with jet-black skins; (b) the kinky-haired blacks of the Equatorial regions. Both types entered into the composition of the Egyptian population.

Melanin Dosage Test

In practice it is possible to determine directly the skin colour and hence the ethnic affiliations of the ancient Egyptians by microscopic analysis in the laboratory; I doubt if the sagacity of the researchers who have studied the question has overlooked the possibility.

Melanin (eumelanin), the chemical body responsible for skin pigmentation, is, broadly speaking, insoluble and is preserved for millions of years in the skins of fossil animals.[20] There is thus all the more reason for it to be readily recoverable in the skins of Egyptian mummies, despite a tenacious legend that the skin of mummies, tainted by the embalming material, is no longer susceptible of any analysis.[21] Although the epidermis is the main site of the melanin, the melanocytes penetrating the derm at the boundary between it and the epidermus, even where the latter has mostly been destroyed by the embalming materials, show a melanin level which is non-existent in the white-skinned races. The samples I myself analysed were taken in the physical anthropology laboratory of the Musée de l'Homme in Paris off the mummies from the Marietta excavations in Egypt.[22] The same method is perfectly suitable for use on the royal mummies of Thutmoses III, Seti I and Ramses II in the Cairo Museum, which are in an excellent state of preservation. For two years past I have been vainly begging the curator of the Cairo Museum for similar samples to analyse. No more than a few square millimetres of skin would be required to mount a specimen, the preparations being a few um in thickness and lightened with ethyl benzoate. They can be studied by natural light or with ultra-violet lighting which renders the melanin grains fluorescent.

Either way let us simply say that the evaluation of melanin level by microscopic examination is a laboratory method which enables us to classify the ancient Egyptians unquestionably among the black races.

Osteological Measurements

Among the criteria accepted in physical anthropology for classifying races, the osteological measurements are perhaps the least misleading (in contrast to craniometry) for distinguishing a black man from a white man. By this criterion, also, the Egyptians belong among the black races. This study was made by the distinguished German savant Lepsius at the end of the nineteenth century and his conclusions remain valid: subsequent methodological progress in the domain of physical anthropology in no way undermines what is called the 'Lepsius canon' which, in round figures, gives the bodily proportions of the ideal Egyptian, short-armed and of negroid or negrito physical type.[23]

Blood-Groups

It is a notable fact that even today Egyptians, particularly in Upper Egypt, belong to the same Group B as the populations of western Africa on the Atlantic seaboard and not the A2 Group characteristic of the white race prior to any crossbreeding.[24] It would be interesting to study the extent of Group A2 distribution in Egyptian mummies, which present-day techniques make possible.

The Egyptian Race According to the Classical Authors of Antiquity

To the Greek and Latin writers contemporary with the ancient Egyptians the latter's physical classification posed no problems: the Egyptians were negroes, thick-lipped, kinky-haired and thin-legged; the unanimity of the authors' evidence on a physical fact as salient as a people's race will be difficult to minimize or pass over. Some of the following evidence drives home the point.

(*a*) Herodotus, 'the father of history', –480(?) to –425. With regard to the origins of the Colchians[25] he writes:

> It is in fact manifest that the Colchidians are Egyptian by race . . . several Egyptians told me that in their opinion the Colchidians were descended from soldiers of Sesostris. I had conjectured as much myself from two pointers, firstly because they have black skins and kinky hair (to tell the truth this proves nothing for other peoples have them too) and secondly and more reliably for the reason that alone among mankind the Egyptians and the Ethiopians have practised circumcision since time immemorial. The Phoenicians and Syrians of Palestine themselves admit that they learnt the practice from the Egyptians while the Syrians in the river Thermodon and Pathenios region and their neighbours the Macrons say they learnt it recently from the Colchidians. These are the only races which practise circumcision and it is observable that they do it in the same way as the Egyptians. As between the Egyptians themselves and the Ethiopians I could not say which taught the other the practice for among them it is quite clearly a custom of great antiquity. As to the custom having been learnt through their Egyptian connections, a further strong proof to my mind is that all those Phoenicians trading to Greece cease to treat the pudenda after the Egyptian manner and do not subject their offspring to circumcision.[26]

Herodotus reverts several times to the negroid character of the Egyptians and each time uses it as a fact of observation to argue more or less complex theses.

Thus to prove that the Greek oracle at Dodona in Epirus was of Egyptian origin, one of his arguments is the following: '. . . and when they add that the dove was black they give us to understand that the woman was Egyptian'.[27] The doves in question—actually there were two according to the text—symbolize two Egyptian women who are said to have been carried off from the Egyptian Thebes to found the oracles in Greece at Dodona and in Libya (Oasis of Jupiter Amon) respectively. Herodotus did not share the opinion of Anaxagoras that the melting of the snows on the mountains of Ethiopia was the source of the Nile floods.[28] He relied on the fact that it neither rains nor snows in Ethiopia 'and the heat there turns men black'.[29]

(*b*) Aristotle, –389 to –332, scientist, philosopher and tutor of Alexander the Great.

In one of this minor works, Aristotle attempts, with unexpected *naïveté*, to establish a correlation between the physcial and moral natures of living beings and leaves us evidence on the Egyptian—Ethiopian race which confirms what Herodotus says. According to him, 'Those who are too black are cowards, like for instance, the Egyptians and Ethiopians. But those who are excessively white are also cowards as we can see from the example of women, the complexion of courage is between the two.'[30]

(*c*) Lucian, Greek writer, +125(?) to +190.

The evidence of Lucian is as explicit as that of the two previous writers. He introduces two Greeks, Lycinus and Timolaus, who start a conversation.

> Lycinus (describing a young Egyptian): 'This boy is not merely black; he has thick lips and his legs are too thin . . . his hair worn in a plait behind shows that he is not a freeman.'
>
> Timolaus: 'But that is a sign of really distinguished birth in Egypt, Lycinus. All freeborn children plait their hair until they reach manhood. It is the exact opposite of the custom of our ancestors who thought it seemly for old men to secure their hair with a gold brooch to keep it in place.'[31]

(d) Apollodorus, first century before our era, Greek philosopher.

'Aegyptos conquered the country of the black-footed ones and called it Egypt after himself.'[32]

(e) Aeschylus, −525(?) to −456, tragic poet and creator of Greek tragedy.

In *The Suppliants*, Danaos, fleeing with his daughters, the Danaïds, and pursued by his brother Aegyptos with his sons, the Aegyptiads, who seek to wed their cousins by force, climbs a hillock, looks out to sea and describes the Aegyptiads at the oars afar off in these terms: 'I can see the crew with their black limbs and white tunics.'[33]

A similar description of the Egyptian type of man recurs a few lines later in verse 745.

(f) Achilles Tatius of Alexandria.

He compares the herdsmen of the Delta to the Ethiopians and explains that they are blackish, like half-castes.

(g) Strabo, −58 to about +25.

Strabo visited Egypt and almost all the countries of the Roman empire. He concurs in the theory that the Egyptians and the Colchoi are of the same race but holds that the migrations to Ethiopia and Colchoi had been from Egypt only.

'Egyptians settled in Ethiopia and in Colchoi.'[34] There is no doubt whatever as to Strabo's notion of the Egyptians' race for he seeks elsewhere to explain why the Egyptians are darker than the Hindus, a circumstance which would permit the refutation, if needed, of any attempt at confusing 'the Hindu and Egyptian races'.

(h) Diodorus of Sicily, about −63 to +14, Greek historian and contemporary of Caesar Augustus.

According to Diodorus it was probably Ethiopia which colonized Egypt (in the Athenian sense of the term, signifying that, with overpopulation, a proportion of the people emigrate to new territory).

> *The Ethiopians say that the Egyptians are one of their colonies*,[35] which was led into Egypt by Osiris. They claim that at the beginning of the world Egypt was simply a sea but that the Nile, carrying down vast quantities of loam from Ethiopia in its flood waters, finally filled it in and made it part of the continent . . . They add that the Egyptians have received from them, as from authors and their ancestors, the greater part of their laws.[36]

(i) Diogenes Laertius.

He wrote the following about Zeno, founder of the Stoic School (−333 to −261): 'Zeno son of Mnaseas or Demeas was a native of Citium in Cyprus, a Greek city which has taken in some Phoenician colonists.' In his *Lives*, Timotheus of Athens describes Zeno as having a twisted neck. Apollonius of Tyre says of him that he was gaunt, very tall and black, hence the fact that, according to Chrysippus in the First Book of his Proverbs, certain people called him an Egyptian vine-shoot.[37]

(j) Ammianus Marcellinus, about +33 to +100, Latin historian and friend of the Emperor Julian.

With him we reach the sunset of the Roman empire and the end of classical antiquity. There are about nine centuries between the birth of Aeschylus and Herodotus and the death of Ammianus Marcellinus, nine centuries during which the Egyptians, amid a sea of white races, steadily crossbred. It can be said without exaggeration that in Egypt one household in ten included a white Asiatic or Indo-European slave.[38]

It is remarkable that, despite its intensity, all this crossbreeding should not have succeeded in upsetting the racial constants. Indeed Ammianus Marcellinus writes: " . . . the men of Egypt are mostly brown or black with a skinny and desiccated look".[39] He also confirms the evidence already cited about the Colchoi: 'Beyond these lands are the heartlands of the Camaritae[40] and the Phasis with its swifter stream borders the country of the Colchoi, an ancient race of Egyptian origin.'[41]

This cursory review of the evidence of the ancient Graeco-Latin writers on the Egyptians' race shows that the extent of agreement between them is impressive and is an objective fact difficult to minimize or conceal, the two alternatives between which present-day Egyptology constantly oscillates.

An exception is the evidence of an honest savant, Volney, who travelled in Egypt between +1783 and +1785, i.e. at the peak period of negro slavery, and made the following observations on the true Egyptian race, the same which produced the Pharaohs, namely, the Copts:

> All of them are puffy-faced, heavy-eyed and thick-lipped, in a word, real mulatto faces. I was tempted to attribute this to the climate until, on visiting the Sphinx, the look of it gave me the clue to the enigma. Beholding that head characteristically Negro in all its features, I recalled the well-known passage of Herodotus which reads: 'For my part I consider the Colchoi are a colony of the Egyptians because, like them, they are black-skinned and kinky-haired'. In other words the ancient Egyptians were true negroes of the same stock as all the autochthonous peoples of Africa and from that datum one sees how their race, after some centuries of mixing with the blood of Romans and Greeks, must have lost the full blackness of its original colour but retained the impress of its original mould. It is even possible to apply this observation very widely and posit in principle that physiognomy is a kind of record usable in many cases for disputing or elucidating the evidence of history on the origins of the peoples . . .

After illustrating this proposition citing the case of the Normans, who 900 years after the conquest of Normandy still look like Danes, Volney adds:

> but reverting to Egypt, its contributions to history afford many subjects for philosophic reflection. What a subject for mediation is the present-day barbarity and ignorance of the Copts who were considered, born of the alliance of the deep genius of the Egyptians and the brilliance of the Greeks, that this race of blacks who nowadays are slaves and the objects of our scorn is the very one to which we owe our arts, our sciences and even the use of spoken word; and finally recollect that it is in the midst of the peoples claiming to be the greatest friends of liberty and humanity that the most barbarous of enslavements has been sanctioned and the question raised whether black men have brains of the same quality as those of white men![42]

To this testimony of Volney, Champollion-Figeac, brother of Champollion the Younger, was to reply in the following terms: 'The two physical traits of black skin and kinky hair are not enough to stamp a race as negro and Volney's conclusion as to the negro origin of the ancient population of Egypt is glaringly forced and inadmissible.'[43]

Being black from head to foot and having kinky hair is not enough to make a man a negro! This shows us the kind of specious argumentation to which Egyptology has had to resort since its birth as a science. Some scholars maintain that Volney was seeking to shift the discussion to a philosophic plane. But we have only to re-read Volney: he is simply drawing the inferences from crude material facts forcing themselves on his eyes and his conscience as proofs.

The Egyptians as They Saw Themselves

It is no waste of time to get the views of those principally concerned. How did the ancient Egyptians see themselves? Into which ethnic category did they put themselves? What did they call themselves? The language and literature left to us by the Egyptians of the Pharaonic epoch supply explicit answers to these questions which the scholars cannot refrain from minimizing, twisting or 'interpreting'.

The Egyptians had only one term to designate themselves: =kmt=the negroes (literally).[44] This is the strongest term existing in the Pharaonic tongue to indicate blackness; it is accordingly written with a hieroglyph representing a length of wood charred at the end and not crocodile scales.[45] This word is the etymological origin of the well-known root *kamit* which has proliferated in modern anthropological literature. The biblical root *kam* is probably derived from it and it has therefore been necessary to distort the facts to enable this root today to mean 'white' in Egyptological terms whereas, in the Pharaonic mother tongue which gave it birth, it meant 'coal black'.

In the Egyptian language, a word of assembly is formed from an adjective or a noun by putting it in the feminine singular. 'Kmt' from the adjective =km=black; it therefore means strictly negroes or at the very least black men. The terms is a collective noun which thus described the whole people of Pharaonic Egypt as a black people.

In other words, on the purely grammatical plane, if one wishes to indicate negroes in the Pharaonic tongue, one cannot use any other word than the very one which the Egyptians used of themselves. Furthermore, the language offers us another term, kmtjw=the negroes, the black men (literally)=the Egyptians, as opposed to 'foreigners' which comes from the same root km and which the Egyptians also used to describe themselves as *a people as distinguished from all foreign peoples*.[46] These are the only adjectives of nationality used by the Egyptians to designate themselves and both mean 'negro' or 'black' in the Pharaonic language. Scholars hardly ever mention them or when they do it is to translate them by euphemisms such as the 'Egyptians' while remaining completely silent about their etymological sense.[47] They prefer the expression Rmt kmt=the men of the country of the black men or the men of the black country.

In Egyptian, words are normally followed by a determinative which indicates their exact sense, and for this particular expression Egyptologists suggest that km=black and that the colour qualifies the determinative which follows it and which signifies 'country'. Accordingly, they claim, the translation should be 'the black earth' from the colour of the loam, or the 'black country', and not 'the country of the black men' as we should be inclined to render it today with black Africa and white Africa in mind. Perhaps so, but if we apply this rule rigorously to =kmit, we are forced to 'concede that here the adjective "black" qualifies the determinative which signifies the whole people of Egypt shown by the two symbols for "man" and "woman" and the three strokes below them which indicate the plural'. Thus, if it is possible to voice a doubt as regards the expression =kme, it is not possible to do so in the case of the two adjectives of nationality kmt and kmtjw unless one is picking one's arguments completely at random.

It is a remarkable circumstance that the ancient Egyptians should never have had the idea of applying these qualificatives to the Nubians and other populations of Africa to distinguish them from themselves; any more than a Roman at the apogee of the empire could use a 'colour' adjective to distinguish himself from the Germani on the other bank of the Danube, of the same stock but still in the prehistoric age of development.

In either case both sides were of the same world in terms of physical anthropology, and accordingly the distinguishing terms used related to level of civilization or moral sense. For the civilized Romans, the Germans, of the same stock, were barbarians. The Egyptians used the expression =nahas to designate the Nubians; and nahas[48] is the name of a people, with no colour connotation in Egyptian. It is a deliberate mistranslation to render it as negro as is done in almost all present-day publications.

The Divine Epithets

Finally, black or negro is the divine epithet invariably used for the chief beneficent gods of Egypt, whereas all the malevolent spirits are qualified as desrêt=red; we also know that to Africans this form applies to the white nations; it is practically certain that this held good for Egypt too but I want in this chapter to keep to the least debatable facts.

The surnames of the gods are these:

=Kmwr=the 'Great Negro' for Osiris[49]

=km=the black + the name of the god[50]

=kmt=the black + the name of the goddess[51]

The km (black) qualificative is applied to Hathor, Apis, Min, Thoth, etc.[52] set kmt=the black woman=Isis.[53] On the other hand 'seth', the sterile desert, is qualified by the term desrêt=red.[54] The wild animals which Horus fought to create civilization are qualified as dešrêt=red, especially the hippopotamus.[55] Similarly the maleficent beings wiped out by Thoth are Des=  =dèsrtjw=thr red ones; this term is the grammatical converse of Kmtjw and its construction follows the same rule for the formation of 'nisbés'.

Witness of the Bible

The Bible tells us: '... the sons of Ham [were] Cush, and Mizraim [i.e. Egypt], and Phut, and Canaan. And the sons of Cush; Seba, and Havilah, and Sabtah, and Raamah, and Sabtechah.'[56]

Generally speaking all Semitic tradition (Jewish and Arab) classes ancient Egypt with the countries of the blacks.

The importance of these depositions cannot be ignored, for these are peoples (the Jews) which lived side by side with the ancient Egyptians and sometimes in symbiosis with them and have nothing to gain by presenting a false ethnic picture of them. Nor is the notion of an erroneous interpretation of the facts any more tenable.[57]

Cultural Data

Among the innumberable identical cultural traits recorded in Egypt and in present-day black Africa, it is proposed to refer only to circumcision and totemism.

According to the extract from Herodotus quoted earlier, circumcision is of African origin. Archaeology has confirmed the judgement of the Father of History for Elliot-Smith was able to determine from the examination of well-preserved mummies that circumcision was the rule among the Egyptians as long ago as the protohistoric era,[58] i.e. earlier than −4000.

Egyptian totemism retained its vitality down to the Roman period[59] and Plutarch also mentions it. The researches of Amélineau,[60] Loret, Moret and Adolphe Reinach have clearly demonstrated the existence of an Egyptian totemic system, in refutation of the champions of the zoolatric thesis.

> If we reduce the notion of the totem to that of a fetish, usually representing an animal of a species with which the tribe believes it has special ties formally renewed at fixed intervals, and which is carried into battle like a standard; if we accept this minimal but adequate definition of a totem, it can be said that there was no country where totemism had a more brilliant reign than in Egypt and certainly nowhere where it could better be studied.[61]

Linguistic Affinity

Walaf,[62] a Senegalese language spoken in the extreme west of Africa on the Atlantic Ocean, is perhaps as close to ancient Egyptian as Coptic. An exhaustive study of this question has recently been carried out.[63] In this chapter enough is presented to show that the kinship between ancient Egyptian and the languages of Africa is not hypothetical but a demonstrable fact which it is impossible for modern scholarship to thrust aside.

As we shall see, the kinship is genealogical in nature.

EGYPTIAN	COPTIC	WALAF
 =kef=to grasp, to take a strip (of something)[64]	(Saïdique dialect) keh=to tame[65]	kef=seize a prey
PRESENT	PRESENT	PRESENT
kef i	keh	kef na
kef ek	keh ek	kef nga
kef et	keh ere	kef na
kef ef	kef ef	
kef es	keh es	kef ef na kef es
kef n	keh en	kef nanu
kef ton	keh etetû	kef ngen
kef sen[66]	keh ey	kef nañu
PAST	PAST	PAST
kef ni	keh nei	kef (on) na
kef (o) nek	keh nek	kef (on) nga
kef (o) net	keh nere	kef (on) na
kef (o) nef	keh nef	kef (on) ef na
kef (o) nes	keh nes	kef (on) es
kef (o) nen	keh nen	kef (on) nanu
kef (o) n ten	keh netsten	kef (on) ngen
kef (o) n sen[67]	keh ney[68]	kef (on) nañu

EGYPTIAN	WALAF
 =feh=go away	feh=rush off

We have the following correspondences between the verb forms, with identity or similarity of meaning: all the Egyptian verb forms, except for two, are also recorded in Walaf.

EGYPTIAN	WALAF
feh-ef	feh-ef
feh-es	feh-es
feh-n-ef	feh-ôn-ef
feh-n-es	feh-ônes
feh-w	feh-w
feh-wef	feh-w-ef
feh-w-es	feh-w-es
feh-w-n-ef	feh-w-ôn-ef
feh-w-n-es	feh-w-ôn-es
feh-in-ef	feh-il-ef
feh-in-es	feh-il-es
feh-t-ef	feh-t-ef
feh-t-es	feh-t-es
feh-tyfy	feh-ati-fy
feh-tysy	feh-at-ef
feh-tw-ef	mar-tw-ef
feh-tw-es	mar-tw-es
feh-kw(i)	fahi-kw
feh-n-tw-ef	feh-an-tw-ef
feh-n-tw-es	feh-an-tw-es
feh-y-ef	feh-y-ef
feh-y-es	fey-y-es

EGYPTIAN	WALAF
 =mer=love	mar=lick[69]
mer-ef	mar-ef
mer-es	mar-es
mer-n-ef	mar-ôn-ef
mer-n-es	mar-ôn-es
mer-w	mar-w
mer-w-ef	mar-w-ef
mer-w-n-f	mar-w-ôn-ef
mer-w-n-es	mar-w-ôn-es
mer-in-ef	mar-il-ef
mer-in-es	mar-il-es
mer-t-ef	mar-t-ef
mer-t-es	mar-t-es
mer-tw-ef	mar-tw-ef
mer-tw-es	mar-tw-es
mer-tyfy	mar-at-ef
mer-*t*-tysy	mar-at-es
	mar-aty-sy
	mar-aty-sy
mer-kwi	mari-kw
mer-y-ef	mar-y-ef
mer-y-es	mar-y-es
mer-n-tw-ef	mar-an-tw-ef
mer-n-tw-es	mar-antw-es
	mar-tw-ôn-ef
	mar-tw-ôn-es

Egyptian and Walaf Demonstratives

There are the following phonetic correspondences between Egyptian and Walaf demonstratives.

EGYPTIAN	WALAF
	ep→w
=pw	p→b
(ipw)→bw	w→w
=pwy	p→b̄
(ipw)→bwy	w→2
	y→y
=pn bané	p→b̄
(ipn)→	n→n
balé	p→b̄
	n→l[70]
=pf bafe	p→b
(ipf)→	f→f
=pf3→bafa	p→b̄
	f→f
	3→a
=pfy	p→b̄
(ipfy)→bafy	f→f
	y→y
=p3→bâ	p→b
	3→á
=iptw→baṭw	p→b
	ṭ→t
	w→w
=iptn→batné	p→b
	ṭ→t
Batalé	n→n
	n→l
=iptf	
=iptf→batafé	p→b̄
	t→t
	f→f

These phonetic correspondences are not ascribable either to elementary affinity or to the general laws of the human mind for they are regular correspondences on outstanding points extending through an entire system, that of the demonstratives in the two languages and that of the verbal languages. It is through the application of such laws that it was possible to demonstrate the existence of the Indo-European linguistic family.

The comparison could be carried to show that the majority of the phonemes remain unchanged between the two languages. The few changes which are of great interest are the following.

(a) The correspondence n (E)→l (W)

EGYPTIAN	WALAF
n	l
=na*d*=ask	la*d*=ask
=nah=protect	lah=protect
=ben ben=wellup	belbel=well up
=teni=grow old	talé=important
=tefnwt=the goddess born of Ra's spittle	tefnit='spit out' a human being. teflit=spittle tefli=spitter
=nebt=plait	let=plait nâb=to plait hair temporarily

(b) The correspondence h (E)→g (W)

EGYPTIAN	WALAF
h	g
=hen=phallus	gen=phallus
=hwn=adolescent	gwné, goné =adolescent
=hor=Horus	gor=vir (? male ?)
=hor gwn=the youth Horus	gor gwne=young man (m.ă.m)

It is still early to talk with precision of the vocalic accompaniment of the Egyptian phonemes. But the way is open for the rediscovery of the vocalics of ancient Egyptian from comparative studies with the languages of Africa.

Conclusion

The structure of African royalty, with the king put to death, either really or symbolically, after a reign which varied in length but was in the region of eight years, recalls the ceremony of the Pharaoh's regeneration through the Sed feast. Also reminiscent of Egypt are the circumcision rites mentioned earlier and the totemism, cosmogonies, architecture, musical instruments, etc., of Africa.[71] Egyptian antiquity is to Africa culture what Graeco-Roman antiquity is to Western culture. The building up of a corpus of African humanities should be based on this fact.

It will be understood how difficult it is to write such a chapter in a work of this kind, where euphemism and compromise are the rule. In an attempt to avoid sacrificing scientific truth, therefore, we made a point of suggesting three preliminaries to the preparation of this volume, all of which were agreed to at the plenary session held in 1971.[72] The first two led to the holding of the Cairo Symposium from 28 January to 3 February 1974.[73] In this connection I should like to refer to certain passages in the report of that symposium. Professor Vercoutter, who had been commissioned by Unesco to write the introductory report, acknowledged after a thorough discussion that the conventional idea that the Egyptian population was equally divided between blacks, whites and half-castes could not be upheld. 'Professor Vercoutter agreed that no attempt should be made to estimate percentages, which meant nothing, as it was impossible to establish them without reliable statistical data'. On the subject of Egyptian culture: 'Professor Vercoutter remarked that, in his view, Egypt was African in its way of writing, in its culture and in its way of thinking'.

Professor Leclant, for his part, 'recognized the same African character in the Egyptian temperament and way of thinking'.

In regard to linguistics, it is stated in the report that 'this item, in contrast to those previously discussed, revealed a large measure of agreement among the participants. The outline report by Professor Diop and the report by Professor Obenga were regarded as being very constructive'.

Similarly, the symposium rejected the idea that Pharaonic Egyptian was a Semitic language. 'Turning to wider issues, Professor Sauneron drew attention to the interest of the method suggested by Professor Obenga following Professor Diop. Egyptian remained a stable language for a period of at least 4500 years. Egypt was situated at the point of convergence of outside influences and it was to be expected that borrowing had been made from foreign languages, but the Semitic roots numbered only a few hundred as compared with a total of several thousand words. The Egyptian language could not be isolated from its African context and its origin could not be fully explained in terms of Semitic, it was thus quite normal to expect to find related languages in Africa'.

The genetic, that is, non-accidental relationship between Egyptian and the African languages was recognized: 'Professor Sauneron noted that the method which had been used was of considerable interest, since it could not be purely fortuitous that there was a similarity between the third person singular suffixed pronouns in Ancient Egyptian and in Wolof, he hoped that an attempt would be made to reconstitute a palaeo-African language, using present-day languages as a starting point'.

In the general conclusion to the report it was stated that: 'Although the preparatory working paper sent out by Unesco gave particulars of what was desired, not all participants had prepared communications comparable with the painstakingly researched contributions of Professors Cheikh Anta Diop and Obenga. There was consequently a real lack of balance in the discussions.'

A new page of African historiography was accordingly written in Cairo. The symposium recommended that further studies be made on the concept of race. Such studies have since been carried out, but they have not contributed anything new to the historical discussion. They tell us that molecular biology and genetics recognize the existence of populations alone, the concept of race being no longer meaningful. Yet whenever there is any question of the transmission of a hereditary taint, the concept of race in the most classic sense of the term comes into its own again, for genetics tells us that 'sickle-cell anaemia occurs only in negroes'. The truth is that all these 'anthropologists' have already in their own minds drawn the conclusions deriving from the triumph of the monogenetic theory of mankind without venturing to put them into explicit terms, for if mankind originated in Africa, it was necessarily negroid before becoming white through mutation and adaptation at the end of the last glaciation in Europe in the Upper Palaeolithic; and it is now more understandable why the Grimaldian negroids first occupied Europe for 10000 years before Cro-Magnon Man—the prototype of the white race—appeared (around −2000).

The ideological standpoint is also evident in apparently objective studies. In history and in social relations, it is the phenotype, that is, the individual or the people as that individual or people is perceived, which is the dominant factor, as opposed to the genotype. For present-day genetics, a Zulu with the 'same' genotype as Vorster is not impossible. Does this mean that the history we are witnessing will put the two phenotypes, that is, the two individuals, on the same footing in all their national and social activities? Certainly not—the opposition will remain not social but ethnic.

This study makes it necessary to rewrite world history from a more scientific standpoint, taking into account the Negro-African component which was for a long time preponderant. It means that it is now possible to build up a corpus of Negro-African humanities resting on a sound historical basis instead of being suspended in mid-air. Finally, if it is true that only truth is revolutionary, it may be added that only *rapprochement* brought about on a basis of truth can endure. The cause of human progess is not well served by casting a veil over the fact.

The rediscovery of the true past of the African peoples should not be a divisive factor but should contribute to uniting them, each and all, binding them together from the north to the south of the continent so as to enable them to carry out together a new historical mission for the greater good of mankind; and that is in keeping with the ideal of Unesco.[74]

Note by the Editor of *General History of Africa* (Unesco, 1981): The opinions expressed by Professor Cheikh Anta Diop in this chapter are those which he presented and developed at the Unesco symposium of 'The peopling of ancient Egypt' which was held in Cairo in 1974. The arguments put forward in this chapter have not been accepted by all the experts interested in the problem.—Gamal Mokhtar.

Plate 1. Protohistoric figure of Tera-Neter, a negro nobleman of the Anous race who were the first inhabitants of Egypt.

Plate 2. A pharaoh of the First Egyptian Dynasty, said to be Narmer.

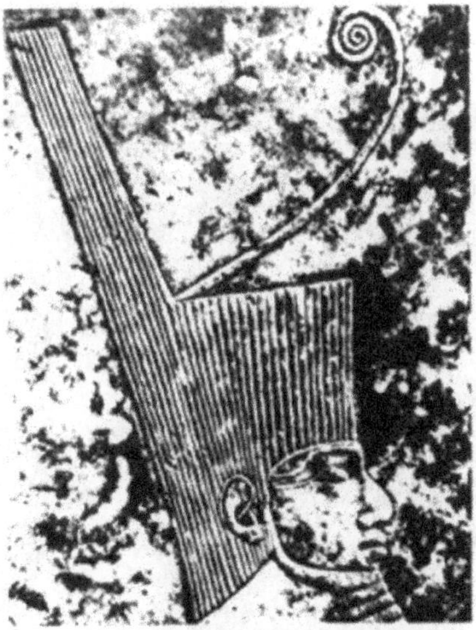

Plate 3. Djeser, typical negro, pharaoh of the Third Dynasty; this ushered in the great age of dressed-stone architecture: the step pyramid and burial complex at Sakkara. By his reign, all the technological features of Egyptian civilization were already developed.

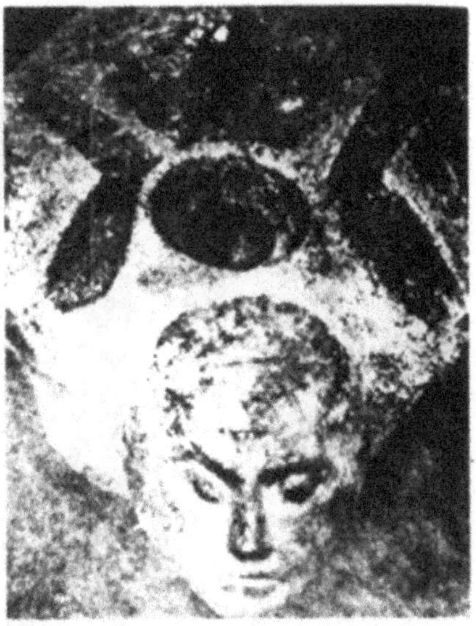

Plate. 4. Door socket from Hierakonpolis, First Egyptian Dynasty.

Plate 5. Libyan prisoner.

Plate 6. Foreigner.

Plate 7. Semitic captive.

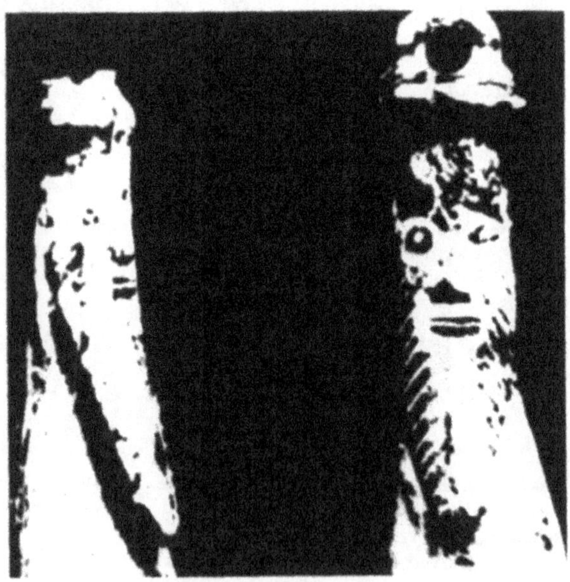

Plate 8. Predynastic figurines.

Plate 9. Indo-European captives.

Plate 10. Indo-European captive.

Plate 11. Indo-European captive.

Plate 12. Cheops, Pharaoh of the Fourth Dynasty, builder of the Great Pyramid.

Plate 13. Semitic captives at the time of the pharaohs; Sinai rock.

Plate 14. Pharaoh Mentouhotep I.

Plate 15. Four Indo-European types (Zeus, Ptolemy, Sarapis, Trajan). Compare with Egyptian groups II and III.

Plate 16. Two Semites. Like the Indo-European type, the Semitic type was totally absent from the Egyptian ruling class, entering Egypt only as war captives.

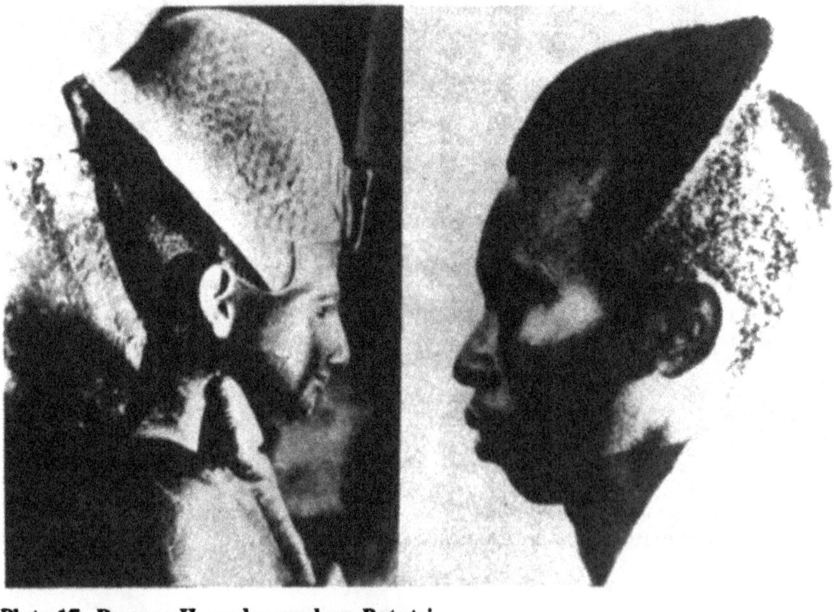

Plate 17. Ramses II, and a modern Batutsi.

Plate 18. Statue of the Sphynx as found by the first French scientific mission in the nineteenth century. The typically Negro profile is thought to be that of the pharaoh Khafre or Khefren (ca.—2600, IV Dynasty), the builder of the second pyramid of Giza.

Notes

1. *Proceedings of the Seventh Pan-African Congress of Pre-History and Quaternary Studies*, December 1971.
2. M.F.A. Montagu, 1960, p. 390.
3. The study of this race's pigmentation can be carried farther by the method described; actually Elliot-Smith often found patches of skin on the bodies and the mummification eethods which cause skin deterioration were not yet in use.
4. D.P. de Pedrals, p. 6.
5. *Géographie*, classe de 5°, 1950.
6. In his 'Lutte des races' (1883) L. Gumplovicz asserts that the diverse classes making up a people always represent different races, of which one has established its domination over the others by conquest. G. de Lapounge in an article published in 1897 postulated no less than a dozen 'fundamental laws of anthropo-sociology' of which the following are typical: his 'law of distribution of wealth' posits that, in countries of mixed European-Alpine populations, wealth is greater in inverse proportions to the cephalic index; the 'law of urban indices' given prominence by Ammon in connexion with his research on Badener conscripts asserted that town dwellers exhibit greater dolichocephaly than the people in the adjacent countryside; the 'law of stratification' was formulated in the following terms: 'the cephalic index decreases and the proportion of dolichocephalics rises the higher the social class, in each locality'. In his 'Sélections sociales' the same writer has no hesitation in asserting that 'the dominant class in the feudal epoch belongs almost exclusively to the variety "Homo Europaeus" so that it is not pure chance which has kept the poor at the foot of the social ladder but their congenital inferiority'.

We thus see that German racism was inventing nothing new, when Alfred Rosenberg asserted that the French Revolution must be deemed a revolt of the brachycephalics of the Alpine stock against the dolichocephalics of the Nordic race.' (A. Cuvillier, p. 155).

7. W.M.F. Petrie, 1939, Fig. 1.
8. ibid., p. 69.
9. ibid., p. 68.
10. E. Amélineau, 1908, p. 174.
11. Pl. 1.2.
12. Pl. 1.3.
13. W.M.F. Petrie, 1939, p. 67.
14. Pl. 1.11.
15. Pl. 1.5.
16. Pl. 1.8.
17. Pl. 1.7 I know that 'Indo-European' is usually said to be a language, not a race, but I prefer this term to 'Aryan' wherever its use causes no confusion.
18. Pl. 1.12.
19. Pl. 1.13.
20. R.A. Nicolaus, p. 11.
21. T.J. Pettigrew, 1834, pp. 70-71.
22. C.A. Diop, 1977.
23. M.E. Fontane, pp. 44-5 (see reproduction: T).
24. M.F.A. Montagu, p. 337.
25. In the fifth century before our era, at the time when Herodotus visited Egypt, a black-skinned people, the Colchians, were still living in Colchis on the Armenian shore of the Black Sea, east of the ancient port of Trebizond, surrounded by white-skinned nations.

The scholars of antiquity wondered about this people's origins and Herodotus in 'Euterpe', the second book of his history on Egypt, tries to prove that the Colchians were Egyptians, whence the arguments we quote. Herodotus, on the strength of commemorative stelae, erected by Sesostris in conquered countries, asserts that this monarch had got as far as Thrace and Seythia, where stelae would seem to have been still standing in his day (Book II, 103).

26. Herodotus, Book II, 104. As with many peoples in black Africa, Egyptian women underwent excision of the clitoris: cf. Strabo, *Geography*, Book XVII, Ch. I.
27. Herodotus, Book II, 57.
28. Seneca, *Questions of Nature*, Book IV, 17.
29. Herodotus, Book II, 22.
30. Aristotle, *Physiognomy*, 6.
31. Lucian, *Navigations*, paras 2-3.
32. Apollodorus, Book II, 'The family of Inachus', paras 3 and 4.
33. Aeschylus, *The Suppliants*, vv. 719-20. See also v. 745.
34. Strabo, *Geography*, Book I, ch. 3, para. 10.
35. My italics.
36. Diodorus, *Universal History*, Book III. The antiquity of the Ethiopian civilization is attested by the most ancient and most venerable Greek writer, Homer, in both the *Iliad* and the *Odyssey*:

'Jupiter followed today by all the gods receives the sacrifices of theEthiopians' (*Iliad*, I, 422).
'Yesterday to visit holy Ethiopia Jupiter betook himself to the ocean shore' (*Iliad*, I, 423).

37. Diogenes Laertius, Book VII, i.
38. The Egyptian notables liked to have a Syrian or Cretan female slave in their harems.
39. Ammianus Marcellinus, Book XXII, para. 16 (23).
40. Pirate gangs who worked from small ships called *Ćamare*.
41. Ammianus Marcellinus, Book XXII, para. 8 (24).
42. M.C.F. Volney, *Voyages en Syrie et en Egypte*, Paris, 1787, Vol. I, pp. 74-7.
43. J.J. Champollion-Figeac, 1839, pp. 26-7.
44. This important discovery was made, on the African side, by Sossou Nsougan, who was to

compile this part of the present chapter. For the sense of the word see *Wörterbuch der Aegyptischen Sprache,* Vol. 5, 1971, pp. 122 and 127.

45. ibid., p. 122.
46. ibid., p. 128.
47. R.O. Faulkner, 1962, p. 286.
48. Wörter buch der ägyptischen Sprache, p. 128.
49. ibid., p. 124.
50. ibid., p. 125.
51. ibid., p. 123.
52. It should be noted that set=kem=black wife in Walaf.
53. Wörter buch der ägyptischen Sprache, p. 492.
54. ibid., p. 493.
55. Dešrêt=blood in Egyptian; deret=blood in Walaf: ibid., p. 494.
56. Genesis, 10: 6-7.
57. C.A. Diop, 1955, pp. 33ff.
58. E. Massoulard, 1949, p. 386.
59. Juvénal, *Satire* XV, vv. 1-14.
60. E. Amélineau, *op. cit.*
61. A. Recnach, 1913, p. 17.
62. Often spelt Wolof.
63. C.A. Diop, 1977.
64. R. Lambert, 1925, p. 129.
65. A. Mallon, pp. 207-34.
66. A. de Buck, 1952.
67. ibid.
68. A. Mallon, pp. 207-34.
69. By extension=love intensely (hence the verb mar-maral) after the fashion of a female animal licking the cub which she has just borne. This sense does not conflict with the other notion which the determinative may convey of a man raising hand to mouth.
70. See below for the explanation of this important law.
71. See C.A. Diop, 1967.
72. See *Final Report of the First Plenary Session of the International Scientific Committee for the Drafting of a general History of Africa,* UNESCO, 30 March-8 April 1974.
73. Symposium of 'The peopling of ancient Egypt and the deciphering of the Meriotic script'. Cf. Studies and Documents No. 1, UNESCO, 1978.

THE ANCIENT WORLD AND AFRICA: WHOSE ROOTS?

Basil Davidson

To a television series about history of the Africans which I lately had the good fortune to be able to present to a wide public in many countries, more than thirty countries I am told, there were of course some protests and objections. Surprisingly, however, these were fewer than I had expected. Mostly they came from persons of evidently fixed opinions who clearly knew little or nothing of the subject of the programmes, and who made up for their astonishment at being shown that Africans have a history of their own by accusing me of bias, exaggeration or sentimental frailty. A few were from white South Africans in this country or former Rhodesian settlers, foreseeably couched in the kind of gutter language one has learned to expect from such quareters. And several were from otherwise sympathetic viewers who had oddly convinced themselves that black history could be written only by a black historian. One of these even went so far, although politely, as to suggest that the series in question should have been presented by my late friend and colleague Cheik Anta Diop, who was certainly a notable historian but who spoke no English.

None of these objections has seemed to me to warrant serious argument, but there was another, far more solidly based in European culture, which undoubtedly does warrant such argument and in which, as I think, one can find some of the crucial origins of established or intellectual denial of value to the cultures of Africa. This objection, heard from a number of viewers in Europe and North America, was against a central theme in the series. This theme portrayed Egypt of the Pharoahs, Ancient Egypt before conquest by the Arabs in the seventh century AD, as a country of black origins and population whose original ancestors had come from the lands of the great interior, and whose links with inner Africa remained potent and continuous. To affirm this, of course, is to offend nearly all established historiographical orthodoxy. The Ancient Egyptians, by that orthodoxy, were not only not black—in whatever pigmentational variant of non-white that Nature may have provided—but they were also not Africans. To say otherwise must be so mistaken, one has gathered, as to be patently absurd.

Reprinted, with permission, from *Race and Class*, XXIX, 2 (1987)

But isn't Egypt. other issues apart, quite simply a part of Africa? That, it seems, is a merely geographical irrelevance. The civilisation of Pharaonic Egypt, arising sometime around 3500BC and continuing at least until the Roman dispossessions, has been explained to us as evolving either in more or less total isolation from Africa or as a product of West Asian stimulus. On the deeply held view, the land of Ancient Egypt appears to have detached itself from the delta of the Nile, some five and a half thousand years ago, and sailed off into the Mediterranean on a course veering broadly towards the coasts of Syria. And there it apparently remained, floating somewhere in the seas of the Levant, until Arab conquerors hauled it back to where it had once belonged.

Now what is one to make of this unlikely view of the case, coming as it has from venerable seats of learning? Does its strength derive from a long tradition of research and explanation? Is it what Europeans have always thought to be true? Have the records of ancient times been found to support it? As Martin Bernal has now most ably shown in his *Black Athena*.* the remarkable book about which I am chiefly writing here, the answer to such questions is plainly and unequivocally in the negative. That the Ancient Egyptians were black (again, in any variant you may prefer)—or, as I myself think it more useful to say, were African—is a belief which has been denied in Europe since about 1830, not before. It is a denial, in short, that belongs to the rise of modern European imperialism, and has to be explained in terms of the 'new racism', specifically and even frantically an anti-black racism, which went together with and was consistently nourished by that imperialism. I say 'new racism' because it followed and further expanded the older racism which spread around Europe after the Atlantic slave trade had reached its high point of 'take off' in about 1630. Was there no racism, then, before that? The point is complex and can be argued elsewhere: essentially, however, the answer to this is also in the negative. Before the Atlantic slave trade, and before its capitalism, there was plenty of ancient xenophobia, fear of 'blackness', association of blackness with the Devil, and so on and so forth; but none of this was the racism that we know.

The racism that we know was born in Europe and America from the cultural need to justify doing to black people, doing to Africans, what could not morally or legally be done to white people, and least of all to Europeans. To justify the enslavement of Africans, in short, it was culturally necessary to believe, or be able to believe, that Africans were inherently and naturally less than human but were beings of a somehow sub-human, non-human, nature. That was the cultural basis, in this context, of the slave trade and of the modern imperialism in Africa which followed the slave trade. The racism that we know, accordingly, was altogether different from ancient xenophobia or superstitious 'fears of the Dark': its core and motivation were to act as a weapon of dispossession and exploitation. And its success in this dehumanising project needs no demonstration here, for it is obvious in our culture to this day.

The consequences of this need to condemn Africans as less than human—and how otherwise justify enslaving and then invading them?—have been many and various. Among these consequences, logically enough, has been a denial of the Africans'possible possession of histories of their own, and thus of common humanity with other peoples elsewhere. Not surprisingly, this denial began to be heard from eminent spokesmen in Europe as soon as Europe's modern imperialism imposed a corresponding need to structure and systematise its attitudes to overseas conquest and imperialist enclosure. In the year that France invades Algeria, for example, we find Hegel appropriately lecturing at Jena on this very subject. He knows nothing of Africa, has never been there, is oblivious to all the older sources of African knowledge that were extant then as now. Never mind: in 1830 he is able to say, in a course of lectures which were celebrated for generations after they were given, that 'the Negro . . . exhibits the natural man in his completely wild and untamed state . . . for [Africa] is no historical part of the World; it has no movement or development to exhibit . . .' And one grave academic after another, one belaurelled explorer after another returning to the plaudits of a Grateful Nation, went on duly to explain that Africans had no history because Africans were insufficiently human. They were grown-up children who had failed to develop into adulthood. There was something missing in the frontal lobes of the African brain. They might seem to copy but could not invent, and even their copying was a masquerade. Such stereotypes filled book after book.

Then what about Ancient Egypt, universally held before the 1830s to be African, and the source of Europe's own civilising process by way of the Greeks? How could that belief be squared with the 'grown-up children' stereotypes? The questions were heard and briskly dealt with. After the 1830s Ancient Egypt ceased to be seen as part of Africa, and Pharaonic civilisation ceased to be an aspect of Africa's development and initiative. As for the Ancient Egyptians, the builders of the Pyramids and of the greatest civilisation of High Antiquity, they were steadily reduced to the status of a rather feeble bunch of mystics and magicians.

This operation, consciously or not in the minds of those who made it, was the required adjunct of another. It flowed from the need—as we can see it now, the racist-motivated need—to overthrow the hitherto accepted version of Europe's civilising origin and process. This Ancient Model, as Bernal calls it, had accepted as self-evident that European civilisation, launched from Classical Greece in the sixth century BC, was essentially and inseparably though not exclusively the product of older civilisations, above all those of Egypt and Phoenicia. This Ancient Model, as Bernal is careful to insist, gave full credit to the moral and intellectual achievements of Classical Greece, but it still saw these as being initially derived from Egypt, and to a lesser extent from the centres of Phoenician civilisation. It taught that the founding beliefs of Classical Greece, like the mathematics and astronomy of Classical Greece, had for the most part come from Egypt. And Egypt being accepted as an African country, they had thus come from Africa.

Such had been the traditional view of the matter. It had been questioned by no sufficient need to dehumanise Africans, at least until late in the seventeenth century when the slave trade began to prick at Christian consciences; and even as late as that it remained a view of history which was scarcely questioned. And this was not surprising, for the Ancient Model (it is Bernal's useful term) was based on solid historiographical evidence. This evidence was no other and no less than what the historians of Classical Greece had themselves accepted as fact. Without exception, so far as surviving texts can show, every Greek thinker of the Classical Age looked to Egypt for inspiration and guidance, and accepted the cultural primacy of Egypt.

The philosophers and propagandists of the new imperialism could obviously not accept such views. They set about constructing a new model of Europe's civilising process, an Aryan Model (again Bernal's useful term). This proposed, and increasingly asserted with an intellectual arrogance perfectly in tune with the new imperialism, that Classical Greece had been the pure and original source and creator of all that was civilised in Europe: of all the arts of government and the values of freedom, of all the gods that men should worship and the teachings they should follow. These nineteenth-century proponents of racism, of racist discrimination as a systemic weapon of oppression, were thus obliged to shove whatever the ancient Greeks had thought and written about African origins right under their academic carpet, and lose it there. As Bernal says in his illuminating treatment of this operation, 'the more the nineteenth century admired the Greeks, the less it respected their writing of their own history'.

But if this newly created Aryan Model of Europe's civilising origins responded to European nineteenth-century needs, it was not, of course, entirely mistaken. Linguistic studies duly showed that the language of the Classical Greeks, as of modern Greeks, is one of a wide language family which linguists know as Indo-European: speakers of one or other derivative of 'original Indo-European' had ranged from an 'Aryan heartland', never quite fixed but supposedly in Eastern Europe or Western Asia, right across our continent to the shores of the Atlantic, the Celtic languages being those that have survived farthest to the west. It was further found to be true, moreover, that speakers of the Indo-European parent of Greek had entered Greece in large numbers at some time before the emergence of Classical civilisation. The simplicity of the Ancient Model, which had derived Greek civilisation from Egyptian and Phoenician exemplars as well as from Egyptian and Phoenician settlements in pre-Classical Greece, had therefore become clearly insufficient. Bernal deals with all this in lucid fashion and great detail, and proposes a Revised Ancient Model; this maintains the essence of the Ancient Model while accompanying the Indo-European evidence.

My brief foray here into this subject of vast complexity is concerned primarily to draw attention to *Black Athena*, Bernal's far-ranging treatment; and indeed I know of no other work of such value. Bernal asks us to follow him through difficult terrain, but the effort is well repaid. Traveling with Bernal seems to me to offer the same kind of impact, for everyone involved in the problems of race and class, as another moment held for me, long ago, when at last I reached the iron-slag mounds of Meroë and knew that everything the books had taught me about history in Africa would have to be thought anew. This is the main thing I want to say. But I also want to pursue some other points a little further.

* * *

As his title indicates, Bernal's overall objective is to re-establish the place of Egypt, and thus of Africa, in the moral and cultural development of Classical Greek civilisation in which Europe has seen, and generally persists in seeing, its founding parentage. He does this with an immense erudition, respect for sources, and notable linguistic scholarship, and I shall make no effort here to track the route he follows. As he himself remarks, any attempt to summarise 'the complications of this vast and extraordinarily ramified theme can be best described by the Chinese expression "looking at flowers from horseback" '. Even so, some of the flowers along the way are enough to make one pause and dismount.

To begin with, there is the evidence of what the Greeks themselves thought; and this is really very awkward for our racists. The Greeks all agreed upon the cultural supremacy of Pharaonic civilisation, and the ways in which they wrote about this clearly show that they would have thought it absurd to advance a contrary opinion. Herodotus of Halicarnassus in Asia Minor, for example, was born around 490BC and wrote his great world histories some forty years later. Several of his nine books, but especially the second, have much to say on Egypt and Africa, and were composed after the long sojourn in Egypt which all Greek scholars of that time thought desirable or entirely necessary.[1] And they thought this, one may remark in passing, for the most persuasive reason that Egyptian civilisation enjoyed a towering prestige and influence, and seemed of immemorial weight and value. Their grasp of exact historical chronology could not be as good as ours, but they were perfectly alive to Egypt's immense time dimension: not surprisingly, for 2,000 years had passed since the building of the Pyramids at Gizeh, or as much time—even if they knew it less precisely than we do—as has passed for us since the threshold of the Christian era. For the Greeks of the Classical Age, Egypt was where one went to learn history.

The same writers likewise took it for well-established fact that the Greeks had learnt their civilisation from the same source, and that this had come about, in some degree, because Egyptians had formed settlements in Greece in earlier centuries. Herodotus simply assumed that his readers would know this. 'How it happened', he wrote, 'that Egyptians came to the Peloponnese [southern Greece] and formed settlements there, and what they did to make themselves kings in that part of Greece, has been chronicled by other writers. I will therefore add nothing but proceed to mention some points which no one else has yet touched upon.' For example, 'the names of nearly all the gods came to Greece from Egypt'. Moreover, 'it was only, if I may so put it, the day before yesterday that the Greeks came to know the origin and form of the various gods . . . for Homer and

Hesoid, the poets who composed our theogonies and described the gods for us . . . lived, as I believe, not more than 400 years ago.'

The philosophers and mathematicians were in full agreement. Pythagoras spent no fewer than twenty-one years in Egypt. Aristotle said that 'Egypt was the cradle of mathematics'. Eudoxus, Aristotle's teacher and a foremost mathematician of his time, had likewise studied in Egypt before teaching in Greece. Isokrates and Plato were profoundly influenced by Egyptian philosophy. Euclid, again, learned mathematics in Egypt before applying them elsewhere. And who could be surprised? For the pyramids and temples of the Nile were not built by guesswork or rule of thumb. The were built by the use of mathematical propositions which the Egyptians had discovered and proven. How otherwise could it have come about that the difference in length between the shortest base-side of the Great Pyramid at Gizeh (c2600BC) and the longest side (756.08 inches) is no more than a staggeringly accurate 7.9 inches? Herodotus and the men of his time did not know this, but they did know that the Great Pyramid was only one of innumerable mathematical marvels to be found in the land of the Pharaohs.

Yet the Greeks of the Classical Age went further. They also affirmed that Pharaonic culture had derived from inner Africa: from the lands of the 'long-lived Ethiopians', as Herodotus wrote, meaning not the people of the country we nowadays call Ethiopia but in general the country of the blacks. This was another Greek belief that went back to the remote origins of Greek culture. Homer's *Iliad* had said it long before, when recounting the visit of Zeus and the rest of the Greek gods to the annual banquet given for all the gods by the gods of the blacks:

> For Zeus had yesterday to Ocean's bounds
> Set forth to feast with Ethiop's faultless men,
> And he was followed there by all the gods . . .

Many histories written by the Classical Greeks have long been lost to us. But another which has not been lost is the world history composed by Diodorus Sikeliotes of Sicily, in about 50BC.[2] 'Now the Ethiopians [that is, the black peoples of Africa], as historians relate, were the first of all men', writes Diodorus in his second book, 'and the proofs of this statement, they [that is, these same Greek historians] say, are manifest'. As for the people of Egypt, adds Diodorus from the same sources, they 'are colonists sent out by the Ethiopians' after, as he explains, the steady annual accumulation of Nile silt had raised the land of Egypt above the level of the waters. 'And the larger part of the customs of the Egyptians, [these historians] hold, are Ethiopian, the colonists still preserving their ancient manners'. Allowing for all the differences of conception that separate us from Diodorus, this is an astonishingly exact statement of what archaeologists now affirm: i..e., that the cultures of the lower Nile, of Egypt proper, were initially derived from Neolithic cultures which first took shape in the then green Sahara of the fifth millenium BC and earlier. Just as Egypt had been the gift of the Nile, in the splendid phrase of Herodotus, so also was inner Africa the cultural begetter of the peoples who accepted the gift. By a marvellous if infinitely diffuse process of social evolution, the cultures of the Saharan Neolithic led on to those of the Pharaonic Nile. In the amazing harvests of Pharaonic achievement that followed, there was no doubt a place for other formative elements, including several from the Near East and Mesopotamia. But the primary heritage from inner Africa seems to come ever more clearly from the archaeological record.

Yet consider the version offered for so long by our schools and universities. Here we have been presented with another Aryan Model, likewise very dear to imperialism. This has preached that any signs of past progress detectable among the black peoples must have been the fruit of outside intrusion, of northern instrusion: in a word, of 'white' intrusion. This supplementary form of the Aryan Model, so handy for the 'civilising mission' of Europe in Africa, went into countless books and lectures. It was best enunciated in a 'scientific' guise by a British anthropologist of the 1920s, C.G. Seligman, in his *Races of Africa* (London, 1929).

Maintained as proven truth, this view asserted that a people or peoples known as 'Hamites' were responsible for any process of history that might be identifiable in Africa, because the 'Negroes' were too primitive to be able, on their own, to embark on any such process. Apart from relatively recent Semitic influence, Phoenician or Arab, Seligman taught that 'the civilisations of Africa are the civilisations of the Hamites'. And who were and are these pioneering and indispensable Hamites? No problem for Seligman: the Hamites were and are not really Africans at all. They 'are Caucasians, i.e., belong to the same great branch of mankind as almost all Europeans . . .' Or again, just to make sure: 'the incoming Hamites were pastoral Caucasoids—arriving wave after wave—better armed as well as quicker witted than the dark agricultural Negroes'. Seligman was following a well-beaten trail. Years earlier in 1912, for example, the German anthropologist Carl Meinhof had explained that 'in the course of [African] history'—at least he admitted that there had been some!—'it has repeatedly happened that the Hamitic peoples subjugated and, as a ruling people [*Herrenvolk* in Meinhof's original German], have governed dark pigmented Negroes who spoke languages different from that [*sic*] of the Hamites'.

Seligman, in fact, was reflecting the imperialist culture of his times; and this was as pervasive in academic circles as it was passionately advanced. Thus we have H.E. Egerton, when professor of colonial history at Oxford early in the 1920s, publishing a book in which he defends colonialism as 'the right way . . . of dealing with the native problem'. With colonialism, he says, 'What had happened [was] the introduction of order into blank, uninteresting, brutal barbarism'; and one may note in passing just how passionately the adjectives pile up. That was in 1922, and the same theme continued to be struck out loud and clear. So we have Egerton's successor at Oxford, Reginald Coupland, sounding it again late in the 1920s. History in Africa, with him, has to wait to begin until the arrival there of the missionary-explorer David Livingstone. 'A new chapter in the history of Africa began with David Livingstone . . . So far, it might be said, Africa proper had had no history.' Ancient Egypt and All That, presumably, was 'Africa improper'? In any case, until the middle of the nineteenth century, 'the main body of Africans . . . had stayed, for untold centuries, sunk in barbarism. Such, it might almost seem, had been Nature's decree . . . So they remained stagnant, neither going forward nor going back . . . The heart of Africa was scarcely beating.' And so it continued—and these men, after all, were the opinion-makers of their time—until well after the Second World War and the beginnings of anti-colonial change in Africa. Even then there was a rearguard action, notably signalled by Hugh Trevor-Roper (today Lord Dacre) who, when Regius Professor of History at Oxford in 1963, found it perfectly right to provide his own version of Hegel's nonsense of 130 years earlier.

* * *

Now this extension of the European Aryan Model to an entirely comparable African version—to an African Aryan Model for all of Africa-beyond-Egypt—had not been Bernal's concern in this present volume, although he is manifestly well aware of it and of its racist origins and uses. Yet it remains entirely relevant and cognate to Bernal's thesis that this African Aryan Model, as I think he will allow me to call it, has been very largely overthrown during the past thirty years or so. No serious Africanist of today would think of taking Egerton or Coupland or Trevor-Roper for a moment seriously when they speak of Africa's lack of history; and the break-through point here can probably be dated to Onwuka Dike's thesis of 1956 (*Trade and Politics in the Niger Delta*), as well as, in a large archaeological sense, to Libby's demonstration of the early 1950s that the C-14 isotope of carbon can be used to provide approximately probable dates of organic materials in archaeological sites otherwise undateable.

No serious Africanist, by the same token, any longer believes in the 'Hamitic hypothesis' of progress in ancient Africa, or even in the existence, now or in the past, of any people properly definable as Hamites. By a nice coincidence of 1963, as it happens, the abolition of the Hamites—however 'Caucasoid' and 'quicker-witted' as Seligman had reassured his readers—began with the publication in that year of J.H. Greenberg's essential *Languages of Africa*,[3] and has continued ever since. The Hamites were a myth: 'even the linguistic use of the term Hamite', wrote Greenberg with an authority unchallenged in this context, 'should be abandoned'. Likewise, the then fashionable term Hamito-Semitic for major languages in northern and north-eastern Africa should be dropped as misleading. For these languages Greenberg coined a new term, Afroasiatic; and this has since come into general acceptance, being also used by Bernal in this volume. Yet Afroasiatic can also be misleading for the non-specialist, though certainly less so than Hamito-Semitic, for the Asiatic element in Greenberg's classification applies only to one of the five major groupings in this linguistic family, that of the Arabic which became current in north-eastern Africa only after the middle of the seventh century. The other four linguistic elements in Afroasiatic, as Greenberg lists them, are Egyptian (extinct today), Berber, Cushitic in its five derivative variants, and Chadian: all of them, as you see, thoroughly African. But the Hamites and their Caucasoid quick wits have in any case vanished from the scientific scene.

So have other stereotypes of the racist model. The scholarship of the last thirty years and more simply tipped them into the dustbin of exploded fantasies. This was not achieved easily or without a lot of stubborn effort; but it has now been achieved beyond any possibility of reversion to those aforesaid fantasies. It may even be claimed that this achievement is among the most significant intellectual advances of the twentieth century. Yet Bernal's treatment of this important aspect of his own subject is disappointingly deficient, being little more than an afterthought at the end of his book. No doubt he has it in mind to put this right in a later volume. As it is, reading his pages in this respect must leave one without the slightest indication of the fact that the study of African history and humanity, in many disciplines, has become the concern of manifold colleges and universities in all the continents, not least in Africa itself. One could not guess that whole libraries of books and papers are now available in one or other field of Africa-centered and Africa-directed research and debate, Bernal refers very briefly, however, only to two or three American historians apart from Cheik Anta Diop. This is, again, surprising in a writer as conscientious as Bernal, for African studies in the USA, where Bernal teaches, had also become impressively wide in their range and distinguished in their level at least by the middle 1960s, while the forthcoming assembly of the American African Studies Association, due this November of 1987, will be its thirtieth annual meeting. Valiantly toppling the Aryan Model for Europe, this sympathetic writer has not yet had time to notice that its partner for Africa has meanwhile bitten the dust.

Has bitten the dust, that is to say, among all serious students of Africa: not yet, by any means, with the non-specialised serious public and much less with any 'general public' in Europe or North America. Hence the objections to the television series mentioned earlier. The news has evidently yet to get through; but there are explanations for this outside any question or inherited prejudice. One of them concerns our almost total ignorance of the developmental relationship which came to exist between the civilisation of the Pharaohs and the peoples of inner Africa, the peoples of 'the land shadowing with wings which lies beyond the rivers of Ethiopia'.

Here is a subject from which historians and archaeologists have tended to shy away, no doubt because of the formidable influence of schools of Egyptology which have had no interest in the question and which, more or less ferociously, have resisted any 'Africanising' of their field of work. Yet it is now a subject which needs tackling if Aryan mythologies of the Hamite sort are to be finally dismissed. Given, for example, that the origins of Pharaonic civilisation are traceable to the remote Neolithic of the green Sahara, as they increasingly appear to be, what was the manner and the movement of the civilising 'feed back' by that civilisation, in due course of its astonishing development, to the peoples of the continental interior? Or, if peoples in western Africa possess symbols and beliefs which have been exactly parallel to those of the ancient Nile—to mention only two, the serpent and the ram—who acquired them first? Or if people in southern Africa have used headrests exactly comparable with those of Ancient Egypt, has this been mere coincidence of 'separate invention', or, if not, how is it to be explained?

And so on: remote African history is alive with such taunting questions, and very possibly they will never win sufficient answers. Yet it seems to me that their importance in this whole story calls urgently for provisional and tentative answers, and, furthermore, that such answers now begin to be possible. Working suppositions which I believe that many specialists now accept, or more or less accept, are that the geographical locus of all or most of Africa's ramifying cultures lay, as I remarked above, in the long unfolding of the Saharan Neolithic;[4] that these cultures manifestly achieved their greatest elaboration and success in Pharaonic Egypt; and that, in one elusive way or another, the consequential 'feed back' was shuttled to and fro but became ever more tenuous as desiccation after c2500BC severely continued in the lands to the south and west of the Nile. However one may conceive this process, what emerges today is that one has to think of all African cultures, those of the Nile certainly included, as belonging to the same capacious arena of this continent's history.

This is a view of the matter which is still found shocking by the orthodox. That is easily understandable because, like Bernal's Revised Ancient Model, it calls for the radical and therefore painful re-thinking of many received opinions. It asks for the healing of more than one neurosis in the field of 'race relations', above all (at least within Europe, but I suspect elsewhere as well) of the neurosis which has to see black humanity as inherently 'less'—add any substantive that you may wish—than white humanity. Here in Britain it remains so widely spread that we shall have to work away at removing it for a long time before its fevers fall.

* * *

To that end, it seems to me, one cannot sufficiently insist that all such racist opinions and neuroses are relatively new—older than Bernal's Aryan Model, and yet not so very much so. Shakespeare's *Othello*, for example, was written before the great onset of racism in Northern Europe, and it is not a racist play. It is a play about sexual jealousy, careerism, and hatred of competitive foreigners; and if the Moor was certainly black, he was still the powerful and admired commander of the armies of the Venetian Republic, then the strongest of the city-states of the Mediterranean, and greatly trusted by the masters of that republic. At most, *Othello* in 1603 can be interpreted in a racist sense as foreshadowing the coming racism of the Atlantic slave trade in Northern Europe (a racism which appeared somewhat earlier in Portugal). Yet before that? Here is one case, to round off these notes on *Black Athena*, which offers a suggestive answer.

What did Europeans think about black people before the rise of racism? How did they estimate the values of black humanity? There are countless indications in the pictorial arts. Think only of the noble portraits of the black monarch among the three kings who journeyed to salute the birth of Christ. Think of the work of the great masters of the Renaissance who painted black persons. Think of Rembrandt, Velasquez, many more. Each of them, without exception, painted black persons from the same standpoint as they painted white persons, whether either of these, white or black, were kings or merchants or ambassadors or servants. Yet none of these paintings, even so, has seemed to me to possess as much persuasive and explanatory power as a medieval statue in the Magdeburger Dom, the majestic thirteenth-century cathedral of the German city which was then the capital of the Holy Roman Empire. This is the statue of a crusader figure, sculpted life size and wearing the chain mail armour of the period.

The statue in fact is of St Maurice, patron saint of Magdeburg, made for the cathedral in about 1240. That in itself is not in the least surprising, for St Maurice was well known to the Middle Ages as a great military saint, and was in this respect the companion of St George. Whether or not he was a real historical person rather than a pious legend, he was widely revered. Said to have been martyred as a Christian legionary commander of late Roman times—for having refused an imperial order to kill one in ten (that is, *decimate* in the Roman meaning of the word) of the soldiers of another legion which had gone into revolt—St Maurice was always referred to as St Maurice of Thebes. This was the Thebes of Egypt, not of Greece, but Maurice nonetheless had always up to now been portrayed as white. Innumerable icons in the churches of Europe had shown him as being as white as any European saint.

Yet here at Magdeburg in 1240, something new occurred. Overnight, as it were, St Maurice became black. He became an African beyond any doubt; not only that, he very certainly became a Nubian, even down to the lineage cuts upon his forehead. Facing his stern and yet warmly protective gaze, you know that you are looking at a man from Nubia, a Nubian crusader in the chain mail likewise worn in Nubia then, but a Nubian, moreover, very clearly regarded as a friend and ally. Now what had happened, and why was this? Nobody as yet, so far as I know, has provided any satisfactory answers drawn from the history of those times. Within the possible limits of this essay, here is a sketch of what the answer surely ought to be.

A few years before this remarkable statue was carved—so manifestly from the life—and placed in the cathedral of Magdeburg, the Holy Roman Frederick II had led the sixth of the Christian crusades to recover the Holy Land and Egypt from their Muslim rulers. From his point of view, Frederick managed rather good results from this crusade of 1227-9, although the Pope bitterly denounced him for not managing better; ten years of peace ensued in Palestine and a treaty with the sultan of Egypt, warfare being renewed only in 1239. In any case, it was altogether understandable that the crusade should be commemorated in the emperor's principle place of worship, the cathedral of Magdeburg. And what could be more natural, one may ask, than that it should be commemorated in such a way as to celebrate the crusaders' only religious allies in the distant lands to which they had gone? For the twin kingdoms of Nubia, due south of Egypt, were bastions of Christianity in the early thirteenth century, and had been so for more than six centuries.

These Nubian Christian kingdoms have been largely erased from memory since the fifteenth century, engulfed as they were by Islam after about 1450. But in the time of Frederick II they were an integral part of the Eastern Christian Church, and, as such, had been sporadically at war with the Saracen rulers of Egypt for more than a hundred years. What more probable, even if precise proofs are lacking, than that the Christian Nubians were fighting alliance with the Crusaders from the West? (Very suggestive evidence to this effect is in fact available, but I will not go into it here.) What more to be expected, then, than that the crusaders of Magdeburg should wish to celebrate their distant ally? What more understandable than that the citizens of Magdeburg, rededicating their newly rebuilt cathedral of the late 1230s to Saint Maurice, should honour their patron saint as black, as Nubian?

This, in any case, is exactly what they did. And from then onwards the cult of this black St Maurice spread far and wide across Europe. Black icons of the saint supplanted earlier white icons. And it has seemed to me that there could be no more dramatic and instructive an illustration of the mental abyss, in the whole matter of 'white-black relations', which divided the consciousness of the Middle Ages from the racism of later times.

As it happens, there is an unnoticed English footnote to this German illustration of pre-racist attitudes to powers and persons who were black. Let me mention it here, for I have so far tried in vain to find a place to write about it. Medieval England, as everyone knows, shared in the continental European influence and appeal of the Crusades. Knights trekked in from the most remote fiefdoms, and in due course the churches of the period became rich in the effigies of knights who had taken part in the crusading venture. As in many other places, this is what happened in the medieval churches of remote Herefordshire in western England (where, simply to explain, I lately lived). Among these churches is that of the forgotten little parish of Brinsop.

There in Brinsop you will find a superb East Window in which the stained glass of the Middle Ages has wonderfully outlived the assaults of time. And in the centre of this thriteenth-century Brinsop splendour you will see the portrait figure of a knight in armour. About that, in itself, there is again nothing to be surprised—except that the face of the knight is as black as the face of the Magdeburg Maurice. Given the historical context, the conclusion appears so obvious as to be undeniable. No doubt: and yet Brinsop Church is not dedicated to St Maurice, much less to a black St Maurice, nor is there any mention of

Maurice in any aspect of the building. The church is dedicated to St George, a very white saint, while the heraldic banner woven by nineteenth-century Herefordshire ladies, and proudly displayed in the nave, likewise portrays the saint in the window as a saint most properly white. Thus does history get stood upon its head.

Now it cannot be proved that Brinsop Church was originally dedicated to St Maurice, nor that the black saint in the East Window is an echo of the black Maurice of Magdeburg. But the contrary cannot be proved either, the records being lost; and we are simply left with the anonymous face of a black saint. So much, after all, has gone beyond recall. The churches of medieval Herefordshire, like others elsewhere, have many crusaders' effigies; seldom or never can any name be added to them. One of the finest of these effigies, as it happens, is in another thirteenth-century church at Moccas, not far from Brinsop: but to put a name to this crusading knight upon his tomb top has to be merest guesswork. One certain fact at Brinsop is that the saint in the East Window has a completely black face, even though his features have long since blurred away. Another certain fact is that the blackness of this saint, in racist times, had been utterly ignored, just as if it were not there at all.

Now a black St Maurice could in no way have shocked or astonished the congregations of the Middle Ages, as so many black icons are there to show. But in racist times any such icon became unthinkable; and the unthinkable continues. Even the devotedly conscientious Nicolaus Pevsner, in the Herefordshire volume of his monumental *Buildings of England* (Penguin 1963), has nothing to say on the subject. Having examined every feature of Brinsop Church with his always exacting care and expertise, Pevsner passes in silence over the blackness of the saint in question, and simply notes that Brinsop East Window has panels of medieval glass, depicting 'especially a St George'. St George, that is, with a black face: and yet no comment. Pevsner himself was not, of course, a racist: on the contrary, he was a refugee from racism in Nazi Germany. On this occasion he was simply reflecting, for sure unconsciously, the racist culture of the times in which he lived and in which we still live. That is why I said that racism has been a weapon, even when innocently used, to stand history upon its head.

Bernal's book is an attempt, a major attempt, to help old history back upon its feet again so that we may better understand later history and our own history. It is a profoundly liberating work because it sheers through the murk of racism, academic or otherwise, that has obscured and confused our conceptions of intercontinental history, just as racism, consciously or not, does this still. I hope that Bernal's book will be very widely read and pondered. One need not consent to everything advanced by Bernal: I do not do so myself. One can find some of his arguments insufficient, and some of his arrows wrongly aimed. His is a book to argue with as well as to agree with; and it is indeed in this sense that he tells us he has written it. But his main target: *that* he strikes with unfaltering and powerful skill.

Notes

1. The *Histories* of Herodotus are available in English in an excellent modern translation by Aubrey de Selincourt (London, Penguin Books).

2. English translation in twelve volumes by C.H. Oldfather, *Diodorus of Sicily* (London, Heinermann, and Cambridge, Mass, Harvard University Press, 1967).

3. J.H. Greenburg, *The Languages of Africa* (Bloomington, Indiana University, 1963).

4. For a useful recent summary on the Saharan Neolithic, with a large specialised bibliography, see Marianne Cornevin, 'Les Néolithiques du Sahara Central et l'histoire génerâle de l'Afrique', *Bulletin de la Société Préhistorique Française*, Vol. 79, 10-12.

*Martin Bernal, *Black Athena: the Afroasiatic roots of classical civilisation*. Vol. 1 'The fabrication of ancient Greece, 1785-1985' (London, Free Association Books, 1987).

ANCIENT EGYPTIANS: "THE DARK RED FACE MYTH"

James Brunson

The myth of the Egyptians belonging to the so-called dark-red race was created in the early nineteenth century, and continues to be perpetuated by modern scholars and laymen. This premise is based primarily upon the color generally used to depict the ancient Egyptians on wall and papyrus paintings and statues. I am of the opinion, similarly expressed by late Senegalese scholar Cheikh Anta Diop, that there was no such thing as a dark-red race. This hue in fact, was also used in a symbolic context.

Red ochre, an oxide of iron, was combined with a vegetable gum binder by the ancient Egyptian painter to create the now famous dark-red color. This red ochre was extracted from an iron ore called hematite. Recent archaeological discoveries have yielded evidence of iron ore mines in Swaziland and Zimbabwe, dated to 27,000 B.C. and 41,000 B.C. respectively.[1] Africans had been extracting and using hematite for thousands of years prior to the beginning of Egyptian civilization.

The actual magico-religious symbolism attached to the color red may not have begun in Egypt, but probably came from Inner Africa. during the Paleolithic period (40,000-2000 B.C.) When Aurignacian Blacks invaded Europe, we find that the act of inhumation became a general practice. Corpses were elaborately buried, and sprinkled or painted with red ochre. Some experts conjecture that the application of red ochre to the body of the deceased indicated a belief in a survival of the soul or rebirth.[2]

Soviet scholars have recently pointed out that "Equatorial types" (i.e., Central Africans) reflecting ancient genetic connections to their Aurignacian ancestors, spread from Europe into Asia.[3] As their nomadic lifestyle gave way to a more sedentary existence, this cultural practice of using red ochre in burial customs evolved as well. A Neolithic wall fragment discovered in ancient Turkey, and dated to 5500 B.C. adds significant meaning to the intellectual transition in the usage of red ochre. On this fragment is the depiction of a man and woman, the former painted in red ochre and the latter in yellow ochre. This symbolism which depicts the man as the "blood of life" and the woman as goddess of agriculture, (the yellow representing fertility) predates the identical Egyptian canon of painting.[4] Earlier blacks had used this symbolism several millenia before.

As pointed out by St. Clair Drake in his work "Black Folk: Here and There," Egyptian men were certainly not red in color so the question of its symbolic significance must be explained. "To the African," according to the British Egyptologist Wallis Budge, "the blood represented life, and therefore the spirit of the person to whom it belonged. And as blood carries with it protection, people, and even spirit houses, and the gateways of villages continue to be sprinkled with it by modern Africans."[5]

In their paintings, the Egyptians cared little for whether non-Egyptians would maintain their spirit, thus portrayed them in their natural hues. Furthermore, they knew that they were dark-brown and brown-skinned in complexion. Dark-red was a standard color symbolically used for portraying Egyptian men.[6] Old Kingdom art, in particular, made it a habit of this while depicting the women as yellow. Budge further believed that the earliest Egyptians painted their bodies with red pigment, a practice he noted among central Africans.

Notes

1. Mircea Eliade, A History of Ideas, Vol. I: From the Stone Age to the Eleusinian Mysteries, transl. by Willard R. Trask, The University of Chicago Press, 1978, p. 10-11
2. Ibid.
3. T.A. Trofimova, "Population of Southern Turkmenia in Ancient Times and Its Near Eastern and South Indian Connections According To Paleoanthropological Data," Contributions To The Physical Anthropology of Central Asia And The Caucasus, Russian Translation Series of the Peabody Museum of the Archaeological and Ethnology, Harvard University, Vol. III, No. 2, 1968, p. 327
4. Eliade, p. 10-11
5. Sir Wallis E. Budge, Osiris and the Egyptian Resurrection, Vol. I, Dover Publications, New York, 1973, originally published in 1973, p. 277
6. St. Clair Drake, Black Folk Here and There, Vol. I, University of California, Los Angeles, 1987, p. 267-268

ETHNIC OR SYMBOLIC: BLACKNESS AND HUMAN IMAGES IN ANCIENT EGYPTIAN ART

James Brunson

During the most important Egyptian dynasties (Dynasty I—IV, Dynasty VI, Dynasty XI—XIII, Dynasty XVII-XVIII, and Dynasty XXV), we find that a black-skinned or Africoid people were in power. The pharaoh's theocratic rule and physical well-being was essential to the maintenance of the Egyptian state. In perpetuating pharaonic images critical to his power and authority, the king utilized a strict color canon which celebrated humankind's victory in life and death.

> . . . It seems rather an extraordinary circumstance that the statues of the Gods of the ancients should be represented of a black colour; or that they be made of a stone as nearly black as could be obtained . . . I continually found . . . that my labors terminated with something black.[1]
>
> —Godfred Higgins, *Anacalypsis*

> Black was used extensively by ancient Africans to represent a host of concepts, all of them having in common the concept of seed, archetype or doorway to the collective all, collective unconscious mind.[2]
>
> —Dr. Richard King, *Black Dot*

In 1793, France declared war upon its eternal rival for world domination, Great Britain. Within six short years, Napoleon's imperialistic aims took him to the northeastern part of the African continent. During the ebb and flo of war (which culminated at the Battle of Waterloo in 1815), intrigue brought scholars, scientists, and freebooters from both sides to Egypt, heralding a rediscovery of the mysteries of a long-forgotten civilization. Among these explorers was an amateur British archaeologist, sent by Lord Byron, ambassador to Constantinople, Turkey, on an expedition to Alexandria, Egypt. The mission, according to this agent, was to seize the French collection of Egyptian artifacts. And so, during the British invasion of Egypt in 1801, William Hamilton and a newly acquired colleague, Daniel Clark, succeeded in "stealing from the French" a great many antiquities (among these spoils of war was the famous Rosetta Stone). Using these works of art as a point of reference, Hamilton published in 1809 his Aegyptica, a volume including information on Egyptian history and art.

Perhaps the earliest known modern writer to comment upon the use of black on human figures in Egyptian art (Hamilton toured Egypt several years before Champollion the Younger and attempted an unsuccessful decipherment of the Rosetta Stone), Hamilton was awe struck by several painted bas reliefs depicting "black figures conferring on certain red figures, similarly habited, the instruments of sacerdotal office."[3] The amateur archaeologist went on to postulate a connection between the images and ancient traditions regarding Ethiopia's founding of Egypt.

Eurocentric scholarship has generated controversy in more areas of Egyptological study than one would care to enumerate. Scholarly interpretations of color application to human images in ancient Egyptian art have proven no exception. Red, brown, yellow, green, blue, white, pink, and black were employed by the artist to define neters, women, men, and children. I think that some of these hues do point to racial and ethnic distinctions; however, others were more symbolic and esoteric in meaning. Besides the famous "dark-red" color generally associated with representations of the ancient Egyptians, no hue has caused more heated debate in the depiction of anthropomorphic images than the use of black. While there is no doubt that during the important dynasties the ancient Egyptians were primarily a black skinned people, the actual color black held a significant position in ancient Nile Valley spirituality.

African sensibility perceived the symbolism of blackness as inextricably bound to the conceptual cycle of life, death, and rebirth. The impact of blackness upon ancient Judeo-Christian symbolism focusing upon 'baptism and rebirth,' remains obvious today. Blackness as an ancient Egyptian concept, represented the "Lord of the Hidden Treasure", guardian and divine consciousness which raises the human spirit from obscurity to light. The focus of this essay is two-fold, and its aim must be clarified. Strictly speaking, I will concentrate on human images that are painted coal-black, ink-black, jet-black, or blue-black in hue and described as such by the sources. Secondly, an analysis of its usage will be made in relation to the importance of the figure(s) discussed.

Below, I have listed the generally recognized theories and some of my own observations:

1. Black symbolized the black land, soil of Egypt.
2. Black symbolized divinity, and reverence toward the ancestors—deification.
3. Black had a spiritual or religious connotation, symbolizing rebirth or regeneration; this entailed a rhythmic cycle suspended in eternity, which included plant and animal life.
4. Black symbolized death and the underworld or netherworld, known as Amenta.[4]
5. A connection was made between the black soil which flowed into Egypt from Nubia which occurred during the inundation; a further association was attached to Nubians that were literally black-skinned.
6. Ancient memories and traditions connected the original transmission of

the "gods and goddesses" from ancient Egypt's black-skinned ancestors.[5]

7. Only the king, queen, and neters were allowed the symbolic use of black in funerary ritual; this prior to the advent of the Middle Kingdom, would bar or restrict anyone black in skin tone from being depicted as such.

While I have not specifically mentioned black-skinned people in the above criteria, the idea of possessing coal-black skin and not being considered "anthropologically Africoid" is an absurdity. The bigoted, Austrian Egyptologist Hermann Junker, was chief among those proponents conveniently and ficticiously dividing Africa into "Hamites and Negroes," with the latter having "subnasal prognathism, thick puffy lips, wooly hair, and black skin."[6] The art as it presents itself, particularly some predynastic paintings, does not always allow for anthropological study. But where there is corroborating evidence, being literally black-skinned and ethnically black will be applicable to the discussion.

The artistic development and rise of Egyptian art was inextricably bound to the power of the elite. As with all civilizations, this occupation was financed by the wealthy, the ruling class in particular. Chieftains and Pharaohs of the Nile Valley seized every available opportunity to espouse their theocratic doctrines, using sculpture and painting as one of their vehicles. Central to the success of the nation was the virility of the king, leader of the "flock". As the "Good Shepherd", the Pharoah had to renew or revive his sacred spirit, in order to instill continued hope in the people. Certain Egyptian deities were associated with regeneration, and it appears that the color black was at times used to convey this message. Osiris, Hathor, and Amen/Min are among those neters connected with regeneration and at times appear black-skinned; or they were associated with kings or queens appearing black-skinned in a sacred composition.

Osiris as the Black God King

Osiris, as Lord of the Resurrection, personified the deceased pharaoh of Egypt. His ancient origin has been traced back to central Africa, among the peoples living along the Upper Nile River. In Egyptian art, he has been portrayed as dark-red, green, and blue, but the emphasis will here be on his black aspect (Fig. 1). One of his most ancient epithets, "He who is in God's Tent", has prehistoric and predynastic antecedents. This title emphasized the traditional importance of wrapping the king's body and creating a "tent" or shrine for the ceremonial burial.[7] Artistic evidence beginning with the Predynastic Period and culminating with the end of the New Kingdom, shows a gradual evolution not only of the king's funerary ritual but the importance attached to the image of a black Osiris.

From the earliest available artistic evidence, a sacred boat or barque is seen associated with the deceased king and instrumental to his heavenly journey

Egyptian nobleman and wife presenting offerings to Osiris (New Kingdom)

toward the stars. On a predynastic linen fragment found at Gebelein, Upper Egypt and dating between 3400-3200 B.C., we have a depiction of two boats and several crudely painted stick figures (Fig. 2). On both boats are representations of dark-red oarsmen, but in the lower boat is the first appearance of a "tented" black-skinned figure (Fig. 3). For several reasons, this is without doubt the depiction of a deified ruler: 1.) This fine linen fragment was originally part of a larger blanket found in a tomb wrapped around the human remains of a wealthy man. 2.) Commoners when buried, were wrapped in straw matting, hardly fine materials such as linen. 3.) Another point is the later use of Osirian burial by nobles in the Middle Kingdom. In some tombs, there have been discoveries of small wooden boat models carrying a seated image of the deceased "shrouded and tented" (Fig. 4).

In this predynastic painting, we have our earliest representation of the deceased in the funerary barque en route to a cosmic destination. Thus we find that as early as 3400 B.C., we have the shroud, shrine, funerary barque, and black-skinned Osirian figure—symbols of the resurrection—all depicted in one small fragment. These symbolic images would endure beyond all Egyptian religious and cultural turmoil for the next three thousand years.

By the Middle Kingdom, veneration of the Pharaoh as the personification of

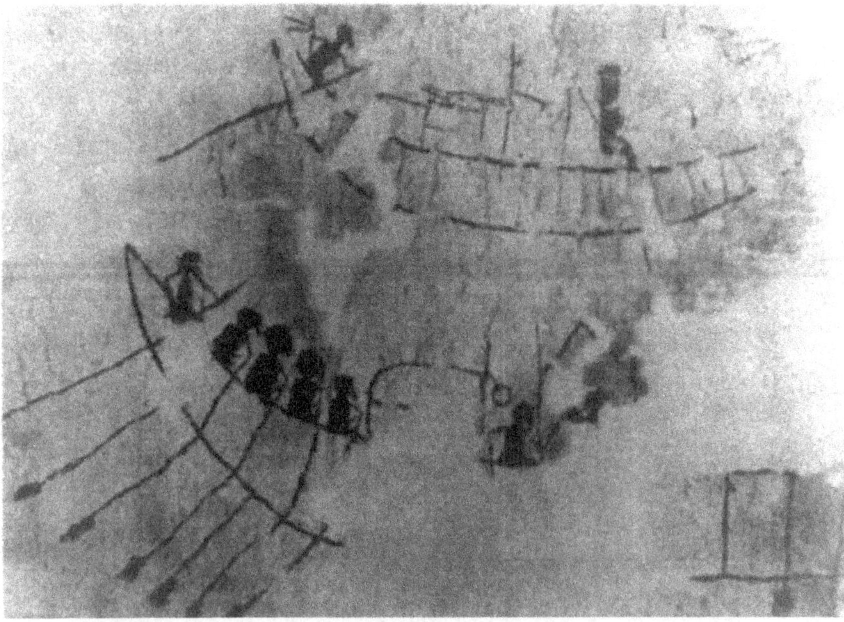

Funerary boat withblack-skinned figure underneath canopy Predynastic 3400-3200 B.C.

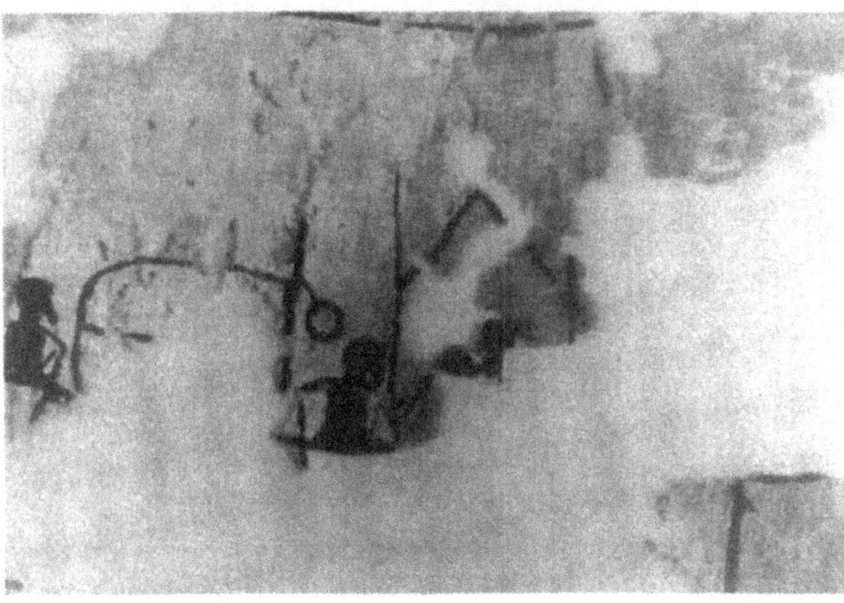

Detail of boat with Black-skinned figure.

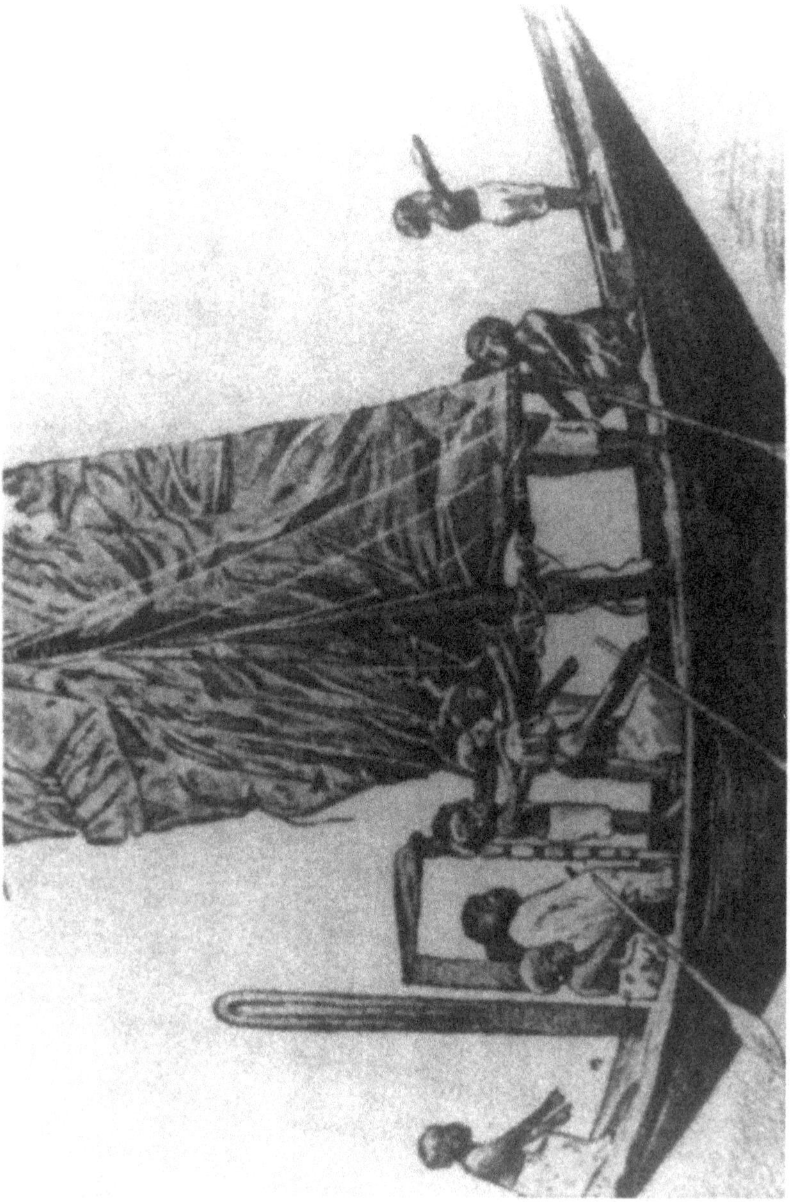

Funerary boat for the deceased, called the Maatit Boat. Middle Kingdom, Dynasty XI.

Osiris, became intimately linked with the rising Nile, whose sustenance brought fertility to all living things in Egypt.[8] While I have come across no evidence of statues or bas reliefs painted in black that date to the Old Kingdom, that does not mean none existed. In fact, evidence from the previously discussed Predynastic Period (3600-3200 B.C.) and Archaic Period (3200-2860 B.C.) support the idea that black-skinned depictions existed of the Pharaoh as the living Osiris (Fig. 5). Mentuhotep I (2060-2010 B.C.), founder of Dynasty XI, erected eight seated and standing statues of himself at the Upper Egyptian mortuary complex at Deir

The black Pharaoh Ba-en-neter of Dynasty II setated in the Osirian pose. Archaic period 3200-2860 B.C.

el Bahari, Thebes. Among them, in one funerary niche, was a 5′9″, seated limestone statue, painted in black skin and wrapped in fine linen bandages.[9] Recovered from a subterranean chamber, this statue was different from the others; it was an image of the Pharaoh's Ka as Osiris [10] (Fig. 6). In his death, the king merged with the black "god," becoming the living Osiris.

Discoveries of mural paintings and life-sized standing statues exhibiting a

Nebhetepre Mentuhotep I, founder of Dynasty XI. Middle Kingdom 2060-2010 B.C.

black-skinned representation of the Pharoah as Osiris, have been more numerous during the New Kingdom. Dynasty XIX mural paintings from the Theban tombs of the Egyptian priest Usherhet (1395 B.C.), and the Vizier Amenmose (1300 B.C.), depict Thutmoses I and Thutmoses III respectively; even though the mural works were conceived well after their reigns (Thutmoses I, 1525-1512 B.C.; Thutmoses III, 1504-1450 B.C.), they support the idea that at one time, life-sized statues painted in black-skin, existed for those sovereigns. In fact, an earlier mural painting from the tomb of the royal official Rekhmire (1504-1453 B.C.), contemporary with the reign of Thutmoses III, depicts royal sculptors creating the black statue of the pharaoh. The depicted image of Thutmoses I (Fig. 7), discovered in Userhet's tomb, rests upon a platform, which was pulled by priests in a ceremonial procession. Verification of this contention is supported by the mural portrait of Thutmoses III, which was found in the tomb of Amenmose.

"Dragging the statue of Thutmoses 1". Painted representation of black skinned Ka statue of Thutmoses I. Tomb of Userhet. Dynasty XVIII. 1395 B.C.

Here, the shrine, sacred barque, and Ka statue are graphically shown (Fig. 8). Although the sledge itself is not actually shown, its presence on the three dimensional statue cannot be doubted.

Physical evidence of authentic three dimensional statues, was recovered from the tomb of the young boy king, Tutankhamen (1363-1352 B.C.). Between 5'6" and 5'7" tall, "they were in the name of 'the royal Ka of Harakhti, the Osiris Tutankhamen'" (Fig. 9). The murals depicting two dimensional counterparts of these statues, were in all probability, made of wood, and coated with black resin. If the "gods" were transported back up the Nile to Nubia, as tradition relates, the resin would survive the deterioration experienced by water-based paint. In each case, the king's Ka strides forward with staff and mace, and sports the uraeus crown—the god Osiris victorious over death. As Tutankhamen's statue was wrapped in linen bandages, there seems to be no reason to doubt a similar arrangement for the others. One cannot help escape similarities to the biblical Lazarus, once dead, but later resurrected, victoriously shedding his dark tomb and linen bandages.

Hathor: Black Goddess and Mother of the King

Of her many epithets, Hathor's role as the "Great Wild Cow", provider of

Detail of Deified Thutmoses III. Painted representation of black-skinned, Ka statue. Tomb of the Vizier Amenmose. Dynasty XIX, 1300 B.C.

Black-skinned Ka statue of Osiris-Tutankhamen. Note the headdress, staff, mace and wooden sledge in comparison to the two previously discussed illustrations. Dynasty XVIII. 1363-1352 B.C.

nourishment for the pharaoh as her young bull, is pertinent to this study. As with Osiris, Hathor's origins may be traced to ancient black peoples living along the Upper Nile in what is now the Sudan. As completely bovine, Hathor is shown merging from either a watery papyrus marsh or canopied shrine. Symbolic of renewed life, Hathor was often represented by black-skinned queens, or central to the resurrection of black-skinned pharaohs.

As early as the Archaic Period (3200-2860 B.C.), Hathor was venerated. However evidence during the Old Kingdom (2360 B.C.), shows that women of the royal court served as her priestesses. The Pharaoh, Pepi I (Dynasty VI, 2335 B.C.), even declared himself a "son of Hathor." Further support of this veneration is prevalent in the Middle Kingdom, where a large Theban shrine was found dedicated to Hathor.

Mentuhotep I, as previously mentioned, erected his mortuary district at Deir el Bahari, which also sanctified the memory of five royal wives, all High Priestesses of Hathor. Among them, representations of Ashayet and Kemset, were painted black; in this instance, I think that the color was symbolic of the neter Hathor (Fig. 10). There is physical evidence that women of Nubian and Central African extraction resided in the royal household at Thebes during this time.[11] An anthropological study of all five queens demonstrated evidence of "Nubian

Protrait of Queen Ashayet, royal wife of Nebhettepre Mentuhotep I, painted in black. Middle Kingdom, Dynasty XI.

blood" or Africoid characteristics. At least two of the women had scarification or tattooing, a distinctive trademark of equatorial Africa. The mummies of Ashayet and Henehet were overwhelmingly Central African in type.[12] In this connection, it is to be noted that black as an ethnic marker as well as symbolic element could be applicable. However, the additional use of dark-red and yellow skin tones to depict Ashayet on other painted reliefs makes this thesis tenuous. Black as a sacred color is, in my opinion, the rationale for its usage here.

Thutmoses III also had a small shrine built for Hathor on the same site, which has yielded a statue and wall relief of this pharaoh painted in black skin.(Fig. 11) In both cases, Thutmoses III strides forward, protected overhead by the cosmic presence of the cow-headed Hathor. It is as if the pharaoh has been revitalized by Hathor, and imbued with a black visage.

Statue of a black-skinned Thutmoses III striding under the protective gaze of the Cow-Goddess Hathor. New Kingdom, Dynasty XVIII

Min: Black God of Regeneration

Min was a prehistoric "god" originally worshipped in Nubia or Punt, and later brought to Akhim and Koptos, Upper Egypt, during the Predynastic epoch. His anthropomorphic and ithyphallic form, which also dates back to this period, depicts a man with one upraised hand holding a flail, and in the other, his erect phallus.

Middle Kingdom texts have described Min as possessing all valuable incense originating from Nubia and Punt, and as being the ruler of the Anti or Nubian bowmen.[13] The connection between Nubia and Min may be signified by the role of a "black man" in extolling the neter with incense. Min was painted dark-red, blue, but also black, with blue and black being sometimes indistinguishable.[14] Our representation of Min (Fig. 12), from Thebes depicts him as black-skinned and wrapped in white bandages. The exact narrative of this fragmentary work, restored by the Pharaoh Horemhab (1348-1320 B.C.), cannot be totally explained. However, similar images of Min, from as early as the Archaic period, show the pharaoh dancing before the "god." Regeneration is again a central theme of images associated with Min.

Portrait of Thutmoses II as the god Min. New Kingdom, Dynasty XVIII

Ahmose-Nefertari

The Queen-mother, Ahmose-Nefertari, was the royal co-founder of Dynasty XVIII (1567-1320 B.C.). Ancestress to a prestigious line of Black Theban royalty and nobility, Ahmose-Nefertari became deified at death, and for her a cult of worship was established. At least five shrines were dedicated to Ahmose-Nefertari, and her son, Amenhotep I, with ancestor worship being strongly attached to a ceremonial procession of cult statues.[15]

As early as the life of Jean Francois Champollion (1790-1832), modern explorers and scholars have written about the black visage of Ahmose-Nefertari depicted in the painted bas reliefs. Attempts to explain this perturbed many, dividing speculation into two distinct theories: one ethnic and the other symbolic. Champollion wrote that she was of the Ethiopian race. William Osburn (1854) described her as a queen "Ethiop in complexion and descent." Karl Lepsius (1810-1884) called her the "Black Queen," while Samuel Birch (1875) wrote, "At the Eighteenth Dynasty . . . the negress mounts the throne." The writings of Henreich Brugsh-Bey (1891) and Ratzel (1896) were among the earliest to postulate a non-ethnic rationale for the use of black. Undeniably caught up in the

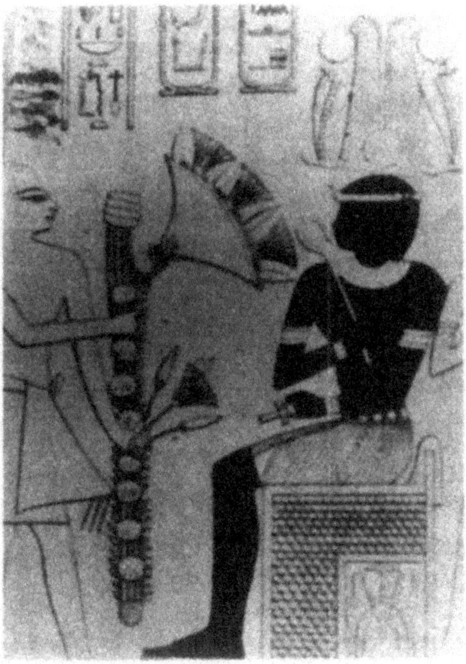

Portrait of Amenhotep I painted in black. New Kingdom. Late Dynasty XVIII.

racism of his day, Brugsh-Bey contended that this blackness symbolized the "dark night of the grave."[16] Ratzel enlarged upon this thesis, connecting blackness with divinity. While a battleground has been established between Euro-centric and Afro-centric scholars regarding blackness and human images, I think that its use in denoting ethnicity is a subject that demands expanded study. Ahmose-Nefertari was depicted in dark-red skin, yellowish-brown, and black skin. However that she was of Africoid ancestry has been proven elsewhere.[17]

Amenhotep I, (Fig. 13) and his mother, Ahmose-Nefertari, were deified in a cult by a guild of Theban craftsmen on the west bank at Deir el Medina. At least five tombs were dedicated to them, containing mural portraits, done well after their deaths. The images are betrayed by the elegant fashions worn by the queen, being styles not worn until late Dynasty XVIII and early Dynasty XIX.

There are at least four known depictions of Thutmoses III painted in black-

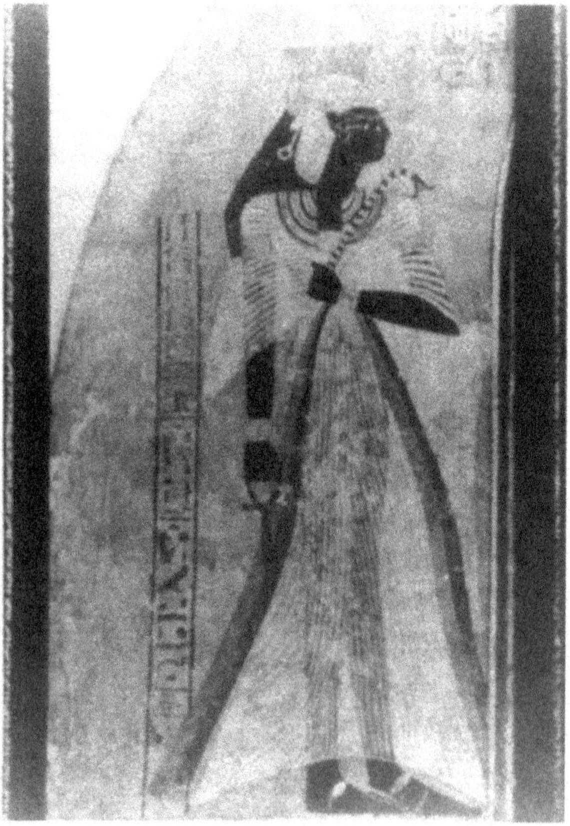

Portrait of Queen Ahmose-Nefertari, co-founder of Dynasty XVIII. New Kingdom (Photo: Larry Williams).

skin, with just as many having been dedicated to Ahmose-Nefertari. As stated, the paintings depicting this queen were completed during late Dynasty XVIII and early Dynasty XIX, and were characterized by a 'spirited bourgeois age.' Elegantly dressed,the queen wears extravagant and contemporary garments, characteristic of the period. One of these portraits (Fig. 14), originates from the tomb of the Two Sculptors (Nabamen and Ipuky) at Deir el Medina in western Thebes. In this portrait, she wears the titulary vulture goddess of Upper Egypt. The flail or "scourge" held by Nefertari takes on the form of the lily. A connection between the flail and Min, dates back to Dynasty I.[18] The flail was used to collect and hold the sticky, fragrant myrrh gum resins,[19] which were tapped lightly onto the skin. This perfume was also connected with Amen (a variation of Min). According to the texts of the woman Pharaoh Hatshepsut, Queen Eti of Punt used myrrh in her sacred offerings to Amen: "Her majesty (Eti) is acting with her two hands, the best of the 'ntyw' (myrrh) is upon all her limbs, her fragrance is divine dew, her odour mingled with Punt."[20]

In the final example, Nefertari and her son, Amenhotep I, affectionately embrace under a pavillion or shrine (Fig. 15). Dated to the time of Rameses VIII (1147 B.C.), this work was discovered in the tomb of Kynebu, a priest residing

Deified portrait of Ahmose Nefertari and her son Amenhotep I, conceived well after their deaths. New Kingdom, Dynasty XIX, 1147 B.C.

over the 'secrets of the estate of Amen.' A black statue may have also existed for Ahmose-Nefertari, for a tomb painting in Amenmose's burial chamber depicts a funerary barge holding a life-sized figure of the deified queen (Fig. 16). Ahmose-Nefertari may have been painted black because she represented the "divine spouse of the god," Amen, as all high-priestesses were recognized.

Bark of Amen greeted by deified statue of Queen Ahmose Nefertari. New Kingdom, Dynasty XIX.

Ethnic or Symbolic: Black Invaders and Southerners

Connections between Egypt and its southern neighbor, Nubia, are not only historically important, but germane to a discussion of human types painted black as well. From prehistoric times down to the historic period of Egyptian history, the "Black Land" and the region to the south of it was viewed more or less as a contiguous region.[21] Those black images of royal and non-royal types, add some insight to what has been previously discussed.

Towards the end of the predynastic Gerzean period (3600-3200 B.C.), armed conflict and conquest emerged, with several kingdoms seeking hegemony over the Nile Valley. One of these kingdoms, originating in Lower Nubia, was in fact ruled by "pharaohs" prior to the unification of Egypt. Archaeologically known as the A-Group culture, "Ta-Zeti" (Land of the Bow) may indeed be the seat of Egypt's founding dynasty.[22] Ta-Zeti ruled the region between El Kubbaniya in Upper Egypt, and the Second Cataract. Further evidence shows that the "Nubians" intruded as far as Hierakonpolis (Nekken), where a royal tomb of A-Group type was discovered.

Tomb Painting 100, as it is called, from Hierakonpolis (3400-3200 B.C.), offers evidence of human figures represented with black skin (Fig. 17). Recognized as the oldest known Egyptian wall painting, this mural thought archaic, clearly depicts red and black-skinned men in armed conflict. Sir Flinders Petrie was the first scholar to suggest a narrative of war between them in which the black men were victorious.[23] Because of recent research,[24] I find it possible to suggest that the black painted figures represent warriors from Ta-Zeti. Significantly, some scholars have pointed out that, for all practical purposes, Hierakonoplis served as gateway to Nubia, throughout Egyptian history.[25]

Human figures depicted on the Tomb 100 mural have been defined as blue-black and red on an ochre background.[26] The artistic canon of the Gerzean period typically demanded the use of red for figures and not black.[27] However this work depicts the aggressors (as black) intruding into Upper Egypt. Much attention has been given to the armed conflict hypothesis and some of the iconographic elements depict black figures in roles later reserved for pharaohs and priests of Egypt:

1. A "leader" (in hierarchic proportion) holding a mace threatens a prisoner.
2. Another wields a mace.
3. A "foreign ship" with a "tented" black-skinned figure.
4. A black-skinned figure extends to a red-skinned figure a leopard's skin.

Based upon similar iconographic images of the Archaic period (ie. the Scorpion Macehead, Narmer Palette, and the Ivory relief of the pharaoh Djer), the enlarged black figure has been interpreted as a king and conqueror.[28] The image of

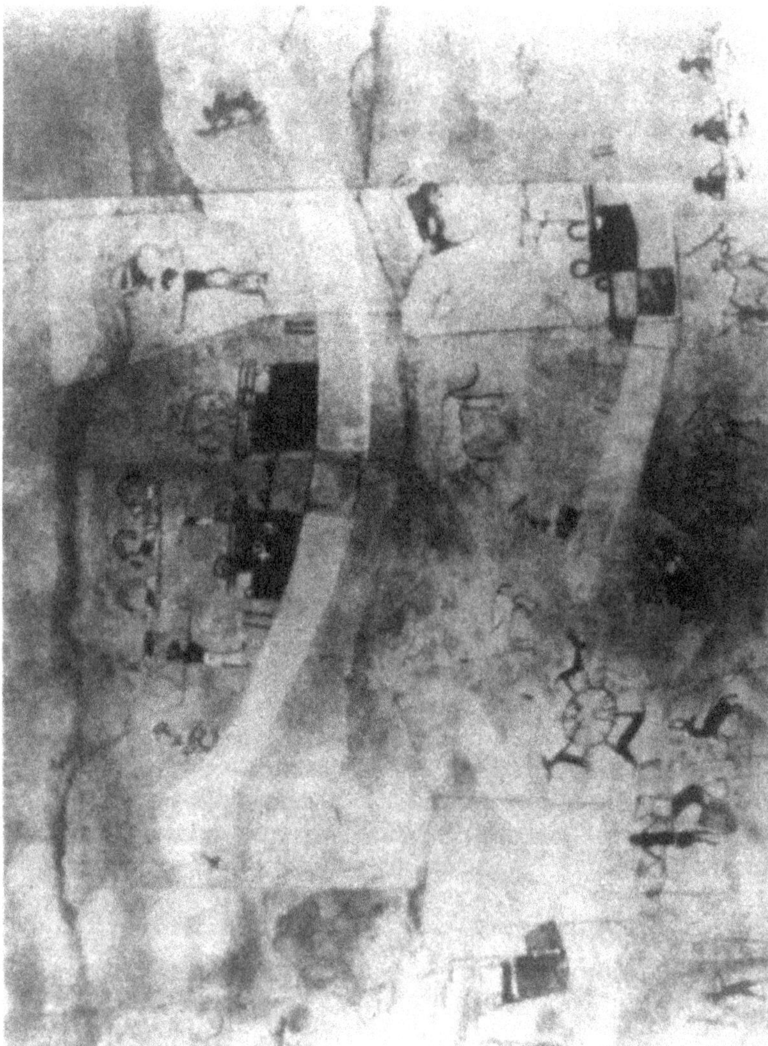

Detail of Predynastic Mural, from Tomb 100. Predynastic Period, 3400–3200 B.C.
From Hierakonpolis

the black figure passing to the red one a leopard skin echoes Hamilton's comment about the former "bestowing the emblems of sacerdotal office."

The hierachic proportions of the black figure raises many questions, among them the question of ethnicity. Had the artistic canon of using dark-red to depict the ancient Egyptians been established as early as the predynastic era? And better still, did the tomb painting belong to a ruler that conceived of himself as black-skinned? If one accepts the theory that this tomb belonged to an individual who conceived of himself as dark-red (ie.Egyptian), why would the mortuary shrine commemorate and honor some black-skinned foreigner? At this time in Egypt's prehistory, Hierakonpolis was probably a vassal of Ta-Zeti, which may have attempted rebellion but was "pacified."

While it cannot be stated with certainty that the dark-red color had been artistically established at this time to depict the ancient Egyptians, evidence from Tomb 100 demonstrates the existence of literally black-skinned people in Egypt from its beginning. The most intriguing possibility suggests that after the unification, black was used solely for gods, and the pharaoh. By the Middle Kingdom however, this right was extended to other members.

Throughout Dynasty XVIII, the territory of Nubia was divided into two distinct regions. The first began near Hierakonpolis, Upper Egypt ending at the Second Cataract: this was Lower Nubia or the kingdom of Wawat. The other region was Kush, a kingdom located between the Second Cataract and Karoy, at the Fourth Cataract.[29] From the beginning, these southern cousins of the Egyptians were "middlemen", integral to the trade of highly prized ivory, ebony, "throw-sticks," incense, vegetables oils, leopard and panther-skins, and agricultural produce.[30] Peace, commerce, warfare, and dispensation were interchangeable variables in the formula which made up Egypto-Nubian relationships.

Nubio-Egyptian relationships were crucial to the economy of the Nile Valley. In the presentations of gifts to the royal court as depicted on Egyptian wall paintings, we reputedly see for the first time, "black royalty" who are actually painted black in complexion. Painted murals from the New Kingdom royal tombs of Rekhmire, Sebekhotep, Huy, and polycrome faience portraits from the palace of Rameses III, provide us with images of blue-black, jet-black, and ebony-black Nubians. From Rekhmire's tomb, we have offering bearers in a wide range of hues. In his recorded inscriptions, Rekhmire called them the Anti of Ta-Zeti, and inhabitants of Khent-hen-nefer.[31] The latter region was known as the "land of the Gods."

A curly-haired, blue-black, offering-bearer, discovered on the tomb mural of Sebekhotep (reign of Thutmoses IV, 1425-1417 B.C.), was depicted with a

Tribute Bearer from the tomb of Sebekhotep. New Kingdom, Dynasty XVIII. 1425-1417 B.C.

straight and arched nose, destroying the myth of "Negroid physiognomy" (Fig. 18). There is no question of the skill of the Egyptian artists in rendering human images in this tomb, because practically all Egyptologists see this tomb as the epitome of the highest achievements of Theban painters.[32] The French Egyptol-

Princes from the kingdom of Kush, from the tomb of Huy New Kingdom, Dynasty XVIII, 1342-1333 B.C.

ogist Vercoutter went so far as to conjecture a kinship between this figure and Nilotic types of the Sudan, that have been classified as "Hamites."

In a procession of kings, offering-bearers, and prisoners from Wawat and Kush, depicted in the tomb of Huy (1342-1333 B.C.), there are representations running the color spectrum of dark-red to blue-black. (Fig. 19) The artist(s) went so far as to creatively alternate black and reddish-brown royal figures to create a dynamic contrast (Fig. 20). Finally, I call attention to the portrait of Prince Hekanenfer, prince of Wawat. The glistening skin of the ebony-black Hekanefer, with a long, arched and pinched nose, greets Huy (Fig. 21).

By the reign of Rameses III (1198-1166 B.C.), a theme of conquered and bound enemies was utilized by the Egyptian artist (Fig. 22). For some reason, not totally clear, the Egyptians stereotyped their southern kinsmen as wearing elaborate wigs, feathers in hair, large gold earrings, full lips, and jet-black skin.[33] A polychrome faience plaque from Medinet Habu (royal palace of Rameses III) portrays such a motif which at this time is found throughout Egyptian art. These representations have been viewed as propaganda, themes of traditional or magical importance. The cosmic functions of kingship required a magical reaffirmation of the triumph of the pharaoh over his enemies.[34] Here, art imitates life: the literally black-skinned type has become a symbol of itself.

"Southern Prisoners" from the tomb of Huy. New Kingdom. Dynasty XVIII, 1342–1333 B.C.

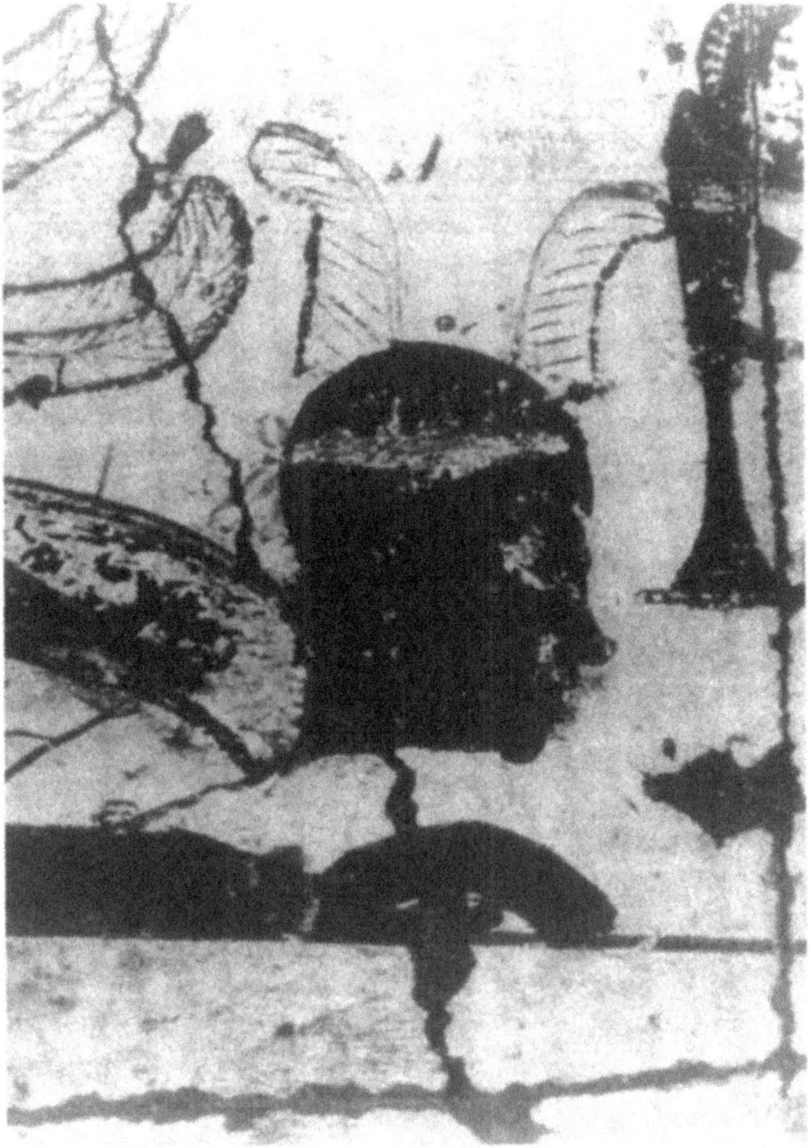

Portrait of Hekanefer, royal prince of Wawat. New Kingdom Dynasty XVIII, 1342-1333 B.C.

A Summary

In the first issue of the *Journal of African Civilizations* (1979), Jules Taylor wrote an article discussing the relationship between blackness and human images. His critical point, in my opinion, is the attempt by scholars to disassociate the blackness of cosmic and divine fertility from the "blackness" of African ethnicity.[35]

A common denominator found among images related to kings and queens, is the association with ceremonial processions presided over by a black deity, or that royal personage serving as symbol of the deity. They are further connected with life-giving sources (water, milk, or semen in the case of Min). The idea of cosmic fluid, spiritual rebirth, and blackness being interrelated is justified in a most unlikely source: the bible. Throughout the Old Testament, references are made to confrontation between a symbolic blackness and the patriarchs. The patriarch Jacob emerges victorious, after crossing a body of water to confront his God, a nocturnally black, but divine adversary.[36] This symbolism had an obvious connection to and origin in, ancient Egyptian magico-religious echatology.

According to Homer, all the gods returned to Ethiopia to bathe and refresh

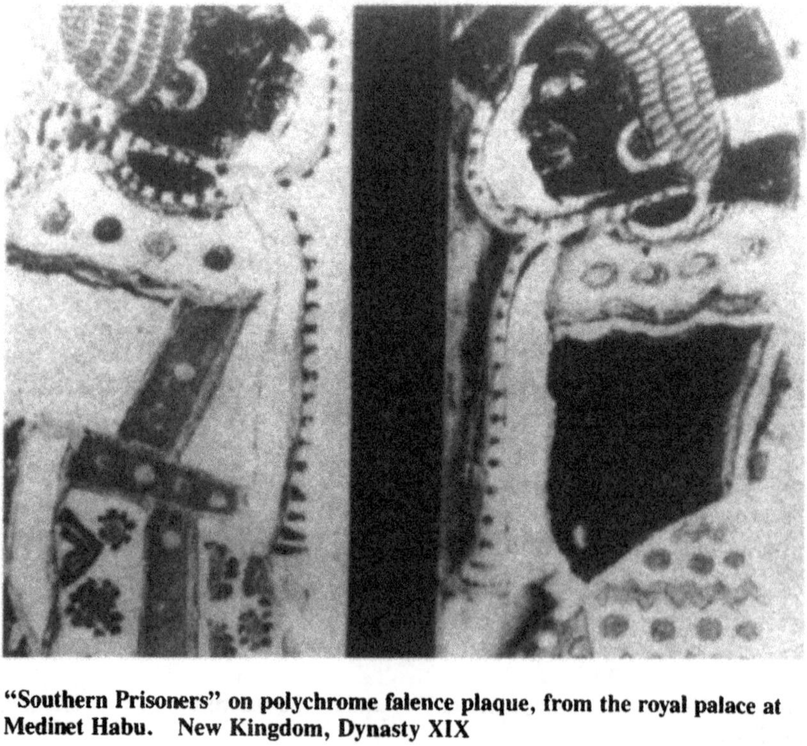

"Southern Prisoners" on polychrome faience plaque, from the royal palace at Medinet Habu. New Kingdom, Dynasty XIX

themselves. In later European symbolism, the black man symbolized water and myrrh (an embalming ingredient used by the Egyptians and Nubians).

The evidence presented amply demonstrates the existence of black-skinned peoples in Egyptian art at the very beginnings of Nile Valley prehistory and throughout Egyptian history. The social historian Bruce Trigger points out that skin color in the Nile Valley tends to darken from "light brown to what appears to the eye as bluish black . . ."[37] This is only partially true, since ancient Egypt prior to Greek, Roman, and Arab invasions, was largely composed of a dark population. While there should be further study of African color symbolism in Egyptian art, we should not lose sight of the critical role played by these Blacks in the building of Egyptian civilization.

Notes

1. Godfrey Higgins, Anacalypsis,Vol. I, London, 1836, p. 134-137
2. Dr. Richard King, Black Dot, 1980, San Francisco, p. 4
3. William Hamilton, "Remarks on Several Parts of Turkey," Aegyptica, Vol. I, London, 1809, p. 830-2
4. Henreich Brugsh-Bey, Egypt Under the Pharaohs, London, 1891, p. 131-3
5. William Leo Hansberry, Africa and the Africans,Vol. II, Howard University Press, Washington D.C., 1981, p. 177
6. Hermann Junker, "The Appearance of the Negroes in History," JEA, VII, Pts. III-IV, Oct. 1921, The Egyptian Exploration Society, p. 132
7. George Hart,Egyptian Gods and Goddesses, Routledge and Kegan Paul, London, Boston and Henley, 1986, p. 154
8. Cyril Aldred, Egyptian Art, Thames and Hudson, 1980, p. 107
9. Sergio Donadoni, Egyptian Museum: Cairo, Newsweek, Great Museums of the World, N.Y., 1978, p. 67-8
10. Ibid
11. William C. Hayes, "The Middle Kingdom in Egypt," Vol. I, The Cambridge Ancient History, Pt. 2A, Cambridge University Press, Cambridge, 1980, p. 488
12. Herbert Winlock, The Rise and Fall of the Middle Kingdom, N.Y.,The MacMillan Co., 1947, p. 26-7
13. Hart, p. 124
14. G.A. Wainwright, "Some Aspects of Amun," JEA, Vol. XX, Nov. 1934, Egyptian Exploration Society, p. 140
15. Miriam Stead, Egyptian Life, Harvard University Press, Cambridge, Mass., 1986, British Museum, p. 65
16. Brugsh-Bey, p. 130-2
17. Legrand Clegg, "Black Rulers of the Golden Age," JAC: Nile Valley Civilization, ed. Ivan Van Sertima, 1985
18. Percy Newberry, "The Shepherd's Crook and the So-Called 'Flail' or 'Scourge' of Osiris," JEA, Vol. XV, 1929, Egyptian Exploration Society, p. 86
19. A. Lucas, "Notes on Myrrh and Stacte," JEA, June, 1937, Vol. XXIII, The Egyptian Exploration Society, p. 32
20. Nigel Groom, Frankincense and Myrrh, Longman, London, and New York, Librarie du Liban, Beirut, Lebanon, 1981, p. 25
21. Bruce Williams, "The Lost Pharaohs of Nubia," Archaeology, Vol. 33, Nov. 5, 1980
22. Bruce Williams, "Forebears of Menes in Nubia: Myth or Reality," JNES, Vol 46, Jan. 1987,

The University of Chicago Press, Chicago, Illinois, p. 15-26

23. Sir Flinders Petrie, The Making of Egypt, London: Sheldon Press, 1939, p. 13

24. Bruce Williams and Thomas J. Logan, "The Metropolitan Museum Knife Handle and Aspects of Pharaonic Imagery Before Narmer," JNES, October 1987, Vol. 46, University of Chicago Press, Chicago, Illinois, p.245-285

25. Humphrey Case and Joan C. Payne, "Tomb 100: The Decorated Tomb at Hierakonpolis," JEA Vol. 48,Dec. 1962, The Egyptian Exploration Society, p.17

26. P.T. Ridley, The Unification of Egypt, Melbourne, Australia, 1974, p. 22-4

27. Case and Payne, p. 17

28. Ibid., p. 12

29. Christiane Desroches-Noblecourt, Tutankhamen, New York Graphic Society Ltd. 1963, p. 192

30. Bruce Wiliams, Nubia: Its Glory and Its People, 3500-1200 A.D., exhibition pamphlet, The Oriental Institute of the University of Chicago and the Oak Woods Cemetary Association, 1987, p.6

31. Jean Vercoutter, "The Iconography of the Black in Egypt: From the Beginnings to the Twenti-fifth Dynasty," The Image of the Black in Western Art, Vol. I, Pt.I, 1976, Menlil Foundation, Houston, Texas, p. 291, footnote 3

32. Ibid., p. 50

33. Ibid., p. 76

34. Jean Leclant, "Egypt in Nubia During the Old, Middle, and New kingdom," Africa In Antiquity: The Essays, the Brooklyn Museum, 1978, N.Y., p. 69

35. Jules Taylor, "The Black Image in Egyptian Art," JEA, Vol. I, 1979, ed. Ivan Van Sertima, p. 38

36. "Genesis 13-30," The Holy Bible: The King James Version, The World Publishing Co., Cleveland, Ohio

37. Bruce Trigger, "Nubian, Negro, Black, Nilotic?" Africa in Antiquity: The Essays, Brooklyn Museum, N.Y., 1978, p. 27, There are depictions of black-painted figures dated to the Middle kingdom, other than royalty. "On the east wall of the chapel (at Aswan) appear black-skinned bowmen, as at Mialla and Gebelein."—William Stevenson Smith, The Art and Architecture of Ancient Egypt, p. 152

BLACK DYNASTIES AND RULERS

BLACK DYNASTIES AND RULERS

Introduced by Ivan Van Sertima

This second section is devoted to summaries and surveys of the dynasties. The "recorded" history of Kemet stretches over three thousand years and it is impossible to cover it, even in a dozen volumes. This, therefore, should be seen simply as an introduction to the highlights of the dynasties and, in some cases, that is all that survives of the history of great civilizations.

Runoko Rashidi, in collaboration with James Brunson, provides us with a "working chronology" of the Kemetic dynasties. It is called a "working" chronology because it is not a complete list. It is the only one, however, that scholars can "work" with at the moment since the original, more extended, list has been destroyed. It is invaluable as a reference guide for students of the subject. It begins where revised chronologies of Nile Valley dynasties will in future begin—not in Egypt but in Nubia—two centuries before the first historic dynasty of Kemet.

In 1962 an American archeological expedition under Keith Seele discovered the birthplace of pharaonic civilization. This was at a place called Qustul in Nubia where a pharaonic dynasty had been established—the oldest monarchy found so far in the world—several generations before the first historic Egyptian dynasty. Bruce Williams, who is now in charge of the archeological survey in that area describes in detail in "The Lost Pharaohs of Nubia" the range of finds at Qustul. There the American team racing against time as waters threatened to rush over the area with the completion of the Aswan dam, came upon a cemetery of 33 large tombs, as large as the Egyptian tombs of Ka and Narmer at Abydos, in a place where advanced political organization was not believed to have come until 2,500 years later.

The Nubians had always been portrayed as poor neighbors of the Egyptians and the Nubian pharaohs were not supposed to have come into their day of power save in the twilight years of the Egyptian empire—the Twenty-Fifth dynasty—but here, for the first time, we were given direct and irrefutable evidence that they were the powers in the dawn—that Nubian kings reigned in the Nile Valley before the earliest Egyptian kings.

And it was not simply a matter of their precedence but their seminal influence on the structure of pharaonic civilization itself. Here were found the first kings linked to the falcon-god Horus, incense burners incised with serekhs, representations of panelled palace façades—all the definitive symbols of royalty. Here too were the beginnings of the hieroglyphs and the first appearance of the white crown of the south that was later to sit beside the red crown of the north on the head of Egyptian pharaohs. Ta-Seti (The Land of the Bow) in fact, boasted of a dozen black pharaohs, the last of whom coincided with the emergence of the first of the northern kings.

What is equally significant is the more recent discovery that there was some pharaonic-type civilization developing parallel to Egypt through the centuries. Bruce Williams, in a letter to me in 1984, maintained that a Kushite continuity sustained the pharaonic impulse through the ages, from A-group (3,300 B.C.) right through to X-group (550 A.D.) This, to put it in his own words, "represents a new departure in the examination of Egypt's place in the African context."

Wayne Chandler, in his study of the accomplishments of the Old Kingdom—the Pyramid Age—raises questions about the chronology of Egypt. As we pointed out above, the dynastic list, although now generally accepted, is really a shortened version of the original list of pharaohs. The most complete list (the Royal Papyrus of Turin) by which we should have made our calculations, was accidentally destroyed in the 19th century. We have had to depend, therefore, on a list by the Egyptian priest Manetho. Although flawed by serious gaps, it has been used so far as the standard, in the absence of a more complete list. The debate over how old dynastic Egypt was, will be continued in the next volume but it is important to note two things in this connection. One, it further invalidates any claim to Sumerian or Mesopotamian primacy or any significant influence on the Egyptians of the pyramid age—the earliest hard dating of materials found at Ur, the first Sumerian city-state, is 2,600 B.C. whereas the most conservative date for the first Egyptian dynasty is 3,100 B.C. Two, it does not affect the dating of the first pharaonic dynasty in Nubia since the methods used to arrive at that dating would still place Ta-Seti at least 200 years before the first Egyptian dynasty (whatever that date may be). Discussions with Dr Bruce Williams has established that very clearly.

Chandler goes on to deal with some of the mythical figures that dominated the Egyptian imagination—Osiris, Isis and Horus (the divine trinity) and Thoth, who is really a constellation of centuries of early African scholarship, to whom we owe the word "thought" itself.

He then highlights the extraordinary accomplishments of the early Pharaohs and touches upon the moral code and character of the Egyptian state, exploding myths about slaves as the mainstay of the working force. This is most important to students since it needs emphasizing that technical accomplishments, however impressive, do not, in themselves, constitute civilization. Civilization after all is the humanization of the human and the building of an ethical code of human conduct is just as important as the building of a pyramid. As Chandler, citing

Brugsch-Bey, records: "In the schools the poor scribe's child sat on the same bench as the offspring of the rich . . . Above all things they esteemed justice, and virtue had the highest value in their eyes. The law which ordered them to honor the dead, give bread to the hungry, water to the thirsty, clothing to the naked, reveals to us one of the finest qualities of old Egyptian character—pity towards the unfortunate."

Their science startles us even to this day. Scholars have expounded all sorts of improbable theories to explain how the early Egyptians built the pyramids but Chandler shows how the Japanese experiment in 1978 has humbled and astounded us all. Cheikh Anta Diop had argued that the iron hoe found in the interstices of the Great Pyramid represented an early process of metal-smelting and was not merely a result of accidental fusion, as Professor Leclant had claimed (see "Iron in the Ancient Egyptian Empire" in *Great African Thinkers*). Diop had based these assertions not only from an examination of this tool, dismissed as a fragment, but from other iron objects of exquisite craftsmanship found in the pharaonic period. The cutting and burnishing of granite, such as we witness in the pharaonic world, required knowledge, perhaps even an advanced knowledge, of iron-smelting. But Leclant, Mauny and others had tried to argue all this away. And so the Japanese, following conventional wisdom, tried to cut the stone in the Egyptian quarries with the best tools they thought were available in the Pyramid Age.

Chandler shows step-by-step the folly of these still generally accepted assumptions. The Japanese eventually had to resort to twentieth-century technology, using air-jackhammers to cut the stone. Then they tried to load it on barges which capsized, made unstable by the weight of the stone. They had to resort to steamboats. Then they found they could not transport it from the boat to the shore—the stone sank in the mudsilt of the riverbanks and even in the sand. Then, after the usual Hollywood reconstruction of thousands of muscled supermen pulling tons of rock to the building site they brought today's most powerful lifting cranes and helicopters. All to no avail. Not only were the stones badly scratched, chipped and broken (compared to the perfect casing stones of the early Africans) but the Japanese could not align the stones. Chandler reveals to us that the early engineers aligned them within 1/1000 of an inch of mathematical perfection, a precision achieved today only by jewelers with microscopes cutting gems.

This introduction to the pyramid age, which raises other provocative questions (Why were they built? Were they really simply tombs?) is accompanied by a remarkable gallery of African faces. Chandler points to the progressive intermixture over the centuries between the indigenous African and other races coming into the Nile Valley but he holds, and his photographic evidence is the best argument in the end, that the dominant ruling figures of the age remained African.

Of the Middle Kingdom less is popularly known. It was founded by African nobles from Southern Egypt. Runoko Rashidi provides us with a detailed family tree of its rulers and guides us through a photo gallery of the Middle Kingdom Pharaohs. What is remarkable about this period, which runs from 2130 B.C. to 1786 B.C. is the fact that the great science of the Pyramid Age did not die as many people believe. No pyramid of the magnitude of the Great Pyramid of Giza was built in this time but, in the reign of King Amenemet 111, a 27 mile-long embankment was constructed around Lake Moeris in Middle Egypt. This embankment secured 27,000 acres of fertile land, and, at the Nile's entrance to Lake Moeris, a dam was built to regulate the river's flow. On the south side of the Lake the Africans built the Labyrinth, the largest single building in world history. Herodotus said it surpassed the pyramids. It contained 3000 rooms, 1500 above and 1500 below the ground. This is not just a legend. Rashidi cites Petrie, who excavated it in 1888 and declared that all the temples on the east bank of Thebes and the largest one on the west bank could be placed together in this colossal building.

Thebes is the focus of our next essay on the dynasties. Today's Luxor, it was known originally as *Waset* among the early Egyptians.

Asa Hilliard focuses on this great city of the south, the cradle of Black leadership in Egypt. Although the Pharaohs of dynastic Egypt ruled from the north, a strategic center of empire in terms of its location, they were never to forget their origins in the south. Khenti, meaning south, is also the word for first, foremost, origin. The tomb of the legendary Osiris is to be found in the Holy City of Abydos, also in the south. Almost all the Pharaohs had a tomb in that sacred place even if their actual remains were buried in the Sakkara cemetery of the north.

The south, therefore, was always the spiritual center. Waset was more than that. Hilliard demonstrates that it was the center of political power as well. Although very old, it did not become prominent in the written record until the Middle Kingdom. By then it was the greatest city in the world. Within its walls lie the remains of the finest temples that have survived the march of time—the Southern Ipet (Luxor Temple) and the Ipet Isut (Karnak Temple). They were both religious and educational institutions. The kings and queens, priests and priestesses, that can trace their origin to this city were to affect the Middle Kingdom (11th and 12th dynasty), the New Kingdom (18th and 19th dynasty) and the Late Kingdom (the 25th dynasty) the period of the Nubian Renaissance. The first two kingdoms were ruled from Waset physically while the last was dominated by the spirit of its culture, shining like the sun going down in a blaze in the evening of the Egyptian world.

But it is important to note, beyond these periods we have specified, that as Hilliard points out, "Kemet was liberated or established from the south for each of its Golden Ages or Kingdoms. Mena [Menes] who in the First Dynasty founded the Old Kingdom, was a Southerner. The Intef and Mentuhotep founders of the Middle Kingdom were Southerners. Sequen-en-re Ta'o, the 17th dynasty liberator who started the war of liberation and made possible the founding of the New Kingdom was a Southerner. Finally, the Twenty-Fifth Dynasty, the Late Kingdom (the Restoration Kingdom) was initiated by Southerners.

Legrand Clegg 11 introduces us to major figures of the Seventeenth and Eighteenth dynasties. This was the noonday of classical Egypt. The Seventeenth dynasty, which has its origins in Nubia, began a major war of liberation against the hated Hyksos, invaders of Egypt, a war that ended victoriously in the founding of the Eighteenth. This dynasty "brought Egypt to new heights of technical achievement and military might, marking the first time that any nation expanded its borders to encompass a vast world empire". Clegg meticulously builds up the family tree of the great kings and queens of this "golden age", tracing their African ancestry. His photos of Akhenaton, his daughters, Queen Tiye, the boy-king Tutankamun, his wife Queen Ankhesenamon, Queens Hatshepsut and Ahmose-Nefertari (wife of Ahmose 1) clearly support his conclusions about their ethnicity.

Our survey of the dynasties ends with the Twenty-Fifth during which most historians agree that Ethiopians controlled the Egyptian empire. Phaon Goldman (Tarharka) who has taken the name of the most illustrious of these pharaohs of the Twenty-Fifth, tells the story of their reign. He establishes, as I had done in my own work, that this was no period of decline but a renaissance, the revival of the very best in classical Nile Valley civilization.

THE LOST PHARAOHS OF NUBIA

By Bruce Williams

A newly discovered ancient kingdom is always a matter of intense interest, but when it precedes the earliest known monarchy, the unification of Egypt in the fourth millennium B.C., then history itself is reborn. The place is anient Nubia at Qustul, where the investigation of archaeological materials recovered during the great 1960's rescue effort has recently unveiled a birthplace of pharaonic civilization several generations before the rise of the first historic Egyptian dynasty. This finding is rendered even more startling by the fact that advanced political organization was not believed to have come to Nubia, or anywhere south of Egypt, for another 2,500 years.

Transforming prehistory into history is always an enormously complex task, even in Egypt whose earliest written records rival those of ancient Mesopotamia. The firm progression of contemporary records from pharaoh to pharaoh trails off rapidly into obscurity just before the beginning of the First Dynasty. The establishment of this dynasty in about 3200-3150 B.C.—marking the political unification of Upper and Lower Egypt—is believed to have been achieved by the first pharaoh of both lands, Aha, in the conquest virtually completed by his predecessor Narmer. Much of the evidence for this period at the edge of history stems from great tombs dated to Aha and his successors in the First Dynasty. They were found with tombs of their predecessors, Ka and Karmer, at Abydos, the ancient holy city of the god Osiris, located 100 miles down the Nile from Luxor, and at Saqqara outside of Cairo. Farther upstream at Hierakonpolis in Upper Egypt, another great find was made in the beginning of this century—a major cache that included large stone palettes and maceheads associated with both Narmer and yet another predecessor, Scorpion, and some of even earlier times. The most important of these was the great stone Narmer Palette. Although shaped like other smaller stone palettes then used for grinding cosmetics, this one was inscribed with representations and symbols in bas relief that told of a triumph of the Upper Egyptian king over part of Lower Egypt, with the king's name, Narmer, spelled out at the top. In addition to this all important evidence, other monuments of Narmer and Scorpion document aspects of the unifying thrust northward. New excavations now in process at Hierakonpolis should add even more evidence.

Otherwise, there are only frustratingly enigmatic fragments from the Pre-

Reprinted from *Archeology Magazine*, volume 33, no. 5.

dynastic period—serekhs, palace façades symbolic of royalty, that were scratched on pottery, as well as a small group of other seemingly royal palettes showing evidence of warfare, and an earlier group depicting animal struggles. Since none of the palettes and maceheads were found in their original contexts, no precise chronological relationship for the various fragments can be established. Later king lists refer to whole dynasties before the unification of Egypt, but the names cannot be connected to any specific monuments, events or people. They are dynasties without substance preceded by the entirely mythological kingship of the gods. Until now, the lack of direct evidence has made the study of these early sovereignties largely speculative.

1.
The Narmer palette is one of the most famous and ambitious commemorative stone objects for the period just before Egypt's First Dynasty. In the main scene (top), Narmer, wearing the White Crown of Upper Egypt, smites a defeated enemy. The scene is labeled from above by a group which shows a falcon holding a rope leading from a main's head. This head is combined with a "land" sign and papyrus plants to make a personification of Lower Egypt. On the opposite side (bottom), Narmer, wearing the Red Crown of Lower Egypt and accompanied by standards and servants, reviews the slain enemy beside his ship.

In the last few years all this has sudenly changed. Direct evidence for kings in the Nile Valley before the reign of Narmer has finally emerged in context, but in a place and culture that no one had expected—Qustul in Lower Nubia, very near the present-day border of Egypt and the Sudan. The inhabitants of Lower Nubia in this period, whose cultural remains are called A-Group by archaeologists, were long thought to have had too simple a culture and too small a population to establish and support the complex political institutions and centralization implied by the presence of pharaohs. How could they possibly have achieved some "first dynasty" of their own? Even though the A-Group culture was substantially derived from that of Upper Egypt in the early Predynastic period, called Naqada I or Amratian after major sites in Egypt, by middle and late Predynastic times (the Naqada II and III or the Gerzean period), native objects are not Egyptian and many reveal characteristic traits from the Sudan. Based on the poverty of the country and the mixed character of the culture, archaeologists have concluded that A-Group Nubia was at most a scattered group of chiefdoms or, more likely, a loose collection of kin groups.

In an ironic twist, the startling evidence that reverses this thinking entirely was retrieved just when excavation at Qustul was all but doomed. In 1962, when an eleventh-hour international archaeological team set out to rescue ancient remains threatened by the rising waters of the Aswan Dam, the area of Qustul near the river was considered to be unworthy of further excavation. Keith C. Seele, then director of the University of Chicago's Oriental Institute Nubian Expedition, decided otherwise. After clearing sites and cemeteries of all pre-Islamic periods, in the last months of the last possible season, the expedition found a cemetery of A-Group tombs as large as those of Ka and Narmer at Abydos. Seele was immediately impressed with the importance of this site, which he designated Cemetery L, although every tomb in it had been plundered and the contents were mostly smashed and burnt. The immense bulk of material recovered put off any systematic consideration of Cemetery L, so only a preliminary partial assessment could be made on the basis of the 33 tombs and the registry of special objects in them. As a result, and because no explicit evidence of royalty could immediately be detected, Seele's early suggestion that these tombs might be those of Predynastic Nubian "princes" or "kings" was totally ignored—neither Qustul nor Cemetary L is mentioned in recent major discussions of A-Group or Predynastic civilization.

But by 1977—sadly, only a few years after Keith Seele's untimely death—the project of publishing the materials recovered by the Oriental Institute's Nubian Expedition turned to the systematic investigation of the remains from Cemetery L. The first and most daunting task was to make sense of the piles of sherds and fragments of stone vessels. Several years earlier these had been searched for "joins" but, for lack of time, had not been compared with one another to isolate the unconnected fragments from single vessels. A necessary process in even roughly determining the original number of objects in the tombs, distinguishing the fragments of one vessel from another was facilitated both by the distinctive designs on the numerous A-Group painted bowls, and by the variable texture of the "alabaster" calcite of which most of the stone vessels were made. Although the dedicated volunteer who had searched the collection for joins years before, Elizabeth Tieken, had warned that many sherds matched no others, no one even remotely expected the large numbers of objects that would appear; painted vessels are uncommon and stone vessels are rare in other A-Group sites. During weeks of comparing, counting and cross-checking, it became increasingly apparent that the Qustul collection contained greater numbers of both kinds of vessels than had ever been found before in Nubia—all told, more than 1,000 complete and fragmentary painted pots, and over 100 stone vessels. The range of these and other fragments from the plundered cemetery began to indicate a wealth and complexity that could only be called royal.

The pottery falls into five major groups distinguished by manufacture and decoration. By far the most numerous vessels, the painted pottery bowls, are sometimes decorated with elaborate overall patterns reminiscent of ripple burnishing, a practice that apparently had been abandoned earlier in Egypt and was reintroduced to Lower Nubia from Sudan. Most of this painted pottery is decorated with geometric or linear patterns in horizontal bands that resemble no other painted pottery of the period. It may be modeled after the well-known band incised pottery from Sudan to the south, or perhaps was inspired by the patterns of net slings used to carry the vessels. One smaller group of vessels may actually have been of Sudanese origin or may have been made at Qustul, copying a specifically Sudanese style with broad bands of incised decoration and zig-zag rocker-stamp patterns so well known in the south.

Thick, soft, poorly fired shallow bowls with incised and stamped decorations on a burnished surface represent another tradition. Some of these bowls are decorated with serpents in reserve, outlined against the impression-filled background, a motif strikingly similar to serpents found on black-incised bowls of the C-Group—the name for the culture that occupied Lower Nubia from the Late Old Kingdom to the start of the New Kingdom (ca. 2300-1500 B.C.). These bowls so closely resemble their C-Group counterparts, they must be considered part of a long-standing, unbroken tradition. The entire manufacturing technique and style is so different from any other A-Group material that they must have been imported from the home of the later C-Group, probably in the west.

After the A-Group painted vessels, Egyptian pottery is the most common. Distinctive pieces clearly match pottery from the Naqada III period, the last phase of Predynastic culture in Egypt. These pieces include small to monumental bowls; miniature lentoid flasks; narrow-necked bottles; cylindrical jars with incised wavy bands, including one from a late tomb with painted lattice decoration; spouted jars; and large heavy storage jars, 23 of which were found intact in the trench of one monumental tomb. Four of these great storage jars—which have a modified shape found in the latest Predynastic royal tombs of Abydos—were in-

2. The central portion of a seal from Siali in the northern part of Lower Nubia clearly shows a man saluting a serekhor palace façade with a falcon above it, labeled by a bow over a rectangle as the Horus of Ta-Seti. This indicates that Nubia was a territorial state. It is assembled from three sealings and was corrected by eliminating a probable crack in the original seal down the center of the palace façade. The falcon and the palace façades above the man are partially restored.

cised with inscriptions that clearly represent an early form of hieroglyphic writing. A substantial number of the Egyptian vessels are painted, mostly with groups of wavy lines that characterize late Predynastic vase painting. A few of these pots are decorated with groups of figures that proved to be extremely significant.

The last group came from the Levant and was made in the tradition of Syro-Palestinian vessels dating to the Early Bronze I period (before ca. 3200/3150 B.C.). Almost all of these were found in a single early Cemetery L tomb and represent a type that has never been found in Egypt—although close parallels have been found on the Asiatic coast.

In addition to the large group of pottery and 100 stone vessels, other badly damaged objects of local A-Group, Egyptian and Sudanese origin give eloquent testimony to the thorough plundering of the cemetery. Their special quality and unusual number tell a story. Some of the small stone A-Group palettes, for example, were made of highly polished, hard, colored quartz. Large mortars were generally carved to precise shapes from an extremely hard quartzite; sometimes simple spiral decorations were added. But most important are the distinctively A-Group incense burners—cylindrical objects made of local sandstone or a mixture of clays and sepiolite (meerschaum)—found at Qustul in numbers several times greater than ever before in all of Nubia. Several of these incense bur-

3. The preserved part of a bowl from Qustul shows the typical late prehistoric motif of two giraffes flanking palm trees. The crowns of the trees have been replaced with representations of historic significance. Vultures tear at fallen enemies, here partly obliterated. On the right, the enemy, who has fallen forward, is labeled Upper Egypt, the first mention of this region as a political entity. On the left, the victim appears to be Libya. This scene, together with the label on another Qustul jar, which shows a vulture attacking Hierakonpolis, links the more allegorical representations of cultures attacking serpents on slightly earlier objects to specific scenes of royal victory.

ners were incised and carved with the representations and symbols of Egyptian royalty—a decisive indication of the true meaning of the size and wealth of the Qustul tombs.

A number of small objects reflect a third tradition, and one that stems from a most interesting source. The most common of these are small hooklike objects carved from seashells, with tapered heads and pointed shanks that varied from a short spike to a long, curved semicircle. Hooks, studs and tokens of this type are relatively rare in Egypt and occur only in a few poor graves. They are almost entirely missing from any excavated A-Group tomb in Numia. Early forms of these same objects, however, mostly in stone, are common farther upstream at Shaheinab in Sudan where they probably originated. Although many of these small pieces were found throughout Cemetery L, the only totally unlooted pile of shell objects contained more than 1,650 as well as 2,600 other objects of unknown purpose usually called "lip plugs," which were also common at Shaheinab but rare in Egypt and Lower Nubia. Although no clear evidence for the purpose of the small plugs or tokens is known, they could hardly have been intended for use in very large numbers. It is clear that the more than 4,000 objects found in this pile may be tokens of wealth in other materials.

Tombs of this size, wealth and date in Egypt would have been immediately recognized as royal. Their extraordinarily varied contents would have been taken as evidence of a complex culture exposed to wide outside connections. But be-

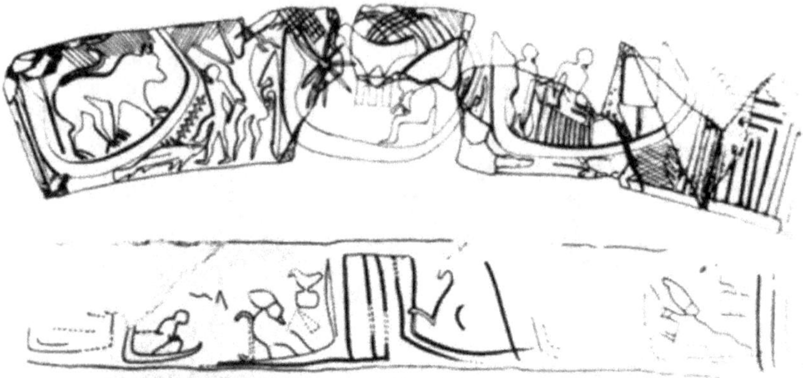

4. The Archaic Horus Incense Burner (*bottom*), named after the Horus clearly present in the last ship, shows two royal processions of three ships, but most of the passengers are difficult to locate in the badly crumbled surface. The presence of Horus emphasizes the development of official religion at Qustul of a type later characteristic of dynastic Egypt. Preserved measurement, 7.5 by 15.3 centimeters.

cause the discovery was made in Nubia at a time and a place when kingship was thought impossible, further proof of royalty is necessary. Fortunately, such crucial supporting evidence was on hand in the form of the incense burners incised with serekhs, the representations of paneled palace façades. Definitive symbols of Egyptian royalty, serekhs appear in late Predynastic times often surmounted by a falcon-Horus symbol of the Pharaoh; later they are used to enclose Horus names of Egyptian pharaohs, the major royal name used during the first and Second Dynasties. The palace façades on the incense burners are similar to the simplest examples found incised on Predynastic pottery in Egypt. Some of these façades are associated with ship processions, and in two cases are especially elaborate. In fact, the most interesting and precious object found at Qustul, the largest, finest and most elaborately decorated of all the A-Group incense burners, has the best example of such a scene incised in a sunk silhouette style related to rock drawing. It was found in one of the earliest and richest tombs of Cemetery L, dating to about four generations or more before the time of the Egyptian King Ka, six or seven generations before the start of the First Dynasty. The Oriental Institute researchers quickly recognized that this incense burner showed a procession of three ships with their tall sterns and bent prows going toward a palace façade. Investigators also noted both the curious concentric design of the serekh and possible Mesopotamian connections for it and the ships. But because only one occupant of the three ships was known, and the passengers of the other two seemed unrestorable, the Qustul incense burner remained an enigma. Later, however, when the incense burner was reexamined in the light of the obviously royal stature of the people buried in Cemetery L, the essential restoration of the missing elements was immediately clear.

In the first ship, a prisoner is kneeling on a palanquin or litter held by a rope in the grasp of a guard with a mace. Although the figure in the middle ship is almost completely destroyed, the white crown of Upper Egypt clearly stands out above the ship. In front of it is the tail of a falcon—another sign of kingship. The crown indicates that the figure is a king, and the falcon should be seen as perched on a serekh, together a characteristic representation in early dynastic Egypt. In front of the falcon is a rosette, a symbol of royalty before the First Dynasty. The pair, bound prisoner and pharaoh, are well known in early Eygptian iconography, but are represented somewhat unusually here. During the First Dynasty, scenes of the two are static with the king and prisoner both firmly placed on dry land—but on the incense burner from Qustul, generations before, they are transported by ship. The early date of the Qustul incense burner is further reflected by other figures that have important connections to middle and later Predynastic art—an unnamed feline deity (determined by a falcon on a standard); a man saluting in a pose and style typical of Naqada II vase painting; and two animals, an antelope and carnivore, cavorting around the central royal ship. They pose in the characteristic manner of early palettes which show groups of struggling animals; this type precedes those with scenes of historical events. Its date provided by context, style and composition, the Qustul burner furnishes the earliest definite representation of a king in the Nile Valley or anywhere. This conclusion is further supported by several other incised incense burners depicting a combination of ships and palace façades in royal procession. However, their designs are so simple or poorly preserved that they were difficult to recognize until the Qustul incense burner was deciphered.

As the weeks and months wore on, the continued reevaluation of the Qustul objects began to indicate a sequence that led generation by generation from Cemetery L to the time of the last pre-First Dynasty tombs at Abydos. The people buried at Qustul were obviously kings with the full wealth expected of royalty, and had even far wider cultural contacts than has ever been thought possible for such a remote place. But what is known about this new kingdom? What relationship did these first pharaohs have with their subjects and surrounding political entities? Perhaps the most troublesome question was why nothing of this kingdom had been known until now. Actually, the truth is that evidence, other than the cemetery at Qustul, has been known for some time but it has been either ignored or wrongly interpreted and dated. The greatest example is the large Gebel Sheikh Suleiman monument located south of Qustul. Originally, this inscription was thought to have been made by the Egyptian pharaoh Djer, the second king of the First Dynasty, identified by his Horus name in a serekh. But the incisions across the lower body of the falcon perched on the serekh, which have been taken to be Djer's name, are actually part of an animal common in rock graffiti if Nubia. In fact, there is no room for a name on this serekh, and it must be dated with other unlabeled ones to the Predynastic period. The nameless serekh presides at a battlefield scene including fallen enemies, two bound prisoners and a

5. The incense burner from Tomb L24 is the most vivid evidence of kingship at Qustul (*top, bottom and opposite page, top*). Made of a mixture of fine clay minerals, it is an ancestor of the slate palettes and monumental maceheads that show royal events and ceremonies in Egypt. The scene shown here is a royal sacrifical procession of three ships going toward a palace façade. The completed restoration (*opposite page, top*) shows a bound prisoner held by his guard in the forward vessel: a pharaoh, indicated by the White Crown of Upper Egypt and the falcon, in the middle ship; and a feline deity with a falcon standard in the third. About 8.5 by 15.5 centimeters.

royal ship. Interestingly, these enemies have labels that do not seem to be associated with Nubia. In addition, one is being physically bound, rather than labeled, by a bow, which is significant because the "Land of the Bow" is the earliest hieroglyphic name for Nubia and, later, is the actual name for the southernmost nome or province of Egypt. By acting as agent of the pharaoh, the bow marks the ruler as one of Nubia, and makes this an A-Group rather than an Egyptian monument.

6. **Pottery from the A-Group royal tomb at Qustul includes large amounts of fine painted pottery (*left*), with one large bowl decorated with rows of palace façades; a Syro-Palestinian Early Bronze I jug (center); and Egyptian pottery (*right*). Height of handled jug, 17.7 centimeters.**

The bow appears elsewhere in prehistoric monuments—for example, on a seal impression found in a A-Group storage cache at Siali far to the north of Qustul. This sealing had been misinterpreted as a result of a crack in the original ivory or wood seal, which made a concentric serekh appear to be a plant and thus was overlooked as a reference to kingship. Its central subject, however, is undoubtedly a concentric serekh surmounted by the familiar falcon symbol. Although a number of aspects of this seal are still difficult to verify, certain features of the iconography are fairly certain, including representations of incense burners in use; D-shaped altars or pylons associated with the Heb-Sed festival, the jubilee celebrated by a pharaoh first in his thirtieth year and periodically thereafter; and a man seated in a chair saluting the bow symbol. This time, however, the bow hovers over a shortened rectangle which in this period represents land. The obvious interpretation is that the man is saluting the name for Nubia—Ta-Seti, or "Land of the Bow"—as a kingship and territorial state. Obviously, Nubia was a sophisticated political order of an actual and not embryonic rule.

Three objects from Cemetery L relate even more directly to the history of the kingdom of Ta-Seti. The first is a large Egyptian bowl from tomb L23 which has an elaborate painting of a processional scene leading to a shrine made of poles. Three vultures appear, two of them holding serpents in their talons and attacking

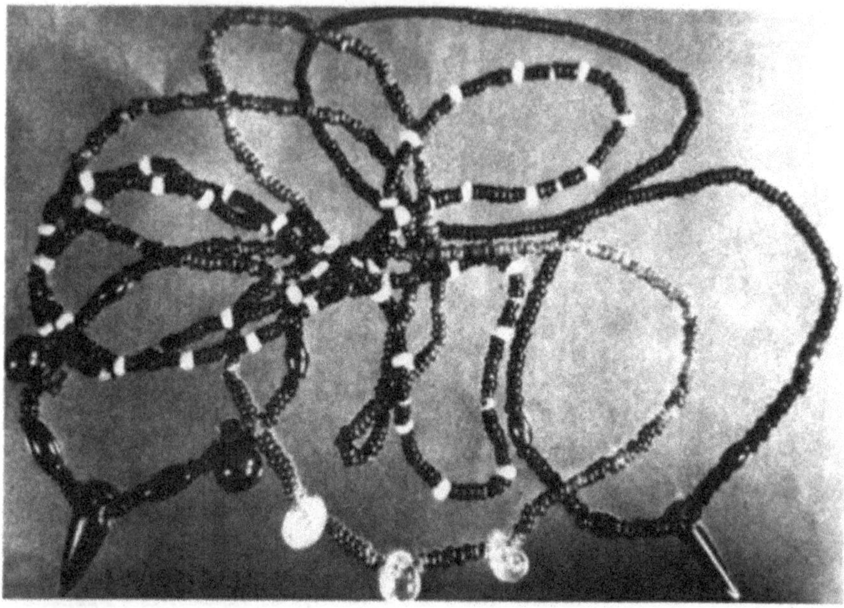

7. **Little jewelry remained in the plundered royal cemetery at Qustul, but what did survive was of high quality, including carnelian, amethyst, faience and rock crystal.**

them with their beaks. An identical motif is found on other vessesl and occurs in simplified form on a series of famous Predynastic Egyptian ivory objects decorated with elaborate rows of animals. Aside from this connection, the specific occurrence of this motif on the Qustul bowl allows us to follow a chronological progression in the development of this motif on two other important objects. One of these is also a large bowl; the other is an Egyptian storage jar with a faded black ink label on its shoulder from tomb L6, an animal sacrifice burial contemporary with L23. Because this label was applied after firing, it was most likely done locally and could hardly have referred to an Egyptian event. It shows a vertical pole with an oval object on it that is being attacked by an elongated, vulture-like bird. The back and neck of the bird are stretched in an exaggerated arc, like that made by the tails, backs and necks of the vultures on the bowl from L23. The oval under attack contains two diagonal lines, clearly the sign for Nekhen or Hierakonpolis, the late prehistoric site that has yielded so much evidence for the rise of the Egyptian pharaohs.

The third piece of evidence, from tomb L19, is a large bowl somewhat smaller than the example from L23. Painted on the sides are static heraldic groups, consisting of two giraffes facing a tree with at least one animal above and behind them. Groups of this kind are already well known from two monumental palettes, one depicting the early animal hunt group, and the other from the later historical series. Both the shapes of the giraffes and the roots of the tree indicate that this

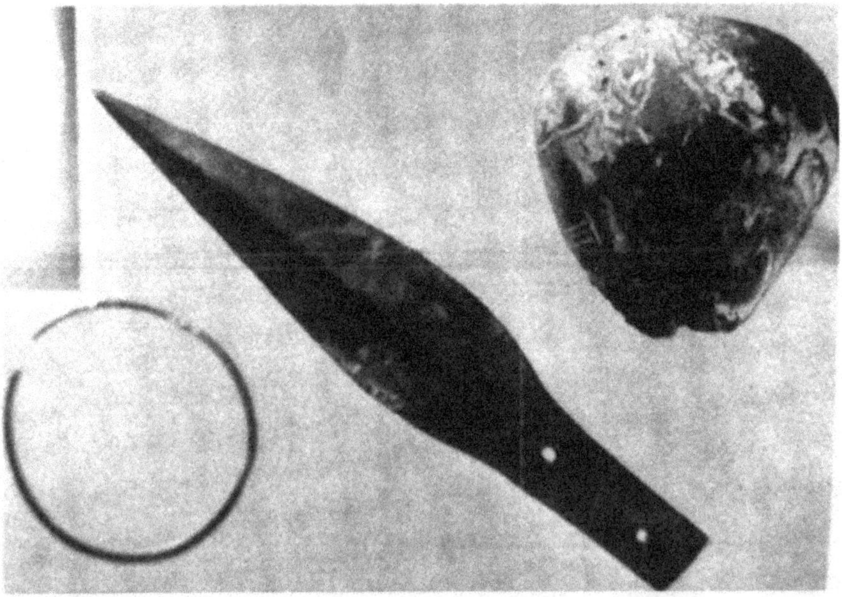

8. Few weapons remained in the robbed tombs at Qustul, but they included this spearhead and macehead. The bracelet is made of gold or electrum. Length of spearhead, 15.5 centimeters.

representation belongs to the early group. It seems that the paint was applied after firing, for much of it has been removed and what remains is vulnerable to contact with water. Since the paint was so delicate, it could hardly have been put on anywhere but in the immediate vicinity of Qustul because it would not have been able to stand the rigors of travel. In fact, so much of the paint has disappeared that the design could not have been followed if the background around the painted areas had not faded, leaving a traceable shadow of the original design.

The most striking feature of this decoration is the crown of the palm tree between the giraffes which has been supplanted by an animal group including the now familiar vulture. Here, the bird tears not a serpent or symbol, but a fallen man, a group seen elsewhere on the "Lion Palette" in England, one of the later palettes which show historical events. On the L19 bowl, the fallen man is labeled below his knee with the familiar oval land sign—without the two diagonal marks. Instead, a plant extends at an odd angle from the left end of the oval, presumably because it had been displaced from the vertical by the man's torso which can no longer be seen. The plant has three opposed pairs of short leaves (now partially obliterated) and a broad stalk that curves sharply to a point. Although the leaves are short and the stalk broad, this plant is clearly an early form of the symbol for Upper Egypt. The plant, together with the land oval, can plausibly be read one way only—the fallen enemy is labeled Ta-Shemau or Upper Egypt. Although the second group remaining on this bowl is fainter than the first, it can be seen that

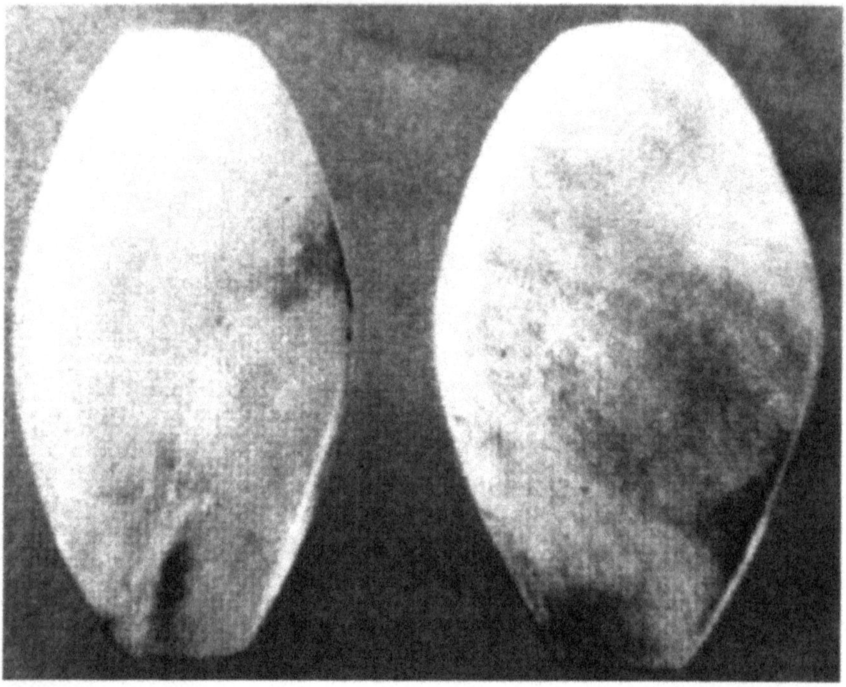

9. Some of the palettes from Qustul used to grind malachite for eye paint were made of special colored quartz and were given a jewel-like polish. Average length, eight centimeters.

"the enemy" has fallen on his back rather than forward. The long flat sign (land) extends from the enemy's knee and the unimpeded vertical identifying sign appears to make a kind of question mark above—this, in all probability, is the label Ta-Tjemeh or Libya.

All of these complex parts comprise the great legacy of the cemetery at Qustul—the eloquent remains of a remarkable civilization that rose out of both Egyptian and Sudanese heritages and had contacts as far away as Libya and western Asia. For nine generations or more, according to the sequence of tombs in Cemetery L, some twelve kings at Qustul participated with other kings in Upper Egypt in the creation of a unified culture. For Egypt, they helped fashion pharaonic civilization and thus a legacy for the First Dynasty which the world has marveled at for millennia. For Nubia, they established an early political unity and led that country to its first cultural distinction. Sifting through the individual artifacts, one can recreate the grand chain of events from the broken fragments.

In the first and second generation, the seal from Siali shows a king ruling Ta-Seti even before the unification of Upper Egypt. The actual king appears in the "third generation" figure on the Qustul incense burner, and is a link in the successive royal monuments both in Nubia and Egypt that culminate in the rise of the First Dynasty as shown on the Narmer Palette. The faded ink label of the Qustul storage jar, by describing the conflict with Hierakonpolis in Egypt, takes us to the fourth generation and, most important, the earliest known recorded event. In the fifth generation, this conflict grows ominously to include a now possibly united Upper Egypt. At about the same time, the Gebel Sheikh Suleiman monument seems to specify the places and/or people against whom the pharaohs of Ta-Seti fought. Whether it refers to actual events or is merely propaganda, the records of their victories are repeatedly asserted, and A-Group tombs, including one of royal size and design, have been found at Hierakonpolis itself. In the sixth generation, perhaps due to reverses in battle, the tombs at Qustul diminish sharply in size, possibly reflecting a reduction in stature of those buried in them.

The next generation, finally, appears to be contemporary with the first great royal burials at Abydos and the last Egyptian pharaohs before the First Dynasty. At Qustul, the royal cemetery continued for another two generations with the tombs growing ever smaller until no more were made, and the sepulchres were pillaged and burned. Apparently, the demise of Qustul coincides with the campaign of Aha in Nubia, the first king of the Egyptian First Dynasty, who recorded the smiting of Ta-Seti. Afterward, the A-Group culture ceased to exist in Lower Nubia. It may be that the remarkable adventure in political organization that began at Qustul and had such fateful consequences for human history was also terminated at this time. But striking parallels between the much later royal cemetery at Kerma, just south of the Third Cataract, and Cemetery L show another possibility: perhaps the survivors of the A-Group went south, beyond the reach of First Dynasty conquerers to the area even south of modern Lake Nasser. Although the chronological gap between the A-Group and Kerma is great and needs to be filled in by systematic field research, the present lack of evidence by no means rules out this possibility. After all, the kingdom at Qustul was not thought possible at that time or place. Given such a sudden and complete reversal of assumptions, there is reason to believe that knowledge of the achievements that created and sustained Egyptian civilization penetrated even further south than Qustul at a very early time. There must be a new search.

Bibliography

FOR FURTHER READING on Nubian kingship in general: William Y. Adams, *Nubia, Corridor to Africa* (Princeton University Press, Princeton 1978), for a current reconstruction of social organization in A-Group Nubiam this is a large-scale discussion of all periods of history in the region; A.J. Arkell, *A History of the Sudan to A.D. 1821* (Athlone Press, University of London 1961, second edition), a thoughtful work, but based on a much smaller body of evidence; Hans-Ake Nordstrom, *Neolithic and A-Group Sites* (Scandanavian Joint Expedition to Sudanese Nubia Vol. 3, Uppsala, Sweden 1972); Boyce Rensberger, "Nubian Monarchy Called Oldest" (*The New York Times*, March 1, 1979, A1 and A16), except for other short notices in the press, no other publication available to the public refers to the possibility of kingship in Nubia during the A-Group; Bruce G. Trigger, *History and Settlement in Lower Nubia* (Yale University Publications in Anthropology, No. 69, New Haven 1965), discusses A-Group culture generally.

On the "new chronology for the Egyptian Predynastic period: Elise J. Baumgartel, "Predynastic Egypt" (Cambridge Ancient History, Vol. 1, Chapter IXa, Cambridge 1970); *Die altorientalischen Reiche I; vom Paläolithikum biz zur Mitte des 2. Jahrtausends* (Fischer Bucherei K.G., Frankfurt A.M. and Hamburg 1965), accepts an alternative reconstruction which recognizes late predynastic (Naqada III or Late Gerzean); Werner Kaiser, "Stand und Probleme der ägyptischen Vorgeschichtsforschung" (*Zeitschrift für ägyptische Sprache* 81 (1956): 87-109 and "Zur inneren Chronologie der Naqadakultur" (*Archaeologia Geographia* 6 (1957): 69-77, propose this alternative reconstruction; "Einige Bemerkugen zur ägyptische Frühzeit," parts I-III, *Zeitschrift für äyptische Sprache, vols.* 84 (1959), 85 (1960), 86 (1961) and 89 (1964), discusses pharaonic culture in late predynastic and early dynastic times.

A WORKING CHRONOLOGY OF THE ROYAL KEMETIC DYNASTIES

Runoko Rashidi
With the Collaboration of James E. Brunson

Kingdom of Ta-Seti
Nubian Dynasty (Qustul): ca. 3400 (?)—3200 B.C.E.

Kemetic Dynasty I: ca. 3200 (?)—2890 B.C.E. (Selected Monarchs)
Thinite Dynasty

King Narmer (Menes) rules over united Kmt.
The White Wall (Memphis) is established as Kmt's administrative capital.
Temples erected and dedicated to Ptah at the White Wall (Memphis) and Neit at Sau (Sais).
King Aha ('The Fighter')
King Djer (Athothis) reigns 47 years.
Books written on anatomy.
King Djet
King Den (Udimu) experiments with stone as a building material.
Queen Mer-neit
King Anedjib
King Semerkhet
King Qaa reigns 25 years.

Kemetic Dynasty II: ca. 2890—2686 B.C.E. (Selected Monarchs)
Thinite Dynasty

King Hotepsekemui
King Reneb
King Nynetjer reigns approximately 38 years.
King Peribsen—Strong Advocate of Set
King Khasekemui

Kemetic Monarchs of Dynasties I and II buried in mastaba tombs at Sakkara.

Royal Cenotaphs (false tombs) constructed at Aabdju (Abydos).

Kemetic Dynasty III: ca. 2686—2613 B.C.E. (Selected Monarchs)
Memphite Dynasty

King Sanekht establishes a Kemetic presence in the Sinai Peninsula.
Bedjmes (Noted Ship-Builder)
King Zoser—Construction of the 'Step Pyramid' (World's first massive stone building).
Imhotep (Brilliant Administrator, Architect, Author, Physican and Priest)
King Sekhemkhet begins the construction of a step pyramid at Sakkara.
King Khaba—Construction of the 'Layer Pyramid' at Zawiet et Aryan.
King Huni—Construction of a major pyramid at Meydum.
Solar Calendar utilized in Kmt.
Important Gods: Atum, Hathor, Horus, Neit, Ptah, Re and Set.

Kemetic Dynasty IV: ca. 2613—2494 B.C.E.
Memphite Dynasty

King Nae-maet Sneferu—Construction of the 'Bent Pyramid' at Dahshur.
Construction of the 'Northern Stone Pyramid' (First true pyramid) at Dahshur.
Queen Hetepheres (Greay Royal Wife of Sneferu; Mother of Khufu)
Military conflicts between Kmt and Ta-Seti.
Active commercial relations between Kmt and Phoenicia.
Military conflicts between Kmt and Libya.
King Khufu—Construction of the 'Great Pyramid' at Khem (Giza).
The Instruction of Prince Hardjedef recorded.
King Dedefre reigns eight years.
Rising power of the Priesthood of Re at Northern Anu (Heliopolis).
King Khafre—Construction of the 'Second Pyramid' of Khem (Giza).
Hor-m-akhet (Sphinx of Giza) carved in the image of King Khafre.
Kingh Menkaure—Construction of the 'Third Pyramid' of Khem (Giza).
King Shepseskaf—Buried in a distinct bomb known as 'Mastabet el-Fara'un.'
Hesyre (Outstanding Physician)

Kemetic Dynasty V: ca. 2494—2345 B.C.E.
Heliopolitan Dynasty Sons of Re

King Userkaf—Introduction of sun-temples.
Construction of a pyramid at Sakkara.
King Sahure—wars with Libyans: Construction of a pyramid at Djedu (Abusir).
Expedition to Punt ('God's Land') on the Somali coast.

King Neferirkare Kakai—Construction of a pyramid at Djedu (Abusir).
The Royal Annals of the Palermo Stone inscribed.
King Shepseskare Isi reigns seven years.
The Admonitions of the Vizier Kagemni recorded.
King Nyuserre—Construction of a pyramid at Djedu (Abusir).
Construction of a splendid stone sun-temple at Abu Ghurab.
King Menkauhor Akauhor reigns eight years.
King Djedkare Isesi reigns 39 years.
Construction of the 'Pyramid of the Sentinel.'
Construction of the last known sun-temple.
Expedition to Punt ('God's Land') on the Somali coast.
The Maxims of Ptahhotep recorded.
King Unas inscribes his tomb with the earliest known *Pyramid Texts*.

Kemetic Dynasty VI: ca. 2345—2181 B.C.E. (Selected Monarchs)
Memphite Dynasty

King Seheteptowy Teti reigns twelve years.
Weni (Governor of Upper Kmt)
King Merire Pepi I reigns 49 years.
Major African military operations against Asiatics.
King Merenre Antyemsaf I journeys to the First Cataract to meet the Nubian Monarchs.
Harkhuf, the Kemetic governor of Ta-Seti, leads four expeditions to Yam (Inner Africa).
King Neferkare Pepi II reigns longer (94 years) than any monarch in history.
Tax immune status granted to the Temple of Min at Gebtu (Koptos).
Queen Regent Nitocris
Climatic conditions worsen steadily; Usurpation of power by provincial leaders.
Dynasty VI Monarchs buried in small pyramid tombs at Djedu (Abusir) and Sakkara.
Important Gods: Atum, Hathor, Horus, Isis, Min, Neit, Osiris, Ptah, Re and Sebek.

Kemetic Dynasty VII: ca. 2181—2173 B.C.E.
(?) Memphite Dynasty

King Neferkare ('The Younger')
King Neferkare Neby
King Djedkare Shemay
King Neferkare Khendu
King Meryenhor

King Neferkamin
King Nykare
King Neferkare Tereru
King Neferkahor
Appearance of early *Coffin Texts* in Kemetic tombs.

Kemetic Dynasty VIII: ca. 2173–2160 B.C.E.
Memphite Dynasty

King Wadjkare Pepysonbe reigns four years.
King Neferkamin Anu reigns two years.
King Kahare Ibi—Construction of a small pyramid near Sakkara.
King Neferkare reigns two years.
King Neferkauhor Kapuibi reigns for little more than a year.
Kmt experiences widespread internal disorder; Asiatics settle in Northern Kmt.

Kemetic Dynasty IX (Selected Monarchs)
Herakleopolitan Dynasty House of Akhtoy

King Kheti I
King Kheti II

Kemetic Dynasty X (Selected Monarchs)
Herakleopolitan Dynasty House of Akhtoy

King Neferkare
King Kheti III
King Merikare

Kemetic Dynasty XI: ca. 2130–1991 B.C.E.
Theban Dynasty

King Tepya Mentuhotep I
King Sehertowy Intef I
King Wahankh Intef II
King Nakhtnebepnefer Intef III
King Nebhepetre Mentuhotep II reunites Kmt in 2040 B.C.E.
Waset (Thebes) becomes the Kemetic capital.
Queen Ashayet (Great Royal Wife of Mentuhotep II)
Queen Kawit (Great Royal Wife of Mentuhotep II)
Asiatics driven from Kmt's Eastern Delta.
Reestablishment of strong central monarchy.

Construction of a distinct rock-cut tomb surmounted by a pyramid at Waset (Thebes).
King Sankhkare Mentuhotep III—Major expedition to Punt on the Somali Coast.
King Nebtowyre Mentuhotep IV reigns briefly.
Amenemhet (Vizier of Kmt during the reign of Nebtowyre Mentuhotep IV)
Widespread democratization of Kemetic religious beliefs.
Important Gods: Amen, Hathor, Montu, Osiris and Re.

Kemetic Dynasty XII: 1991—1786 B.C.E.
Theban/Ta-Seti Dynasty

King Sehetepibre Amenemhet I moves the capital of Kmt north to It-Tawy.
Queen Neferu (Great Royal Wife of Amenenhet I)
King Kheperkare Senusret I orders the Temple of Amen at Ipet-sut (Karnak) rebuilt in stone.
Red granite obelisks erected at Northern Anu (Heliopolis).
Major expedition to Punt ('God's Land') on the Somali Coast.
The Story of Sunuhe composed.
King Nubkaure Amenemhet II dedicates a temple in Sinai to the goddess Hathor.
Construction of 'The White Pyramid' at Dahshur.
Regular commercial relations with Punt.
King Khakheperre Senusret II—Kemetic relations with Minoan Crete.
Construction of 'The Shining Pyramid' at El Lahun.
Queen Nefert (Great Royal Wife of Senusret II)
Resumption of expeditions to Punt on the Somali Coast.
King Khakaure Senusret III—Military campaigns against Nubians and Asiatics.
Erection of strong Kemetic defensive fortifications along the Nubian frontier.
Major reorganization of Kmt's administrative system.
King Nymare Amenemhet III reigns 47 years.
Construction of 'The Black Pyramid' at Dahshur.
Construction of a major pyramid at Haware.
Construction of the 'Egyptian Labyrinth' (The largest building in antiquity).
Exploitation of copper mines in the Sinai Peninsula.
Massive irrigation and land reclamation projects in the Fayum Oasis.
King Makherure Amenemhet IV reigns eight years.
Queen Regent Sobkkare Sebeknefrure (Daughter of Amenemhet III)
Kemetic Monarchs of Dynasty XII buried in pyramid tombs near Ineb-hedj (Memphis).

Kemetic Dynasty XIII: ca. 1786—1700 B.C.E. (Selected Monarchs)
Theban Dynasty

King Sebekhotep I reigns five years.
King Awibre Hor reigns only seven months.
King Userkare Khendjer—Construction of a small pyramid near Dahshur.
King Khasekhemre Neferhotep I reigns eleven years.
King Khaneferre Sebekhotep IV reigns eight years.
King Khahetepre Sebekhotep VI reigns four years.,
King Wahibre Yayebi reigns ten years.
King Merneferre Iy reigns 23 years.
King Nehesi reigns in Southern Kmt.
Important Gods: Amen, Hathor, Montu, Osiris, Re and Sebek.

Kemetic Dynasty XIV: ca. 1730—1680 B.C.E.
(?) Memphite Dynasty

Few significant monuments constructed; Collapse of central government.
Asiatic Hyksos invade from the East and occupy Kmt for more than a century.

Dynasty XV: ca. 1730—1680 B.C.E. (Selected Monarchs)
Hyksos Dynasty

King Khyan
King Apophis I
King Apophis II

Dynasty XVI: ca. 1680—1560 B.C.E. (Selected Monarchs)
Hyksos Dynasty (Authority limited to Northern Kmt)

King Semqen
King Amu
King Apophis III
Nubians ransack and burn Kemetic fortresses in Ta-Seti

Dynasty XVII: ca. 1650—1560 B.C.E. (Selected Monarchs)
Kemetic Theban Dynasty (Authority limited to Southern Kmt)

King Nubkheperre Intef VI
King Senakhtenre
The scribe Ahmose copies the *Rhind Mathematical Papyrus*.
King Seqenenre Tao I ('The Elder')—Queen Tetisheri
King Seqenere Tao II ('The Brave')—Queen Ahhotep I
King Wadjkheperre Kamose escalates Kmt's war of liberation against Hyksos.

Kemetic Dynasty XVIII: ca. 1560–1295 B.C.E.
Theban Dynasty

King Nebpehtyre Ahmose I ('The Liberator')—Queen Ahmose-Nefertari
Expulsion of Hyksos; Reunification of Kmt.
Queen Regent Ahmose-Nefertari
King Djeserkare Amenhotep I reigns twenty years.
Amen becomes the state god of Kmt.
King AkheperkareThutmose I extends Kemetic military power to the River Euphrates.
Kimg Akheperenre Thutmose II reigns four years.
Makare Hatshepsut ('The Female Horus') reigns 21 years.
Major expeditin to Punt ('God's Land') on the Somali coast.
Senemut (Overseer of Works during the reign of Hatshepsut)
Nehesi (Chief Treasurer of Kmt during the reign of Hatshepsut)
Enormous obelisks raised at Ipet-sut (Karnak).
Senenmut designs a distinct mortuary temple for Hatshepsut at Waset (Thebes).
King Menkheperre Thutmose III directs the furthest extensions of Kemetic military power.
General Amenemhab (SuperiorArmy Officer and Confidant to King Thutmose III)
Kemetic relations with Minoan Crete.
Expedition to Punt ('God's Land') on the Somali coast.
Table of Karnak King-List recorded.
King Akheprure Amenhotep II continues the military policies of Thutmose III.
Commercial relations with Punt.
King Menkheprure Thutmose IV—Evcavation of Hor-m-akhet (Sphinx of Giza).
King Nebmare Amenhotep III ('The Magnificent') reigns 38 years.
Queen Tiye (Great Royal Wife of Amenhotep III; Mother of Amenhotep IV/Akhenaten)
Construction of the 'Colossi of Memnon.'
Kmt achieves enormous power and prosperity.
King Amenhotep IV/Akhenaten renounces Amen; Aten established as the sole god.
Queen Nefertiti (Great Royal Wife of Amenhotep IV/Akhenaten)
Kemetic capital transferred to Akhetaten (El Amarna).
Naturalism adopted in Kemetic art.
Ankhkheprure Smenkare (Coregent for three years with Akhenaten)
King Nebkheprure Tutankhamen restores the national supremacy ofAmen.
Kemetic capital returned to Waset (Thebes).
King Kheperkheprure Ay reigns two years.
King Djeserkheprure Horemheb—Strong Advocate of Amen

Important Gods: Amen, Amen-Re, Aten, Hathor, Isis, Osiris, Ptah and Thoth.

Kemetic Dynasty IXX: ca. 1295—1187 B.C.E.
Ramesside Dynasty

King Menpehtyre Ramses I has brief reign.
King Menmare Seti I ('Bringer of the Renaissance')
Military campaigns against Libyans and Hittites.
Queen Tuya (Great Royal Wife of Seti I; Mother of Ramses II)
Construction of the 'Osireion' temple at Aabdju (Abydos).
Table of Abydos King-List recorded.
King Usermare Ramses II ('Ramses the Great') reigns 67 years.
Queen Nefertari (Great Royal Wife of Ramses II)
Queen Istnofret (Great Wife of Ramses II; Mother of Khaemwaset and Merneptah)
Kemetic capital relocated to Pi-Ramses in the Eastern Delta.
Historic battle of Kadesh fought along the banks of the River Orontes in Syria.
Historic peace treaty concluded between Kmt and the kingdom of Hatti.
Construction of the 'Ramesseum' (The mortuary temple of Ramses II).
The Tale of the Two Brothers (A Kemetic Fairy Tale) composed.
Prince Khaemwaset (Administrator, Archaeologist, Magician and High Priest of Ptah)
Construction of major temples in Ta-Seti (Lower Nubia).
Commercial relations with Punt ('God's Land') on the Somali coast.
Prince Khaemwaset repairs numerous Old Kingdom pyramids and sun-temples.
Turin Canon of Kings recorded.
King Baenre Merneptah repels a major invasion of Kmt by the Sea Peoples.
Revolt in Ta-Seti crushed.
King Menmire Amenmesses reigns briefly.,

King Userkheprure Seti II-Queen Tawosre (Great Royal Wife of Seti II)
King Siptah reigns six years.
Queen Regent Tawosre reigns eight years.

Kemetic Dynasty XX: ca. 1187—1180 B.C.E.(Selected Monarchs)
Ramesside Dynasty

King Userkhaure Sethnakhte reigns two years.
King Usermare-Meryamen Ramses III repels three invasions of Kmt. by Libyans and Sea Peoples.
Major expedition to Punt ('God's Land') on the Somali coast.
Kmt experiences prolonged labor troubles and turbulence among government workers.

Kmt experiences an inflationary rise in wheat prices.
Kmt experiences a sharp decline in the value of copper and bronze.
King Hiqmare Ramses IV reigns six years.
Gradual weakening of central authority.
Kemetic royal tombs robbed with impunity by high officials.
King Neferkare Ramses IX reigns nineteen years.
Kmt experiences severe famine.
Craft of mummification reaches its zenith.
King Ramses XI proclaims a Kemetic renaissance.
Herihor rules over Upper Kmt and Ta-Seti.
Smendes rules over Lower Kmt.
Kemetic Monarchs of Dynasties XVIII-XX buried in rock-cut bombs at Waset (Thebes).
The *Book of the Dead* found in Kemetic tombs.
Important Gods: Amen, Amen-Re, Hathor, Khonsu, Mut, Osiris, Ptah and Set.

Kemetic Dynasty XXI: ca. 1080–945 B.C.E. (Selected Monarchs) Theban/Tanite Dynasty (Authority divided between Theban Priesthood and Delta Princes)

Herihor (First Prophet of Amen)
Smedes
The Journey of Wenamen to Phoenicia composed.
Psusennes I
Pinudjem I (First Prophet of Amen)
Usermare Amenemope
Menkheperre (First Prophet of Amen)
Pinudjem II (First Prophet of Amen)
Psusennes II
Tanite Monarchs of Kemetic Dynasty XXI buried in sunken tombs in the Eastern Delta.

**Kemetic Dynasty XXII: ca. 945–817 B.C.E.
Libyan Dynasty**

King Sheshonq I attacks Palestine and plunders Jerusalem.
King Osorkon I
King Takelot I
King Osorkon II
Civil war rages intermittently in Kmt for 25 years.
King Sheshonq II
The power of Assyria grows steadily.
King Takelot II

King Sheshonq III reigns 52 years.
Prince Osorkon becomes First Prophet of Amen at Waset (Thebes).
King Pami
King Sheshonq IV

Kemetic relations with Spain.
Kemetic capitals at Dja'net (Tanis) and Bast (Bubastis).

Kemetic Dynasty XXIII: ca. 817 (?)—730 B.C.E.
Tanite Dynasty

King Pedibast I
King Sheshonq
Local rulers proliferate in Kmt.
King Osorkon
King Takelot
Kemetic capital at Nay-ta-hut (Leontopolis)

Kemetic Dynasty XXIV: ca. 730—715 B.C.E.
Saite dynasty

King Tefnakhte makes a treaty with Hosea of Samaria against Assyria.
King Bakenrenef (Boccaoris) supports the King of Isreal against Assyria.

Kemetic Dynasty XXV: ca. 750—656 B.C.E.
Kushite Dynasty

King Alara
King Kashta
Amenirdas I (Divine Wife of the God Amen)
King Piye (Piankhi) conquers Upper and Lower Kmt; Rules from Kush.
King Shabaka completes the total reunifiction of Kmt; Rules from Waset (Thebes).
Recording of the ancient creation story known as the *Memphite Theology.*
Prince Taharqa commands African invasion of Spain.
King Shabataka—Introduction of demotic script.
Capitals at Ineb-hedj (Memphis), Waset (Thebes) and Napata.
King Taharqa commands African military campaign in Palestine.
Assyrian armies invade Kmt and sack Ineb-hedj (Memphis) in 671 B.C.E.
Assyrian armies invade Kmt and sack Waset (Thebes) in 663 B.C.E.
King Tanwetamani severely defeated by Assyrians.
Kushite Monarchs of Dynasty XXV buried in pyramid tombs at El Kurru and Nuri.

Kemetic Dynasty XXVI: ca. 656–525 B.C.E.
Saite Dynasty

King Psametik I
King Necho
Kemetic military defeated by Babylonians at Carchemish in 605 B.C.E.
Kemetic naval exploration of African coasts.
King Psametik II
King Apries
Thales in Kmt.
King Ahmose II (Amasis)
Pythagoras in Kmt.
King Psametik III
Deification of Imhotep.
Jeremiah in Kmt.

Dynasty XXVI Monarchs buried in the Temple of Neit at Sau (Sais).

Persian invasion and conquest of Kmt under Cambyses II in 525 B.C.E.
Kmt incorporated into the Persian Empire

Dynasty XXVII: 525–404 B.C.E.
Persian Dynasty

Cambyses II
Darius I
Xerxes
Herodotus in Kmt.
Ataxerxes
Darius II

Kemetic capital at Susa or Babylon.

Kemetic Dynasty XXVIII: ca. 404–390 B.C.E.
Saite Dynasty the Amyrtaios

King Amyrtis

Kemetic Dynasty XXIX: ca. 390 (?)–378 B.C.E.
Memphite Dynasty

King Nepherites I

King Nepherites II
King Achoris
Plato in Kmt.

Kemetic Dynasty XXX: ca. 378—341 B.C.E.
Last Native Kemetic Dynasty

King Nectanebo I
Kemetic capital at Tjebnutjer (Sebennytos).
King Teos
King Nectanebo II defeated by Persians under Ataxerxes III in 343 B.C.E.

Alexander of Macedon defeats the Persian Army at the Battle of Issus.
Greek invasion and occupation of Kmt under Alexander of Macedon in 322 B.C.E.

Dynasty XXXI: 323—30 B.C.E.
Ptolemaic Dynasty

Ptolemy I (Soter)
Alexandria becomes the Kemetic administrative capital.
Manetho (Famous African Scholar-Priest) writes a *History of Egypt (Aegyptiaca)* in which he divides the Kemetic royal families into dynasties.
Ptolemy II (Philadelphus) opens ports at Arsinoe, Myos Hormos and Berenice.
Alexandrian Museum and Library founded.
Eratosthenes (Celebrated African Scholar and the First Librarian at Alexandria) accurately charts the earth's circumference and writes the *Canon of the Kings of Thebes*.
Ptolemy III (Euergetes)
Ptolemy IV (Philopator)
The Rosetta Stone (A bilingual decree of Ptolemy IV) inscribed in 196 B.C.E.
Ptolemy V (Epiphanes)
Ptolemy VI (Philometor)
Ptolemy VII (Neos Philopator)
Ptolemy VIII (Euergetes II)
Ptolemy IX (Soter II)
Ptolemy X (Alexander I)
Ptolemy XI (Alexander II)
Khaemwaset and Na-nefer-ka-Ptah and *Khaemwaset and his son Si-Osiri* written.
Ptolemy XII (Neos Dionysos)
Cleopatra VII commits suicide.
Augustus Caesar claims Kmt as a province of the Roman Empire in 30 B.C.E.

OF GODS AND MEN:
EGYPT'S OLD KINGDOM

Wayne Chandler

> *And, I say unto you, that through the inspirational writings of him who is my word unto the nations, shall the land of Khem be caused to give forth those secrets to mankind which I shall cause to be hidden there . . .*[1]
>
> Osiris, The Book of Truth

In this paper I hope to demonstrate that the origin of the civilization of Egypt (Khem) was black African, specifically Ethiopian or Anu. In order to understand the progression of events which I hope will lead us to the revision of Egypt's history, I will give an overview of archaeology in Egypt. In order for the reader to fully appreciate the achievements of Egyptian civilization, I will summarize the notable accomplishments of the early Egyptians.

For centuries, countries too numerous to mention have competed for the right to lay claim to Egypt, the birthplace of science, philosophy, art, and yes, the very genesis of civilization as we know it. Those origins which have become most popular over the centuries are India, Sumeria, Mesopotamia, and Arabia. Ironically, with the advent of the archaeologist, the historical perspectives became even more confusing. For this pioneering school, trying to solve the archaic mysteries of this culture became more a cause of frustration than a source of adventure. Too often were archaeologists confronted with pieces of a puzzle that did not seem to fit. In what finally became an historical frenzy to make sense of data accumulated from temple, tomb, and terrain, archaeologists committed the cardinal sin of sanding square pegs so they might fit into round holes. Personal bias and racial prejudice prevented most of these scientists, many of whom were great scholars, from seeing the obvious—that Egypt was born and culturally nurtured from the very womb of Africa herself! In the words of Chiekh Anta Diop, ". . . The history of Black Africa will remain suspended in air and cannot be written correctly until African historians dare to connect it with the history of Egypt."[2]

The 1900's ushered in a new era of archaeological exploration. For the first time since the inception of Egyptology several historians began to paint a more accurate account of Egypt's historical record. Leaving behind them the racially tainted perceptions which were characteristic of the 1800's, these erudite explorers withstood a barrage of vehement criticism as they dared to connect Egypt with black Africa. The debates that were waged in the early 1900's between these two factions attracted the attention of the few outstanding black historians then residing in the U.S. With fresh historical perspectives, individuals such as Drusilla D. Houston, W.E.B. DuBois, and J.A. Rogers (the father of anthrophotojournalism), initiated a virtual revision of black history the world over.

As Egyptology forged ahead into the mid-1900's, the general consensus of the field's leading scholars was that Egypt's origin was still Euro-Asiatic. Even with an abundance of new information which repeatedly contradicted their convictions, their minds remained hermetically sealed. This state of confusion continues to the present day. Today, as one examines the current state of Egyptology, one cannot help but see the fundamental inconsistencies and profound voids which abound in this field. It is unfortunate that most of the available information regarding Egypt is biased, very conservative, and insufficient. In 1984 Geo Magazine printed a revealing article on the British Museum. When the curator was asked about the thousands of artifacts housed in the museum's basement he matter-of-factly noted that they had collected enough material over the years to literally rewrite history. As students of Egyptian history, we now find ourselves standing at a historical cross-road: one road well traveled, although very convoluted, a road turned into a dead-end by a mind-set that has no place in our present or our future; the other road wide open with the exhilarating promise of new perspectives and discoveries.

Statement of Purpose

In the next several pages we will examine critical issues in the light of these new perspectives. We will consider the correct chronology of Egypt, the true origin of Egypt, and the identity of the first Egyptians. We will also look at the men who lived before the first dynasty, who later became gods, and men after, who became legends. Their achievements in the arts and sciences will all be points of discussion. Finally, we will explore the creation of the pyramids.

I. The Chronology of Egypt

The chronology of the "Old Kingdom" is by far the most perplexing of all the periods of Egypt. How old is it really? The documents which we have at our disposal all have certain and definite limitations which hamper the establishment of a viable chronology. The most important of these documents are the Tablet of Karnak, the Tablet of Abydos, the Table of Saqqara, the Papyrus of Turin and the chronology of the Egyptian Priest, Manetho. Wallis Budge, noted Egyptologist and historian, wrote of these tablets: "Until we have more evidence of a definite character on the general facts of Egyptian history, and a more accurate means for finding the date of the starting point of Egyptian civilization, we shall have to be content with a system of chronology which contains several gaps and a series of minimum dates for the greater number of the reigns of the kings, for the beginning of which an exact date cannot be assigned."[3]

Egyptologist Roger Moorey points out his difficulty in devising Egypt's chronology. "Elsewhere in Western Asia prehistoric chronology is largely based on the analysis of the layers of debris from successive settlements in one place (stratigraphy) which have formed a mound or *tell*. These are virtually absent in Egypt."[4] Hence the emphasis on tablets and ruler chronology. Traditionally, the key to establishing the approximate age of Egypt has been to reconstruct the chronology of her kings. However, this has proved to be a frustrating and impossible task. The most complete list of kings known appeared in the Royal Papyrus of Turin, which assigned in order of dynasty the names of over 130 kings. Unfortunately, when it was shipped to Turin in the early nineteenth century, it disintegrated into thousands of tiny pieces. A reconstruction was attempted in 1826 by a linguist named Seyffarth, but his knowledge of hieratic characters was very limited and his efforts have been deemed worthless. Current opinion maintains that the most important single document of all has been given to us by the Egyptian Priest Manetho, which encompasses both prehistory and the dynastic period. In it, Manetho named over a hundred kings and divided them into thirty dynasties; this system is still employed to this day. The main drawback of this chronology is that it has come down to us by word of mouth. The two most complete versions of his list are those quoted by Julius Africanus and by Eusebius. Much to our despair these two lists differ in the arrangement of the dynasties, the lengths of the reigns of the kings and in the number of kings assigned to the different dynasties. According to Julius Africanus, 561 kings reigned for approximately 5,524 years in total. Eusebius, on the other hand, states 361 kings ruled in 4,780 years. Budge states that of the two versions Julius Africanus is "clearly the more accurate of the two". The biting irony in all of this is that many of our top scholars in the field feel that Manetho's work as handed down to us is short of useless, *yet Manetho's scheme of thirty dynasties is still employed!*

This problem of chronology is further compounded by the presence of two major eras known as Egypt's "dark eras". These periods existed on either side of the Middle Kingdom and are traditionally called the first and second Intermediate Periods. James Henry Breasted, famed Egyptlogist and historian, says of these periods: "It was a period of such weakness and disorganization that neither king nor noble was able to erect monumental works which might have survived to tell us something of the time. How long this unhappy condition may have continued it is now quite impossible to determine."[5] These remarks by Breasted indicate the possibility that these periods may have spanned several centuries. If this is indeed the case it would push the Pyramid Age and the age of Egypt proper into a more remote antiquity.

Cheikh Anta Diop, egyptologist, linguist, physicist, and historian, allows 10,000 years for the cycle of Egyptian civilization. His logic is pure and simple and hard to refute. The Egyptian calendar was based on the cycle of the star Sirius whose rise coincides with the sun every 1,461 years. Now any astronomer will verify the fact that it takes thousands of years to study the stellar movement of celestial bodies before one may acquire information accurate enough to develope a calendar. Dr. Diop says, and I quote: "This civilization called Egyptian in our period developed for a long time in its early cradle . . . This cycle of civilization, the longest in history, presumably lasted 10,000 years. This is a reasonable compromise between the long chronology (based on data provided . . . by Manetho [which] places the beginning at 17,000 B.C.) and the short chronology [3100 B.C.] of the moderns—for the latter are obliged to admit that by 4245 B.C. the Egyptians had already invented the calendar (which necessarily requires the passages of thousands of years)."[6] Thus, if the Egyptians had the calendar in 4245 B.C. and it took the passage of several thousand years to amass enough data to create it, then it is only rational that we adhere to the logic of Professor Diop. Diop goes on to say, "The official date, adopted until now for no special reason wavers between 3100 B.C. and 3000 B.C. In actual fact, the choice of 3100 B.C. results from no necessity but that of synchronizing Egyptian and Mesopotamian chronology."[7] Continuing, Diop goes on to point out, "The motivating idea is to succeed in explaining Egypt by Mesopotamia, that is, by Western Asia, the original habitat of Indo-Europeans. The chronology of Viktor Christian, who relies on Kugler's astronomical calculations, dates the start of the first Ur dynasty between 2600 and 2580, [B.C] which would thus also be the period of the so-called 'royal' tombs".[8] Therefore the fixed date of Mesopotamian civilization at 3100 B.C. is incorrect and purposely misleading. In essence what is being stated here is that this information implies a much greater antiquity than the poor few thousand years accorded Egypt by the world's Egyptologists.

What of the Egyptians themselves? How did they perceive their own chronology? When Herodotus was in Egypt in the fifth century B.C., he was informed of Egypt's great antiquity. The "Father of History" was told that the first man to rule Egypt was Min, who lived so long ago that Egypt was still under water: "in (Min's) time the whole country, except the district around Thebes, was marsh, none of the land below Lake Moeris, was then showing above water. To this place from the sea [Now] is seven days passage up the river . . ."[9] Later Solon, en route from Greece, happened upon an Egyptian priest of Sais. Trying to engage him in an historical debate the priest answered thus, "You Greeks are novices in all knowledge of antiquity. You are ignorant of what passed here or among yourselves in the days of old. The history of eight-thousand years is deposited in our sacred books, but we can ascend to much higher antiquity and tell you what our fathers have done for nine-thousand years. I mean their institutions, their laws, and their brilliant accomplishments."[10] According to Diodorus' sources, which corroborate those of Herodotus, the Ethiopians began to migrate into Egypt while some of it was still underwater: "They even allege that this country was originally under water, but that the Nile, dragging much mud as it flowed from Ethiopia, had finally filled it in and made it a part of the continent."[11] There is ample evidence that the Mediterranean still covered Egypt while the rest of the continent was already dry, and that the first of the new Egyptians began to build as the waters receded.

Herodotus, as we have already said, was told that the first ruler Min lived at this time, and recorded his own conclusion: "I not only believe the people who gave me this account of Egypt, but my own conclusions strongly support what they said . . . Now it is my belief that Egypt was originally an arm of the sea."[12] In support he noted "I have observed for myself that Egypt at the Nile Delta projects into the sea beyond the coast on either side; I have seen sea shells on the hills and noticed how salt exudes from the soil to such an extent that it affects even the pyramids; I have noticed too, that the only hill where there is sand is the hill above Memphis, and that the soil of Egypt does not resemble that of the neighboring country of Arabia, or Libya, or even of Syria . . . but is black as one would expect of an alluvial soil . . ."[13] More evidence comes from the books of Thoth (Hermes). It describes one of the pyramids as standing upon the sea-shore, "the waves of which dashed in powerless fury against its base."[14]

Modern scientists confirm these ancient writers. An archaeologist, Dr. H. Getzinger produced startling photographs of one of the sides of the Great Pyramid revealing the incrustation of sea-shells at a certain level quite above the present level of the base of the structure. Dr. R. Rennel an American geologist substantiates this by saying "The configuration and composition of the low lands of Egypt leave no room to doubt that the sea once washed the base of the rocks on which the pyramids . . . stand; the present base of which is reached by the inundations of the Nile at an elevation seventy or eighty feet above the Mediterranean."[15]

II. Origin of Egypt

Apart from the question of Egypt's chronology, there remains the intriguing question as to who were the Egyptians and from where did they originate? In reviewing Egypt's beginnings, we find an advanced civilization already intact from the earliest Dynasty. This fact has perplexed historians down through the ages. Common sense dictates that if Egypt began fully mature, then its civilization must have originated elsewhere. "We find when we discover Egypt in what we call the First Dynasty, under Menes, that it is at its absolute zenith of culture in painting, sculpture, architecture. From this peak period, the Egyptian culture steadily declines. It is very much as if the Egyptians found themselves the inheritors of a great ready-made culture of which they could take advantage, which they could utilize and even to some degree emulate, but which they themselves did not create . . . This very strongly suggests that it drew its greatness from a source higher than itself . . ."[16]

In 1962 a new discovery occurred which shed some light on this puzzle. An excavation team headed by Keith C. Seele, then Director of the University of Chicago's Oriental Institute, had set out to salvage ancient remains in Nubia which were in danger of rising flood waters. There they found the birthplace of a pharaonic-centered civilization several generations older than the first historic Egyptian dynasty. There in Qustul, Nubia, prehistory was transformed into history, for it had previously been believed that advanced political organization did not enter Nubia or anywhere south of Egypt for another 2,500 years. This discovery, along with information excavated from tombs, proved that Egyptian civilization and culture had not only originated in the south, but that in some remote period of antiquity the inhabitants of Egypt and Nubia were one and the same.

Diodorus of Sicily informs us that "the Ethiopians say that the Egyptians are one of their colonies which was brought into Egypt by Osiris . . . They add that from them, as from their authors and ancestors, the Egyptians get most of their laws. It is from them that the Egyptians have learned to honor kings and gods and bury them with such pomp; sculpture and writing were invented by the Ethiopians. The Ethiopians cite evidence that they are more ancient that the Egyptians, but it is useless to report that here."[17]

At this juncture, we should explore more deeply into the nature of the Ethiopians who emigrated to Egypt. First we must clarify some terminology. The word "Ethiopian" is Greek, stemming from the words "aithein" which means to burn, and "ops" which means face. Therefore the term burnt face or Ethiopian was applied very broadly to all black peoples who inhabited Africa and Asia. The blacks of ancient Ethiopia referred to themselves as the Anu. When Osiris brought forth this exodus out of Ethiopia into Egypt we must almost remember that the term Egypt did not exist, for it too is Greek. Though the ancient Egyptians called their land Khem, Kemit, or Kmt, (which means black in their language or land of the blacks) never did those blacks of the Old Kingdom refrain from identifying themselves with the Anu.

Abbe Emile Amelineau (1850-1916) is credited with the discovery of the Anu and their contribution to Egyptian civilization.[18] It was Amelineau who designated the first black race to occupy Egypt as the Anu. He followed their path along the Nile, and revealed that they built the cities of Esneh, Erment, Qouch, and Heliopolis. According to Amelineau, "All those cities have the characteristic symbol which serves to denote the name Anu."[19] Citing evidence uncovered in

Basalt statue of a pre-dynastic figure adorned with a false beard, which later became a pharaonic symbol, and a penis-sheath. ***Courtesy of Wayne Chandler and Gaynell Catherine.***

Pre-dynastic statuette of a woman from the Temple at Hierakonpolis. *Courtesy of Wayne Chandler and Gaynell Catherine.*

his excavations he continues: "These Anu were agricultural people, raising cattle on a large scale along the Nile, shutting themselves up in walled cities for defensive purposes. To this people we can attribute *without fear of error*, the most ancient Egyptian books, The Book of The Dead and the Text of the Pyramids, consequently, all the myths or religious teachings. I would add almost all the philosophical systems then known and still called Egyptian. They evidently knew the crafts necessary for any civilization and were familiar with the tools those trades required. They knew how to use metals . . . They made the earliest attempts at writing, for the whole Egyptian tradition attributes this art to Thoth, the great Hermes, an Anu like Osiris, who is called Onian in chapter fifteen of *The Book of the Dead* and in the *Texts of the Pyramids*. Certainly the people already knew the principal arts; it left proof of this in the architecture of the tombs at Abydos, especially the tomb of Osiris, and in those sepulchers objects have been found bearing the unmistakable stamp of their origin—such as carved ivory, or the little head of a Nubian girl found in a tomb near that of Osiris, or the small wooden or ivory receptacles in the form of a feline head . . ."[20]

Of course, if the Egyptians were Anu people, like the Ethiopians, they would also be black. Ancient writers as well as modern ones, led of course by Diop, confirm this. The ancient testimonies include writers who were contemporary with the dynastic Egyptians and represent some of the most respected explorers, historians, and Egyptologists of the last 2,000 years. Gaston Maspero (1846-1916) summarizes how the writers of antiquity viewed the ancient Egyptians. "By the almost unanimous testimony of ancient historians, they belonged to a Negro race which first settled in Ethiopia, on the Middle Nile; following the course of the river, they gradually reached the sea . . ."[21] Another scholar, Count Constantin de Volney was imbued with all the racial prejudices which were characteristic during his time. Embarking upon a sojourn to Egypt in the year 1783 (the slave trade was at its zenith) he made a discovery about the African race that would forever change his outlook: ". . . all [the inhabitants] have a bloated face, puffed up eyes, flat nose, thick lips; . . . I was tempted to attribute it to the climate, but when I visited the Sphinx, its appearance gave me the key to the riddle. On seeing that head, typically Negro in all its features, I remembered the remarkable passage where Herodotus [5th century B.C.] says: 'As for me, I judge the Colchians to be a colony of the Egyptians because, like them, they are black with wooley hair. . . .' In other words, the ancient Egyptians were true Negroes of the same type as all native-born Africans . . . Just think that this race of black men, today our slaves and the object of our scorn, is the very race to which we owe our arts, sciences and even the use of speech! Just imagine, finally, that it is in the midst of peoples who call themselves the greatest friends of liberty and humanity that one has approved the most barbarous slavery and questioned whether black men have the same intelligence as whites!"[22] This profound revelation is all the more remarkable for one previously inflicted with the virus of racism. Finally this is all substantiated in the text "A Comparative study of Racial Analysis" by B.K. Chatterjee and G.D. Kumar. They compared the mean values of different cranial, facial, nasal, and orbital measurments of skulls related to various areas and periods of Egyptian civilization. Cranium material was analyzed from the pre-historic sites of Egypt Naqada II, Egypt Badari, plus Nubia Ariba, and were then compared with skulls from the Twelfth and Thirteenth Dynasties and Saqqara, (Old Kingdom). The archaeologists found that all of these skulls in respect to "long head, broad face, low orbit, and broad nasal aperture have the characteristic features of the Negroid type".[23]

III. The Men Before the First Dynasty

"Myths are things which never happen but always are"

—Salustius

In Egyptian history Osiris was enshrined as a god, a legend or myth, if you will. But in all actuality he existed as a historical figure as did Menes, and many of the other kings of the Old Kingdom, who found their way to immortality through deification. Egyptologist Heinrich Brugsch notes "Frequent mention is made in the old records of royal gods, as of real personages. Besides the name of their dynasty they have a second name of honor, and, just like the Pharaohs, they bear respectively the authentic title under which the god Tehuti [Thoth], the sacred scribe of the gods, registered each of them in the 'Book of Kings,' at the command of the sun god, Ra. They have their individual history, which the scribes wrote down in the temple books; they married royal brides, and begat a very numerous posterity".[24] The part Osiris played in Egyptian history is obscure. Outside of what legend has bequeathed us, we know that he was part of a triad which included his spouse Isis, and son Horus, all of whom were deified during a later period. Another eminent figure who played a prominent role during this era was Thoth, or Hermes as he was known to the Greeks.

Egypt's greatest Masters, Osiris, Hermes, Isis, and Horus all belonged to "the old race", the black Anu. It was through these sovereign rulers that the very core of Egyptian philosophy and science (in all of its aspects) was created and maintained. Each of these great individuals played a particular role in not only Egypt's history, but the histories of many nations which were to later arise. We have not the time or space to include the history and legends which accompany these deities, but a brief overview is appropriate.

Once again we must turn to Amelineau for it was he that discovered the tomb of Osiris at Abydos. Because of this discovery Osiris could no longer be considered a mythical hero. The magnitude of this discovery cannot be stressed enough. Another incredible find may also be attributed to Amelineau, the dis-

Proto-dynastic life-sized figure of Osiris, from Abydos. ***Courtesy of Wayne Chandler and Gaynell Catherine.***

Close up of Osiris, showing negroid features. ***Courtesy of Wayne Chandler and Gaynell Catherine.***

Old Kingdom statue of Isis and Horus, the original black madonna, dated circa 2635 B.C. ***Courtesy of Wayne Chandler and Gaynell Catherine.***

Isis and Horus, Saite Period. *Courtesy of Wayne Chandler and Gaynell Catherine.*

covery of the head of Osiris. Found in a jar in the necropolis of Abydos, Amelineau says, "I myself have found other shrines during the preliminary excavations which culminated in the royal necropolis, before unearthing the shrine where the skull of the god I believed I had found was preserved."[25] Being the scientist that he was he sought to verify his finding. Referring to the papyrus in the Museum of Leiden, he found that it expressly stated that the god's head was preserved at Abydos, a place designated on the papyrus as "the necropolis of Abydos".

Amelineau must have been overwhelmed with excitement. The fact that he may have found the head of Osiris was numbing. Still uncertain he sought further confirmation. The papyrus was written in demotic so he conferred with one Eugene Revillout who was an expert in the field of ancient languages and scripts. Revillout verified the validity of the document and the fact that it mentioned the head as being located at Abydos. This proved to be a discovery of great importance. In brief, the legend of Osiris states that he was the god of transformation and immortality, King of the other world (death). In life he was the lord of creation, became king of Egypt and taught the people science, husbandry, and established a code of laws. Having made Egypt peaceful and prosperous he embarked on journeys to instruct other nations of the world. In his absence his spouse Isis ruled the kingdom. On the 28th year of his reign Typhon, Set, or Seth, as he was known, plotted with Aso, the Queen of Ethiopia, to murder Osiris. Having done this they then hoped the kingdom would fall into disarray. When Isis learned of Osiris' death, her lamentations were so terrible that one of the royal children died of fright. Later Osiris was avenged by his son Horus who fought Seth several times. Osiris, Isis, and Horus, comprise the divine Trinity of father, mother, and son. Their story is purely allegorical and symbolic. What is known of them historically amounts to very little. Osiris was the greatest god of Egypt, son of Saturn, celestial fire, reincarnation, etc. Isis is the Virgin Mother, and personified nature. She is described as the woman clothed with the Sun of the land of Khemi. Together Isis and Horus form the first and original Black Madonna. Horus was next to last in the line of divine sovereigns of Egypt. He is called the "loved of heaven" and "beloved of the Sun". He is the subjugator of the world, being born from the womb of the world. Horus is also the substance of his father, that is, being related to death and time—the material manifestations. By him the world is judged by that which it contains.

Thoth, Thot, or Hermes as he was known to the Greeks is the last divine personage of the ancient pre-dynastic Anu. Much like Osiris, historical information about his personal life is extremely scarce. But what the ancient temples of Egypt have been able to divulge about him for the most part is clear and concise. He was called Hermes Mecurius Trismegistus by the Greeks which means "the thrice great" "the great great"; "the greatest great"; and "THE MASTER of MASTERS". To Thoth we may attribute writing, medicine, chemistry, law, rhetoric, the higher aspects of mathematics, astronomy and astrology, not to mention the early Egyptian understanding of the intricate dynamics of universal order. Thoth or Thot was divine mind. He was known as the messenger of the gods, and became Mercury to the Romans who revered him through the planet Mercury because its body is nearest the Sun or light, (God). The word 'thought' is derived from this deity's name Thot. Francis Barret said of Thoth "If God ever appeared in man, he appeared in him". Legend holds that Thoth was the grand architect of the Great Pyramid aided by a high priest named Ra or Ra Ta, and Isis, as counselor and advisor. This is said to have taken place in the year 10,490 B.C. The fourth century philosopher Iamblichus (?-A.D. 330), attributes to Thoth the writing of 1,100 books and Seleucus estimates no less than 20,000 of his works were done before the period of Menes. Eusebius saw but forty-two of these books in his time (260, 360-A.D. ?). He also stated that the last six texts on medicine treated that subject with an unbelievable understanding of the body and its functions, and was practiced in the most remote periods. In 1877, the Astor Library of New York was enriched with a fascimile of an Egyptian Medical Treatise dated 1552 B.C. The original was written upon the inner bark of Cyperus Papyrus more than twenty meterslong (approximately twenty two yards) forming one roll divided into one hundred and ten pages. It was purchased in Egypt by an archaeologist named Ebers, and bore internal evidence of being one of the six Hermetic Books on Medicine named by Clement of Alexandria. The text is now known as the Ebers Papyrus, but the general consensus is that it is indisputably one of the six medical treatises written by Thoth (Hermes). Among the fragmentary writings believed to have come from the stylus of Thoth two other works are also known. the first is the Emerald Table, and the second is the Divine Pymander. Another outstanding point of Hermetic lore is that he was one of the few philosopher-priests of pagandom upon whose writings the early Christians did not vent their ignorance through the usual destructive channels. Some of these early Christians arrogantly stated that Thoth exhibited several symptoms of intelligence, and that if he had been born in a more enlightened period he might have benefited from THEIR instruction and become a REALLY great man! Tradition declares that on the dead body of Thoth, at Hebron, was found by an initiate, the tablet known as the Smaragdine (the Emerald Table). Characteristic of Thoth, the first sentence merely states that it speaks not fictitious things, but that which is true and most certain. From this tablet evolved the key to comprehending the axioms of the universe and how they affect mankind; the book came to be known as the KYBALION. It is interesting to note that the last poem of America's beloved poet, Henry Wadsworth Longfellow, was a lyric ode to Thoth-Hermes.

IV. The Dawn Dynasties and Old Kingdom of Ancient Egypt (3000-2150 B.C.)

In the words of Cyril Aldred, "There is a clear gap between the prehistoric periods in ancient Egypt and the culture of the dynastic age that succeeded them."[26] Tradition holds that there are four major periods which lead up to dynastic Egypt. These are as follows: Badarian—before c. 4000 B.C.; Naqada I (Amratian) c. 4000-3500 B.C.; Naqada II (Gerzean) c. 3500-3100 B.C.; and finally what is known as Naqada III c. 3100-3000 B.C. Where these periods fit in the predynastic chronology in all reality is very uncertain. Dates before 3000 B.C. are approximate, and the unearthing of new information threatens to push these periods back into an abyss of complete ambiguity. In fact, all we are really certain of is that somewhere in Egypt's remote antiquity a nebulous monarch appears known as Narmer-Menes, or as the Greeks called him Min, Mena, Menes. Narmer in the Egyptian language translates into "Catfish". Originally, Menes or Narmer was thought to be the first king or pharaoh of Egypt. We now know that this is not the case. Besides the dynastic discoveries in Nubia at Ta-Seti, we are aware of another king who preceded Menes known as "Scorpion".

As with much of the information obtained from the ancient world, the fact that this king was mentioned in the pharaonic lineage was not enough for early historians. Keeping in custom with the narrow-mindedness that has characterized Egyptology, most historians preferred to view Menes as mythical, purely a figment of the Egyptians' imagination. With the discovery of what has come to be known as Narmer's Tablet, this king was instantly catapulted from wonderland into official Egyptian history. Although the importance of this epoch in Egyptian history has only been revealed in fragments, it is nonetheless clear that Narmer's or Menes' achievements changed forever the face of Egypt's African culture and civilization.

Before we examine in detail the accomplishments of Narmer-Menes, let us peruse what little biographical information we have on him. Because of what Narmer-Menes has come to symbolize, like Egypt proper, many nations have tried to claim him as their own. In his rather presumptuously titled text "Egyptian Civilization—Its Sumerian Origin & Real Chronology", L.A. Waddell states emphatically that Menes was Mesopotamian, the son of Sargon the great Akkadian ruler. Waddell goes on to impress upon the reader that Narmer-Menes was of Aryan descent and explains how he annexed and civilized Crete and extended his rule westward to the pillars of Hercules and Britin.[27] Unfortunately these phantasmagoric assertions did not stop here. East Indian author and historian, Collouca Batta, also professed that Menes was of Asian descent. In his book "History of India", he states "Under the reign of Viswamitra, first king of the Dynasty of Soma Vanga, on consequence of a battle which lasted five days, Manu Vina, heir to the ancient kings, being abandoned by the Brahmans, emigrated with all his companions, passing through Arya, and the countries of Barria, till he came to the shores of Masra".[28] He goes on to say that Manu Vina

Narmer-Menes, first historic king of Egypt, creator of the dynastic system, the delta, and the city of Memphis; circa 3168 B.C. ***Courtesy of Wayne Chandler and Gaynell Catherine.***

and Menes, the first Egyptian king, are identical. Of course with the discovery of Menes's Tablet these far fetched delusions came to an abrupt halt.

In fact, Menes was born in the south of Egypt, (which later came to be known as Upper Egypt), in a small town called Tini located west of the Nile. This name would later be changed by the Greeks to This or Thinis. Tini was the ancient metropolis of the eighth district or nome, lying near to Abydos, revered city of Egypt's most celebrated. Though both cities have now vanished, their legacy will last an eternity. Tini was held in special honor by the Old Race, the Anu. The fame and glory bestowed on Tini in later years was surely by reason that it had not only been the cradle of Egypt's first historical monarch, but it became the hereditary seat of his successors for two dynasties as well. Egyptologist Heinrich Brugsch exclaims "even under the sovereigns of the Nineteenth Dynasty, the highest servants of the state, of Pharaoh's own . . . were denoted by the title of 'King's son of Tini', a distinction which elsewhere occurs only in the titles 'King's son of Cush, or of the land of the Ethiopians, . . ."[29]

There is no doubt that Narmer-Menes was a genius in many respects. We find proof that he was better acquainted with hydrostatics and hydraulic engineering than we were in the early 1900's. The herculean task of diverting the course of the Nile was done with a degree of skill and precision that still eludes us to this day. ". . . the river flowed entirely along the sandy ridge of hills which skirts Egypt on the side of Libya. Narmer-Menes, however, by banking up the river at the bend which it forms about a hundred furlongs south of Memphis, laid the ancient channel dry, while he dug a new course for the river halfway between the two lines of hills. To this day, the elbow which the Nile forms at the point where it is forced aside into the new channel is guarded with the greatest care by the Persians, and strengthened every year . . ."[30] Thus it was this feat of hydrostatic ingenuity that created the delta and allowed Menes to build a city on the land which had been drained by the diversion of the river. In time, this city stretched over twenty square miles and was known as Men-nefer, the 'good place' which the Greeks altered to Memphis. Prior to this period, this land which was later to be desginated as Lower Egypt was no more than a swamp.

Menes has been recognized as the king who first ushered in the Proto-Dynastic system which contained the First and Second Dynasties (3000-2365 B.C.). This system contained within it several rulers known as pharaohs. The term 'pharaoh' used to refer to these rulers of ancient Egypt is in fact a biblical term extracted from the Old Testament. The Egyptian word 'per-'o' originally referred not to an individual but rather to their palace (Great House). Only after circa 1400 B.C. did it begin to signify the rulers themselves as in the biblical accounts of Moses and Joseph.

Historically, Menes is credited with the unification of two kingdoms (Upper and Lower Egypt), which in effect created the first nation-state. At this junction it becomes very important for the reader to understand the powerful significance of this enactment. Many students of Egyptian history have been led to believe more or less that there were unruly Egyptians in the northern territories which Menes had to subdue. This could not be further from the truth. In actuality there was no kingdom in the north in the proper sense of the word, only pastoral bands of Euro-Asian barbarians. These tribes were a source of great agitation for the Egyptians. Attracted by the wealth of the southern inhabitants, these tribes continuously raided their settlements; consequently, travel was becoming a dire undertaking. Historically, these Tamahu, as the Egyptians called them, were described as having white skin, red to blond hair, and blue eyes.[31] In the Egyptian language "Tama" means people created and "Hu" is white, light, or ivory.[32]

Narmer-Menes Tablet, frontal view, circa 3168 B.C. ***Courtesy of Wayne Chandler and Gaynell Catherine.***

Narmer-Menes Tablet, rear view. ***Courtesy of Wayne Chandler and Gaynell Catherine.***

Much later in history the Tamahu would be known as the Libyans. Egyptologist Alexandre Moret wrote the following comments concerning the plight of the ancient Egyptians: "Against the background of the fertile loams of the valley, these Libyans and Troglodytes assume the mien of starveling pillagers, always on the lookout for a chance to raid the Egyptian fellah, peaceful and absorbed in the task of farming. They were never a source of real danger to the Egyptians, for they had as yet no swift mount . . . Egypt was ever watchful and on guard . . ."[33] How great a threat the Libyans really were is not entirely clear. Apparently, they were more formidable in some historical periods than others.[34]

The impact these Euro-Asiactic raiders had on the Old Kingdom was of minimal proportions, especially in respect to its ruling class, who remained of black African descent (as the photos will verify) throughout the Sixth Dynasty. As previously mentioned there were a few exceptions to this rule and kings of mixed parentage did sometimes ascend the throne. Regardless, Narmer-Menes' rule was one of glory and vast accomplishment. His reign was one of the longest in history, lasting sixty-two years. He died after conducting a campaign against hostile Libyan tribes in the north; while traversing a river, he was seized and devoured by a crocodile. Narmer-Menes was succeeded by his son Teta, who was brilliant physician and built the royal palace in Memphis. Little is known of these first and second dynasty kings. Although several artifacts which display their visage have been found, extensive damage has rendered their cartouches unidentifiable. One thing that can be said of these old dynasty kings is that they viewed themselves as lawgivers or enforcers, implementing a grid of protecting that they felt would last forever. Thus Narmer-Menes was the 'constant'; Teta, 'the smiter'; Ka, 'the bull of bulls'; Senta, 'the terrible'; Djet, 'the serpent'; and Hui, 'the hewer'. Through these kings the foundation of Egypt's Old Kingdom was laid.

The Egyptians of the Old Kingdom made commendable forays into the arts and sciences. The old saying that nothing is new under the sun is surely reflected in the accomplishments of the first six dynasties. A powerful cure for severe cases of leprosy was discovered in a writing case underneath the feet of the divine Anu, in the town of Sekhem. The Egyptians also had an understanding of optics, surgery, and magnification. The Ebers Papyrus states that the Egyptians used pain killers, flea powders, and hair dyes and invigorators. The son of Menes, Teta, developed a formula for making the hair grow. Their architectural feats went unsurpassed. Champollion, who passed almost his entire life in the exploration of archaeological remains, described one of the great temples of ancient Egypt as being so overwhelming that the Cathedral of Notre Dame might stand in it and not touch the ceiling, but merely be considered a small decorative ornament in the center of the hall. The proof that they were proficient in mathematical sciences lies in the fact that those ancient mathematicians we regard as the fathers of geometry went to Egypt to receive instruction; for example, Pythagorus

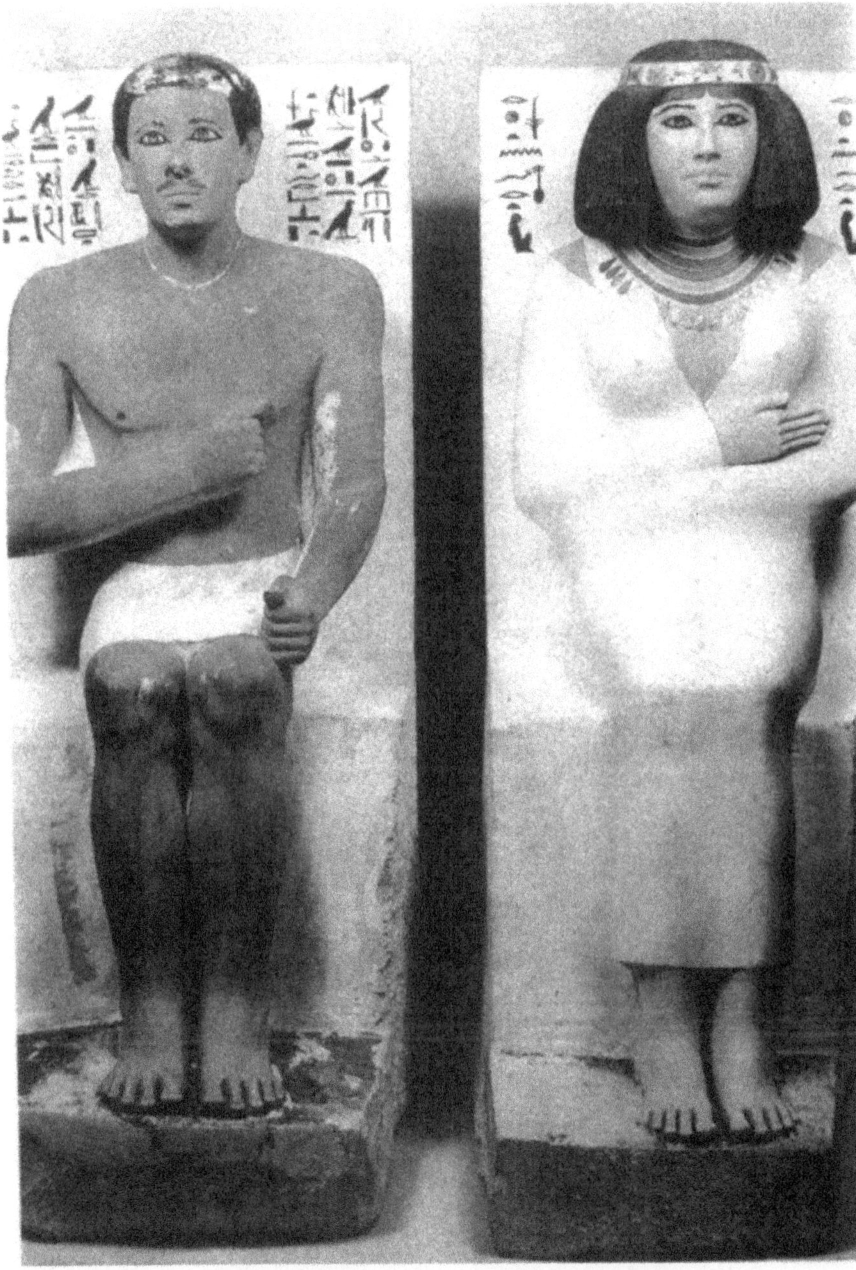

Two statues depicting mixed Libyan types, figures are Rehotep and his wife Nofret, circa 2630 B.C. ***Courtesy of Wayne Chandler and Gaynell Catherine.***

Statue of King Khasekhem from Hierkonpolis, Dynasty II, crica 2710 B.C. ***Courtesy of Wayne Chandler and Gaynell Catherine.***

studied in Egypt twenty two years. As one historian noted, the number of Greek scholars visiting Egypt gave rise to the saying that "the geometrical knowledge of the pyramid builders began where Euclid's ended." Advances were made in astronomy that truly staggered the minds of our contemporary scientists. Herodotus wrote in the fifth century B.C. ". . . the Egyptians by their study of astronomy discovered the solar year and were the first to divide it into twelve parts—and in my opinion their method of calculation is better than the Greek; for the Greeks, to make the seasons work out properly, intercalate a whole month every other year, while the Egyptians make the year consist of twelve months of thirty days each and every year intercalate five additional days, and so complete the regular cycle of the seasons".[35] The Egyptians also brewed the best beer of the ancient world. They made paper of such excellent quality that it was immune to the vestiges of time.

But what of their temperament? History tells us that the typical Egyptian of the Old Kingdom was of a relatively gentle and charitable nature. Although future events would modify these characteristics, this man seemed made for peace and not for war. In fact, men eligible for service would occasionally take refuge in the hills at the time of army recruitment. Brugsch remarks that ". . . in the schools the poor scribe's child sat on the same bench beside the offspring of the rich . . . Above all things they esteemed justice, and virtue had the highest value in their eyes. The law which ordered them to honor the dead; to give bread to the hungry, water to the thirsty, clothing to the naked'—reveals to us one of the finest qualities of old Egyptian character—pity towards the unfortunate."[36] In regards to the status of women, Egypt followed the social pattern characteristic of black culture, originating from a strong matrilineal foundation. "The queen and the other ladies of the royal family were for the most part honored with sacred dignity of 'prophetess of the goddesses Hathor and Nit;' . . . Ba-en-neter enacted as a standing rule forever, that women should inherit the throne. The working of this new custom had important consequences in the establishment of many a dynasty . . . [and] According to the ancient custom the mother's pedigree had great weight in the order of inheritance".[37] Roles in the Old Kingdom appear to have been interchangeable; men often worked at the loom and women frequently managed the business.

The design of Egyptian homes showed no small degree of skill. Constructed of sun dried bricks, they were generally square of two stories in height with an open gallery above. There were many latticed windows and the rooms were built on the periphery of an open courtyard with anywhere from three to four sides. Contained within this courtyard were trees, cisterns, and fountains.[38] All in all, the social, family, and business life of Egypt's Old Kingdom inhabitants reflected a great deal of harmony.

When examining Egyptian history as a whole, a historian will discover areas where the historical record becomes convoluted and nebulous. Religion is one

Bas-relief of daily life. *Courtesy of Wayne Chandler and Gaynell Catherine.*

such area of ambiguity. Sir Wallis Budge in his text *Osiris and the Egyptian Resurrection* tells us that "the knowledge of the Egyptian priests of the real meaning of their religion after 1200 B.C. seemed extremely vague and uncertain. The early beliefs became buried in magic spells and amulets."[39] Budge goes on to say that only a few retained the doctrine of the old faith. What was the old faith and from whence did it come? Budge continues, ". . . all characteristics indicate that the Egyptian religion was of African rather than Asiatic origin. Its true form died about 3000 years ago. The best explanation of the Egyptian religion could only be obtained from the religion of the Soudan."[40]

Most authorities on the subject would insist that the Egyptian religion was thoroughly pagan, consisting of a mixture of polytheism and magic. A notable exception is Champollion, renowned Eyptologist and historian, who has declared that the ancient Egyptians were "profoundly monotheistical." Egyptian records support the notion of Egyptian monotheism with references to one supreme god. The Ebers Papyrus contains the following: "I came from Heliopolis with the great ones from Het-aat, the Lords of protection, the masters of eternity and salvation. I came from Sais with the Mother-goddesses, who extended to me protection. THE LORD OF THE UNIVERSE told me how to free the gods [man] from all murderous diseases".[41] In addition, the following extracts from the Hermetic Philosophy, taken from the book Pymander, make several references to the one god, even referring to him as "the father"; other similarities with Christian philosophy are striking:

> "Truth alone is eternal and immutable; truth is the first of blessings; but truth is not and cannot be on earth: it is possible that God sometimes gives a few men together with the faculty of comprehending divine things with that of rightly understanding truth; but nothing is true on earth, for everything has matter on it, clothed with a corporeal form subject to change, to alteration, to corruption, and to new combinations . . . the things of earth are but appearances and imitations of truth; they are what the picture is to reality. Death, for some persons, is an evil which strikes them with profound terror. This is ignorance . . . Death is the destruction of the body; the being in it does not die . . . the spirit ascends to heaven to become a harmony. The spirit thus purified by the . . . celestial harmonies, returns once more to sing eternally the praises of the FATHER. Hitherto, he is placed among the powers, and as such has attained to the supreme blessing of knowledge. He is become a God! . . . No, the things of earth are not the truth."[42]

Such was the wisdom of the Ancients.

Herodotus, Thales, Parmenides, Empedocles, Orpheus, and Pythagoras, all made their pilgrimages into Egypt to be instructed in Natural Philosophy and Theology.[43] Even Moses, who is credited with the dissemination of monotheism in the Old World, acquired his wisdom of this concept in Egypt. In Acts chapter seven verse twenty two, "And Moses was learned in all the wisdom of the Egyptians . . ." Jesus also passed his earlier years in this land. In his book *Egypt*

Old Kingdom bas-relief of women making perfume. *Courtesy of Wayne Chandler and Gaynell Catherine.*

under the Pharaohs, Brugsch says, "The forty-two commandments of their religion, which are contained in the 'Book of the Dead', are not inferior to the precepts of Christianity; and in reading the old inscriptions concerning morality we are tempted to believe that Moses modelled his teachings on the patterns given by those old sages."[44] Thus it is no accident that Moses, in all his glory, did no more than impart to his people a long standing doctrine of Egyptian philosophy. Moses lived during the time of Tell el Amarna, circa 1400 B.C., in King Akhnaton's (Amenophis IV) City of Dreams. During this period, Akhnaton, who was known as the heretic king, was trying to resurrect the monotheism of the Old Kingdom in order to counter the corruption of Egypt's priests. Apparently, Akhnaton felt that the empire needed a centralized religion to reestablish the moral fabric of its inhabitants. Thus exposed to the idea, Moses adhered to monotheism and began to preach it to the Hebrews. Clearly, the implications are that both Judaism and Christianity have their roots in Egyptian religion.

IV. The Pyramid Age: 2635-2450 B.C.

Before delving into the dynastic succession, I would like to address two very important issues which relate to the pyramids of Egypt so please bear with me. The twin mysteries of the pyramids—who built them, and why,—have puzzled both casual visitors and serious scientists for literally thousands of years. Therefore these are questions we must examine before we proceed.

In thinking about the original purpose and construction of the pyramids, it is important to remember that the pyramids today are but shadows of their former selves. Originally, the four sides of the Gizeh pyramids were covered with huge blocks of fine white limestone. The largest of these casing blocks as they are called weighed in at sixteen tons each. These blocks were highly polished, polished to such an extent that the brilliance of their luster could literally be seen for miles. In the fourteenth century A.D., the Moslems ripped these white casing blocks from the bodies of the Gizeh pyramids and used them to build their homes and Mosques in Cairo.

Who built the pyramids? As children we have all heard the spiritual 'Let My People Go', which exhorts the hearer to "go down, Moses, way down in Egypt's land and tell ole Pharaoh to let my people go". For centuries we have been led to believe that the pyramids were built by the brawn of slave labor. This is an historical fallacy. Upon being witness to a Jewish Sater one year, I was somewhat dismayed to find that much of the ceremony was based on the premise of Jewish slaves building the pyramids! This is also historically incorrect. There is no evidence whatsoever to suggest that slavery existed in the first six dynasties of Egypt. To the contrary, what we now know from the Armana letters, and other documentation, is that not only were there no slaves but those individuals commissioned to work were PAID for their labor! Dr. H.S. Smith, Professor of

Close up of Great Pyramid showing remaining casing blocks at its base. ***Courtesy of Wayne Chandler and Gaynell Catherine.***

Egyptology in London states in his book *Ancient Centres of Egyptian Civilization*, "It is now clear that unfree labour, slaves, did not play a role in Egyptian society during the Old Kingdom . . ."[45] In fact, for the Jewish people to have played any kind of a role in the Old Kingdom is an impossibility for there is no record of their existence until after circa 1674 B.C. Josephus, (37-100 A.D.) Jewish statesman and historian commented that the Hyksos were the ancestors of the Israelites, "The Egyptians took many occasions to hate and envy us: in the first place because our ancestors, the Hyksos, or shepherds had dominion over their country . . ."[46] As modern historians will now attest this fact is undoubtedly true. The Hyksos invaded Lower Egypt following the Thirteenth Dynasty. They pillaged and destroyed thousands of the statues, maimed and killed an undisclosed number of Egypt's inhabitants and mercilessly raped the women of the kingdom. This domination of Lower Egypt persisted for two centuries! How ironic; the Jewish people identify themselves as the former slaves of Egypt, when in fact their ancestors, the Hyksos, ruled and enslaved Egyptians for 200 years (the dates of Hyksos rule have ranged from 400 to 150 years, depending on the author quoted).

Of the several pyramids that were built during the Old Kingdom, those that rose in the Fourth Dynasty on the sands of Gizeh are the most outstanding; and of those pyramids which comprise the Gizeh legacy the Great Pyramid of Khufu (Cheops), is by far the most remarkable. Therefore, we shall use the Great Pyramid as our example, although it should not be forgotten that the overall mystery which applies to one applies to all. Herodotus stated that 100,000 men constructed the Great Pyramid in a period of twenty years. Though this has been the accepted theory for several centuries in all reality it is somewhat absurd. Simple mathematics will show us why. In 20 years there are 7305 days. There are about 2,300,000 blocks of stone in the Pyramid, most averaging 2.5 tons in weight. The accepted theory requires at least 315 of these 2.5 ton blocks to be placed in the pyramid every day. Because of the pyramid's basic structure, its incline etc. the ramp that they employed would have to be lengthened and heightened every day as they completed each level worked upon! "To carry an inclined plane to the top of the pyramid at a grade of one in ten requires starting the ramp 6000 feet away in the Nile Valley. The volume of such a ramp would have been 75,000,000 cubic feet, or nearly the volume of the pyramid itself—some 88,000,000 cubic feet. Since the pyramid would have been built more carefully than the ramp, it may be supposed that only one third of the total time was used in building the ramp. If we proportionally decrease the number of working days allotted to the pyramid by one third, only 4870 days remain, and this implies that 472 blocks (averaging 2.5 tons each) were placed in the structure each day when work was not taking place on the ramp. Assuming they worked 12 hours a day, this means that between 39 and 40 blocks were positioned each hour, a rate of one block every 91.5 seconds!"[47] The incredible skill evidenced in the building of this pyramid would make such an effort an impossibility.

Also, if there were 100,000 stone haulers as Herodotus reports, then we would have to incorporate several thousand more workers because stone hauling is just one facet of the work load. Thus in proportion there would have to be 100,000 quarrymen, 100,000 men pulling the stones to the barges, 200,000 sailors rafting the full and empty barges up and down the Nile, another 200,000 loading and loading at both ends, 100,000 men building and repairing the barges, sleds, ropes, etc. etc. The list would be endless.

That this was an impossible task was demonstrated in 1978 by the Japanese. The Nippon Corporation of Japan, with permission from the Egyptian Government, embarked upon a project that would prove to be extremely humbling. Their mission (if they chose to accept it), was to build a pyramid of lesser proportions on the Gizeh desert just southeast of the third pyramid of King Menkaure. Their focus was not to build for size but to build for technique, following the method expounded upon by Herodotus. They were to quarry the stone out of the nearby hills, float it down the river, hire Arab workmen as haulers using ropes and pulleys to drag the blocks onto and up the ramps, putting them in place manually with the aid of levers.

Upon beginning construction the Japanese found that they were faced with insurmountable problems. First and foremost, the duplicated hand tools the men were provided with could not cut the stone, so the workers had to resort to the use of air jackhammers. Secondly when the boulders were placed on the rafts another problem arose. They could not prevent the barges from capsizing, since they were soon overrun with water and could not be handled properly. They became unsafe for the men, due to the instability created by the weight of the rock. Therefore the quarried boulders had to be transported across the Nile by steamboat. Upon reaching the shore they ran into a third problem: the limestone boulders began to sink into the river silt and the sand of the desert, and those that did not sink were of no consequence for the men could not budge them. Once again modern technology was called upon in the way of trucks and land rovers to move the stone to the designated site. Finally, adding insult to injury, the great numbers of men that they had amassed, could not lift the blocks by pulley, levers, nor ropes, and as a result, power cranes plus helicopters were contracted to do the job. *Even then*, employing the use of today's most powerful lifting machines, those blocks set in place were greatly out of alignment, and many (if not most) were broken, chipped, and badly scratched, due to improper handling. Finally, the Egyptian Government interceded and put an end to their agony. The unauthorized use of the heavy land equipment had torn asunder large stretches of desert land which had become quite an eye sore. The project was terminated and the pyramid, what little was intact, was dismantled. What the world learned from this endeavor were two things—one; that the simple methods conservative scholars have for so long said were utilized were totally inadequate, falling way short of the mark—and two; even with the aid of modern technology in regards to transportation, lifting, quarrying, and placing these two ton blocks the job done left much to be desired!

In comparison, the ingenious masonry work exhibited in the construction of the pyramids, especially the Great Pyramid, far surpassed the meager attempts made by the Japanese. When archaeologists removed one of the few remaining casing stones, (the stones that at one time covered the entire pyramid) on the north side of the pyramid at its base they were shocked at what they discovered. None of the underlying blocks examined had chipped edges, cracks, or even scratches: they were perfect! In reference to the casing stones, one of the world's greatest Egyptologists, Flinders Petrie, found that the faces and butting surfaces of these 16 ton blocks were cut to 1/100 of an inch of mathematical perfection. He reported, "the mean variation of the cutting of the stone from a straight line and from a true square is but .01 inch in a length of 75 inches up the face, an amount of accuracy equal to most modern opticians' straight edges of such a length. These joints, with an area of some 35 square feet each, were not only worked as finely as this, but were cemented throughout. Though the stones were brought as close as 1/500 of an inch, or, in fact, into contact, and the mean opening of the joint was 1/50 of an inch, yet the builders managed to fill the joint with cement, despite the great area of it, and the weight of the stone to be moved—some 16 tons. To merely place such stones in exact contact at the sides would be careful work, but to do so with cement in the joints seems almost impossible."[48] Thus the builders of these great monoliths quarried and cut approximately 80 acres of casing stone within 1/100 of an inch of perfection, and raised a man-made mountain as meticulously as we cut gems.

There are approximately 2,300,000 blocks of stone which comprise the Great Pyramid. These individual blocks weigh from 2.5 tons to 70 tons (as much as a railroad locomotive) and originally covered an area of 13.11 acres. The Great Pyramid contains more stone than all the churches, chapels and cathedrals built in England since the time of Christ. If all the stone in the pyramid were sawed into blocks one foot on an edge and these were laid end to end, they would stretch two thirds of the way around the globe at the equator. The Great Pyramid contains enough stone to construct thirty Empire State Buildings. When you take its perimeter (3023.13 feet) and divide it by twice its height (480.95 feet), you acquire an engineer's working approximation of the universal equation pi (3.1428). The Great Pyramid is a scale model of the hemisphere, incorporating the geographical degrees of latitude and longitude. "Gizeh is at the center of the land mass of the earth, which means that if one identifies the lines of latitude and longitude which pass over more of the earth's land surface than any other such lines, they cross near Gizeh. The Great Pyramid is built on the closest suitable site to that intersection."[49] The perimeter of the Great Pyramid equals a half minute of equatorial latitude or 3023.13 feet. The perimeter of the sockets equals a half minute of equatorial longitude, or 1/43,200 of the earth's circumference.

Photograph showing the optician's seam of two adjoining casing blocks; coin which straddles the seam is equivalent in size to a US quarter. ***Courtesy of Wayne Chandler and Gaynell Catherine.***

2nd Great Pyramid of Khafre which indicates the immense number of stone necessary in its construction. *Courtesy of Wayne Chandler and Gaynell Catherine.*

The height of the pyramid, including the platform, equals 1/43,200 of the earth's polar radius. Calculating from only these three geodetic measurements (measurements which relate to the size and shape of this planet), one can estimate the size and shape of our earth, including the equatorial bulge and the flattening at the poles.[50] Note that modern scientists did not arrive at such accurate figures until the advent of sophisticated satellite surveying in the 1970's.

For what purpose were the pyramids created? While this question is impossible at present to answer fully, we can dispel some common myths. The idea that the pyramids were tombs has been espoused by nearly every Egyptologist from Harvard to Cairo, but whatever you may have been told, or whatever you may have read, that assertion is incorrect. First of all, the pyramids were not tombs! No mummy has ever been removed from the Great Pyramid, nor from the second or third pyramids. In 1837 Colonel Howard-Vyse discovered bones, a sarcophagus, and part of a coffin lid in the third pyramid. Upon close examination, archaeologists found the lid to be a forgery and the sarcophagus a "forced" burial, meaning that whoever entered the pyramid forced their way in at a latter period. Eventually the bones were carbon dated, and the test results showed that they came from the early Christian era. There were at one time anywhere from forty-five to eighty pyramids in Egypt. Most of them are poorly constructed and are now no more than mounds of dust or rubble. But, according to contemporary Egyptologist Mark Lehner, the results at Gizeh are typical: ". . . no original burial has EVER been found in ANY pyramid in Egypt." Some have sought to attribute the dearth of evidence of mummies to the activities of grave robbers. But why would thieves seeking valuables steal corpses as well?

The tomb 'theory' stemmed from the massive burial intrusions of the Twenty-sixth, or Saite Dynasty (663-525 B.C.). During his period, interest in the pyramids were revived. Having lost their true meaning several centuries earlier, the Egyptians of the Saite Dynasty began to utilize them as tombs to bury their dead. We have several examples of this. The coffin lid fragment discovered in the third pyramid is in the style of the Saite era, although the accompanying bones appear to be more recent. Another example was unearthed in 1837, when sixty mummies were uncovered in a large burial gallery under the Stepped Pyramid of King Djoser. Carbon dating techniques identified the mummies as Saite, and the gallery itself appeared to have been dug during that same period.

The "tomb theory" suffers not only from a lack of mummies, but also of sarcophagi. For in all of Egypt, only three pyramids harbor what we have surmised as the kings' sarcophagi: the Great and second pyramids of Gizeh and the pyramid of Sekhemket at Saqqara. The sarcophagus of the Great Pyramid was built into what we call the kings' chamber and therefore could only be removed by smashing it to pieces. This in itself would have been quite an undertaking since this sarcophagus is made of solid granite; Petrie estimated that a pressure of two tons would have to be placed on modern gem-tipped drills to cut through this granite. The other two sarcophagi in the remaining pyramids could be removed but only with great difficulty.

If it is true that the pyramids were built as tombs to protect the remains of Egypt's chosen kings, then they were great failures. In 1925 a tomb was unearthed which reputedly dated from the Old Kingdom. Some have speculated that it belonged to Hetepheres, Khufu's mother. Regardless, when the site was excavated, jewelry, pottery, an alabaster box with the internal remains of the occupant in a preservation solution and other personal belongings were discovered in it. There was also a large stone box or sarcophagus with the lid perfectly sealed. When the seal was broken and the lid removed, they found to their dismay an empty box! This is not the only recorded case of this kind; there are two others on the books as well. What we may construe from this is that whatever these large stone boxes were used for, they were not used to hold corpses. You may now ask yourself, well were do the mummies discovered come from? The answer is simple, graveyards! The most important royal graveyard is in the Valley of the Kings, across the Nile from modern Luxor 450 miles south of Gizeh. The term necropolis which is often found when studying Egyptian history simply means a large burial area for the dead.

The study of pyramids is a science in itself. We can only guess at their original symbolic or practical purpose, but in doing so our perspective should be elevated and lofty, not limited by ignorance and egomania. There are myriads of fables regarding what the pyramids were or were not: huge water pumps, or Joseph's granaries, or landing sites for extraterrestrials, or tombs for the dead. The stories are endless. All of the above information on the pyramids is documented. It is the result of years of study and painstaking analysis by those in the field of Egyptology, Pyramidology, and Archaeology, and therefore is not to be taken lightly. In regards to their esoteric meaning, the pyramids appear to have symbolized the fusion of heaven and earth or, more correctly stated, spirit and matter. This is seen in the Hermetic symbol of the interlaced triangles (now erroneously called the star of David). One triangle pointing up reflecting the ascent into spirit, and one pointing down representing the descent into matter. Known by the Egyptians as the star of creation, it also embodies the axiom 'as above, so below'. That which we see in our solar or macro system with the Sun as its center and the several planets which orbit around it, we also see in the micro system or cosm in the minute atom with its nucleus, and the protons, electrons, and neutrons, which likewise orbit around it. I personally believe the pyramid holds the answer to many of earth's mysteries, but this is my conjecture. As to the question of how the pyramids were built, no one has really answered that. All possible avenues of conventional theory have been explored. We have made substantial investments with no returns. Legend is all we have at our disposal to date that might explain this vast undertaking. The tenth century Coptic historian Al Masudi retained an ancient Egyptian tradition of how these mountains of stone were raised. The legend states that after the stones were quarried they were laid on sheets of metal inscribed with symbols and floated along roads also inscribed with symbols. The high priests who alone held the key to this science, would strike each sheet of metal with a vibrating rod of specific length. This in turn would cause the sheets to vibrate and would then lift the stones into the air by their own power and transport them down the road a distance which was equivalent to one bow shot of an arrow. Of course what is being described here is the technique of levitation and of course we know this is totally absurd, or do we?

With these perplexing issues settled, let us return to the dynastic succession. The advent of the Third Dynasty brought changes to the Old Kingdom circa 2639 B.C. The capitol was shifted from Tini to Memphis concurrent with the first of the Memphite Dynasties. Monumental structures were blueprinted and made ready for construction: it was the era of the pyramid builders, it was the time of Djoser. Djoser, (pronounced Zoser) was the first great ruler of the Third Dynasty. Djoser, or Neterikhet as he was known in his lifetime, ascended the throne under the auspices of his parents Queen Nemathap and King Khasekhemui, the last rulers of the Second Dynasty. He accomplished much in his nineteen years as king. He first established a firm Memphite supremacy, then he continued the exploitation of the copper mines in the Sinai, while in the south he extended his frontier to the first cataract. Djoser's reign marked the beginning of extensive building in stone and it is here that his story really begins. It is known all too well that Djoser's success is due in part to a great wise man who became Djoser's chief advisor. His name was Imhotep, divine priest of the Third Dynasty.

A key figure in Egyptian history, Imhotep was God of medicine, prince of peace, and the first Christ-figure. Known as he REAL Father of Medicine, Imhotep is the first physician to stand out clearly in the annals of antiquity. Little is known about his personal life: his father was an architect named Kanofer; his mother was Khreduonkh; and his wife Ronfrenofert. However, his professional achievements became legendary. Imhotep is said to have treated more than 200 diseases, among them fifteen diseases of the abdomen, eleven of the bladder, ten of the rectum, twenty nine of the eyes, and eighteen of the skin. He, as well as other physicians in Egypt, were learned in the science of facial analysis, which allows a trained physician to detect a malady through shape, condition, and complexion of the patient's features. Imhotep knew of the circulation of the blood 4,000 years before it was known in Europe. He was worshipped as a god for the next 3000 years; first as a medical demi-god, from 2650 B.C. to 525 B.C., and then as a complete deity, from 525 B.C.- 550 A.D. Breasted said of Imhotep, "In priestly wisdom, in magic, in the formulation of wise proverbs; in medicine and architecture; this remarkable figure of Zoser's reign left so notable a reputation that his name was never forgotten . . . 2,500 years after his death he had become a god of medicine in whom the Greeks, who called him Imouthes,

Djoser, King of the Third Dynasty, initiator of the Step Pyramid, circa 2635 B.C.
Courtesy of Wayne Chandler and Gaynell Catherine.

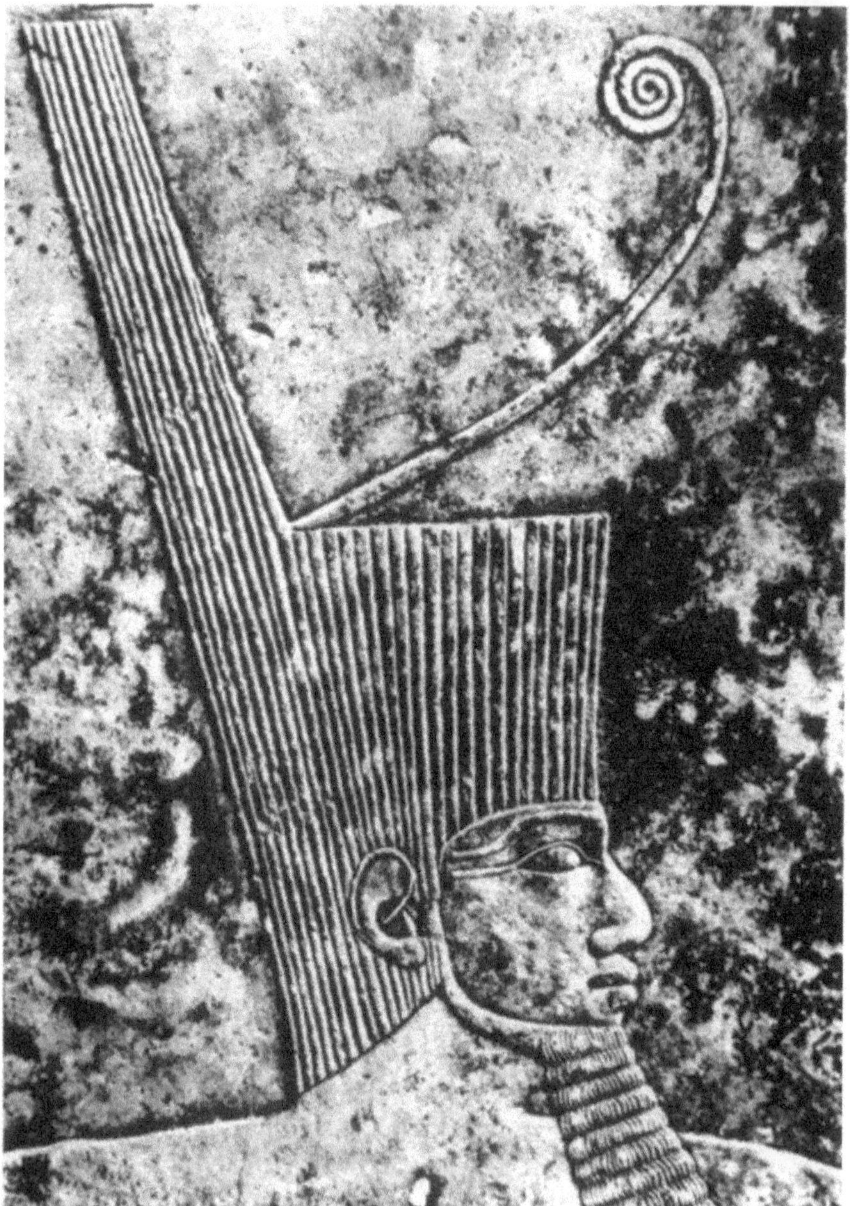

Bas relief of King Djoser, circa 2635 B.C. *Courtesy of Wayne Chandler and Gaynell Catherine.*

Close up of Old Kingdom statuette of Imhotep, showing pronounced negroid features. *Courtesy of Wayne Chandler and Gaynell Catherine.*

recognized their own Asklepios."[51] Later in history his fame spread to Rome and there too he was deified. Even early Christians worshipped him as the Prince of Peace.

In addition to his responsibilities as chief physician to Djoser, he was also sage, scribe, priest, grand architect, astronomer, and philosopher. He was also a poet, and some of his work has managed to live on in the present day; the saying "eat drink, and be merry, for tomorrow we shall die" is said to be taken from his work. In the twenty-seventh century B.C., Imhotep created for Djoser a monument that became the wonder of its age. Known as the terraced or stepped pyramid it dominated the skyline of Saqqara, the necropolis of the capitol Memphis. Done in six stages, the completed structure ascended two hundred and four feet in height. The original base was some twenty six feet high and two hundred and twenty-seven feet wide. Upon this base five rectangular additions were added, each one smaller in size than the one which preceded it. This pyramid was the first monolithic stone structure known in history.

The wealth and power which characterized the reign of Djoser continued throughout the duration of the Third Dynasty. To these great kings we may attribute other forays into pyramid construction, although most of these were never completed. The Third Dynasty came to a close with the reign of King Huni. He also built a pyramid, which is to be found at Meydum. An old papyrus states "Then died the holiness of King Huni. Then was raised up the holiness of King Sneferu as a good king over the whole country."[52] At the close of the dynasty widespread prosperity enveloped the land.

We begin the start of the Fourth Dynasty with Sneferu. He immediately began to set the standard that would epitomize the cultural and political atmosphere of the Fourth Dynasty. "He built vessels nearly one hundred and seventy feet long, for traffic administration upon the river; he continued the development of the copper mines in Sinai, . . . a thousand years later it is his achievements in this region, with which the later kings compared their own. He regulated the eastern frontier, . . . and roads and stations in the eastern delta still bore his name fifteen hundred years after his death."[53] Sneferu was responsible for the building of the bent pyramid at Dashur. This pyramid was the greatest building thus far created, and would pave the way for what would become one of the seven true wonders of the world.

After the passing of the great family of Sneferu, the king next to succeed the throne was Khufu, or Cheops of the Greeks. Khufu was born in a town close to present day Beni Hasan in Middle Egypt. Because of this fact Khufu did not consider himself a Memphite and retained a strong allegiance to the south. In terms of hardcore evidence we honestly know nothing about the times in which Khufu reigned, nor do we really know anything about the king himself! Historians are aware that the Egyptians enshrined in carved marble, granite, alabaster, and diorite the great men of their kingdom. One would think that in the case of

Step Pyramid of Djoser. ***Courtesy of Wayne Chandler and Gaynell Catherine.***

Bent Pyramid of Sneferu. ***Courtesy of Wayne Chandler and Gaynell Catherine.***

Khufu, the acclaimed builder of the Great Pyramid, that Egypt would be overrun with his image. Well this is not the case. All that we have in the way of identifying this monarch is a small four-inch ivory statuette. In contrast to the many impressive statues of Old Kingdom kings, this is both pathetic and unbelievable. The statuette of which I speak was found in Abydos, far to the south of where Gizeh lies. The name Khufu and Khnum-Khuf has been found in various locations throughout Egypt. Though they appear together it is not really known if Khnum-Khuf is another name for Khufu or if it is truly another individual. Both of these names appear in the Great Pyramid but the cartouches of Khnum-Khuf are far more numerous. As stated earlier, we know virtually nothing of this king, with the exception that he is purported to have built the greatest structure on earth.

Dedefre, or Radedef as he was also known, was the next king in line of the great Fourth Dynasty monarchs. Even less is known of this personage than Khufu. He built his pyramid north of Gizeh at Abu Roash. In the not too distant past, a team of archaeologists excavated what was called the 'boat pit' in front of the Great Pyramid. The name of this king, Dedefre, was the only royal name found which was discovered on its roofing stones. What this may imply I can only speculate. Some historians have tried to suggest a bitter feud between him and Khufu based on the premise that he did not build his pyramid at Gizeh. This of course is pure speculation, and it would seem invalid in light of the fact that he had something to do with the boat pit which was an integral part of the pyramid.

Head of unidentified king, presumed by Cyril Aldred to be the visage of Sneferu, the Fourth Dynasty king and builder of the Bent Pyramid; crica 2570 B.C. ***Courtesy of Wayne Chandler and Gaynell Catherine.***

Khufu (Cheops), King of the Fourth Dynasty, builder of the Great Pyramid. *Courtesy of Wayne Chandler and Gaynell Catherine.*

Red quartzite head of King Djedefre, circa 2575 B.C. *Courtesy of Wayne Chandler and Gaynell Catherine.*

Next to ascend the throne was Khafre, or the Chefren of the Greeks. It is possible that he was the son of Dedefre for their names translate into the same meaning, "His Shining is Ra". Also like Dedefre, there seemed to be a strong connection with the priests at Heliopolis. Khafre's wife was named Meri-s-ankh, and she appears to have been a devout patron of the Old Kingdom's religion. Khafre's pyramid stands next to that of Khufu and was designated by the ancients 'the Great'. This pyramid is smaller and not quite as well constructed as Khufu's, but it remains just as imposing. Discovered in a building of immaculate design, close to the Sphinx, were several statues of this king thrown piece-meal into one of its chambers. Most of them were destroyed by the fall but those that survived constitute some of the most beautiful of all Egyptian sculpturing. From east to west, almost in line with Khafre's pyramid, lies the Great Sphinx for which this king is given credit for building. This is due mainly to an inscription engraved between its paws during the reign of Thutmose IV in the Eighteenth Dynasty, which implies Khafre had something to do with its construction. The Sphinx supposedly protects the records of man's true genesis and the origins of the earth, which are contained in several underground chambers. Some have proposed a connection between the Sphinx and Poseidia, the last fragmented remains of Atlantis. One thing is certain: chambers do exist beneath the Sphinx. Archaeologists have been using electronic sensing devices over the last fifteen years. In 1977 the Stanford Research Institute conducted several such tests and the results were promising. Using techniques in electrical resistivity and acoustic reverberation they discovered the location of a number of such chambers. These tests suggest that there are least four shafts and tunnels around the Sphinx, one lying right beneath the right paw. There is also a room more than 60 feet under the second pyramid of Gizeh and another under the King's Chamber in the Great Pyramid. Only time will tell what we may discover in and around the Sphinx. Excavating this area will be difficult for most digging sites are consumed by water after only a few feet of earth has been removed.

The next Great Pyramid to rise on the sands of Gizeh belonged to King Menkure who was the Mycerinus of the Greeks. Though he tried to maintain the building splendor of his predecessors, Khafre and Khufu, his pyramid in comparison leaves much to be desired. Most historians feel that by the time Menkure became sovereign over Egypt the kingdom's resources had been greatly depleted by the raising of Gizeh's first two pyramids, not to mention the pyramids of Snefru and Djoser. Though his efforts may have been meager in comparison, his achievement has stood the test of time, unlike many pyramids that succeeded him. His pyramid in the Egyptian language was called Her, 'the high one'. This may have reflected the character of the man rather than the pyramid itself, for he was known to be just and forthright. He was reputed to have been of mild temperament and industriously studied the religious writings of his time. His epitaph stated that he was known as King Men-kau-Ra, the deified.

Khafre or Chephren, builder of the Second Great Pyramid of Gizeh. ***Courtesy of Wayne Chandler and Gaynell Catherine.***

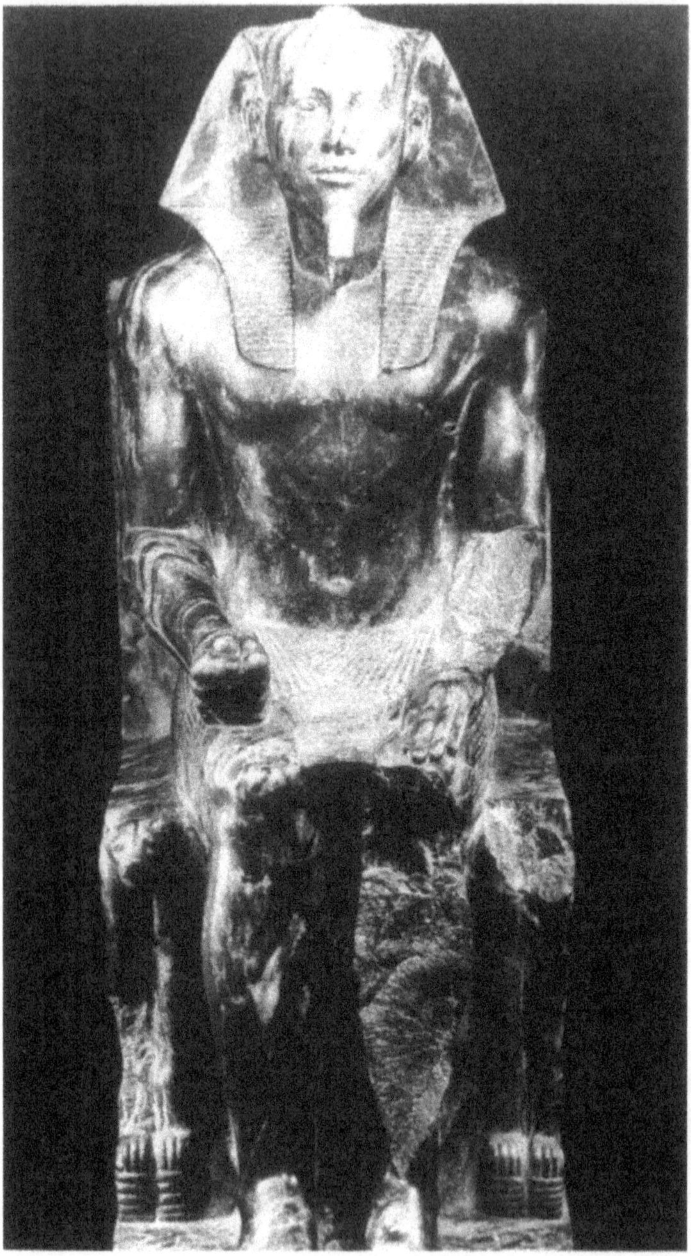

Striking life sized diorite statue of Khafre, Fourth Dynasty. ***Courtesy of Wayne Chandler and Gaynell Catherine.***

The Sphinx, built by Khafre, supposedly in his image. ***Courtesy of Wayne Chandler and Gaynell Catherine.***

Shepes-Ka-F succeeded Menkure, and by all accounts was his adopted son. Shepes-Ka-F also built a pyramid, but it has since succumbed to time and weather. We have no idea where it stood, for there is not even a mound of rubble to identify it. What we do know is the name of his pyramid which was Qebeh, 'the cool'. The close of the Fourth Dynasty marks the pinnacle of prosperity in the Old Kingdom. This period, which had lasted over one hundred and fifty years, contained unprecedented splendor and glory that would never be eclipsed.

With the commencement of the Fifth Dynasty, a new theology took hold of the kingdom. Previously, many of the kings were recognized as 'the sun god original', symbolized in the deity of Horus; sometime in the Fifth Dynasty, the priests of Heliopolis demanded that the kings become the embodiment of the son of Ra. This belief, that every king is the bodily son of Ra, the sun-god, was maintained from this point on throughout Egyptian history.

The kings of the Fifth Dynasty continued to reign in the vicinity of Memphis. Several magnificent temples were erected by these Fifth Dynasty monarchs, and most of them were dedicated to Ra. As Breasted states, "Enjoying wealth and distinction such as had been possessed by no official god of earlier times, Ra gained a position of influence which he never again lost."[54] In the myth of the sun, Ra was king of both Upper and Lower Egypt. Ironically enough he ruled with Thoth as his vizier, which of course in another tradition, the two of them collaborated to build the Great Pyramid.

Significant changes also occurred in the pattern of royal succession and governmental procedure. The king's eldest son no longer assumed the role of vizier and chief judge, which were two of the most powerful positions in the state. Instead, this role became the prerogative of another noble family, and from then on remained hereditary. This thrust the king into an awkward situation of having to negotiate with a noble family as viziers to his domain. Those governors in each individual district became independently powerful as generations passed and son succeeded father. This process of fuedalization weakened the king's authority.

Userkaf was the first king of this dynasty. Though little is known of his exploits, he seems to have properly secured the succession of his royal line. Sahure followed Userkaf, and established Egypt as the earliest known naval power in history. He dispatched a fleet of ships to the north coast to subjugate bands of Syrian Semites. This is the oldest known record of sea going-ships. Sahure also ventured by sea into Punt, which the Egyptians called Somalia. We can only surmise what transpired during the reigns of the next four kings. One thing we can discern about this period is that its prime objective was to conserve its internal wealth and draw from resources in distant regions; this mercantilist strategy made possible a cohesive, cultured, and powerful state. There is also further evidence of the waning of pharaonic influence as it applies to the official classes of the land. An example of this was seen in military campaigns. In the

Menkure or Mykerinus of the Greeks, builder of the Third Great Pyramid, Fourth Dynasty. Here he is shown standing with Hathor, center, and personified Hare-Nome left. Circa 2530 B.C. ***Courtesy of Wayne Chandler and Gaynell Catherine.***

Upper portion of colossal alabaster statue of Menkure. ***Courtesy of Wayne Chandler and Gaynell Catherine.***

Fifth Dynasty head of unknown king. Though this head has found its way through the many successive dynasties which date from the Late Period to the Middle Kingdom, Cyril Aldred states "the handling of this head seems to be in the style of a similar head in diorite which has been dated very plausibly to the Old Kingdom." ***Courtesy of Wayne Chandler and Gaynell Catherine.***

Another unidentified Fifth Dynasty king, wearing the white crown of Upper Egypt. ***Courtesy of Wayne Chandler and Gaynell Catherine.***

past, it was customary for the designated official to honor the king by proclaiming him (the king) the victor and conqueror, even though in actuality the king did not play a role in it. Now, these nobles, more assured of their power, began to take credit for carrying out these campaigns, making themselves increasingly prominent in all records of the royal achievements. Pyramid building degenerated into an inferior science, with their cores being largely composed of sand and rubble.

Unis was the last king of the Fifth Dynasty. Of his feats and accomplishments we know very little. Historians state that he was the last king in the traditional line of Narmer-Menes, exclaiming that this line went uninterrupted from the onset of the First Dynasty. What this simply implies is that all kings from Narmer-Menes to Unis were of black African descent, with strong ties to Egypt's southernmost frontiers. To quote Breasted, "Moreover the kings still feel themselves to be kings of the South governing the North."[55]

With the close of the Fifth Dynasty a dangerous political situation developed in the Egyptian territories. The local governors had finally broken the political harnesses imposed upon them by the king. Consequently, the governors, though independently in control of their own districts, moved as a unit and succeeded in overthrowing the Fifth Dynasty. The northern governors, some of whom were of Euro-Asiatic or Libyan descent, were not indoctrinated with a strong nationalistic perspective. This was the first time an entirely new lineage, in regards to racial composition, ascended the throne. "The shape of the skulls subsequent to the Sixth Dynasty are different from those that preceded it. This was a period of absolute decadence and must represent the domination of some other race."[56]

The many officials of their various districts, or nomes as they were called, renounced the term governor and replaced it with the title "great chief". They brought in emigrants to settle in those nomes or districts which needed a transfusion of social, economic, and cultural life. Teti II was the first king to usher in the Sixth Dynasty. Though his reign is obscure it is possible that he served as a puppet king to the district governors of the land. Egyptologists have indentified another king, Ati, who may have been the real founder of the Sixth Dynasty. He seems to have reigned simultaneously with Teti, though his domain was located in the South.

From out of the chaos arose Pepi I, an Egypto-Nubian with strong ties to Upper Egypt. The Wady-Magharah which contains many memorials to the ancient kings says that Pepi I was the conqueror of the foreign people (Euro-Asiatics), who in his time dwelt in the valley of caverns (cavemen). He succeeded Teti II as king of the newly formed Sixth Dynasty. Though these 'Chiefs' retained control of their various districts, the powerful Pepi I possessed the necessary force to hold them well in hand. Pepi I seeing the potential turbulence ahead, began to create an entourage of family and friends who would be unswervingly loyal. One of his first major appointments was Uni, who under Teti

Alabaster statue of King Pepi I, Sixth Dynasty. ***Courtesy of Wayne Chandler and Gaynell Catherine.***

II was a mere custodian of the royal domains. Pepi I now appointed him as judge and gave him rank at the royal court, not to mention an inflated income as a priest of the pyramid-temple. He deemed Hatnub as governor of the South, to oversee the southern districts. He then proceeded to marry two sisters from Tini or Thinis of the same name, (Enekhnes-Merire) who of course became his queens. These women became the mothers of the two kings who would eventually succeed Pepi I as king. Pepi ruled for twenty years and in that time he firmly established his family at the head of state, thus solidifying their power within the Sixth Dynasty.

Pepi I's son, Mernere, became heir to the throne and, though he was but a child, ruled Egypt. Mernere's age did not hinder his judgement, for he immediately appointed Uni, Pepi I's trusted servant of the royal house, as governor of the South. Ironic as it may seem, these powerful nobles of the South embraced the young king, showing him much respect for his courage and audacity. Uni was dispatched on several military campaigns of which all were successful. The young king later commissioned Uni to open a succession of canals, connecting the great granite barrier of the first cataract with these waterways. In Mernere's fifth year he did what no king before him had done, or even attempted to do. He appeared at the first cataract in person to receive tribute from the kingdoms of the South which included Nubia. Uni, his trusted companion, friend, and commander, being somewhat up in years, finally met his demise. His responsibilities were transferred to a lord of Elephantine by the name of Harkhuf. Harkhuf and his family of nobles were daring and adventurous, but most importantly loyal to the king. Many exceptional campaigns were implemented by Harkhuf, but his exploits were cut short by the untimely death of his king. Mernere died in his fifth year as king, still a youth.

Mernere was followed by his half brother Pepi II. He ascended the throne at six years of age, still a baby. Pepi II was the son of Enekhnes Merire, the second sister of the Tinite nomarch, whom Pepi I had taken as his queen. Pepi II appointed his uncle, Zau, as vizier, chief judge, and governor of the residence city. He therefore had command of the state while Pepi II was being nurtured and refined for his royal position as king. During this period Egypt carried on without upheaval, and Harkhuf made extensive military campaigns into the deep interior of Africa. The conquests of Pepi II became so geographically overwhelming that he had to create a new office which held the title "governor of foreign countries." The countries of Wawat, Punt, Nubia, and Irthet all succumbed to the might of this great king. Pepi II enjoyed the longest reign of any monarch in history, ruling ninety-four years. This dynasty, the Sixth, had endured for a period of over one hundred and fifty-five years. With the death of Pepi II, Egypt was again subjected to the treachery of the various district barons who were steadily regaining control of the kingdom. The last sovereign of this dynasty was Queen Nit-Aqert, the Nitocris of the Greeks. She ascended the

Statue of King Pepi I, kneeling to offer libation vessels. ***Courtesy of Wayne Chandler and Gaynell Catherine.***

throne after her brother was assassinated and ruled for twelve years. She avenged her brother's death but by then the governors had already seized control. She committed suicide as the Sixth Dynasty took its last gasp. Finally, the districts or nomes gained their independence and the Old Kingdom, like a delicate fabric, was torn asunder. Soon to follow was an era of immeasurable darkness. This was Egypt's first intermediate period (2150-2040). Thus the temples echoed this dismal epitaph:

> "Thieves become proprietors and the former rich are robbed. Those dressed in fine garments are beaten. Ladies who had never set foot outside now go out. The children of nobles are dashed against the walls. Towns are abandoned. Doors, walls, columns are set aflame. The offspring of the great are thrown into the street. Nobles are hungry and in distress. Servants are now served. Noble ladies. . . . [their children] cringe in fear of death. The country is full of malcontents. Peasants wear shields in the fields. Man slays his own brother. The roads are traps. People lie in ambush until [the farmer] returns in the evening; then they steal whatever he is carrying. Beaten with cudgels, he is shamefully killed. Cattle roam at will; no one attends them. . . . Each man leads away any animals he has branded. . . . Everywhere crops are rotting; clothing, spices, oil are lacking. Filth covers the earth. The government stores are looted and their guards struck down. People eat grass and drink water. So great is their hunger that they eat the food intended for swine. The dead are thrown into the river; the Nile is sepulcher. Public records are no longer secret."[57]

Decadence and anarchy descended upon the Old Kingdom and the flame of civilization that had burned so brightly for one thousand years was then extinguished. The incursion of the Euro- Asiatics into the Delta dealt Egypt's Old Kingdom its final blow. As one author states, "It had been a thousand years of inexhaustible fertility when the youthful strength of a people of boundless energy had for the first time found the organized form in which it could best express itself."[58]

Conclusion

"The Pharaohs, to whom the unparalleled grandeur of this age was due, not only gained a place among the gods in their own time, but two thousand years later, at the close of Egypt's history as an independent nation, in the Twenty Sixth Dynasty, we still find the priests who were appointed to maintain their worship."[59] Egyptian civilization would rise again with the birth of the Middle Kingdom. Once more blacks from the South, like the winds of March, would blow over their Egypt and resurrect her from this state of suspended animation. These powerful kings swept out of Egypt the cultural ineptitude that had desecrated her, thus making way for Egypt's first "Golden Age". The high points of Egyptian civilization, her Golden Ages, were always attained through emulation

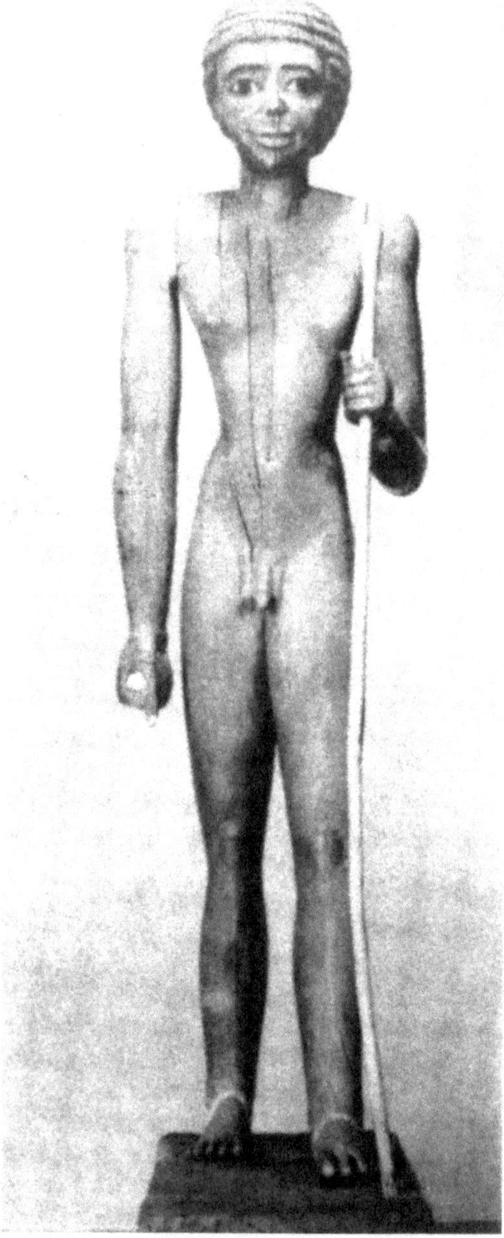

Royal statue carved in wood of King Meh-y-erah, end of Dynasty VI. ***Courtesy of Wayne Chandler and Gaynell Catherine.***

of the Old Kingdom. This is true for the Eleventh and Twelfth Dynasties, as well as the Seventeenth and Eighteenth, and the Twenty-fifth. It is also of great importance that the reader understand that all of the dynasties that constituted the three "Golden Ages" were founded by her indigenous black inhabitants to the South.

What I have tried to do in this chapter is to make evident the incredible voids which exist within Egyptian history as a whole. Chronology is a good example of this; adjustments must be made if we are to fully understand the nature of the beings who achieved things we still hold today as improbable. In the several books that I used as references, each chronological table was different, sometimes radically so! To participate in such exaggerated conjecture that is stated as fact is unbefitting to those who deem themselves scholars. It is because of this speculation, or rather to the degree that this speculation abounds, that these vast inconsistences continue to exist in this field. A barrier of several phobias, passed from one generation to the next, also stands in the way of the conventional Egyptologist. That ancient Egypt was an advanced civilization in many respects comparable to ours constitutes one of these fears; that Egypt was an advanced civilization which in some ways eclipsed ours is another; that this advanced civilization, from which we inherited the foundation of our laws, arts, and sciences, was BLACK, is yet another. Egypt to many symbolizes a door of time, a door which allows us to look backwards into a world apart from ours, but in many ways just as advanced. A world which goes far beyond the 3000 years we've so graciously allotted it. Thus it is no surprise that a 2500 year old model glider is housed in the Cairo Museum, and has been investigated by aeronautical engineers including officials from NASA. Among them are Dr. Gamal Mokhtar and Michael Frenchman, who stated that this glider "bears a close resemblance to the American Hercules transport aircraft . . . "[60] There is not one person that I know of who has looked at the pyramids and NOT thought that they looked other worldly. We know nothing of the "world" that came before us which has come to be known as the antediluvian world or world before the flood. That Egyptians extend their history into that forgotten epoch is no mystery. Why is it that contemporary historians have accepted Herodotus' version of the building of the pyramids when they don't believe anything else he said? The answer is simple: it allows them to sleep at night thinking that we have not been outdone by primitives. Of the many things Herodotus has been accused of falsifying, his account of how the pyramids were constructed should head the list! Herodotus by his own admission was inducted into the Egyptian mystery school. Therefore he was sworn to secrecy about anything that pertained to the secret, hidden, or symbolic methods that the Egyptians used in their rites of initiation. What else could he say? He knew he would be asked about the pyramids. Try to imagine Herodotus conversing with a congregation of Greek senators, statesmen, and scientists, all of whom are still somewhat underdeveloped in their knowledge of history, science, philosophy, law, mysticism, and the earth in general, and telling them that the pyramids were built by levitation. He would have been burned in the same fashion that they burned Pythagoras—as a warlock!

I do not wish to take anything away from man's more recent achievements. What we've accomplished is astounding: abundant electronic gadgetry, amphibious automobiles, laser beam surgery, communications via satellite, walks on the moon, flights faster than the speed of sound. But in all of modern man's creations, he has yet to build a single pyramid!! The truth of the matter is that we do not possess the machinery or technical skill at present to accomplish such a feat. Thus I leave you with this thought: *"the farther back you look, the further forward you'll be able to see"*.

Notes

1. Randall Stevens, *Osiris—The Book of Truth*, (London: The Camelot Press Ltd., 1976), pg. 115
2. Cheikh Anta Diop, *The African Origin of Civilization Myth or Reality*, (Westport: Lawrence Hill & Company, 1974), p. xiv
3. E.A. Budge, History of Egypt, (New York: Dover Publications, Inc. 1912) pp. 113-114.
4. P.R.S. Moorey, *Ancient Egypt*, (Oxford: Ashmolean Museum Publications, 1988), p. 7
5. Wallis Budge, *History of Egypt*, (New York: Dover Publications, Inc., 1912) pg. 125
6. Cheikh Anta Diop, *The African Origin of Civilization: Myth or Reality*, (Westport: Lawrence Hill and Company, 1955), p. 22
7. Diop, *Op Cit.*, p. 105
8. Cheikh Anta Diop, *The African Origin of Civilization Myth or Reality*, (Westport: Lawrence Hill & Company, 1974), p. 105
9. Herodotus, *The Histories*, (Harmondsworth, Middlesex, U.K. Penguin Books, 1983), pg. 131
10. Drusilla Dunjee Houston, *Wonderful Ethiopians of the Ancient Cushite Empire*, (Baltimore: Black Classic Press), 1985, pp. 70-71
11. *Ibid.*, p. 1
12. Herodotus, *The Histories*, (Harmondsworth, Middlesex, U.K. Penguin Books, 1983), pg. 131
13. Ibid., p. 133
14. John H. Everard, Translator, The Divine Pymander (Los Angeles, California: Wizard Books) 1968 p.9
15. Drusilla Dunjee Houston, *Wonderful Ethiopians of the Ancient Cushite Empire*, (Baltimore, Black Classic Press, 1985), p. 67
16. Jalandris, *The Hall of Records: The Hidden Secrets of the Pyramid and Sphinx*, (San Francisco: Holistic Life Travels, p. I980) p. 4
17. Diop, *Op Cit.*, pp. 1-2
18. Amelineau was a great Egyptologist and archaeologist. He excavated at Om El'Gaab, near Abydos, and discovered a royal necropolis where he was able to identify the names of sixteen kings more ancient than Menes. He discovered four royal tombs of the kings Ka, Den, the Serpent King Djet, and one king who remains unidentified.
19. Abbe Emile Amelineau, *Nouvells Fouilles d'Abydos*, (Paris, Paris Press, 1899), pp. 248
20. *Ibid.*, p. 247
21. Gaston Maspero, *The Dawn of Civilization*, (New York, Frederick Unger Press, 1968), p. 15
22. Diop, *Op Cit.*, p. 27
23. B.K. Chatterjee and G.D. Kumar, Comparative Study and Racial Analysis of the Human

Remains of Indus Valley Civilization. (Calcutta, Sol Distributors, W. Neuman, 1965), p. 17

24. Heinrich Brugsch, Egypt under the Pharaohs, (London: John Murray), 1891, p. 14

25. *Ibid.*, p. 158

26. Cyril Aldred, *Egyptian Art*, (New York: Oxford University Press), 1980, p. 931

27. L. A. Waddell, *Egyptian Civilization: Its Sumerian Origin and Real Chronology* (Hawthorne, California: Christian Book Club, 1926), p. ix

28. Collouca Batta, *The History of India*, (Calcutta: Calcutta Press, 1936), p. 27 An expanation of the terms used by Batta is in order. Arya, is Eran or Persia; Barria, is Arabia, and Masra, was the name of Cairo.

29. Heinrich Brugsch-Bey, *Egypt under the Pharaohs*, (London: John Murray, 1891), p. I9

30. Herodotus, *The Histories*, (Harmondsworth: Penguin Classics) p. 148

31. A. Rosalie David, *The Making of the Past: The Egyptian Kingdoms*, (Turnhout, Belgium: Eisevier-Phaidon, 1975), pp. 13-14

32. Gerald Massey, *Book of Beginnings*, (Voll University Books, 1881), p. 27

33. Alexandre Moret, *Le nil et la civilisation egyptienne*, p. 122, as quoted in Chiekh Anta Diop, *The African Origin of Civilization: Myth or Reality*, (Westport: Lawrence Hill and Company, 1974), p. 97

34. Cheikh Anta Diop, *The African Origin of Civilization Myth or Reality*, (Westport: Lawrence Hill & Company, 1974), p. 78

35. Herodotus, *The Histories*, (Harmondsworth, Middlesex, U.K. Penguin Books, 1983), pg. 130

36. Heinrich Brugsch, *Egypt under the Pharaohs*, (London: John Murray), 1891, p. 10

37. Heinrich Brugsch, *Egypt under the Pharaohs*, (London: John Murray), 1891, pp. 24-29

38. Drusilla Dunjee Houston, *Wonderful Ethiopians of the Ancient Cushite Empire*, (Baltimore: Black Classic Press), 1985, p. 85

39. Wallis Budge, *Osiris and the Egyptian Resurrection*, (New York: Dover Publications, Inc., 1968) Preface IX

40. Wallis Budge, *Osiris and the Egyptian Resurrection, (New York: Dover Publications, Inc., I968) Preface IX*

41. C.P. Bryan, *The Papyrus Eberus* (London: London Press), 1930, Plate 1

42. John H. Everard, Translator, *The Divine Pymander*, (Los Angeles, California: Wizard Books), 1968, pg. 63

43. Heinrich Brugsch, *Egypt under the Pharaohs*, (London: John Murray), 1891, pp. 10

44. Heinrich Brugsch, *Egypt under the Pharaohs*, (London: John Murray), 1891, pp. 10-11

45. Professor H.S. Smith and Miss Rosalind M. Hall, *Egyptian Centers of Civilization*, (Windsor Forest: The Kensal Press) 1983, p. 29

46. Flavius Josephus, *Against Apion* (Book One), (New York: Reinland Press), 1976, p. 25 Josephus was born in Jerusalem in 37 A.D. After studying the tenets of the sects of Judaism, the Essenes, Sadducees, and the Pharisees, he became a Pharisee. At the beginning of the war between the Romans and Jews he was appointed governor of Galilee. Though he fought with valor his battle was lost. Ironically, he won favor with the Roman general and was given the name Flavius.

47. William R. Fix, *Pyramid Odyssey*, (Urbanna, Virginia, Mercury Media), 1984, p. 42

48. Flinders Petrie as quoted by Charles Smyth, *Our Inheritance in the Great Pyramid*, (London: A. Straham and Co.), 1874, p. 20

49. William R. Fix, *Pyramid Odyssey*, (Urbanna, Virginia: Mercury Media), 1984, p. 5

50. William R. Fix, *Pyramid Odyssey*, (Urbanna, Virginia: Mercury Media), 1984, pp. 230-22

51. James Breasted, *A History of Egypt*, (New York: Charles Scribner & Sons), 1909, pp. 112-113

52. Heinrich Brugsch, *Egypt under the Pharaohs*, (London: John Murray), 1891, pp. 32

53. James Breasted, *A History of Egypt*, (New York: Charles Scribner & Sons), 1909, p. 115

54. James Breasted, *A History of Egypt*, (New York: Charles Scribner & Sons), 1909, p. 126

55. James Breasted, *A History of Egypt*, (New York: Charles Scribner & Sons), 1909, p. 132

56. A.H. Sayce, as quoted by Drusilla Dunjee Houston, *Wonderful Ethiopians of the Ancient Cushite Empire* (Baltimore: Black Classic Press), 1985, p. 76

57. Temple inscriptions as quoted by Cheikh Anta Diop, *The African Origin of Civilization Myth or Reality*, (Westport: Lawrence Hill & Company, 1974), p. 205-206

58. James Breasted, *A History of Egypt*, (New York: Charles Scribner & Sons), 1909, p. 143

59. James Breasted, *A History of Egypt*, (New York: Charles Scribner & Sons), 1909, p. 144

60. Drs. Messiha, Mokhtar, and Frenchman, African Experimental Aeronautics: A 2,000-Year Old Glider, Blacks in Science-Ancient and Modern. Edited by Ivan Van Sertima,(Transaction Books, Rutgers U.) 1984 p. 92

THE MIDDLE KINGDOM OF KEMET: A PHOTO ESSAY

Runoko Rashidi

Ancient Kmt's Middle Kingdom, the significant period in Kemetic history encompassing Dynasties XI (ca. 2130-1991 B.C.E.) and XII (1991-1786 B.C.E.) was one of the most remarkable epochs in the long history of the African people. The Middle Kingdom was founded by the Mentuhoteps and Intefs—a distinguished and aggressive family of African nobles from Waset, the then unheralded city in Kmt's Scepter Nome that the Greeks were to call Thebes. When Nebhepetre Mentuhotep II assumed the Upper Kemetic throne about 2060 B.C.E., the Thebans were only able to claim hegemony over Southern Kmt. Under his determined leadership however, this situation changed dramatically and quickly, and early in his reign the Thebans began their most sustained, and ultimately successful, drive for the reunification of all Kmt. This was accomplished in 2040 B.C.E., along with reestablishment of a strong central monarchy. Immediately, Waset (Thebes) became the Kemetic capital, and the Asiatics were driven from Kmt's Eastern Delta.

After subduing his Kemetic rivals, Nebhepetre proceeded to pacify Kmt's frontier regions. Crushed in the Northwest were the unruly Libyan tribes of the Western Desert. In the Sinai Peninsula, in order to guarantee the safety of Kmt's overland trade routes, major punitive expeditions were carried out against the Asiatics. The Blacks also had to be particularly vigilant of their own Eastern Delta. This area had been heavily settled by Asiatics during the First Intermediate Period. The foreign infiltration and settlement of the Eastern Delta, and subsequently all of Lower Kmt, was a constant problem for the Africans and eventually proved a decisive factor in Kmt's demise.

In the South, Nebhepetre struck against Nubia. The outstanding Afrocentric historian Chancellor Williams argues that this military policy was dictated by economic factors. According to Prof. Williams:

> Southern Ethiopia (Nubia or Cush and Abyssinia) had to be more firmly integrated with the North, no matter how black the pharaohs of the time

Dedicated to John Henrik Clarke and John G. Jackson

Mentuhotep II

might be—and also for economic reasons. For the South actually had all Egypt at its mercy. The South was the real source of Egypt's wealth as it had been of Egypt's civilization. The gold mines were there, and also it was where the vast stone quarrying, copper and tin mining were carried on. Here were most of the papyrus plants from which the Blacks invented paper and built the first and finest boats from the same tough leaves. Here in the South

> was all the ivory and the only source of the then prized ostrich feathers, etc. In short, Egyptian foreign trade depended almost entirely on Southern Ethiopia. Added to these economic imperatives, there was an even greater danger felt in the North. This was the control of the Nile, almost all of which—over 3,000 miles—flowed through Southern Ethiopia.[1]

Nebhepetre also became famous for his splendid and highly distinct mortuary temple at Deir el-Bahri, in the cliffs of Western Waset (Thebes). Mounted on a rectangular podium on top of the rock-cut temple was a small pyramid. There is little doubt that it was this building that served as both the guiding inspiration and rock quarry for the splendid mortuary temple of Kemetic Monarch Makare Hatshepsut. This was constructed by Senenmut in the glory days of the XVIIIth Kemetic Dynasty. The Nubian queens Ashayet and Kawit were the Great Royal Wives of Mentuhotep II.

Queen Kawit

Of Nebhepetre's successors little is currently known. Sankhkare Mentuhotep III ascended the Kemetic throne in 2009 B.C.E. He was apparently already past middle-age, and ruled for twelve years.

King Sankhare Mentuhotep III. (Limestone) Now in Brooklyn

His reign was characterized by relative peace and prosperity. Sankhkare also reinstituted Kemetic expeditions to Punt on Africa's Somali Coast—a prized, honored and fabulous region known as the "Land of the Gods."

Following Sankhkare was Nebtowyre Mentuhotep IV. Nebtowyre appears to have only ruled for about six years. Numerous scholars have suggested that he was a weak and ineffective ruler, and that during his reign reappeared the same signs of national discord and decentralization that had marked the end of the Old Kingdom. After this, however, we have only a bit of knowledge. Even the fate of Mentuhotep IV is uncertain. We do know though, that sometime during this

Relief of King Sankhare Mentuhotep III. (Limestone)

brief and troubled period, Nebtowyre's Vizier, Amenemhet, seized the throne for himself and founded the XIIth Kemetic Dynasty.

Like the powerful kings of Kemetic Dynasty XI, Sehetepibre Amenemhet I, 1991-1971 B.C.E., was of southern origins:

> (Then) it is that a king will come, belonging to the south. Ameni [Amenemhet], the triumphant, his name, He is the son of a woman of the land of Nubia. He is one born in Upper Egypt.[2]

After having gained power, Amenemhet took the necessary steps to consolidate it. Right away the capital of Kmt was transferred from Thebes northward to It-Tawy (Holder-of-the-Two Lands), in order to more effectively administer Lower Kmt. To keep the Asiatics out of the Kemetic Delta, Amenemhet constructed a fortress called "The Walls of the Prince." In the South Amenemhet annexed Ta-Seti (Lower Nubia).

Amenemhet I also curtailed the rising power of the feudal nobles, who had gradually come to regard themselves as serious entities that the King had to contend with. While recognizing certain hereditary privileges, Amenemhet managed to restore to the crown much of the divine authority and grandeur that the Old kingdom rulers had possessed. Queen Neferu was the Great Royal Wife of Amenemhet I.

Amenemhet I also initiated the custom of placing his son beside him on the throne as co-regent. Amenemhet I's successor, Kheperkare Senusret I, 1971-1926 B.C.E., was co-regent during the last ten years of Amenemhet I's reign. Senusret was just as energetic as his father had been. As a builder he was grandiose. His pyramid rose to a height of 352 feet, and was the largest such monument constructed in Kmt since the Dynasty V reign of King Neferirkare Kakai, more than 400 years earlier. It was also the largest of the pyramids of the Middle Kingdom.

Among the other major construction projects of Senusret I was the rebuilding in stone of the Temple of Amen at Ipet-sut (Karnak), and the erection of two red granite obelisks at Northern Anu (Heliopolis).

Like most of the Dynasty XII Kings, Senusret pursued an aggressive military policy. In the South, in order to guarantee the commercial exploitation of Nubia, Senusret established the fortress of Buhen, south of Abu Simbel. Senusret also commissioned a major expedition to Punt ('God's Land') on the Somali Coast. The King's activities towards the West seem to have been confined to the maintenance of communications with the oases. His policy with the regions of the Northwest was to defend Kmt's borders, and to continue trading with the countries of Western Asia. Finally, it was during the reign of Senusret I that the famous *Story of Sinuhe* was originally composed.

Nubkaure Amenemhet II, 1929-1895 B.C.E., following the Twelfth Dynasty policy established by his grandfather, acted as co-regent during the last years of Senusret.

He built a pyramid near Dahshur, and worked the turquoise and copper mines

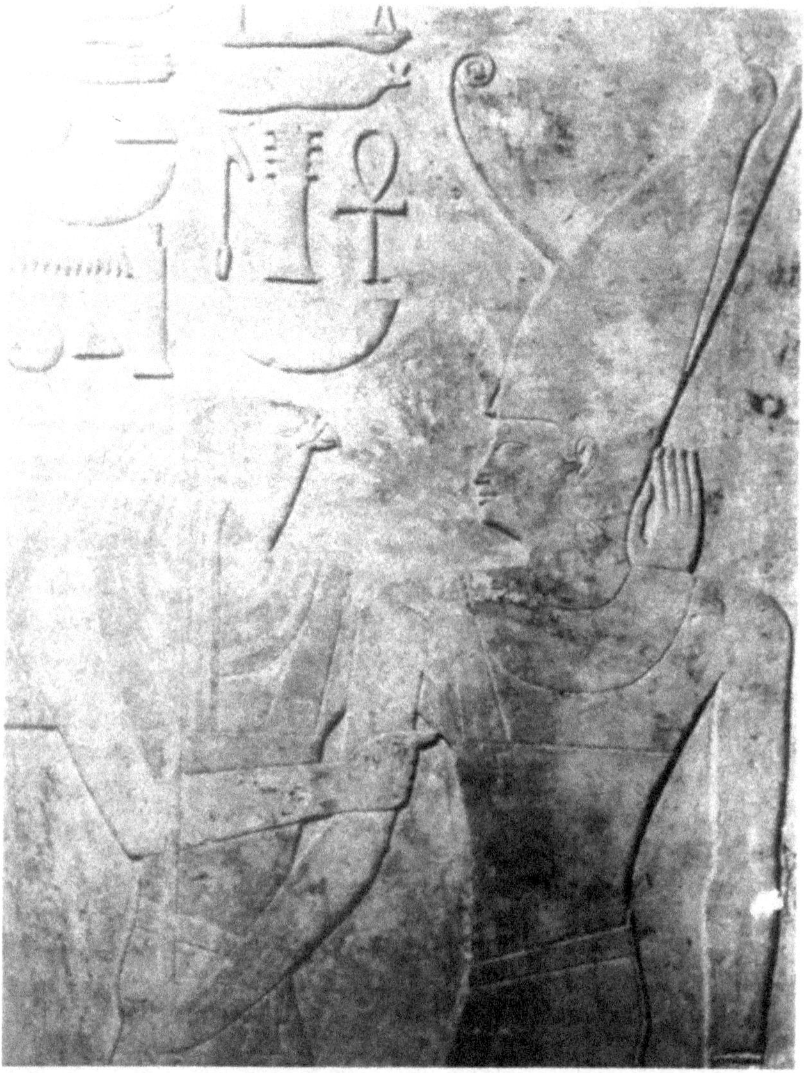

King Kheperkare Senusret 1 and the God Horus. Limestone. Width 42 inches. From a ruined temple at Ipet-Isut (Karnak) Now in Cairo.

of Sinai. Amenemhet II built a shrine to Hathor in Sinai, for Hathor was also known as the "Mistress of Mines." Sinai was generally an extension of Kmt, and the semi-precious stones excavated there figured prominently in the works of Kemetic artists and master-craftsmen. Hathor also had a shrine in the Phoenician

Red granite Sphinx of King Nubkaure Amenemhet II. 88 × 189 inches. Now in Paris.

city of Byblos. She was the major deity there, and was widely recognized as the "Lady of Byblos." Amenemhet maintained regular commercial relations with Punt, and constructed of 'The White Pyramid' at Dahshur.

Khakheperre Senusret II, 1897-1878 B.C.E., increased foreign trade. There is

Golden amulet of Hathor, African Goddess of love and fertility. Excavated in Sinai. Now in Tel Aviv.

evidence of Kemetic relations with the Minoan civilization of Crete during his reign, and the resumption of expeditions to Punt on the Somali Coast. Senusret commissioned the construction of 'The Shining Pyramid' at El Lahun. Queen Nefert was the Great Royal Wife of Senusret II.

Khakaure Senusret III, 1878-1843, B.C.E., was one of dynastic Kmt's most illustrious rulers. A mighty warrior-king, Senusret III directed vigorous military campaigns against Nubians and Asiatics, and erected strong Kemetic defensive fortifications along the Nubian frontier.

Kmt's Middle Kingdom was founded by nobles from Southern Kmt. This period is especially noteworthy, like the Old Kingdom before it, for its tremendous engineering and architectural achievements. The really remarkable phase of this construction occurred during the 47 year reign of King Nymare Amenemhet III. It is the marvelous and monumental works of Kemetic sovereigns such as

King Khakheperre Senusret 11. Gray granite. Height 12½ inches. Now in Copenhagen.

Queen Nefert

Black granite head of King Khakaure Senusret III. Height 11 inches. Cairo.

Amenemhet III, 1843-1797 B.C.E., that have caused great scholars like Champollion to remark that "the Egyptians built like men a hundred feet tall."

Amenemhet III raised two major pyramids, at Dahshur and Hawara. The greatest of these pyramids, at Hawara in the Faiyum Oasis, possessed a sepulchral chamber of yellow quartzite—22 feet long, eight feet wide and six feet high. The total weight of the chamber was 110 tons. The roof of the chamber itself was composed of three massive pieces of yellow quartzite—with a combined weight of 45 tons.

King Nymare Amenemhet III. Yellow limestone. Found near Hawara in 1895. Now in Cairo.

Around Lake Moeris, also in the Faiyum Oasis of Middle Kmt, was constructed a vast embankment which, according to Egyptologist James H. Breasted, was 27 miles long and secured over 27,000 acres of fertile land for cultivation. At the Nile's entrance to the Lake was established a great dam, which regulated the mighty river's flow, and thus minimized the risks of a poor harvest. King Amenemhet's officials at the Kemetic fortress of Semneh, located at the Second Cataract in Ta-Seti, recorded the height of the Nile-the world's mightiest river—on the rocks there.

North of Lake Moeris were placed stone platforms filled with earth. Atop these were added two huge pedestals, each of which held a colossi of the king, 39 feet high. Carved from quartzite and polished until they shone brilliantly, they glittered across Lake Moeris. Fragments of these statues can still be seen in the Ashmolean Museum at Oxford.

King Nymare Amenemhet III. Serpentine. Height 4⅞ inches now in Cambridge.

Pectoral of King Nymare Amenemhet III. Gold inlaid with colored stones. Height 3 inches. Excavated at Dahshur in 1894. Now in Cairo.

On the south side of the Lake stood the Labyrinth. The Labyrinth may have been the largest single building in world history. Herodotus said that it surpassed the pyramids. Herodotus wrote that, "It is beyond my ability to describe. It must have cost more in labor and money than all of the walls and public works of the Greeks put together."[3]

The facing of the building was composed of quartz and alabaster, giving it the appearance of white marble. This huge complex, with twelve individual courts, was dedicated to Sebek, the crocodile-headed deity sacred in the Faiyum Oasis.

The Labyrinth contained 3000 rooms, 1500 below the ground and 1500 above. The building itself was 800 by 1000 feet. The ubiquitous Flinders Petrie, who excavated the site in 1888, provided additional information on this building of buildings:

> The mere figures will not signify readily to the mind the vast extent of construction; but when we compare it with the greatest of the other Egyptian temples it could be somewhat realized. On that space could be erected the great hall of Karnak, and all the successive temples adjoining it, and the great court and pylons of it; and also the temple of Mut, and also the two

Black granite sphinx of King Nymare Amenemhet III. 25 × 49 inches. Excavated by Auguste Mariette at Tanis, 1860-61. Cairo.

> great temples of Luxor; and still there would be room for the whole of the Ramesseum. In short, all the temples of the east bank of Thebes, and one of the largest on the west bank, might be placed together in the one area. . . . Here we certainly have a site worthy of the renown which the Labyrinth acquired.[4]

With the passing of Amenemhet III came the rapid decline of the Middle Kingdom. His son and successor Makherure Amenemhet IV reigned quietly for about eight years. Queen Regent Sobkkare Sebeknefrure (Daughter of Amenemhet III) followed Amenemhet IV. Her obscure reign marks the eclipse of Dynasty XII. The glory of the Middle Kingdom, however, had been firmly implanted in the Kemetic consciousness and did not fade. Over the centuries it was regarded as Kmt's classical period.

Notes

Chancellor Williams, *The Destruction of Black Civilization: Great Issues of a Race from 4500 B.C. to 2000 A.D.* (Chicago: Third World press, 1976), p. 110.

1. James Henry Breasted, *A History of Egypt from the Earliest Times to the Persian Conquest* (New York: Scribner's, 1959), p. 177.
2. Herodotus, *The Histories*, Revised Edition, trans. Aubrey De Selincourt (Middlesex: Penguin Books, 1972), p. 188.
3. Flinders Petrie, *Hawara, Biahmu, and Arsinoe* (London: Leadenhall Press, 1889), p. 4.

A photo-gallery of more Middle Kingdom Figures follows on pages 199-210.

Amenhemet I as scribe photo Wayne Chandler

Sensusret I also known as Sesostris photo Runoko Rashidi

King Mentuhotep III photo Runuko Rashidi

Sphinx of King Amenhemet II photo Wayne Chandler

King Senusret II—also known as Sesostris II photo Wayne Chandler

King Senusret III—also known as Sesostris III photo Wayne Chandler

Sphinx of Senusret III photo Wayne Chandler

Head of king Amenhemet III
photo Wayne Chandler

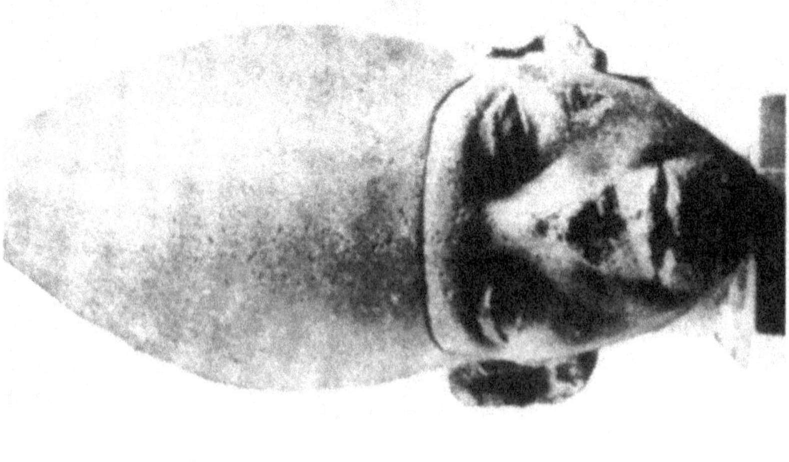

Sphinx of King Amenhemet III
photo Runoko Rashidi

Vizier of the Twelfth Dynasty photo Wayne Chandler

King Sebk-hotep IV Twelfth Dynasty photo Wayne Chandler

Twelfth Dynasty Noble photo Wayne Chandler

King Amenhemet IV photo Wayne Chandler

WASET, THE EYE OF RA AND THE ABODE OF MAAT: THE PINNACLE OF BLACK LEADERSHIP IN THE ANCIENT WORLD

Asa G. Hilliard III

"Waset is holier than any city. Water and land began to exist there . . . . (all cities) are founded after her true name; they are called "cities" after (her) name, and they are placed under the watch of Waset, the eye of Ra.
The Wicked broke loose from Waset. She is the mistress of cities, mightier than any city. She gives the country to one single Master by her victory, she who wields the bow and holds the spear. Near her there is no fighting, for her might is too great. Every city takes pride in her name; she is their mistress, being more powerful than they.
This is (the order) which issued from the mouth of Ra. The enemy of Ra is reduced to ashes, and all belongs to Waset—Upper and Lower Kemet, heaven and earth, the Lower World with its shores, its waters, and its mountains, and all that is brought by the Ocean and the Hapi. All that existed for Geb grows for her, and all belongs to her in peace, wherever the Sun goes round. Every land pays tribute to her as a vassal, for she is the Eye of Ra, *which none resists. . . . Happy is he who comes to die at Waset,* the abode of Maat, *the place of Silence. . . . Evil-doers come not here into the places of Maat. . . . Happiness to him who comes to die here! He will be a divine soul!"*

19th Dynasty Papyrus
(Moret, 1972)

The origin of Kemetic (Ancient Egyptian) civilization is lost in antiquity. Civilization appears full blown at the beginning of Kemet as a nation and before the first dynasty, circa 3,100 b.c.e. (before the common era). Writing, virtually the same calendar that we use today, sophisticated astronomy, the world's parent religion, etc. are all in place.

The developmental period for this civilization must have taken thousands of years. Mer-en-Jehuti, (Manetho) a Kemetic scholar who lived during the Greek period, said that it was over thirty thousand years old. While the nation of Kemet lasted as a political entity for nearly three thousand years, its culture was unbroken for much longer than that. Not only did this culture begin many thousands of years before the establishment of the Kemetic nation, the culture remained intact throughout the entire life of the nation and for hundreds of years after the end of its sovereignty. This record is unmatched in human history!

The center of power, leadership, and spirituality was in the deep south of the nation of Kemet during most of its existence. In the beginning, although the capital of the southern king Mena was located strategically at the apex of the delta (near present day Cairo) of the river in Menefer (Memphis), the southern Holy City of Abdu (Abydos) remained sacred all the way through the Middle and the New Kingdoms. The head or the heart of Asar (Osiris) was said to be buried there in a monumental tomb, made with gigantic limestone blocks. The ruins of this magnificent tomb are still there, and they date from the Old Kingdom. The New Kingdom temple of Seti I and Ra-mes (Rameses II) of the Middle Kingdom are adjacent to it. During the early dynasties, all kings had a tomb at Abdu, even if they had one in the north at the Sakkara cemetery.

During the Middle Kingdom, circa 2,100 b.c.e., the center of government and the center of power came to reside in what was to become the greatest city in the richest and most powerful nation of the ancient world (Cottrell, 1967). It was so great that Homer would sing its praises in *The Illiad* as the "hundred gated" city, as late as 850 b.c.e. During the time of King Amenhotep III and Queen Tiy, that city, Waset, had a population of one million out of the Nation of four million people (Newby, 1980, p.40 and p. 103). Waset (Luxor) today hosts the remains of the finest temples of the ancient world, the Southern Ipet (Luxor Temple) and Ipet Isut (Karnak Temple). Both of these magnificent temples, which served as both religious and educational institutions, were built almost entirely in the Grand Golden Age (The New Kingdom). Waset is located nearly 400 miles directly south from Cairo.

Waset was also referred to in ancient times as Niwt ("The City"). The Hebrews later called it No or No Amon. Chancellor Williams, (1974) called it Nowe or Wose. The Greeks who renamed everything in Kemet, giving them Greek names, including the kings and queens, renamed the city "Thebai," presumably after another of its Kemetic names, "Tapet." From Thebai we get the name "Thebes." (West, 1985, p.236) After the Greco-Roman period, the great Asian immigration occurred. The Arabs gave the city the name "L'Ouqsor", meaning "The Palaces," probably because they believed the temples to be palaces. This name was further Europeanized to "Luxor", the name that it has today.

No one knows how old Waset was. One 19th Dynasty poet said that it had existed since the beginning of time. (Riefstahl, 1964, p.6) However old Waset was, it did not become prominent in the written records and as the political center of Kemet until the Middle Kingdom.

In this essay, we will look more closely at the remarkable role that Waset played in the leadership of Kemet and of the known world. At the same time, we will also look more closely at selected great Kings, Queens and High Priests who ruled during the Waset years. This is important from an African perspective, since we have in the images of these royal and noble persons the best evidence to support of the argument that it was indigenous black Africans who always led their people, the people of Kemet, during Kemet's finest millennia.

On Chronology

To understand Kemetic history and the place of Waset in it, it is important to keep two things clearly in mind. First, the political control of dynastic Kemet was in the hands of Kemetic people for nearly all of Kemetic history from 3,100 b.c.e. to the Persian conquest in 525 b.c.e. During that time, Egyptologists have accepted a division that has three *kingdoms* and three *periods* (the time in between the kingdoms). Kemetic scholars (Africentric) prefer to call them Golden Ages. The First Golden Age, the *Old Kingdom* (the Pyramid age) was from the third to the sixth dynasties (2700 to 2160 b.c.e.). It was followed by a period of disorder that is called the *First Intermediate Period*. The Second Golden Age was the *Middle Kingdom*, the age of classical literature. It included the 11th and 12th dynasties. (2040 to 1784 b.c.e.) It was followed by the Second Intermediate Period, a period of disorder within which occurred a short (150 year) foreign invasion of Asian nomads. They left no significant contributions to Kemetic culture (Steindorff and Seele, 1957, p. 25).

The Third Golden Age is called the *New Kingdom* (The Grand Golden Age), including the 18th and 19th dynasties. (1554 to 1070 b.c.e.) It is followed by a Late Period of declining conditions. Traditional Egyptology has designated the 25th dynasty (760 to 657 b.c.e.) as a "period." However, it should be designated as the Last Golden Age, the *Late Kingdom*, (a Resurrection Kingdom) since that is how it saw itself. That is how it behaved, drawing its cultural inspiration from its ancestors, acting to purify the deteriorated forms of Kemetic culture. The rulers of the 25th Dynasty went back to the Middle Kingdom for its cultural models. Therefore, the last three Golden Ages, including the greatest of the Golden Ages were ruled from Waset either physically, as in the case of the Second and Third Golden Ages, or culturally, as in the case of the Fourth Golden Age.

The second thing to remember is that Kemetic culture preceded, remained intact throughout, and succeeded all the intermediate and late *periods* of dynastic political rule. In other words, even under the rule of conquerors, the Kemetic way of life, its culture, remained unbroken and profoundly influential internationally for more than three thousand years. It was not to be overcome until the massive immigration into the Hapi (Nile) Valley of an Asiatic Arabic speaking population with the new religion of Islam, circa 7th century a.c.e. (after the common era) However, Kemet's purest and loftiest indigenous cultural forms were under the Golden Ages or Kingdoms. For example, here is evidence of the Late Period decadence.

> "In the later period, after the religion had lost more and more of its inner vitality, and the people clung increasingly to outward forms, they carried the animal cults to such extremes that they came to regard each individual of the species in whose form the divinity was believed to reveal himself as sacred and divine.' (Steindorff and Seele, 1957, p.139)

It was under the Golden Ages or Kingdoms, not the periods, that the greatest growth and acceleration of cultural development happened. We may also cite the example from Cottrell (1967) who points out that there are no erotic carved texts in Ancient Kemet. Sex topics were not expressed pornographically, but were treated discretely.

The Primary Waset Kings, Queens and High Priests

Now we can see the indigenous Kemites and their role more clearly. I have chosen to write in more detail about *only the Golden Ages*. Then, within those Golden Ages, I have chosen to show photographs of *only the most significant kings, queens and high priests who ruled from Waset*. To do this is efficient in terms of space. However, this is an even more important way of emphasizing the empirical evidence for the racial make up of Kemet. For we can see clearly with our own eyes that *"racial" identity, as far as it can be determined from the art and the mummies, is least ambiguous when we come to the most important royal figures!*

While we show pictures of rulers and nobles, we must not forget that the whole population of the Hapi Valley was predominantly 'black' during the whole of the dynastic period, as attested to by eyewitnesses, by studies of skeletal remains (Diop, 1987), and by paintings and carvings.

Any visitor to Egypt today will see with their own eyes that in the bustling city of Cairo, a city of nearly 13,000,000 citizens, the population is very mixed racially. Within many families, there is that range in hue from coal black to pallid white. As one moves up the Nile, there is an unmistakable browning of the population, especially noticeable at Luxor. By the time one reaches Edfu, Kom Ombo and Aswan, 600 miles south of Cairo, the population is almost wholly "Nubian," and mainly dark skinned. And this is after nearly 1,500 years of heavy mixing!

The Middle Kingdom 2040 to 1784 b.c.e.

Each major city or nome in Kemet had its own name for The Creator. In each case, The Creator is associated with a maternal deity who is like a Virgin

Mother, who with The Creator has a Son. With the rise of Waset at the beginning of the Middle Kingdom, the whole Nation adopts the name of Waset's God "Amun", "Amon", or "Amen." Strictly speaking, it is not actually a name of The Creator but a description of The Creator's location. Amen means The Hidden Creator whose real name is unknown. Later the Greeks would identify Amen with Zeus, referring to him as Zeus-Amon, and would call the city of Waset the city of Zeus.

Amen of Waset was wed to Mut, the Holy Mother. They have a Son who is called Khonsu. This was the Waset (and the national) Holy Family or Triad. From the start of the Middle Kingdom, the Amen Priesthood centered at Waset held power, down through the Greco-Roman Period. In some cases they even held sufficient power to discipline the King. Even during periods of foreign invasions, these southern Priests kept much of their power.

Menthuhotep II (2010 to 1998 b.c.e.)

Of the 11th Dynasty kings, Menthuhotep II is regarded as the greatest and as the actual founder of the dynasty. (Kamil, 1976, p. 12)

> 'These first kings of the Eleventh Dynasty, Mentuhotep I and Intefs I, II, and III, had small claim to that grandiose title, (King of Upper and Lower Kemet) though they gradually gained control of the Nile Valley to the southern borders of Egypt and began to push the Herakleopolitan kings northward. It was not until about 2,040 B.C. that a king called Neb-hepetre Montuhotep II finally routed the Herakleopolitans and reunited the two lands." (Riefstahl, 1964, p. 16)

The mummy of Menthuhotep II is not shown here. However, his statue reveals that he was almost "coal black" in complexion.

Queen Hatshepsut's dazzling 18th Dynasty mortuary temple is a copy of a smaller temple beside it that was built for Monthuhotep II in the 11th Dynasty. (Simpkins Splendor of Egypt: The Temple of Hatshepsut, no date,) The old name for this Temple was Zosret, meaning "The Holy." Hatshepsut called it Zosret-Zosru, meaning "The Holy of Holies." The two temples together were called Zosreti, meaning simply "The Two Holies." Today the site is called Dier el-Bahari, by its Arabic name.

It must be recalled at this time that Kemet had been the real naval power of the world for at least five hundred years. For example, Seneferu, first king of the Fourth Dynasty, sent 40 large ships in a fleet to Lebanon. (Steindorff and Keith, 1957, p. 50) His son Kufu, builder of the Great Pyramid, was also a builder of *a 140 foot long ship* that is still almost completely intact. It is on display today next to the Great Pyramid! Expeditions to Punt (Somaliland) had been conducted from Kemet from at least as early as the Fifth Dynasty by King Assa Djed-

Mentuhotep II

Ka-Ra. There were many of them. (Rose, 1985) (Newby, 1980, pp. 49 and 54) We may conclude therefore that the Eleventh Dynasty influence extended far beyond the borders of Kemet during the Reign of Menthuhotep II.

Let us now move to the 12th Dynasty, still in the Middle Kingdom. King Seneferu of the Fourth Kemetic Dynasty (2592 to 2568 b.c.e.) is said to have requested of the Priest Neferti of Bastet that he prophesy concerning the future of Kemet. One can understand this great king, the builder of the first true pyramid, the founder of the Dynasty, and the father of King Kufu, as he wonders if the greatness of the kingdom will last for ages. Living in the first "Golden Age," the Pyramid Age, he was clearly the King without peer anywhere in the world.

An Eighteenth Dynasty manuscript, P. Leningrad 1116B, is the earliest surviving record of Neferti's response to Sensferu. Neferti foresaw the disintegration of the power of the central government in the *Old Kingdom*, to be followed by what came to be known as the First Intermediate Period. (Lichteim, 1975, pp. 140-144)

> . . . Rise against what is before you!
> Lo, the great no longer rule the land,
> What was made has been unmade,
> Re should begin to recreate!
> The land is quite perished, no remnant is left,
> Not the black of a nail is spared from its fate.
> (Yet) while the land suffers, none care for it,
> None speak, none shed tears: 'How fares this
> Land!"
> The sundisk, covered, shines not for people to see,
> One cannot live when clouds conceal,
> All are numb from the lack of it.

Neferti continues the gloomy prophesy with specific reference to the identity of the alien destroyers, and even the conditions which permitted the alien destroyers to enter Kemet.

> . . . *A strange bird will breed in the Delta marsh,*
> Having made its nest beside the people,
> The people having let it approach by default.
> Then perish those delightful things,
> The fish ponds full of fish-eaters,
> Teeming with fish and fowl.
> All happiness has vanished,
> The land is bowed down in distress,
> Owing to those feeders,
> Asiatics who roam the land.
> Foes have arisen in the East,
> *Asiatics have come down to Egypt* . . .

Then Neferti prophesies a dramatic turnabout. At the very moment of deepest despair a redeemer will arise. He predicts that the deliverer will be none other than Amen-em-het, a Nubian King.

> *Then a king will come from the South,*
> *Ameny*, the justified, by name,
> *Son of a woman of Ta-Seti, child of Upper Egypt*
> He will take the white crown,
> He will wear the red crown;
> He will join the Two Mighty Ones,
> . . . Rejoice, O people of his time,
> The son of man will make his name for all eternity!
> The evil-minded, the treason plotters,
> They suppress their speech in fear of him;
> *Asiatics will fall to his sword,*
> Libyans will fall to his flame,
> Rebels to his wrath, traitors to his might,
> As the serpent on his brow subdues the rebels for him.
> One will build the Walls-of-the-Ruler,
> *To bar Asiatics from entering Egypt:*
> They shall beg water as supplicants,
> So as to let their cattle drink.
> Then order will return to its seat,
> While chaos is driven away.
> Rejoice he who may behold, he who may attend the king!
> And he who is wise will libate for me,
> When he sees fulfilled what I have spoken!
>
> (Italics mine)

This prophecy was fulfilled and Amen-em-het I (1991 to 1971 b.c.e.) became the founder of the 12th Dynasty. He was followed by two great kings in this Dynasty.

Sen Wosret I (1971 to 1927 b.c.e.)

One of the greatest kings of the 12th Dynasty was Ka-Kepra-Re Sen-Wos-ret I. He is identified by Bernal (1987) as the African king who is mentioned in the ancient Greek legends, 'King Kecrops.' Kecrops is important in that he was said by the Greeks to be the founder of the Greek city-state, Athens. Sen Wosret's predecessor, Amen-em-het I, founder of the 12th Dynasty, was leader during a significant rise in Kemet's international power and influence.

This sphere of power and influence included not only the Red Sea, up to as far as Punt, it also included what today we call the Mediterranean, Libya, Palestine, Syria, Crete, the Agean Islands, and even the mainland of Greece itself! (Kamil, 1976) Sen Wosret inherited this great legacy.

A beautiful "White Chapel" was built for this king at Waset on the site of Ipet Isut Temple (Karnak). It still survives and can be seen, reconstructed from buried fragments, in a slightly new location inside the great Ipet Isut (Karnak) Temple in Waset (Luxor). This White Chapel was actually the earliest surviving building of the greatest university in the ancient world.

Amen-Em-Het III (1843 to 1797 b.c.e.)

Another of the most important kings of the 12th Dynasty was Amen-em-het III. Bernal (1987) identifies him with the legendary Memnon from the Greek Heroic Age. Greeks who came to visit Kemet apparently expected to find evidence of their "Memnon." Since no Greek is known to have learned how to read the Medu Netcher (hieroglyphics), they could not find the real Imnmht (Memnon) or Amen-em-het III. As a result, they made a mistake and identified as "Memnon" the two 18th Dynasty colossal statues of Amenhotep III on the west bank of the Hapi (Nile) opposite Waset. Amen-em-hat was also the king who built the famous Labyrinth.

It is important to recall here that Kemet was liberated or established from the south for each of its Golden Ages or Kingdoms. Mena who in the first Dynasty founded the Old Kingdom, was a Southerner. The Intef and Menthuhotep founders of the Middle Kingdom were Southerners. Sequen-en-re Ta'o (1575 to 1560 b.c.e.), the 17th Dynasty liberator who started the war of liberation and made possible the founding of the New Kingdom was a Southerner. The whole royal family of the New kingdom were Southerners. Finally, the Twenty-Fifth Dynasty, the Late Kingdom (the Restoration Kingdom) was initiated by Southerners from the deep south at Napata and was ruled from the south.

The ancient Kamites regarded themselves and their fellow Kamites as Southerners. Their legends tell of their origins in the south at the sources of the Hapi. Rose (1985) cites the Edfu text as authority for the legend of a southern origin of the pre-dynastic Kemites. The land "up south" was called Ta Ntr, or the land of God. They faced to the south to get their bearings. The word for "left hand" and the word for "east" are the same, as are the words for "right hand" and "west." (Newby, 1980, p. 15) The southern part of Kemet was the most frequent place origin for the kings. (Riefstahl, 1964, p. 13)

With this information and insight, we can move on from Amen-em-hat III and from the Middle Kingdom to the New Kingdom.

The New Kingdom 1554 to 1070 b.c.e.

The Middle Kingdom was started after the Second Intermediate Period, a period that included the first meaningful invasion of Kemet by a group of Asian "Hyksos Kings." They established their capitol in the Delta region of the river.

Senwosret I

Amenemhat III

Amenhemet III (side-view)

It is important to note that they never established effective control over the southern provinces. A subdued but unconquered Waset maintained its cultural and partial political leadership.

Seqen-En-Re Ta'O (1575 to 1560 b.c.e.)

The fight to expel the hated Hyksos invaders began with this Seqen-en—Re Ta'o. The story is told of an argument between Seqen-en-Re and the Hyksos King Apopi (Apophis), who lived several hundred miles away down north in the delta region. Apopi is said to have sent a message to Seqen-en-Re complaining about the noises being made by a hippopatamus at Waset, obviously a taunt. Seqen-en-Re's verbal reply to this thinly veiled challenge was not saved in the records.

Seqen-en Re's mummy was found with the collection of royal mummies in the royal cache at Deir-el Bahari in the Valley of the Kings, on the west bank of the Hapi (Nile) opposite Waset. His mummy, like virtually all of the old royal mummies, is black. Some say that the facial features resemble those that are quite typical of the Masai. His son Wadj Kheper Re Ka-mose by his Queen Ah-hotep, usually called Kamose, continued the liberation war to prepare for his brother, Neb-Pehti-Re Ah-mes. Ah-mes was the founder of the 18th Dynasty and initiator therefore of the New kingdom.

Ah-Mes Nefer-Ta-Re (Circa 1550-1500 b.c.e.)

The great Queen Nefertari (Nefer-ta-Re) was the sister of King Ah-mes and his Great Royal Wife. She also served as co-regent with her son Amen-hotep I, second king of the 18th Dynasty. Both she and her son were later worshipped as God and Goddess. Queen Nefertari, Queen Hat-shep-sut and Queen Tiy were the three most powerful queens of the great 18th Dynasty.

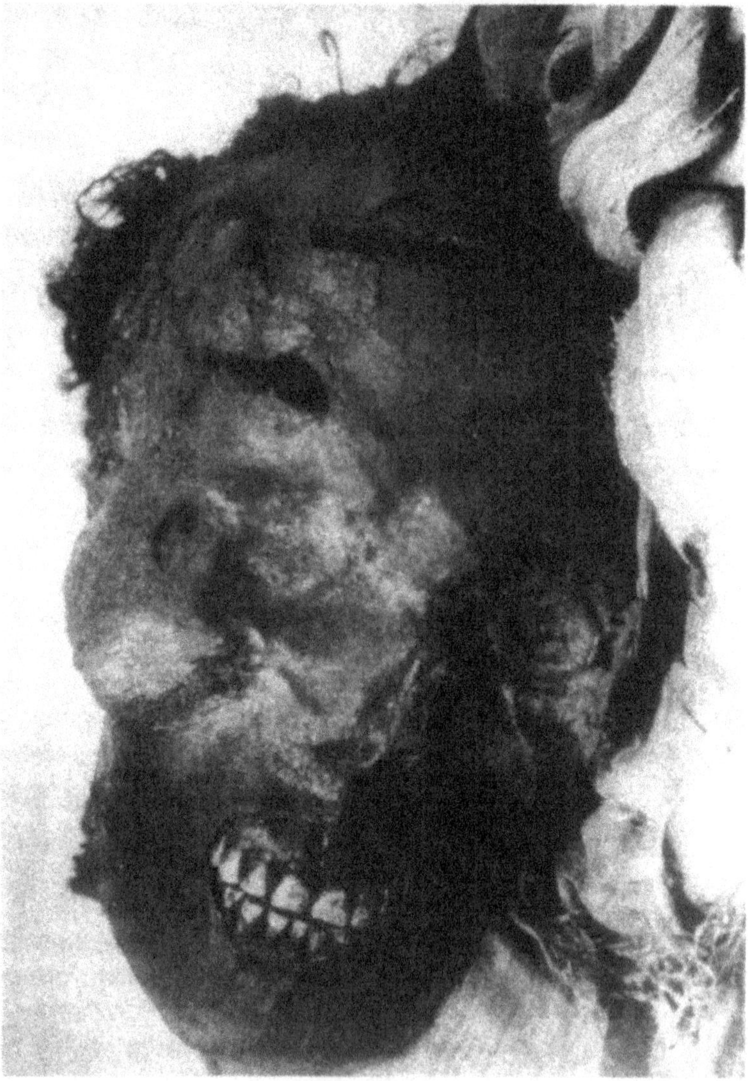

Sekenenre Tao

Queen Nefertari

Maat-Ka-Re Hat-Shep-Sut (1484-1462 b.c.e.)

Queen Hat-shep-sut is well known to students of Kemetic history as the Queen who ruled as a king, and not merely as a regent. She was the daughter of King Thut-mes I and Queen Ah-mes. Some say that she co-reigned with her father and with her half brother and husband Thut-mes II. However, she did seize the throne from her nephew Thut-mes III (Thutmosis III).

Many students of Kemetic history believe falsely that Hat-shep-sut was the first Queen to rule in her own right. She was neither the first nor the last. (Rose, 1985) (Wimby, 1984) However, she was certainly the most powerful and daring. She had the most magnificent funerary temple in the Valley of the Kings. A record of the expedition that she sent to Punt (Somaliland) is preserved in her temple. This expedition is important for what it tells us about her view of the south. To Hat-shep-sut, the south was the Holy Land, Punt in particular. She ordered many things from Punt, including the vegetation of Punt which she placed around her mortuary temple. She said that she wanted to "create a Punt in Kemet" Some of the remains of things that were planted from Punt are said to be still in their place, though long dead. Nowhere in the Kemetic literature do we find such references to any places in the East.

Her mummy has not been found and many of the images of her were destroyed by her nephew Thut-mes III. She described herself as follows.

> "Her fragrance was like a divine breath, *her skin made of gold, it shines like the stars*. She is a great marvel . . . She was selected for the protection of Egypt . . . for arousing bravery among men. She lives, she is stable, she is in good health. She is . . . forever and ever." (Simpkins, no date, p. 4) (Italics nime) Her name is omitted from the kings list at Abdu (Abydos). Yet, she was indeed a superior "King."

Men-Keper-Re Thut-Mes III (1483 to 1429 b.c.e.)

Thut-mes III is said to have been the greatest, the most powerful king of all. It was during his reign that Kemet reached the peak of its imperial power. At one time Thut-mes III's army numbered nearly 700,000 men (Steindorff and Seele, 1957, p.66) Kemet embarked upon a phase of imperialism because of the invasion of the Hyksos. It sought to establish a buffer to thwart further attempts at invasion.

At the height of its power, under the leadership of Thut-mes III, Kemet controlled the known world, at a time when Asia had yet to develop its great civilizations. The rule of Thut-mes III reached all the way to the Agean, to mainland Greece, and to the Euphrates River. He like all the other Thut-mes kings followed the diplomatic practice of marrying Asian wives, the daughters of foreign kings, as extra wives. Thut-mes III had three asian wives. Neither be-

Hatshepsut

Thutmosis III

came his Great Royal Wife (Steindorff and Seele, 1957). With the exception of Akh-en-aten and Thut-mes IV, who married the daughter of the King of Mitanni, no Kemetic king took foreign wives as their Great Royal Wife. Perhaps this was because the African custom was that the royal bloodline ran through the female or the Queen, the Great Royal Wife.

Thut-mes III is remembered among other things by certain monuments. It is ironic that two of the principal ones, his giant tenkenu (obelisks) today are called by names that ignore him.

> "One of the Theban obelisks was taken by order of the emperor Constantine the Great to Byzantium, the eastern capital of the Roman Empire, which had been renamed Constantinople in his honor: it was not, however, until the year 390 that the emperor Theodosius caused it to be erected in the Hippodrome, where it stands to this date. The mate to this obelisk- a shaft a hundred and five feet in height- . . . was removed to Rome and set up in the Circus Maximus about 363. It was overturned in some manner, however,and lay buried in rubbish for centuries, until Pope Paul V excavated it in 1588 and had it erected on a new foundation before the palace of St John Lateran. Still more remarkable were the wanderings of the two Heliopolitan obelisks. By order of the prefect Barbarus they were brought in the eight year of Augustus (23 B.C.) to the Egyptian capital Alexandria in order that they might be erected before the Caesareum in the new surburb of Nikopolis. These shafts are the famous *"Cleopatra's Needles,"* as they were named for the great queen by the Arabs. But they were were destined for still further travels. After one of them, a shaft of about sixty-eight feet in length, had lain on the ground for over a thousand years, it was presented by Muhammed Ali to the British government and removed at the expense of a private citizen to London in 1877, to be erected on the Thames Embankment, where, nearly ruined by smoke and soot, it stands today. Its mate was brought in 1880 to New York as a gift of the Egyptians to the United States government, and has now become one of the most famous landmarks of Central Park. (Steindorff and Seele, 1957, pp. 63-63)

And so in death and across the ages, King Thut-mes III, The Great, rules in spirit in four major cities of the world, Constantinople, Rome, London and New York.

TIY (Circa 1390S to 1340S b.c.e.)

Queen Tiy, Great Royal Wife and virtual co regent with Amen-hotep III, mother of King Ankh-ewn-aten, *was perhaps the greatest Queen of the entire Kemetic historical period. She reigned at the peak of Kemetic imperial power and during the cultural flowering of its greatest golden age. Both during the time of her husband's reign and her son's reign, it was she to whom the kings of foreign lands wrote when they were desperate.* She is shown with her husband in a colossal statue in the Cairo museum. They are seated side by side and are the same size, indicating equal status according to the Kemetic canon.

Her likeness is not familiar to most persons who are interested in Kemet. It is not shown frequently in books about Kemet. This likeness and other pictures of primary source material that are presented here, destroy convincingly the myth of Kemet as a nation of "white" people, establishing it as clearly "black", and that during the periods of its greatest achievements.

Queen Tiye

Amen-Hotep Son of Hapu

Amen-hotep son of Hapu lived during the time of Amen-hotep III. He was a man of lowly birth who had risen to great heights and the High Priest at Waset. He is said to have been the architect who established the canon for the building of the great University of Ipet Isut. (Karnak Temple)

> "In the early years of his reign the king's attention had been directed to this man because of his exceptional knowledge of the "divine words" (the hieroglyphics), and he had appointed him to an undersuperintendency of royal scribes. After a period of loyal service, as we learn from his autobiography, Amenhotep was promoted by the king to the position of "Chief Royal Scribe of Recruits.". . . But all of Amenhotep's achievements as an administrative official and military leader were greatly surpassed by his accomplishments in his third sphere of activity as chief architect. "My lord honored me a third time . . . He appointed me overseer of all works, and I perpetuated the name of the king forever. I did not imitate what had been done before.' (Steindorf and Seele, 1957, pp.76-77)

In later years Amen-hotep Son of Hapu would be revered as a wise man and would be worshipped as a God.

Amenhotep—son of Hapu

Anut Tawi

Sometimes during the 18th Dynasty, Anut Tawi functioned as a priestess of Amun. (Identification of the mummy in this photograph from the archives of the Cairo Museum in Egypt was made by the Director of the Museum to me in the Summer of 1986.) No other details of her life were made available to me. Additional research is being done to get more information.

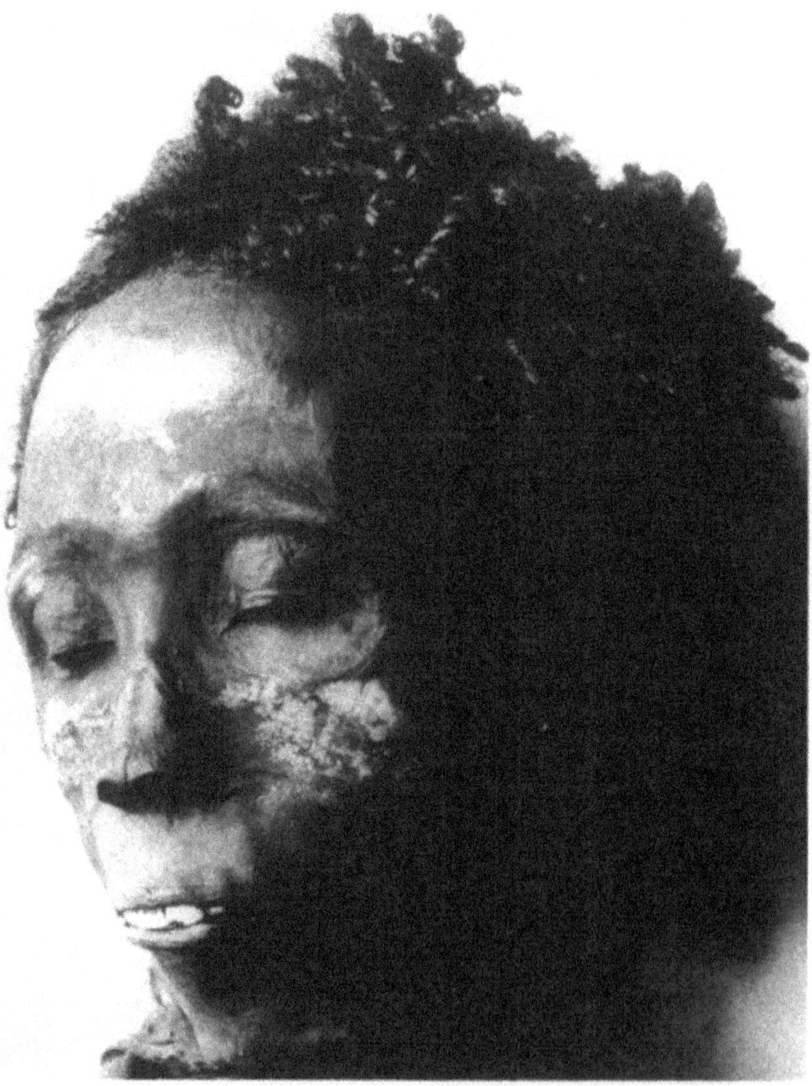

High Priestess Anut Tawi

Nefer-Kheperu-Re-Wah-In-Re Akh-En-Aten (1358 to 1340 b.c.e.)

Born Amen-hotep IV, Ank-en-Aten is best remembered for changing both his name and, more important, for changing the national religion of Kemet.

It is wrong to say that he changed it from polytheism to monotheism, since at no time in Kemetic history was the Nation anything other than monotheistic.

'Both the Aten heresy and its great rival the Amun orthodoxy believed in a Supreme creator, a Sole One, who was hidden or far off. Both were solar cults, but the new religion placed rather more emphasis upon the visible image of godhead in the light that radiated from the sun disk, the Aten." (Aldred, 1973, p. 12) The ancient roots of monotheism is best shown by reference to a summary of the citations from the Per-em-hru, (Egyptian "Book of the Dead," really the Book of Coming Forth from Darkness into The Light).

> 'God is one and alone, and none other existeth with him-God is the One, the One who hath made all things—God is a spirit, a hidden spirit, the spirit of spirits, the great spirit of the Egyptians, the divine spirit-God is from the beginning, and He hath been from the beginning, He hath existed from old and was when nothing else had being. He existed when nothing else existed, and what existed He created after He had come into being, He is the Father of beginnings—God is the eternal One, He is eternal and infinite and endureth for ever and aye—God is hidden and no man knoweth His form. No man hath been able to seek out his likeness; He is hidden to gods and men, and He is a mystery unto His creatures. No man knows how to know Him-His name remaineth hidden; His name is a mystery unto his children. His names are innumerable, they are manifold and none knoweth their number—God is truth and He liveth by truth and He feedeth thereon. He is the king of truth, and He hath stablished the earth thereupon—God is life and through Him only man liveth. He giveth life to man, He breatheth the breath of life into his nostrils—God is father and mother, the father of fathers, and the mother of mothers. He begetteth, but was never begotten; He produceth, but was never produced; He begat himself and produced himself. He createth, but was never created; He is maker of his own form, and the fashioner of His own body—God Himself is existence, He endureth without increase or dimunution, . . . God is merciful to those who reverence Him, and He hearteth him that calleth upon Him. God knoweth him that acknowledgeth Him, He rewardeth him that serveth Him, and He protecteth him that followeth him." (Budge, 1967, pp. xcii-xciii)

And so we have in the words of the Kamites themselves unmistakable proof that monotheism predates Ankh-en Aten by at least 1500 years.

Ankh-en-Aten is well known as the husband of Nefertiti. He is described as a visionary. He was the son of Queen Tiy and Amen-hotep the III. He was the brother of King Tut-Ankh-Amun.

Ankh-en-Aten did lead a religious revolution toward a new form of monotheism. This religion of Aten, using the sun as the symbol of the one God, did not

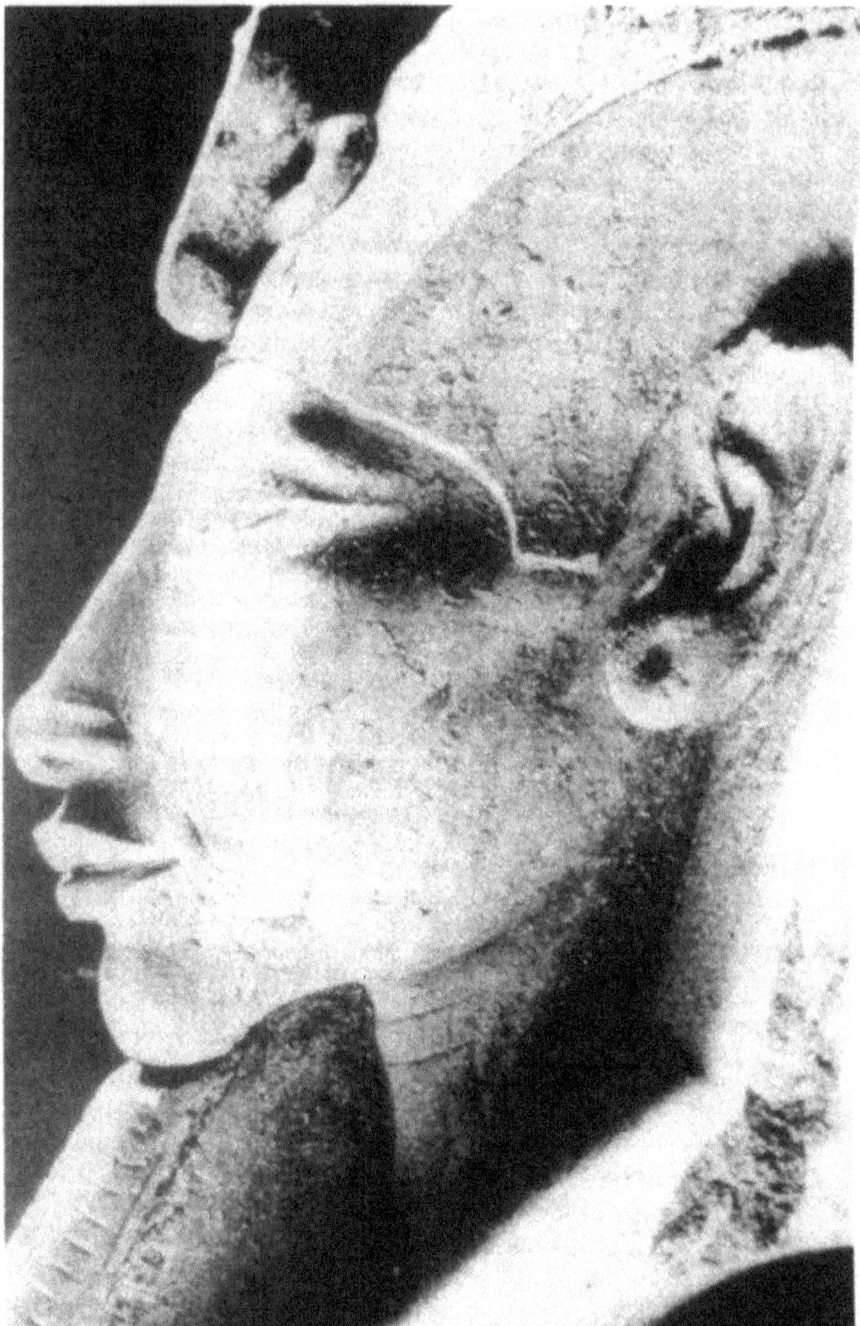

Ankhenaten

survive him as the national religion. Some believe that the Prophet Moses was a student of this religion, if not a student of Ankh-en-Aten. In the New Testament Book of Acts, the Seventh Chapter and the 22nd Verse, we are told that Moses was "learned in all of the wisdom of Egypt." Sigmund Freud has done a detailed study of the relationship of Moses to the Kemetic religion. (Freud, 1967)

Ankh-en-Aten did not rule from Waset, having changed the Capital to a city named for himself, further north. Yet he never really preempted the power of the Waset priesthood. Nevertheless, we include him in the Waset gallery.

Nefer-Titi (Circa 1350S to 1340S b.c.e.)

All the world recognizes the face, the Berlin Bust, a small statuette that is reported to be the image of Queen Nefertiti. She was the wife of King Ankh-en-Aten. Both of them were key players in an attempted religious revolution, changing from the religion of the Amen priesthood to the newly created religion of Aten, the solar disk.

But just who was Nefertiti? What did she really look like? Why is the Berlin Bust accepted as authentic and projected worldwide as "the most beautiful" queen ever, and more as the single image that calls Kemet to mind? Why does she eclipse all of the images like those others presented here?

Ankh-en-aten and Nefertiti changed the royal residence from Waset to the city of Ankhenaten to the north. Ankh-en-aten took, as we shall see, a foreign woman as his Great Wife. He and Tuth-mes IV were the only kings in the 18th Dynasty to do so. These moves by Ankh-en-aten weakened the power of the Waset Priesthood temporarily. So the new religion that this royal pair, Ankh-en-aten and Nefertiti, initiated was alien and foreign to Kemet. Was Nefertiti herself also alien and foreign?

Alexandre Moret said that Nefertiti was a daughter of a foreign king.

> "The breach with tradition was already marked by a first innovation-the Mitannian marriages. Scruples regarding purity of Solar blood, complicated calculations of dynastic rights, according to the decree of heirship on the mother's side, all the centuries old jurisprudence of the royal family, yielded to political necessities when the Pharaohs decided to take Mitannian princesses as their Great Royal Wives.Thothmes IV married the daughter of Artama, King of Mitanni, and she was treated as the true Queen of Egypt, where she bore the name Mutemuia. Amenhotep III, at the height of the glory of the Egyptian Empire, took into his harem first the sister and then the daughter of Dushratta, King of Mitanni, but his Great Royal Wife was Tii, who was not "born" at the court, a foreign lady, whose father, Iuya, was probably Syrian. *Their son, Amenhotep IV, took as his Great Wife Nefertiti, as the Egyptians called Tadukhipa, Dushratta's daughter; she having been sent to Egypt to marry Amenhotep IIi a few days before his death, married his son instead.*" (Moret, 1972, p. 316, italics mine)

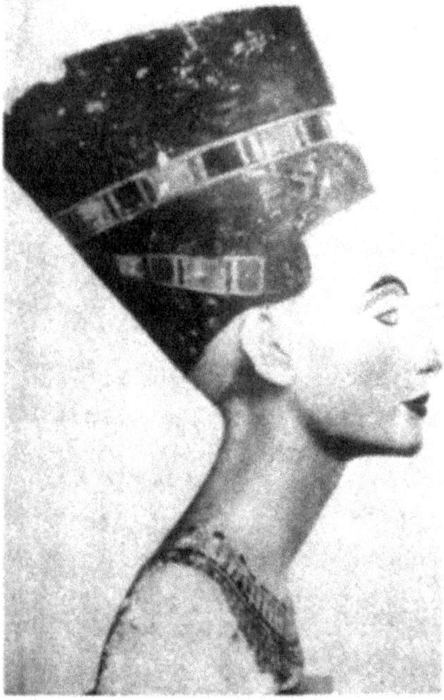

Nefertiti

Nefertiti (from her temple)

The bust that we recognize today as that of Nefertiti was found 1912 to 1913 in grid 47 at Armana by professors Hermann Ranke and Ludwig Borchardt (Vandenberg, 1978). It was out of circulation from that time until 1920, when it was found in Berlin. It has no inscriptions. Identification of this as a bust of Nefertiti is done mainly by reference to the royal headdress and by its proximity to a destroyed bust of Ankh-en-aten in an artist's workshop. Also, it is inlaid with lapis lazuli, an expensive precious stone that was reserved for royalty. What is important is that there are numerous wall reliefs that depict Nefertiti with certainty, yet they are very different from the Berlin Bust. One of them is shown above.

Several Egyptologists claim that Nefertiti was Kemetic. Cotrell (1967) says that Queen Tiy's brother was Ay, later to become the King, and that Ay was the father of Nefertiti. Alfred (1973) also says that Nefertiti was Ay's daughter, since he is referred to in some inscriptions as the "Father-in-law of the King." However, since most 18th Dynasty kings had many wives, the reference to a single father-in-law as certainly the father of the one queen Nefertiti cannot be a confident one. John Anthony West (1985) had this to say.

> "The famous bust of Nefertiti, Akhenaten's wife, and one of the most beautiful women ever depicted, is in all likelihood not Nefertiti. This bust

> was found with other treasures, in the abandoned sculpture studio at Akhenaten. Since Nefertiti disappeared from the inscriptions some seven years prior to the disbanding of Akhenaten's city, the bust, unfinished at the time and still being worked on, is almost certainly not Nefertiti, but perhaps one of her daughters." (p.217)

Given the history of attempts in Germany, beginning in the mid 1700s to degrade and to distort Kemetic history (Bernal, 1987), and given the racism permeating German culture at the time of the find of the bust, one must be very cautious with speculations by professors Ranke and Borchardt, and indeed the entire community of Egyptologists.

To say that Nefertiti was a beautiful woman is one thing. To say that the "Berlin Bust of Nefertiti" was the most beautiful image of a woman in Kemet, and perhaps the most beautiful image of a woman ever is a bit much. Beauty is in the eye of the beholder. Was Queen Tiy not beautiful? Is this European image found in the midst of Africa felt to be beautiful mainly by comparison to African women?

It is an irony of ironies that the world "knows" an alien woman and an alien image as the most famous symbol of Africa's Grand Golden Age!

Neb-Kheperu-Re Tut-Ankh-Amen (1338 to 1328 b.c.e.)

One of the best known kings of Kemet is the boy king Tut-ankh-Amen, known to the world by a nickname, "King Tut." He was approximately nine years old when he became king. He died as a teenager. However, since his tomb with all its incredible riches was discovered intact, it attracted the attention of the world. King Tut-ankh-Amen's mummy was found. However, the image that the world knows is that of the Golden Mask that was on the mummy.

With the rise of King Tut-ankh-Amen, whose original name was Tut-ankh-Aten, signifying his identification with Ankh-en-Aten's God Aten, the old time religion of Amen returned to power. It is hard to believe that the boy King was exercising real leadership. His significance as a King, therefore, does not go beyond the fact that so much information about his times came from the analysis of the materials in his tomb.

User-Maat-Re-Setep-En-Re Ra-Mes-Es (1279 to 1213 b.c.e.)

Ra-Mes-es II is well known, mainly for his military exploits and for an extensive building program, as well as for claiming to have built things that he did not build. He was important as a 19th Dynasty King. His mummy was found.

Ra-mes-es II and the people of his times were not so much cultural innovators as producers of things in quantity. In fact, the quality of things seemed to suffer during this time. A clear example of this deterioration in quality can be seen in

Tutankhamun

the Temple of Seti I, the father of Ra-mes-es II. The temple is in two major parts, the first part having been built by Seti I. It is the part that has the most perfectly executed bas reliefs. As Ra-mes-es II added to his father's temple, the workmanship was clearly inferior to the old part of the temple. However, Ra-mes-es II deserves to be cited as a great Waset King because of his Power and vast building schemes.

Conclusion

Waset was called the *Eye of Ra* and the *Abode of Maat*. It was a special place. It was the home of the most powerful rulers during two Golden Ages. When we view these rulers, their mummies or their images, we see that they were indigenous African people. Moreover, we see that they were world leaders. Most important of all, they were world leaders at a time when the head of state truly was regarded as the representative of the One God on earth at the city that was the very Eye of Ra. For the Ancient Kemite, this meant that God's law, Maat (Meaning truth, justice, balance, order, reciprocity, and righteousness) ought to be manifest in the lives of the people, and especially so in the life of the Son of Ra, the King.

Africans ruled from Waset. The monuments, tombs, temples, papyri, paintings, carvings and remains in general speak eloquently to the fact that, as much as anywhere in the ancient world, Maat prevailed.

References

Aldred, Cyril (1973) *Akhenaten and Nefertiti*. New York: The Viking Press

Bernal, Martin (1987) *Black Athena: The Afroasiatic Roots of Classical Civilization, Volume I, The Fabrication of Ancient Greece 1785-1985*. London: Free Association Press

Budge, E.A. Wallis (1967) *The Book of the Dead (The Papyrus of Ani) Egyptian Text Transliteration and Translation*. New York: Dover

Carruthers, Jacob H. *Essays in Ancient Egyptian Studies*. Los Angeles: Timbuktu Publishers

Cottrell, Leonard (1967) *Lady of the Two Lands: Five Queens of Ancient Egypt*. New York: The Bobbs-Merrill Company

Diop, Cheik Anta (1987) "Origin of the Ancient Egyptians," in Van Sertima, Ivan and Williams, Larry (Eds.) *Great African Thinkers, Vol I: Cheik Anta Diop*. New Brunswick: Transaction Books, pp. 35-63.

Diop, Cheik Anta (1974) *The African Origin of Civilization: Myth or Reality*. Westport: Lawrence Hill and Co.

Foster, John L. (1974) (Translator) *Love Songs of the New Kingdom*. New York: Charles Scribner's Sons

Freud, Sigmund (1967) *Moses and Monotheism*. New York: Vintage

Harris, James E. and Wente, Edward F., An (1980) *X-Ray Atlas of the Royal Mummies*. Chicago: University of Chicago Press

James, George G.M., (1985) *Stolen Legacy*. San Francisco: Julian Richardson (First published, 1954)

Kamil, Jill (1977) *Luxor: A guide to Ancient Thebes, Second Edition*. London: Longman

Lichtheim, Miriam (1975) *Ancient Egyptian Literature, Volume I: The Old and Middle Kingdoms*. Berkeley: University of California Press

Mokhtar, Wafaa Moh (no date) *Karnak*. Cairo: Al-Helal Trading and Press

Moret, Alexandre (1972) *The Nile and Egyptian Civilization*. New York: Barnes and Noble (First published 1927) [The proper names Thebes, Egypt, Nile, and Justice have been changed in the quotation to the Kemetic originals, Waset, Kemet, Hapi, and Maat, respectively.]

Newby, P.H. (1980) *Warrior Pharaohs: The Rise and Fall of the Egyptian Empire*. London: Faber and Faber

Prichard, James B. (1973) (Ed.) *The Ancient Near East, Volume I: An Anthology of Texts and Pictures*. Princeton: Princeton University Press

Riefstahl, Elizabeth (1964) *Thebes in the time of Amunhotep III*. Norman, Oklahoma: University of Oklahoma Press

Romer, John (1981) *Valley of the Kings*. New York: William Morrow

Rose, John (1985) *"The Sons of Re": Cartouches of the Kings of Egypt*. Cheshire, Great Britain: JR-T Deanprint Ltd.

Sauneron, Serge (1969) *The Priests of Ancient Egypt*. New York: Grove Press

Simpkins Splendor of Egypt (no date) *The Temple of Hatshepsut*. Cairo

Simpkins Splendor of Egypt (no date) *The Temple of Luxor*. Cairo:

Spence, Lewis (1929) *The Mysteries of Egypt: or the Secret Rites and Traditions of the Nile*. London: Rider and Co. (Reprinted by The African Publication Society)

Stiendorff, George and Seele, Keith C. (1957) *When Egypt Ruled the East*. Chicago: University of Chicago Press

Van Sertima, Ivan and Williams, Larry (1987) *Great African Thinkers, Volume I: Cheik Anta Diop*. New Brunswick: Transaction Books

Vandenburg, Philipp (1978) *Nefertiti: An Archaeological Biography*. New York: J.B. Lippincott

West, John Anthony (1985) *The Travelers Key to Ancient Egypt*. New York: Alfred A. Knoph

Wimby, Diedre (1984) "The Female Horuses and Great Wives of Kemet," in Van Sertima, Ivan (Ed.) *Black Women in Antiquity*. New Brunswick: Transaction Books (*Journal of African Civilizations*. 6,1, pp. 36-48.)

BLACK RULERS OF THE GOLDEN AGE

By Legrand H. Clegg II

> *When Asia overwhelmed Egypt, Egypt sought refuge in Ethiopia [Nubia] as a child returns to its mother, and Ethiopia then for centuries dominated Egypt and successfully invaded Asia.*
>
> —W.E.B. DuBois, *The World And Africa: An Inquiry into the Part Which Africa Has Played in World History*, New York: International Publishers, 1961, p. 117.

Over the past quarter of a century during which Americans and Europeans have gradually lost their total monopoly on the study and interpretation of world history (and such allied fields as anthropology, archaeology and paleontology), there have emerged two distinct positions on the racial identity of the ancient Egyptian people. One view, which was introduced by Nineteenth Century Egyptologists and has dominated Western scientific thinking ever since, is that "the people who lived in Ancient Egypt were 'white,' even though their pigmentation was dark, or even black, as early as the predynastic period. Negroes made their appearance only from the XVIIIth Dynasty onwards."[1] Little evidence has ever been presented in support of this position, but it has survived largely, if not entirely, on the strength of the reputation, power and influence of the scientists and scholars who espouse it. The opposing view, which holds that "ancient Egypt was peopled, 'from its neolithic infancy to the end of the native dynasties,' by Black Africans,"[2] appears to have been the only opinion on the subject from the time of the ancient Hebrews[3] and Greeks[4] until the birth of the science of Egyptology in Europe over a century ago.

During the 20th Century the latter view has been resurrected in the writings of such African-American scholars as W.E.B. DuBois, William L. Hansberry, J.A. Rogers, Carter G. Woodson, Chancellor Williams, Yosef Ben Jochanan and John Henrike Clark and a number of African scholars, including Cheikh Anta Diop and I. Obenga. One of the major periods in Egyptian history that these scholars have considered in support of their opinion is that of the Seventeenth and Eighteenth Dynasties (Egypt's "Golden Age") which is the focus of this paper.

Undoubtedly because of their defensive position in the face of the awesome might of Western scholarship, the advocates of a Black Egypt have been most meticulous in proving their case as they seek to change prevailing opinion. Chief among these scholars is Diop, probably the world's greatest living historian and certainly the foremost contemporary authority on African History and culture. He relies on anthropology, iconography, melanin dosage tests, osteological measurements, blood groupings, the testimony of classical writers, self-descriptive Egyptian hieroglyphs, divine epithets, Bibical eyewitnesses, linguistics and various cultural data in support of his opinion regarding the ethnicity of the ancient Egyptians.[5]

We enter this controversy as proud disciples of Dr. Diop and the other distinguished scholars who have relied on evidence rather than passion in their pursuit of the truth with respect to the racial identity of the ancient Egyptians. While we understand why the advocates of a Black Egypt have persisted in pressing for the overall acceptance of their position by the moguls of Western academia, we are disinclined to follow this course. It is clear to us that Western authority, as a whole, has conspired to suppress, distort or ignore African history with the intent of perpetuating white historical supremacy; and that this deeply entrenched practice will not give way to the truth simply because the truth is right, just or supported by solid evidence. Therefore, this paper is not intended as another debate with Western scholars over whether the ancient Egyptians as a general rule were blacks. In our opinion, this issue has been settled in the affirmative.

Nevertheless, all points of view should be periodically updated and refined in order to maintain their scientific accuracy. Hence, in further support of our opinion that the ancient Egyptians were essentially a Black people, we hereby propose that a new, comprehensive ethnic examination be undertaken of the general Egyptian population during the Old, Middle and New Kingdoms, the First and Second Intermediate Periods, the Nubian Renaissance (Twenty-Fifth Dynasty) and the period of decline. We also recommend that a similar analysis be made of every possible ruler of each dynasty from the time of Menes in the First Dynasty to the conquest of Egypt by Alexander of Macedonia. This will probably require years of research and it is made difficult by the paucity of available evidence; yet the task must be undertaken if we intend for our work to supplant the lies and inaccuracies of prevailing opinion in African history.

In keeping with the above proposal, our specific intent in this brief paper is to undertake a scientific evaluation of the racial characteristics of the rulers of Egypt's Seventeenth and Eighteenth Dynasties. We have chosen this period because of its significance in African history and world affairs. The Seventeenth Dynasty began a major war of liberation which ended victoriously in the founding of the Eighteenth. This succeeding royal family brought Egypt to new heights of technical achievement and military might, and marked the first time that any nation expanded its borders to encompass a vast world empire. We believe that our scrutiny of the familial ties of the rulers of these two great dynasties will establish a concrete and verifiable genetic continuum that may well remove the ethnicity of these royal families from the realm of speculation.

Background

But in order to lay the foundation for our case here, we must look beyond both the Seventeenth and Eighteenth Dynasties into the Twelfth Dynasty of the Middle Kingdom (circa. 2000-1780 B.C.) at which time Egypt had lapsed into confusion, contention and internal strife that ultimately led to what is called the Second Intermediate Period (i.e., the Thirteenth through the early Seventeenth Dynasties, c. 1786-1567 B.C.). Manetho, an Egyptian priest (ca. 300 B.C.), wrote an historical treatise on Egypt which includes this period, but it has perished. Fortunately, however, Jewish historian Flavius Josephus quotes a portion of Manetho's account of the Hyksos invasion which was the most significant event of the Second Intermediate Period and which transformed Egyptian History. "[A] blast of God smote us," Manetho states, "and unexpectedly from the regions of the East, invaders of obscure race marched in confidence of victory against our land. By main force they easily seized it without striking a blow; and having overpowered the rulers of the land they then burned our cities ruthlessly, razed to the ground the temples of the gods, and treated all the natives with a cruel hostility, massacring some and leading into slavery the wives and children of others . . . Finally, they appointed as king one of their number whose name was Salitis."[6]

Manetho designated these invaders as "Hyksos," which he interprets to mean "king-shepherds" in the Egyptian language.[7] Today the word Hyksos is more generally interpreted as "rulers of foreign lands."[8]

These invaders were largely Semitic foreigners driven from Western Asia into Africa by instability and famine. They appear to have established themselves in Lower Egypt and may have extended their influence, if not their actual rule, over much of the remainder of the country.[9]

Although Manetho holds that the Hyksos dominated Egypt for 511 years,[10] modern scholars generally believe that they ruled for no more than about two centuries.[11] During this period their cultural impact was most unremarkable. "The Hyksos left no literary evidence of their occupation of Egypt. Indeed, they left practically no large monuments at all. What we know about them has been painfully gleaned from a host of scarabs . . . . cylinder seals, and few other isolated objects . . ."[12]

The Hyksos are of particular significance to us here, however, because they appear to have expelled the native African royal family from Egypt and to have driven its members far to the south. How far southward this family was driven and what ultimately became of its members and their descendants are critical issues.

A number of scholars believe that during the Hyksos period (i.e. the Fifteenth through the Seventeenth Dynasties), "the members of the [Egyptian] royal family retired to Kush [i.e. Nubia] where they lived as guests and wards of the Kushites for many years."[13] In other words, the native rulers were expelled from Egypt entirely and then "sought refuge in Ethiopia [Nubia] as a child returns to its mother"[14] until Egypt could be liberated from foreign domination.

Other authorities hold, however, that Hyksos domination was not nearly so pervasive as had been reported. Diop, for example, insists that the Hyksos "occupied only the eastern region of the Delta, with Avaris as their capital'' and that ''the Black dynasty'' remained strong in upper Egypt.[15]

What appears to be relatively certain is that during the period of Hyksos occupation the peoples of Upper Egypt and Nubia (the country immediately south of Egypt) grew close together in the apparent recognition of a common enemy—the Semitic invaders. From this Black interdependence appears to have come much ''cross-breeding,'' cultural interchange, trading and the forging of strong political alliances. Redford has commented on the special relationship between Egypt and Nubia at this time:

> During the Seventeenth Dynasty a good deal of contact took place between the peoples of Nubia and the Egyptians of the incipient Theban kingdom. Egyptian freebooters and adventurers drifted south out of Upper Egypt into the wilds of the transcataract region to hire themselves as soldiers to the king of Kush [Nubia] while an opposite movement brought Nubian mercenaries of Medja extraction into the service of the Seventeenth Dynasty. In numbers the latter migration far outweighed the reverse movement of Egyptians. At numerous sites in Upper Egypt as far north as Asyut the Medja have left behind the remains of their settlements and their shallow pan-graves. So large was the body of Medja mercenaries present in Egypt at this time that they formed a whole contingent of the army Kamose led north against the Hyksos.
>
> It is inconceivable that so sizeable a settlement of Nubians inside the narrow confines of the 'head of the south' should have left the culture of the tiny Theban state unaffected. Although the extent of the influence will probably never be known correctly, not a few of the distinctive features of New Kingdom society and religion may have appeared through contact with Nubia.[16]

This prolonged contact between the Egyptians and Nubians also resulted in considerable intermingling between the two royal houses. So much so that scholars do not know whether the actual founders of the Seventeenth Dynasty were pure Nubians or Egyptian nationals of Nubian lineage.[17] The emphasis here on the Nubian origin of the Seventeenth and Eighteenth Dynasties should not be taken to suggest that the Nubians and Egyptians were of separate racial stocks. Both appear to have been Black people—the Egyptians having become hybridized by Asian immigrants, while the Nubians retained the physical characteristics of the old Egyptian (i.e., African) stock. Therefore, when scholars speak of Egyptians with ''Nubian features'' or ''Nubian admixture,'' they are referring to Egyptians of ''unmixed'' African type. The ''purity'' of Nubian ancestry provides a strong case for unmistakable Black lineage, while references to Egyptian roots alone—at this time in history—leaves some room for ethnic speculation.[18]

Historian William Hansberry quotes British Egyptologist Flinders Petrie as stating that ''the Kushite [Nubian] characteristics of so many members of the 18th Dynasty stemmed from the fact that many of their ancestors had 'mingled their blood with the natives' of Nubia during the period of Hyksos domination.''[19] Redford adds that ''[i]t is not unlikely, in view of the heavy influx of

Nubians into Upper Egypt, that the family of the Seventeenth Dynasty could boast of a large admixture of Nubian blood.''[20]

The Seventeenth Dynasty

Is there solid evidence on which to base Petrie and Redford's opinions as to the Black roots of the 17th and 18th Dynasties? In search of such evidence, one must focus attention on each of the rulers of this period. As has been noted, the Second Intermediate Period was a time of great confusion. So much so that few details have survived concerning events that transpired during the Thirteenth, Fourteenth, Fifteenth, Sixteenth and early Seventeenth dynasties—all of which fell between 1786 and the late 1500's B.C. Scholars are generally agreed, however, that about 1600 B.C., around the time of the late Seventeenth Dynasty, there arose a family in Upper Egypt that would be strong enough to expel the Hyksos and ultimately consolidate Egypt. Two commoners, Senakhtenre Tao and his wife Tetisheri, became rulers of Upper Egypt at this time. No one is certain how they achieved this power, but James Harris and Kent Weeks note that ''[Senakhtenre] Tao may have been related to an earlier king of the Seventeenth Dynasty, Antef V, or he may have usurped the throne. In any case it is clear that he and his wife founded the most powerful line of rulers Egypt was ever to know. Their descendants reigned for three hundred years.''[21]

While no mummy has been brought to light that can be identified as that of Senakhtenre Tao, Tetisheri's mummy has been found; unfortunately, however, nothing has been said about its racial characteristics. This royal couple, nevertheless, were the direct forebears of each of the other rulers of the Seventeenth Dynasty; and it has particularly been noted that ''Tetisheri's role as mother of the line was strengthened because both males and females of the next several generations could trace their ancestry directly to her.''[22] It may be reasoned, then, that evidence of the racial type of the descendants of Senakhtenre Tao and Tetisheri will shed light on the ethnic category into which these founding parents should be placed.

Senakhtenre Tao was succeeded by his son Seqenenre Tao who married his full-blooded sister Ahhotep I. This royal couple began the great war of liberation against the Hyksos people. As a matter of fact it is believed that Seqenenre Tao died in battle[23] and, following his death and the death of his son Kamose,[24] Ahhotep I ''rallied the Upper Egyptian soliders to continue to fight the enemy and rid the land of them in order to clear the way for this native dynasty to rule over a united Egypt.''[25]

The mummy of Seqenenre Tao has been found and a number of authorities have commented on it. ''From the Berber type of [Seqenenre],'' writes Petrie, ''it seems probable that the [Seventeenth] dynasty had come from Ethiopia . . . and the earlier part of it . . . of which we have no names, may have dwelt in Nubia, and only harassed the Hyksos from thence.''[26] Hansberry has commented on the "obvious Kushite [Nubian] traits" of the remains of "Seqenenra III" [Seqenenre].[27] And Harris and Weeks have taken special notice of this pharaoh's mummy:

> Of particular interest and importance are the physical features revealed by [Seqenenre] Tao's mummy . . . His entire lower facial complex, in fact, is so different from other pharaohs (it is closest to that of his son Ahmose) that he could be fitted more easily into the series of Nubian and Old Kingdom Giza skulls than into that of later Egyptian kings. . . . Various scholars in the past have proposed a Nubian—that is, non-Egyptian—origin for Seqenenre and his family, and his facial features suggest this might indeed be true. If it is true, the history of *the family that reputedly drove the Hyksos from Egypt, and the history of the Seventeenth Dynasty, stand in need of considerable re-examination*.[28]

The mummy of Seqenenre Tao's wife Ahhotep I has been found, but, as in the case of her mother's remains, no direct mention has been made of Ahhotep I's racial characteristics. This, too, can be inferred, however, from the description given the mummies of two of the children of Seqenenre Tao and Ahhotep I. The royal couple had at least six children, of whom three survived childhood; and it was these offspring, according to most scholars, who succeeded in driving the Hyksos from the Nile Valley.[29] Kamose, the eldest surviving son, followed his father into battle and died shortly thereafter. "How he died is not known, since his mummy was in extremely poor condition when found; it crumbled to dust in the excavator's hand."[30]

Ahmose I, the youngest son of Seqenenre and Ahhotep, continued the war of liberation and finally drove the hated Hyksos out of Egypt. According to Petrie:

> The history of the war of independence then seems to have been, that perhaps for twenty or thirty years before 1600 B.C. the *Nubian princes of Thebes* had been pushing their way northward against the decaying power of the Hyksos. Active warfare was going on at about 1600 B.C.; and a sudden outburst of energy, under the active young leader Aahmes [Ahmose I], concluded the expulsion of the foreigners, and the capture of their stronghold, within a few years, ending in 1582 B.C.[31]

Harris and Weeks have noted similarities between the remains of Ahmose I and those of his father Seqenenre: "Ahmose [I] and Seqenenre Tao shared many general physical features that were strikingly different from those of later Egyptian rulers. . . [O]ne wonders if both were not genetically influenced by peoples of the south [Nubia]."[32]

The only surviving daughter of Sequenenre Tao and Ahhotep was Ahmose-Nefertari, whom Petrie has described as "the most venerated figure of Egyptian history."[33] While we shall give considerable attention to this queen at a later point in our paper, it is important at this time to consider some observations that have been made regarding her mummy. British anatomist Grafton Elliot Smith was one of the first scientists to examine the great queen's remains. He reported in part that "Nofritari [Ahmose-Nefertari] had very little hair on her head and the vertex was quite bald. Elaborate pains had been taken to hide this deficiency. Twenty strings, composed of twisted human hair, were placed across the top of her head . . . *The appearance of these plaits is not unlike that of the modern Nubian women's hair.*"[34] Hansberry has noted that "the queen's teeth were large and healthy, her nose rather short and broad, her mouth wide, her lips full, and her jaws—particularly her upper jaw—tended toward marked prognathism."[35]

The foregoing observations regarding Ahmose-Nefertari's mummy are critical because of her direct familial ties to her predecessors, particularly in the female line. Harris and Weeks have noted the similarity in the physical types of the three queens who stand at the head of this extended family:

> Her head [the head of Tetisheri], broken from the badly damaged body, was one of the first studied. X-rays showed the same prominent dentition, the same type of malocclusion, and the same shape of the skull as the women found in the royal caches of the next four generations. The moderate wear on her teeth and even an impacted third molar, which lay at a very disfunctional angle in the jaw, were the same sort of problems found among her descendants. A comparison of this mummy, now confidently called Tetisheri, with those of her daughter Ahhotep and her granddaughter Ahmose-Nefertiry [Nefertari] showed how well she fit this family group.[36]

It would appear logical to conclude that the physical similarities of the three queens do not end with the observations recorded by Harris and Weeks. In other words, one can infer from their published reports that the mummies of Ahmose-Nefertari's female predecessors bear the same marked Nubian physical features that Hansberry noted in the mummy of Ahmose-Nefertari. As a matter of fact, Harris and Weeks clearly imply this in their references to the possible Nubian origin of this entire family—including patriarch Senakhtenre Tao and his male descendants—on the basis of the mummified remains of the family members whom the two scientists have examined.[37]

While the Nubian origin of the Seventeenth Dynasty is strongly suggested by the remains of the rulers of that period, there is additional evidence that may be even more persuasive. First, the female rulers of the dynasty wielded great power vis-à-vis their husbands and children.[38] This has been a strong characteristic of royal houses in Nubia from ancient through modern times, but it was rather unusual in ancient Egypt.[39] Secondly, there is evidence in the Seventeenth Dynasty of personal names compounded with *I 'h, k3* and *Ghwty*. "These theophorous names," writes Redford, "presuppose a strong attachment to a lunar cult, and there is no reason to believe that it was a Hermopolitan or a Theban one. The moon cult flourished in Nubia, too, and personal names of the Second Intermediate Period compounded with lunar elements are found in Nubia."[40] Redford further notes that "the early Eighteenth Dynasty image of the royal family as carrying on the traditions of the Twelfth Dynasty finds no explanation if the Seventeenth Dynasty was of Theban origin—the connexions of the Twelfth Dynasty were all with the Faiyum area. But if the [Senakhtenre] Ta'o's were in whole or in part of Nubian origin, an explanation could easily be found in the strong impression left by the Amenemhet's and Senwosret's [rulers of the Twelfth Dynasty] in Nubia, where the forts they had built continued to be used during the Hyksos period, and where their deified persons were already ranked alongside the local pantheon."[41]

On the basis of the foregoing evidence it seems probable that the uninterrupted Seventeenth Dynasty, which appears to have been founded by Senakhtenre Tao and his wife Tetisheri, was of Nubian origin—and it is almost certain that each member of this royal family was black. This conclusion is critical to any discussion of the ethnicity of the Eighteenth dynasty—Egypt's new kingdom; because, as Redford points out, "the royal family of the two dynasties is the same: Ahmose [I], the king who in Manetho's list stands at the head of the Eighteenth is a full-blooded scion of the Seventeenth."[42]

The Eighteenth Dynasty

While Ahmose I may indeed have founded the Eighteenth Dynasty, it was his wife-sister, Queen Ahmose-Nefertari, whom the Egyptian people deified as the great ancestress of this family line. We have noted on the basis of their mummies that this royal couple were most probably of Nubian lineage. In the case of Ahmose-Nefertari, this assumption would appear to be reinforced by the fact that in most pictorial representations she is depicted as a woman with black skin. She is so represented in the tomb at Deir el-Medineh and on walls in ruins at Nibnutiru, Unnofir and Sheikj Abd el-Qurnah. A statue in the Turin museum portrays her with Black skin, a wide mouth, full lips, a rather thick nose and more or less prognathous jaws. She is depicted in a similar manner in a bust molded in relief on her mummy case discovered at Dier-el-Bahari.[43]

A number of Egyptologists and historians have taken note of Ahmose-Nefertari's black complexion. "At the Eighteenth Dynasty," writes Samuel Birch, "the negress mounts the throne."[44] Rawlinson observes that Ahmose-Nefertari "is represented on the monuments with pleasing features, but a complexion of ebon (sic) blackness."[45] Osburn speaks of the queen as being "an Ethiop (sic) in complexion and descent."[46] DuBois has stated that "this queen with a black skin has . . . been regarded as a Negress;"[47] and Maspero has noted that Ahmose-Nefertari is generally "painted black."[48]

Ironically, some scholars hold that the fact that Ahmose-Nefertari is generally depicted with black skin is not necessarily conclusive evidence that she was indeed Black. Egyptologist Jules Taylor, for example, has noted that frequently Black Egyptians "are not represented black, but brown, red or yellow . . .;" while the color black is often used to depict "individuals regardless of their own personal coloration, in ritualistic black guise."[49]

Plate 1. Queen Ahmose-Nefertari (chief queen of King Ahmose I).

The foregoing is of particular significance in the present case when we note that Ahmose-Nefertari appears to have been the fullblooded sister of Ahmose I;[50] yet she is always painted black, but he is depicted in the traditional reddish-brown of the Egyptian male. Historian Lester Brooks has offered some very interesting insight into this whole question:

> [Ahmose-Nefertari] is often shown in pictures of the court with a dark, almost black skin. This is highly unusual, for Egyptian tradition always assigned a fair skin to females, whatever their actual color, and a reddish-brown skin to males. One explanation for the unusual treatment of [Ahmose-Nefertari] by artists is, of course, that because she was so highly regarded, they painted her in her 'true colors', faithful to her real skin tone. Another is that as she became more and more venerated she was assigned divine status and was shown as one of the gods of the Underworld, represented in blueblack colors.[51]

Whatever one believes about the significance of the pictorial representations of Ahmose-Nefertari, when all of the evidence is taken as a whole it is apparent that both she and her husband-brother, co-founders of the Eighteenth Dynasty, were Blacks. And, as we shall see, the evidence also suggests that they were succeeded by rulers of the same racial stock.

Ahmose I, whose name, according to Rawlinson, signifies "child of the moon,"[52] ruled from 1570-1546 B.C. His Chief Queen, Ahmose-Nefertari, bore for him at least four sons—of whom all but one predeceased their father—and two daughters. The surviving son, Amehotep I (1546-1526), continued the reorganization begun by his father following the expulsion of the Hyksos.

The "badly battered" mummy of Amenhotep I was found in the Deir el-Bahri cache where it had been placed by priests of the Twenty-First Dynasty.[53] Unfortunately, nothing has been said about the mummy's racial characteristics, but it would stand to reason that Amenhotep I inherited the African features of his parents.

A painting of Amenhotep I and his mother was found by an early Prussian Expedition on the wall of a tomb at Gournon, "the burial place of Thebes."[54] It is now in the Berlin Museum. Noting the pharaohs's racial characteristics as depicted by the ancient Egyptian artist, Osburn states that "he [Amenhotep I] has himself a noble countenance, but his complexion has the sickly, pallid tint which denotes a mulatto."[55] This is a curious observation since there is no evidence whatsoever that either of the pharaoh's parents was Caucasian.

While Amenhotep I probably had several children by one or more of his sister-wives, none of them survived. The pharaoh was therefore forced to designate his brother-in-law, Thutmosis, to succeed him.

The ascension of Thutmosis I (1526-1512) to the throne represents the first break in the royal family line since the Seventeenth Dynasty co-fo[illegible] Senakhtenre Tao and Tetisheri. But even here the Black genetic contin[illegible]p-pears to remain intact. While Thutmosis' origin is unknown, his m[illegible]y has been examined and has been described by Hansberry as presenting "[illegible] noticably Negroid or Kushite cast."[56] The remains of the great pharaoh's two wives, Ahmose and Mutnofret, have not been found, but their parentage leaves little doubt as to their ethnic origin. Both were daughters of Ahmose I and Ahmose-Nefertari and sisters of Amenhotep I.

Thutmosis I also had a number of children, but only two are of significance here: Hatshepsut, the daughter of Thutmosis and his Chief Queen Ahmose; and Thutmosis II, the son of Thutmosis I and his lesser wife Mutnofret.

When the elder pharaoh, a great militarist who revived Egypt's glory, died, his sickly son, Thutmosis, ascended the throne and ruled as Thutmosis II (1512-1504). Here, again, we have a pharaoh whose mummy has been described as "noticably Negroid" and whose ancestry is clearly black.[57] His wife and half-sister, the famous Queen Hatshepsut (1503-1482), who succeeded him to the throne and ultimately ruled as pharaoh, bore for Thutmosis II at least two daughters, Neferure and Meryetre-Hatshepsut.

Plate 2. Queen Hatshepsut.

Although Hatsheput's mummy has not been found, it is clear that she is the granddaughter of Ahmose and Ahmose-Nefertari and the daughter of Thutmose I and Mutnofret. From this one can readily infer that she, too, in Hansberry's words, "was neither a blond nor a brunette but rather a person who was in all liklihood either dark-brown or black."[58]

Thutmosis III was the son of Thutmosis II and his lesser wife Isis. Scholars believe that, upon his father's death, little Thutmosis ascended the throne with his step-mother/aunt, Hatshepsut, serving as co-regent. However, "during the second year of her stepson's reign she took over all authority from the young ruler and was crowned King of Upper and Lower Egypt."[59]

Following Hatshepsut's death, Thutmosis III finally achieved independent power. This pharaoh, who earned the reputation of being Egypt's "greatest and most powerful ruler," reigned from 1504-1450 B.C. His roots also appear to have been black. According to Diop, Isis, the mother of Thutmosis III, was from the Sudan.[60] DuBois has stated that the pharaoh's "granite head in the British Museum has distinct Negro features."[61] And Maspero has commented on the great king's mummy: "His [Thutmosis III] statues, though not representing him as a type of manly beauty, yet give him refined, intelligent features, but a comparison with the mummy shows that the artists have idealized their model. The forehead is abnormally low, the eyes deeply sunk, the jaw heavy, the lips thick, and the cheekbones extremely prominent; the whole recalling the physiognomy of Thutmose II [Thutmosis II], though with a greater show of energy. Thutmose

Plate 3. Temple of Queen Hatshepsut at Luxor.

III [Thutmosis III] is a fellah of the old stock, squat, thickset, vulgar in character and expression, but not lacking in firmness and vigour.''[62]

Thutmosis III was succeeded to the throne by Amenhotep II, a son borne for him by his half-sister Meryetre-Hatshepsut, the daughter of Queen Hatshepsut. Amenhotep II's uneventful reign extended over a period of about twenty-five years. From his mummy it has been noted that this pharaoh was ''taller than both his father and his son [Thutmosis IV];''[63] but nothing has been said regarding the king's racial characteristics. However, both of the pharaoh's parents appear to have been black or ''Negroid'' and the same may be confidently said of him. The surviving statues of Amenhotep II seem to confirm this hypothesis.[64]

Amenhotep II's chief queen, about whose origin little is known, was Tia. She bore Thutmosis IV, who succeeded his father to the throne. This pharaoh ruled from 1425-1417 B.C. His emaciated mummy has also been found and Harris and Weeks have noted its strong ''resemblance to Amenhotep II, a fact that helps confirm the known order of royal succession.''[65] Just as in the case of his father, nothing has been said regarding the racial characteristics of the mummy of Thutmosis IV. As the grandson of Thutmosis III and his Chief Queen Meryetre-

Plate 4. Queen Tiye (chief queen of Amenhotep III).

Plate 5. King Akhenaton (son of Amenhotep III and Queen Tiye).

Hatshepsut, however, it may be inferred that Thutmosis IV inherited considerable African genetic material.

The final rulers of the Eighteenth Dynasty were the descendants of Thutmosis IV. At this time a new infusion of Nubian "blood" appears to have entered the royal family through Mutemwiya[66]—the wife of Thutmosis IV; and through Yuya and Thuya, the parents of Queen Tiye and the pharaoh Ay.[67]

Amenhotep III, "the magnificent" (1417-1379 B.C.), was the son and successor of Thutmose IV and Mutemwiya. This king married the beautiful Queen Tiye and, according to early scholars, she bore for her husband the successive rulers of Egypt—Amenhotep IV (Akhenaton), Smenkhare and Tutankhamun.[68]

A number of scholars have described Amenhotep III as Black. "The features" of this monarch, writes British Egyptologist John Wilkinson, "cannot fail to strike everyone who examines the portraits of the Egyptian kings [as] having more in common with the Negro than those of any other pharaoh."[69] Massey notes that the sculptures of Amenhotep III "show the Aethopic [Nubian] type."[70] DuBois adds that the king "inherited his mother's Negroid features."[71] And Rogers concludes that "[t]he Eighteenth Dynasty was of almost unmixed Negro strain; in fact, its two principal representatives, Amenophis III [Amenhotep III] and his son, Akhenaton, seem to have had no 'white' blood."[72]

Much the same has been written of this great pharaoh's chief queen, Tiye. Desroches-Noblecourt has noted, for example, that during this period "the Nubians played a part about which too little has been said. They enjoyed exceptional privileges at the court of Malkata. It was ruled by a queen almost certainly of their own race, as some portraits of Tiye, such as the little ebony head now in the Berlin Museum show her to have been.''[73] Tiye's ''southern looks are even more pronounced on a pendant (the *Menat* counterpoise) . . . and another similar portrait found at Tell El Amarna. Finally there is little room left for doubt when one studies the small sardonyx tablet, now in the Metropolitan Museum, which depicts the queen as a female sphinx. The face clearly betrays her origins; it was recently compared with another image of her still to be seen at Sedeinga in Northern Sudan in the ruins of the temple, dedicated to Tiye. Even the wigs of the royal ladies at Malkata as well as Tell el Amarna were inspired by the short neat coiffures of the Nubians.''[74]

Rogers has described Tiye as a ''full-blooded African;''[75] anthropologist Ivan Van Sertima refers to the queen as ''the Negroid mother of Tutankhamen;''[76] historian Alexander Von Wuthenau states that Tiye was of ''pure black stock.''[77] But it is probably Brooks who has provided the most graphic portrayal of this great queen; ''Any Sunday morning you may see her modern counterpart proudly entering America's Negro churches across the land.''[78]

The mummy of Amenhotep III has been found, but nothing has been recorded regarding his racial characteristics. In 1978, a team of scientists reported that a ''royal'' mummy, whose identity had been in dispute for over seventy years, was thought to be the remains of Queen Tiye. Regrettably, this team has also failed to publish any information regarding the racial characteristics of this mummy.[79] At least one authority contends that the mummys of Tiye's alleged parents, Yuya and Thuya, have Nubian traits,[80] while another strongly disagrees.[81] It would appear that, whatever one's opinion may be with regard to existent mummys, whose identities may justifiably be questioned,[82] the iconographic evidence with respect to the racial characteristics of Amenhotep III and his chief queen Tiye are most persuasive, and serve to strengthen our position that the Eighteenth Dynasty was essentially Black and largely of Nubian origin.

Amenhotep IV, who later changed his name to Akhenaton (1379-1362), succeeded his father to the throne. This great reformer of Egyptian art, literature and religion inherited his parent's African racial features. Egyptologists Cyril Aldred and A.T. Sandison note that Akhenaton's ''face is shown to be elongated with a prominent prognathous or progeniac jaw, large full lips, a coarse nose, large ears, and oblique eyes.''[83] Another Egyptologists, Edward Wente, speaks of Akhenaton's ''elongated skull, protruding jaw [and] thick lips;''[84] while Osburn observes that the pharaoh's ''dusky complexion, high cheekbones, projecting jaws and thick lips, call forcibly to mind the features of the true Negro;''[85] and Rogers adds that Akhenaton's ''skull . . . is what some scientists call that of a typical Negro. The jaw is exceedingly prognathous. His lips, as seen in profile, are so thick that they seem swollen.''[86]

The skull to which Wente and Rogers refer is apparently that associated with the mummy once thought to be Akhenaton's, but which is now identified as that

Plate 6. King Tutankhamun (ebony statue).

Plate 7. King Tutankhamun and Queen Ankhesenamon.

of his immediate successor, Smenkhare (1364-1361).[87] This ruler, whom traditional scholars believe to have also been the son of Amenhotep III and Tiye, inherited the racial characteristics of his parents. Harris and Weeks have noted that his "skeleton and broken skull . . . reveal a man who resembles the Thutmosid line,"[88] which, as we have seen, was decidedly "Negroid." Moreover, the paintings and sculptures of Smenkhare clearly depict his African features.[89]

Upon Smenkhare's death, his younger brother Tutankhamun (1361-1352 B.C.) ascended the throne. Events of the life and death of this king are so widely known that we need not recount them here. If we accept the traditional view, that King Tutankhamun was the son of Amenhotep III and Queen Tiye, his ethnic affinity is obvious and requires no further elaboration. Even if we adhere to the theory that Tutankhamun was the son of Akhenaton by one of his lesser wives,[90] it is still most probable that the boy-king was Black. As a matter of fact, given Tutankhamun's immediate and distant ancestors, his surviving mummy and the valuable relics that depict his facial features, one cannot escape the conclusion that Von Wuthenau has reached: "The features of this Egyptian king, whose mother was of pure black stock, are almost as Negroid as the ones of his captured Nubian enemies."[91]

The great royal wives of the successors of Amenhotep III also played prominent roles during the reigns of their consorts. However, no mummies of these queens were found. Nevertheless, a persuasive case can be made for the opinion that they too were either Black or "Negroid." Nefertiti, Chief Queen of Akhe-

Plate 8. Queen Nefertiti (chief queen of Akhenaton).

Plate 9. Daughters of Akhenaton and Nefertiti .

naton, appears to have been the granddaughter of Yuya and Thuya and the daughter of their son Ay.[92] We have mentioned the possible Nubian affinities of Yuya and Thuya. One Egyptologist, William Osburn, claims to have observed, or at least to have knowledge of, the physical characteristics of the mummy of Nefertiti's father. Speaking of the pharaoh's tomb, Osburn says, "The Negro countenance of the King was the most remarkable thing in it."[93] Unfortunately, nothing is known about the mother of Nefertiti.

Most paintings and sculptures of Nefertiti depict her as having decidedly African features—often with the same elongated skull, protruding jaw and thick lips that characterize her husband Akhenaton.[94] All of the couple's daughters, including Meryet-Amon, who was the Chief Queen of Smenkhare, and Ankhesenamun, the Chief Queen of Tutankhamun (and later, following his death, the wife of King Ay) also appear to have had African physical features. Proof of this is found in full detail in the large collection of photographs published in Cyril Aldred's *Akhenaton* and *Nefertiti*.[95]

The final rulers of Egypt's Eighteenth Dynasty were Ay (1352-1348 B.C.) and Horemhab (1348-1320 B.C.). Ay was an old man upon ascending the throne and his reign lasted only four years. Horemhab, who had once served as a general under Akhenaton and Tutankhamun, returned Egypt to its traditional and formerly stable ways. While we have mentioned Ay's mummy and his ancestry, little is known of Horemhab's family except for the fact that he married Mutnodjme, the sister of Nefertiti. Nevertheless, it must be pointed out that the published depictions of Horemhab suggest that he too falls within the ethnic spectrum of his predecessors of the distinguished Eighteenth Dynasty.[96]

Conclusion

The evidence presented in this paper tends to indicate that the Seventeenth and Eighteenth Dynasties of ancient Egypt were of Nubian origin and that each of the rulers of these extended families was either Black, "Negroid" or of Black ancestry. We believe it most probable that any newly discovered evidence will support our general premise and will probably also shed more light on the Black (and perhaps Nubian) origin of the first several dynasties, the Middle Kingdom and, of course, the Twenty-fifth Dynasty or renaissance period.

We therefore urge objective scientists to take a new, hard look at Egypt from an African perspective and to discover a whole new universe which the arrogant giants of Western scholarship have grown too blind to see.

Notes

1. Symposium on "The Peopling of Ancient Egypt And The Deciphering of the Meroitic Script" by the International Scientific Committee For The Drafting of a General History of Africa (United Nations Educational Scientific And Cultural Organization), Cairo, January 28 through February 3, 1974. Transcript of symposium distributed in limited numbers: SHC - 73/CONF. 812/4, Paris, June 28, 1974, page 3.

2. Ibid. We are well aware that the new anthropological party line is that "there is no such thing as 'race,'" and that it is now unscientific to delimit mankind on the basis of "race." We do not accept this point of view for the following reasons: First, three major subspecies of the human family, i.e., the Africoid ("Negroid"), Caucasoid and Mongoloid are readily distinguishable and can be scientifically defined without the absurd assumption that racial "purity" is widespread in either category. Secondly, it appears that the abandonment of the study of "race" by modern science is not so much an attempt to stress the unity of the human species as it is to focus away from the inevitable conclusions that such study has forced upon the academic community. Eighteenth century scientists embarked on the study of human subspecies in order to prove the superiority of the white race and it is no accident that, as their modern disciples come to the startling realization that the human family was born in Africa, that the first homo sapiens were probably Black and that Caucasians probably sprang from prehistoric Black people as a genetic mutation to albinism, these scientists are eager to suppress this information. Finally, as long as the world is dominated by White people, as long as those White scientists—who now claim that there is no validity to the study of race—continue to practice racism socially and academically; and, most important, as long as the Black race bears the universal badge of inferiority forced on it by scientists who have distorted or suppressed Black history, we shall not only include race as an integral part of our historical writings, but we shall prominently focus on it whenever and wherever the truth can be told until sincere men of science return the Black race to its former position of respect and reverence on the earth.

As for the Black or "Negro" race, we accept the definition of Cheikh Anta Diop: "Anticipating the agreement of all logical winds, I call *Negro* a human being whose skin is black, especially when he has frizzy hair." Cheikh Anta Diop, *The African Origin of Civilization: Myth Or Reality?* New York, Lawrence Hill & Co., 1974, p. 136. We also agree with DuBois' position that "[t]here was and is wide mingling of the blood of all races in Africa, but this is consistent with the general thesis that Africa is predominantly the land of Negroes and Negroid peoples, just as Europe is a land of Caucasoids and Asia of Mongoloids. We may give up entirely, if we wish, the whole attempt to delimit races, but we cannot if we are sane, divide the world into whites, yellows and blacks, and then call blacks white." W.E.B. DuBois, *The World And Africa: An Inquiry Into The Part Which Africa Has Played In World History*, New York, International Publishers, 1961, p.119.

Finally, we are aware that there is an intermediate view (between the two extremes presented in the text) regarding the racial type of the ancient Egyptians—i.e., the Egyptians were neither Black nor White, but a mixed type. We have omitted this position from our discussion mainly because it is generally presented as nothing more than a variation of the first point of view, i.e., the Egyptians were "mixed Caucasoids."

3. Diop, *The African Origin of Civilization*, pp. 5-9.

4. Ibid., pp. 1-5.

5. Cheikh Anta Diop, "Origin Of the Ancient Egyptians," *General History of Africa*, Ed. G. Mokhtar, UNESCO 1981 Vol. 11, pp. 27-55.

6. *Manetho*, Edited by T.E. Page et al., with an English translation by W.G. Waddell, Cambridge, Harvard University Press, MCMXL, pp. 79-81.

7. Ibid., p. 85.

8. George Steindorff and Keith C. Seele, *When Egypt Ruled The East*, Chicago, the University of Chicago Press, 1942, p. 24. This appears to be the more correct translation of the Egyptian *heku shoswet*.

9. Ibid., p. 26.

10. Manetho, pp. 85-87.

11. Steindorff and Seele, *When Egypt Ruled The East*, pp. 30 & 274.

12. Ibid.

13. William L. Hansberry, "Africa's Golden Past," *Ebony*, November, 1964, p. 37. The names Nubia and Kush (and sometimes Ethiopia) are often used interchangeably to describe the region south of the Nile's First Cataract and sometimes known as Wawat, a land rich in gold. To the east of Nubia, extending along the Red Sea in what today is the coast of Sudan, Ethiopia and Somalia, was the land which the ancients referred to as Punt. The word Ethiopia, which is Greek for "land of burnt faces," was also once used to designate all of Africa.

14. W.E.B. DuBois, *The World and Africa*, p. 117. DuBois was one of the earliest modern scholars to resurrect the ancient view that Egypt was originally a colony of Ethiopia. Also see W.M. Flinders Petrie, *A History of Egypt During the XVIIth and XVIIIth Dynasties*, London, Muthen and Co., Ltd., 1896, p. 4.

15. Cheikh Anta Diop, *The African Origin of Civilization*, p. 209.

16. Donald B. Redford, *History and Chronology of the Eighteenth Dynasty of Egypt*, University of Toronto Press, 1967, p. 67. Kamose, who is mentioned in this quotation, was the third ruler of the Seventeenth Dynasty.

18. Chancellor Williams, *The Destruction of Black Civilization: Great Issues of A Race From 4500 B.C. to 2000 A.D.*, Chicago, Third World Press, 1974, pp. 62-124. Also see Ivan Van Sertima, *They Came Before Columbus*, New York, Random House, 1976, p. 111. We shall not here indulge in the silly argument over whether the ancient Nubians were actually Black people anymore than present-day scholars feel compelled to defend the foregone conclusion that the Greeks and Romans were white Europeans. For a discussion on the racial identity of the ancient Nubians, one may consult *They Came Before Columbus*, pp. 123-138.

19. Hansberry, "Africa's Golden Past," p. 38.

20. Redford, *History and Chronology of the Eighteenth Dynasty of Egypt*, p. 68.

21. James E. Harris and Kent R. Weeks, *X-Raying The Pharaohs*, New York, Charles Scribner's Sons, 1973, p. 120.

22. Ibid.

23. Steindorff and Seele, *When Egypt Ruled The East*, p. 29.

24. Ibid., p. 31.

25. Barbara S. Lesko, *The Remarkable Women of Ancient Egypt*, Berkeley, Scribe Publications, 1978, p. 4.

26. Petrie, *A History of Egypt During The XVIIth And XVIIIth Dynasties*, p. 17. Petrie's reference

to Seqenenre as being of the "Berber type" should not be cause for confusion. He apparently believed the Berbers, Ethiopians and Nubians to have been Black people and, on page 337, he specifically refers to Seqenenre as Black.

27. Hansberry, "Africa's Golden Past," p. 37. Professor Hansberry refers to a Seqenenre III. At one time it was believed that three pharaohs of the Seventeenth Dynasty bore the name Seqenenre. Scholars are generally now agreed that there was only one Seqenenre and his father bore a similar but different name, Senakhtenre.

28. Harris and Weeks, *X-Raying The Pharaohs*, pp. 123-124. Emphasis added. We would take the two scientists' position a step further and say that the history of the Eighteenth Dynasty is also in need of reexamination.

29. Ibid., p. 125.

30. Ibid.

31. Petrie, A History of Egypt During the XVIIth And XVIIIth Dynasties, p. 23. Emphasis added.

32. Harris and Weeks, *X-Raying The Pharaohs*, p. 127.

33. Petrie, *A History of Egypt During the XVIIth And XVIIIth Dynasties*, p. 41.

34. Grafton Elliot Smith, "The Royal Mummies," *Catalogue General Des Antiquités du Egyptiennes du Musée du Caire*, nos. 61051-61100, Cairo, Service des Antiquites de l'Egypte, 1912, p. 13. Emphasis added.

35. Hansberry, "Africa's Golden Past," p. 37.

36. Harris and Weeks, *X-Raying The Pharaohs*, p. 121.

37. Ibid., pp. 123, 127 & 135.

38. Lestor Brooks, *Great Civilizations of Ancient Africa*, New York, Four Winds Press, 1971, p. 49. Also See Redford, *History And Chronology of the Eighteenth Dynasty of Egypt*. pp. 65-69.

39. Brooks, Great Civilizations of Ancient Africa, p. 49. Also see Redford, *History And Chronology of the Eighteenth Dynasty of Egypt*, pp. 65-69.

40. Ibid., pp. 68-69.

41. Ibid., p. 69.

42. Ibid., p. 28. According to this author, Manetho placed Ahmose at the head of a new dynasty "only because he put an end to Hyksos rule in Egypt and inaugurated a period of independence."

43. Hansberry, "Africa's Golden Past," p. 37.

44. Samuel Birch, *Ancient Egypt From The Monuments, Egypt From The Earliest Times to B.C. 300*, New York, Scribner, Armstrong & Co., 1875, p. 83.

45. George Rawlinson, *History of Ancient Egypt*, New York, American Publishers Corp., 1880, Vol. II, p. 114.

46. William Osburn, *The Monumental History of Egypt*, London, Trubner & Co., 1854, p. 175.

47. DuBois, *The World And Africa*, pp. 126-127. DuBois also refers to the now outmoded view to which many early scholars subscribed, i.e., that, because of her color, Ahmose-Nefertari was not Egyptian by birth, but the daughter of a Nubian monarch with whom Ahmose I had entered an alliance for assistance in expelling the Hyksos rulers. The young princess, according to this view, was married to Ahmose I in order to strengthen the Egypto-Nubian alliance.

48. Gaston Maspero, *The Struggle Of The Nations*, New York, D. Appleton & Co., 1877, pp. 98-99.

49. Jules Taylor, "The Black Image In Egyptian Art," *Journal Of African Civilizations*, April, 1979, Vol. I, p. 27. It should be noted that, while many Egyptologists might object to any consideration of iconographic material to verify the racial characteristics of the ancient Egyptians, J. Vercoutter and N. Blanc have stated that "[t]he incongraphic material available . . . has extremely significant characteristics from the XVIII Dynasty onwards." Symposium on "The Peopling of Ancient Egypt And The Deciphering Of The Meroetic Script," p. 3.

50. For an opposing view, i.e., Ahmose-Nefertari may have been the half-sister of Ahmose I, see Petrie, *A History of Egypt During The XVIIth And XVIIIth Dynasties*, pp. 9 & 337; and Harris and Weeks, *X-Raying The Pharaohs*, p. 128.

51. Brooks, *Great Civilizations of Ancient Africa*, p. 50.

52. Rawlinson, *History of Ancient Egypt*, Vol. II, p. 112. This in itself, according to Redford, strongly suggests that Ahmose I was of Nubian origin. *History And Chronology of The Eighteenth Dynasty*, pp. 68-69.

53. Harris and Weeks, *X-Raying The Pharaohs*, p. 129.

54. Osburn, *The Monumental History of Egypt*, p. 175.

55. Ibid.

56. Hansberry, "Africa's Golden Past," p. 38.

57. Ibid.

58. Ibid.

59. Harris and Weeks, *X-Raying The Pharaohs*, p. 134.

60. Diop, *The African Origin of Civilization*, p. 12.

61. DuBois, *The World And Africa*, p. 128.

62. Gaston Maspero, *The Struggle Of The Nations, Egypt, Syria And Assyria*, London, Society for Promoting Christian Knowledge, 1910, p. 289.

63. Harris and Weeks, *X-Raying The Pharaohs*, p. 138.

64. Cyril Aldred, *New Kingdom Art in Ancient Egypt*, London, Alex Tiranti, Ltd., 1951, figs. 49, 50 &51.

65. Harris and Weeks, *X-Raying The Pharaohs*, p. 139.

66. Rawlinson states, "Born, as it would seem, of an Ethiopian mother, Mutemua [Mutemwiya], Amenophis [Amenhotep III] had a somewhat foreign physiognomy." *History of Ancient Egypt*, Vol. 2, p. 261. Also see Gerald Massey, A Book of The Beginnings, Secaucus, New Jersey, University Press, Inc., 1974, Vol. II, p. 405.

67. Christiane Desroches-Noblecourt, *Life And Death of A Pharaoh*, New York, Graphic Society, 1963, p. 116.

68. Ibid., pp. 120-121. Many scholars no longer accept this view. Wente, for example, and a number of others, now hold that both Smenkhare and Tutankhamun were sons of Akhenaton by minor wives.

69. John G. Wilkinson, *The Ancient Egyptians*, London, 1878, Vol. I, p. 42.

70. Massey, *A Book Of The Beginnings*, Vol. II, p. 405.

71. DuBois, *The World And Africa*, p. 129.

72. J.A. Rogers, *Sex And Race, Negro-Caucasian Mixing In All Ages and All Lands*, New York, published by the author, 1944, Vol. 1, p. 54.

73. Desroches-Noblecourt, *Life And Death of A Pharaoh*, p. 121. Also see Grafton E. Smith, *Tomb of Queen Tiyi*, London, Constable & Co., 1910.

74. Ibid.

75. J.A. Rogers, *World's Great Men of Color*, New York, Collier Books, 1972, Vol. II, p. 63.

76. Van Sertima, *They Came Before Columbus*, p. 29.

77. Alexander Von Wuthenau, *Unexpected Faces in Ancient America*, 1500 B.C.–A.D. 1500, New York, Crown Publishers, 1975, p. 136.

78. Brooks, *Great Civilizations of Ancient Africa*, p. 58.

79. James E. Harris et al., "Mummy of the 'Elder Lady' in the tomb of Amenhotep: Egyptian Museum Catalog Number 61070," *Science*, June 9, 1978, vol. 200, p. 1149.

80. Desroches-Noblecourt, *Life And Death of A Pharaoh*, p. 116.

81. Barbara Mertz, *Red Land, Black Land*, New York, Dodd, Mead & Co., 1966, 1978, pp. 11-17.

82. The mummified remains of the kings and queens of the New Kingdom of Egypt (c.1575 B.C. to 1070 B.C.) were first examined by the French Egyptologist Gaston Maspero in 1889 and the English anatomist Grafton E. Smith in 1912. The mummies had been deposited in two hiding places at Thebes. In 1881 the first cache was discovered in the reused tomb of Queen Inhapy at Deir el-Bahari. The second find, reportedly made in 1898, was in the tomb of King Amenhotep II of the middle Eighteenth Dynasty. "From these two caches were recovered the mummies of most of the kings of

the New Kingdom and a number of the queens. The mummies had been hidden in these two tombs about 3000 years ago after robbers had plundered the original tombs of the kings and queens in the Twentieth Dynasty. During the Twenty-First Dynasty, the mummies were collected and restored or rewrapped, since for the most part they had been badly damaged by tomb robbers looking for treasures placed on the mummies beneath the wrappings

"In a number of cases no identification whatsoever was found on the wrappings or coffins of these mummies. This should not be completely surprising since the grave robbing had occurred over a long period of time, and the royal mummies, after having been badly damaged at the hands of the grave robbers, had been moved from place to place for safety. The priests of the Twenty-First Dynasty were rewrapping mummies some of which were even then as old as 500 years." Harris, "Mummy of the 'Elder Lady'...," vol. 200, p. 1149.

Certain scientists have raised questions concerning the integrity of the white Egyptologists who exhumed the ancient mummies and thereafter indentified them. In this vein, Dr. Diop has written:

> It is customary to mention the straight hair of certain carefully chosen mummies, the only ones found in museums, to affirm that they represent a prototype of the white race, notwithstanding their prognathism. These mummies are displayed conspicuously in an attempt to prove the whiteness of the Egyptians. The very coarseness of their hair precludes acceptance of that contention. When such hair exists on the head of a mummy, it merely indicates the Dravidian type, in reality, whereas the prognathism and black skin—pigmented, not blackened by tar or any other product—excludes any idea of a white race. The meticulous selection process to which they have been subjected ruled out any possibility of their being a prototype. In fact, Herodotus told us, after seeing them, that the Egyptians had wooly hair... [One] may well wonder why mummies with such characteristics are not exhibited. Those that should be most numerous are currently the least discoverable, and when we are lucky enough to stumble upon one, we are assured that it represents a foreign type. *The African Origin of Civilization,* p. 165.

83. Cyril Aldred and A.T. Sandison, "The Pharaoh Akhenaton, A Problem in Egyptology and Pathology," *Bulletin of the History of Medicine,* XXXVI (1962), p. 305. We should point out here that Aldred, Sandison and a number of others have speculated that Akhenaton's "grotesque," "appalling" and "frankly hideous" facial features as rendered by Egyptian artists are a "distortion of the human form," or on the other hand, may be an accurate depiction of a pharaoh who suffered some physical malady. Most scholars explain away the king's apparent "Negroid" features in this manner. We reject this in its entirety because we do not believe that science must resort to conjecture in order to explain Akhenaton's features. He was a black African who chose to be depicted "true to form" rather than to be represented in the traditional nondescript Egyptian fashion. It is highly possible that other pharaohs had physical characteristics similar to those of Akhenaton but chose, for whatever reasons, not to be portrayed as they actually appeared. Even if we accept the far-fetched theory that Akhenaton was truly "deformed," this still need not carry him out of the Black race. Is it not possible for him to have been a Black man with "exaggerated" facial characteristics?

84. Edward F. Wente, "Tutankhamun And His World," p. 23.

85. Osburn, *Monumental History of Egypt*, Vol II, p. 329.

86. Rogers, *World's Great Men of Color*, vol. I, p. 63.

87. Harris and Weeks, *X-Raying The Pharaohs,* p. 146.

88. Ibid., pp. 146-147.

89. Cyril Aldred, *Akhenaton And Nefertiti,* New York, Brooklyn Musuem in association with Viking Press, 1973, pp. 98 & 101.

90. Edward F. Wente, "Tutankhamun And His World," p. 26.

91. Von Wuthenau, *Unexpected Faces in Ancient America,* p. 136.

92. Harris and Weeks, *X-Raying The Pharaohs,* p. 189.

93. Osburn, *Monumental History of Egypt*, vol. II, p. 341.

94. Cyril Aldred, *Akhenaton and Nefertiti*. We are aware that a number of scholars believe that the art of this period was stylized and therefore the representation of the ruling family with "exaggerated

Negroid'' features was a distortion of its actual appearance. Here, as in our reference to Akhenaton, we find it quite possible to believe that the artists were simply depicting Black people in an accurate manner. But, even if we assume that the artwork was stylized, is it not possible for Black people to have stylized art? Does stylized Greek art mean that the people generally depicted were not White Europeans?

95. Ibid.

96. Cyril Aldred, *New Kingdom Art in Ancient Egypt*, fig. 174. Also see Maspero, *Struggle of Nations*, p. 348.

THE NUBIAN RENAISSANCE

By Phaon Goldman (Tarharka)

Due to the great dearth of inscriptions from the end of the New Kingdom to the beginning of the Twenty-fifty Dynasty, precious little is known about this epoch, but in the early years of the Eighth Century B.C., an Ethiopian (or Kushite) king named Kashta penetrated and subdued the kingdom of the Pharaoh.[1] From his capital of Napata Kashta pushed as far north as Thebes—the Capital of Upper Egypt. In this way the Princes of Kush became kings of both Egypt and Nubia and, in fact, permanently moved the capital of the Empire from Napata to Thebes in order to have firmer control over the administration of the now-subject Fatherland of the Pharaohs.

Shabaka, one of Kashta's sons, has been accorded the honor of being the first ruler of the Twenty-fifty or Ethiopian Dynasty, in the opinion of many antiquarians.[2] Herodotus spoke of Shabaka as neither barbarian nor tyrant but rather a benefactor to the nation through the construction of hydraulic irrigation systems. George Rawlinson, oft-quoted translator of *The History of Herodotus*, remarked respectfully that this African lord was a sovereign of great humanity, exhibiting deep understanding for and deference to Egyptian customs while he reigned as an Ethiopian king over Egypt. Diodorus Siculus said, "... (he) went beyond all his predecessors in his worship of the gods and in his kindness to his subjects." Legend has it that he retired from the throne, "lest he should commit an act of injustice."

By sponsoring a cultural revival, among other acts, Shabaka attempted to rekindle the withering fortunes of Egypt. In erecting chapels and refurbishing temples, he, like the rulers of this Dynasty to follow him, kept the language of their inscriptions and the architecture of their buildings and memorials purely Egyptian—an attribute of governing that affirmed the fact that they considered themselves true Egyptian Pharaohs. Perhaps in a deliberate move to highlight the racial ties between this clan of Ethiopian monarchs and earlier Egyptian royal families with claims of southern extraction, these emperors, in many details, pointedly resurrected the linguistic and artistic style of Old and Middle Kingdom pharaohs.

Piankhy was the next son of Kashta to accede to the throne of the Nubian-

This chapter on the Twenty-fifth Dynasty was excerpted from *Black Manhood*, published in 1979 by University Press of America.

Egyptian nation. At his birth black bards exulted, "Happy is the mother that bore you. . .she has borne a Bull!"

The pioneer Egyptologist, Dr. Margaret A. Murray, reiterated, with regard to Piankhy, the phrase about "that certain claim" which we authenticated in an earlier chapter as giving evidence of ancestral and racial ties between Upper Egyptian Blacks and other ruling clans of Egypt. Speaking of the years in which Piankhy reached his majority, Dr. Murray bore witness that, "Ethiopia was in a flourishing state, and the Ethiopian kings had a certain claim to the throne of Egypt. Piankhy of Napata, therefore, set out to enforce the claim, and he left a detailed account of his invasion . . . ."[3]

The account of which this archeologist spoke was known as Piankhy's "Conquest Stela" and it was discovered quite by accident in 1862 by an Egyptian army officer on military assignment in the Sudan which was then under Egyptian suzerainty. The hieroglyphic text finally reached the eminent French archeologist and Egyptologist, Auguste Edouard Mariette, who recognized in a trice that this cryptograpy represented the lengthiest and most detailed narrative of the mastering of Egypt by the Kushites that had yet to come to light.

The beginning lines of this memorial pillar recited a litany engaged in by the Commandant and his regiments during their preparation for the battles sure to come. Leading his troops in prayer in the Temple of Amon, the War God, Piankhy intoned:

> *Amon is the God who has sent us!*
> *He makes the weak strong, so that a multitude flees before the feeble, and one man takes a thousand captive.*[4]
>
> *O Open thou the way before us, and*
> *Let us fight under the shadows of thy sword, for*
>
> *A child if he be sent forth by thee*
> *Shall overcome him that hath overcome multitudes.*

And then he charged his assembled mass of men to stay in a state of readiness to:

> *Delay not, day or night . . .*
> *Fight at sight . . .*
>
> *Yoke the warhorses!*
> *Draw up the line of battle!*

As was their custom when their god-king and war-lord concluded his leadership of this entreaty, the contingent of men-of-war fell to their stomachs before the Emperor and extolled him with this dramatic stanza:

> *Behold, O King*
> *Thy name fills us with might and thy counsel*
> *is the mooring-post of thy army*

It is thy valor that giveth us might
And there is strength in the remembrance of thy name . . .
Thou art the overseer of the operation of war;
Verily thou art a strong king . . .
Who is like unto thee?

Following this service of devotion and charge to valor, Piankhy and his legions sailed down the Nile to either augment his forces already in Middle Egyptian townships—but under seige—or to overpower additional, key metropolises of Egypt.

The "Conquest Stela" extended the story of this jet-black ruler of Egypt with another instance, this one delineating the saga of the Governor of Heracleopolis, a deputy of Piankhy, whose enclave had been under heavy pressure from a covetous Libyan Prince who had just recently consolidated Lower Egypt under his power and was even now encircling cities in Middle Egypt. This stone tablet told how Governor Pefnefdebast of Heracleopolis had been so profundly relieved to have been rescued from certain death that he prostrated himself before his saviour and vociferated:

Hail to thee O mighty King;
Thou are the Bull who conquerest Bulls!
Piankhi, Son of the Sun, King of the North and the South;
Indeed thou art like the warrior-god Montu–a
Bull of mighty arm.[5]

I was sunk deep down . . .in Hell;
But now light hath been made to shine upon me.
I found no friend in the day of evil and none
to uphold me in the day of battle, except thee,
O Mighty King . . . .

Henceforward, I shall be thy servant;
All my possessions are thine and the city of
Heracleopolis shall pay tribute unto thee.

Behold, thou art of the likeness of . . .(the)
chief of the imperishable stars.
As he was, so art thou O King:
As he perishes not, so shalt thou not perish,
O King of the South and North;
Piankhy, who livest forever!

The monograph continued and recorded that further down the Nile another princeling—Osorken, King of Bubastis—also knelt to pay homage to the regal Ethiopian, proclaiming his desire to "look upon the beauty of His Majesty". It was written that this sachem "sniffed the ground before His Highness" and implored him:

Come thou to my house and draw back the bolts of my Treasury and make thyself its master and I shall give unto thee a mass of turquoise as large as

> *thy head. I will give thee as much gold as thy heart can wish, and the finest horses which are in my stud farm and the best and strongest which are in my stables.*

It came to pass, so noted the Stela, that in the course of his taming of the Libyans and Egyptians, "the legs of his enemies trembled like those of women" and district after district "was on its belly in fear of him."

As a warrior-king, Piankhy could—and did, when events demanded it—strike swiftly and ruthlessly although he certainly was no vandal chieftain, killing wantonly or wreaking havoc in his wake simply to establish a name that was feared near and far. There have been copious testimonials from authorities on Ancient History, for example, that when he became monarch of Egypt he protected rather than laid waste its treasure-swollen temples, and his display of humanity and passion for justice tempered with mercy astonished and pleased his opponents.

Sir Alan Gardiner, author of *Egypt of the Pharaohs* (Oxford: Clarendon Press, 1961), analyzing the character of the man, glowed, "... we can not fail to discern the fiery temperament of the Nubian ruler, a temperament which had also as ingredients, a fanatical piety and a real generosity" (p. 340). The Inspector General of Antiquities of the Egyptian Government recorded in his essay, "The Exploits of a Nigger King," that with Ethiopia's "great and well-trained army of black warriors" Piankhy cowered the satraps of the Nile but, "... the good behavior of himself and his troops caused the Egyptians to regard him almost... (as) a protector from ... Assyria ... and Libya."[6]

As frequently as he dared, the Commander-in-Chief of the Armies of Ethiopia gave the overlords of villages about to be beseiged the option of declaring their municipality an "open city". If the officials took advantage of this offer, their shrines and townsfolk were untouched. If, however, as happened at Memphis, the Kushite General's merciful gesture was ignored, the population suffered grievously. At Memphis the ultimatum was broadcast: "Shut not up! Fight not! Those who wish to go out, let them go out. The people of Memphis shall be safe and sound, not even a child shall weep! Look at the provinces of the South, not a single person has been killed...." But Memphis chose to fight it out and Piankhy had no choice but to assault the city full force. Scribes wrote of this martial episode, "... multitudes were slain therein or brought as living captives to His Majesty."

Success after success soon put Piankhy in control of all Egypt and the East African gladiator became ruler of a commonwealth which stretched from the shores of the Mediterranean to the borders of modern Ethiopia—almost one-quarter of the African continent. Little wonder the Pharaoh began his numerous commemorative plaques erected after these spectacular victories with the self-laudatory phrases, "... I who am celestially born King, the living image of the sun-god, (was) destined to rule from birth ... (as) King of Lower Egypt, or Upper Egypt and of Kash (i.e., Kush, or Nubia, or Sudan)."

Piankhy had subdued sixteen field marshals and was master of both Egypt and Ethiopia before he returned to his home and capital of Napata. When his triumphant armada arrived at this riverside town the populace caused the waters to resound with their rejoicing, shouting with gladness:

Hail divine Governor and Conqueror!
Thou hast come and hast made thyself Governor
of the Land North and South. Thou hast made men to be as women.

Let the heart of the mother rejoice who has
given birth to thee and let the man be happy who begat thee.

Let those who dwell in the valley give praise
to the Cow that hath borne such a Bull!
Mayest thou live forever and may thy strength
endure eternally!

Piankhy, not unlike Amenhotep III, had a fondness not only for women—he had at least seven wives—but for horses as well as evidenced by the fact that those Viceroys whose fiefdoms he saved from the Libyans forthwith offered him spirited, powerful steeds, among other prized gifts. Additionally, in the plot adjoining his grave, archeologists also excavated the tomb of Piankhy's four favorite stallions—each of which had been buried standing erect, facing south and caparisoned in full battle attire.

This Twenty-fifth Dynasty Pharaoh was a pre-eminent individual on every count. His premier act of office, once assured of control of his newly acquired Egyptian domain, was to re-appoint most of the vassal Princes of the North (i.e., Egypt) to their seats with the demand that they now pay tribute to the Ethiopian crown. By initiating this political ploy, the citizenry of Egypt remained peaceful and yet ultimate fiscal and military power lay in Ethiopian hands. Much of Piankhy's reign was devoted to ornamenting the capital of Napata and to embarking upon building campaigns in various Middle Egyptian sectors of his dukedom. So singular was the style and magnitude of these edifices that even centuries later they can still be identified with his paramountcy. The black Prince's crowning accomplishment in this avocation was the part he played in the raising of the monumental Temple of Amon in the splendid religious center at Jebel Barkal, the Sacred Mountain. At the zenith of this constructive era this cathedral was one of the most colossal and sumptuous buildings to be found in the ancient world.

His decisive and speedy mastery of Egypt showed him to be a man of great physical stamina, ready decision and quick mental power. As a military tactician, in the assault on Memphis alone, he earned a high place among the battlefield strategists of all time. A man of action, a soldier with a sense of humanity, a ruler who governed in the interest of all the people, Piankhy's qualities of character have assured him a place of high honor among the monarchs of man's early civilized states.

Piankhy became the father of Tarkarka (the Biblical "Tirhakah"), who, at the

Plate 1. The Nubian Pharoah, Tarharka.

age of twenty was proclaimed King of Ethiopia and Egypt. He ascended the throne about 688 B.C. and, having assured himself of the continued subjugation of both Middle and Lower Egypt, held a coronation for himself not only at Thebes but at Tanis also (in the general vicinity of Port Said), in addition to his first assumption of the crown at Napata in the heart of Kush. This triple ceremony amply enchanced his celebrity and added greatly to the belief that the 25th Dynasty was one of phenomenal strength.

His fame became even more towering by the way he regularly reasserted the combatant power of Ethiopia over Egypt in his many sorties up and down the "Father of Rivers." The Egyptian army, with its core of Ethiopia's dreaded legionnaires, once again—as previously during the rule of Thothmes III—reveled in the universal fear and respect it received from other potentates of the world. In the Royal Court of the Temple of Ramses III at Thebes Tarharka had portrayed memorials of his victories in Asia over the Assyrians for it was during his reign that Sennacherib, their king, threatened to invade Lower Egypt but the Ethiopian war-hero's determined advance into the Middle East foiled the hopes of the Assyrians.

Tarharka's opening years as Pharaoh were so imposing militarily and diplomatically that nations of the East fancied that his vigor betokened the restoration of the traditional power and glory of the Nile Valley. Many nobles entreated him for pacts of non-aggression and the ebony Emperor was invited to become an ally of Hezekiah, King of Judah.[7] Erastosthenes, the Third Century, Greek geographer and librarian at Alexandria was quoted in Strabo as saying of Tarharka that he was, ". . . a warrior who . . . penetrated into Europe as far as the 'Pillars of Hercules' (Gibraltar)—that is as a great conqueror."[8]

Tarharka, following in his father's footsteps, showed his respect for the religion and the customs of the Egyptians by the expansive monuments he raised at Thebes. And in his Ethiopian capital he embellished and made even more resplendent the venerated temple at the Holy Mountain, "Jebel Barkel". "Tirhakah," penned Rev. G.A. Knight, "was a thorough Nubian, as his pronounced negroid features seen in sculpture attest . . .," and from all accounts he was an exceptional ruler who advanced the economic and cultural life of both Egypt and Ethiopia to such a level that a number of Africanists have marked him as without a rival among the Ethiopian Pharaohs.

One English Egyptologist extended him the "left-handed compliment" of saying that his years on the throne represented an "astonishing epoch of nigger domination" of Egypt. Anthropologist-archeologist D. Randall Maciver confessed, "It seems amazing that an African Negro should have been able with any sort of justification to style himself, 'Emperor of the World'".

Sir Wallis Budge, the one-time "dean" of Egyptologists, said of Tarkarka:

> . . .(he was) a capable and energetic king, and under his able rule the country, notwithstanding his wars with the Assyrians, enjoyed a period of prosperity for about 25 years. That he should have been able to offer such steadfast resistance . . .(to the Assyrian kings) says much for his capacity as a soldier and leader of men. There must have been something attractive in his personality, and his deeds appealed so strongly to the popular imagination, at all events in Greek times, that they were regarded as the exploits of a hero,

> and he had the reputation of being a great traveler as well as a great conqueror.[9]
>
> This resourceful leader left inscriptions which indicate that he conquered the Hittites and the Assyrians. His sway was so complete and his power was so absolute that he dubbed himself "Emperor of the World."[10]

The sages have written, "Ethiopia was ruined by its war with Egypt, whom she sometimes subdued and sometimes served." And in verification of this time-honored quotation there are many examples of persons holding the crook and flail of pharaonic power over Ancient Egypt whose visages were thoroughly African; who paid homage to the gods of the Upper Nile; and who were identified with escutcheons of the dark duchies of southern Egypt. There has even been the concession by many Egyptologists that the broad-featured, black-skinned rulers of Ethiopia held "that certain claim" to the throne of Egypt. And yet because of, in some cases honest doubt, and in other instances—for a mixture of racial and cultural reasons—there has been a running dispute about the "Negro'ness" of some of these members of royalty.

There is hardly any controversy, however, over the fact that the 25th Dynasty which impressed its will on Egypt in the Eighth Century B.C. was thoroughly Ethiopian, from Kashta the Kushite, through Piankhy, "the Bull who Conquerest Bulls," to Tarharka, the "Emperor of the World". There is no doubt from the artists' representations left of these overlords or from the ritual of their religious practices, or their deliberate revival of the linguistic and artistic styles of the Old and Middle Kingdom that these ebony ensigns considered themselves culturally and genealogically connected with Egypt's most noteworthy prior ruling families.

Indeed, in the space of the ten chapters making up this, Volume One, of *Black Manhood*—which might fittingly be subtitled, *The Building of Civilization by the Black Man of the Nile*—we have shown that many of the most salient developments and the cardinal personalities in the maturation of the human species and civilization effloresced along the banks of the Nile including the manufacture of tools, the beginnings of agriculture and man's control of fire. These flash points in man's creative growth and the pace setting, ingenious builders of Egypt's civilization have finally been credited to the pioneer folk of mankind's premier continent—Africa.

Human life began in Africa. In response to the imperatives of his early environment this earliest man was what we today would call a "black" man. The fossil, geological and archeological records of prehistoric times, among other proofs, leave it more than reasonably certain that *Homo erectus* followed the flow of the Nile—aptly nicknamed the "Father and Mother of Man"—from its beginning near the Olduvai Gorge, "Garden of Eden," in East Africa through its broad sweep into the Nile Valley. He developed new techniques for survival and more and more resourceful ways of managing much of the environment about him as he descended the Nile. In the course of evolutionary time, he stood more and more erect, grew in cranial capacity and capabilities and developed the rudiments of human culture—in terms of managing agriculture, learning to live according to set patterns and regulations, and practicing various industries, et cetera—all of which culminated in the first civilized state, Egypt.

Up to that time, through the millenia of Ancient Egypt's governments—and, as we have seen in this Chapter, even after the demise of native Egyptian rulership—men and women of African birth or extraction have played an intense, always perceptible, oftimes dominant role in the rise of the civilization we inherit today.

Who can any longer wilfully overlook the negroid visage of the Sphinx—representing King Khafra, a member of the ruling family which gave birth to the timeless pyramids of Egypt? What honest scholar can continue to pigeonhole the copious archeological and literary proofs of the consanguinity of the Middle Kingdom emperors with the black Galla nation to the south of Egypt? And only those who are deliberately duplicitous would refuse to publish the consistently recurring attributions of Negro parentage, or African physiognomy, to a host of the rulers of "the greatest royal family to ever rule anywhere.

We have only been able in these manuscripts to scratch the surface of the renaissance of Ancient Egyptian history which is sure to come now that black men around the world have shown such a heightened interest in their past, and therefore, in their future.

Notes

1. One notable exception to this almost total absence of records was a stela from the reign of Ramses II (Nineteenth Dynasty) which read, in part, "Nubia was governed by a Viceroy of Kush, through whom the Nubians were able to place the priest Herihor on the throne of Egypt in 1035 B.C." (Twenty-first Dynasty).

2. Samuel M. Jackson (ed.), *The New Schaff-Herzog Encyclopedia of Religious Knowledge*, Vol. IX (N.Y.: Funk and Wagnalls, 1911; p. 249), considered Shabaka to have been the King So mentioned in 2 Kings 17:4 in the Holy Bible.

3. Margaret A. Murray, *The Splendor That Was Egypt*, (Copyright © 1963 by Margaret A. Murray by permission of Hawthorn Books, Inc. N.Y.), p. 65.

4. Compare this exclamation with Isaiah 30:17 in the Holy Bible. It reads: "One thousand shall flee at the rebuke of one." There are those men-of-letters who have expressed the feeling that the Biblical rendition is but a re-statement of Piankhy's original counsel.

As mentioned at length in several other Chapters, experts have shown many concurrences between Egyptian literature and scripture from the BIBLE. Space has not permitted us to compare all of them but if we take one more example—Akhenaten's "Hymn to Aten" ("Hymn to the Sun") and Psalms 104:1-24—we can readily see the proximity of ideas and words. One stanza of the "Hymn" reads:

How manifold it is, what thou hast made!
They are hidden from the face of man
O sole god, like whom there is no other!

Thou didst create the world according to thy
desire, whilst thou wert alone: all men, cattle and wildbeasts,
Whatever is on earth, going upon its feet,
And what is on high flying with its wings.

While Psalm 104:1-24 (et passim) reads:

O Lord my God, thou are very great!
. . .who has stretched out the heavens like a tent . . .
who makest the winds thy messengers,
fire and flame thy ministers.

Thou didst set the earth on its foundations,
so that it should never be shaken.
Thou makest springs gush forth in the valleys;
they flow between the hills,
By them the birds of the air have their habitation;
they sing among the branches.
From thy lofty abode thou waterest the mountains;
the earth is . . .satisfied with the fruit of
thy work.

Thou dost cause the grass to grow for the cattle,
and plants for man to cultivate,
that he may bring forth food from the earth . . .

O Lord, how manifold are thy works!
In wisdom hast thou made them all;
the earth is full of thy creatures.

Many Orientalists feel this Psalm was inspired by the Egyptian lyric poetry.

5. A symbol of people of inner-Africa.

6. Arthur Weigall, *Personalities of Antiquity* (Freeport, N.Y.: Books for Libraries Press, 1928), pp. 186-187.

7. Judah was a kingdom in the southern part of ancient Palestine. It is also mentioned in the *Holy Bible* in connection with the invasion of the duchy by Zerah, the Ethiopian (2 Chr. 14:9-14). Zerah was identified by Jean F. Champollion with Osorkon I, the second king of the 22nd Dynasty of Egypt. See, James Hastings (ed.), *A Dictionary of The Bible* . . .(N.Y.: Charles Scribner's Sons, 1902) IV, p. 977.

8. Arnold H. Heeren, *Historical Researches into The Politics, Intercourse and Trade of the Carthaginians, Ethiopians and Egyptians* (Oxford: D.A. Talboys, 1832), I, p. 411.

9. E.A. Wallis Budge, *The Egyptian Sudan: Its History and Monuments*. 2 Vols. (London: Kegan Paul, Trench, Trubner & Co., Ltd, 1907) II, p. 41. Sir Wallis also included this reference in his footnote to this quotations, "See Strabo , i, 3, 21 and xv. 1, 6 where he quotes Megasthenes."

10. This paragraph was also attributed to Budge in Lerone Bennet Jr.'s, "The African Past," *Ebony Magazine* (Chicago: Johnson Publishing Company, Inc., July 1961), pp. 35-36.

PHILOSOPHY AND SCIENCE OF THE EGYPTIANS

PHILOSOPHY AND SCIENCE OF THE EGYPTIANS

Introduced by Ivan Van Sertima

What Theophile Obenga sets out to do in "African Philosophy of the Pharaonic Period" has never before been attempted on such a scale. His intimate knowledge of ancient Egyptian, Greek, Arabic and Bantu languages, his wide continental grasp of the fundamentals of African philosophical systems and cosmogonies, uniquely equip him for this formidable task. We are fortunate that Habib Sy, private secretary to the late Cheikh Anta Diop, has selected for us the keystone chapters in Obenga's magnum opus. What we have translated here is but a day in the week of his work. We are even more fortunate to have at hand the brilliant team of translators, Elizabeth Clement and Irene D'Almeida, thanks to whose meticulousness we miss almost nothing from the author's French. It is amazing that, in a work steeped in concepts so subtle in their abstraction that at times they can only be telegraphed to us by evocative image and symbol, the light can still be made to shine through to us from that ancient African galaxy with the pristine freshness of lightning.

Since the introduction by his colleague, Habib Sy, is fairly comprehensive, I shall only dwell on one aspect of Obenga's work, which we hope to continue translating and publishing in our second issue on Egypt. Nothing has more impressed me than his illumination of how the Egyptians conceived of "the morning of times", the first moment of the Universe. It is so modern, so far in advance of much later visions of god and order and time and the dawn of consciousness. As in modern physics, the early Africans of Kemet saw primal matter—the Nun—uncreated before the Creator. They placed matter at the very beginning, preceding the emergence itself of a Rational Being or Consciousness. It is this Being which did not make but reconstituted the primal elements and set the present Universe on its course. Of course man may never know what really happened in the very first moment of time but the poetry, the intuitive logic, the marvellous consistency of this conception, its amazing modernity in terms of its parallels with the theoretical explanations of modern physics, must surely give us pause.

What is particularly interesting for us is how much of this thinking finds a meeting point with the thinking of the Dogon, the Bambara, and other mainstream African philosophical systems. Obenga's work will help to establish a familial relationship between these and the cosmogony of the ancient Egyptian. It will also force a reexamination of Egyptian philosophical thought within an African context. For, as he so persuasively argues, "Egyptology can only arrive at a real understanding of Pharaonic civilization—its deepest "soul", its "mysteries", its human specificity, its originality, its true face and all its "strangeness" the day it encompasses Ancient Egypt in its native and original context, the Black African world."

* * *

In "Science and Symbol in Egyptian Medicine" Charles Finch introduces us to a series of remarkable breakthroughs in medical science which establishes the primacy of Egypt in this field and its profound impact on early medical science among the Greeks, who are often credited for things which they themselves would not claim. Hippocrates, for example, never gave himself the title of "father of medicine" and only a fraction of the large hippocratic written corpus can be directly attributed to him. As Finch points out, he cannot even claim authorship of the fabled hippocratic oath.

Hippocrates, in fact, did not even advance as far as the Egyptians before him. He never mentions pulse-taking and he thought of the brain as a gland. Several operations performed by the Hippocratic school are identical with those described centuries earlier in the Edwin Smith papyrus and can be explained by cultural borrowing from Egypt. The scientific renaissance of the Alexandrian period was really due, Finch shows, to the Greek world's access to Egyptian discoveries. Under the Ptolemies all the available Egyptian scientific papyri were collected in the library of Alexandria. Many of the so-called Greek discoveries were rediscoveries of Egyptian thought. A glaring example of this is pulse-taking. Herophilus, a Greek of the fourth century B.C. is credited with discovery of the diagnostic application of pulse-taking when more than a thousand years earlier an Egyptian surgeon was translating this from an even earlier manuscript—the Book of the Heart and Vessels.

Finch focuses on the medical papyrus that became known by its finder—Edwin Smith. Breasted, the translator of this papyrus, demonstrated that although it was written during the 18th dynasty (1500 B.C.) it was a later copy of an Old Kingdom manuscript. It reflects knowledge, Finch claims, that goes back even before the Old Kingdom. "It is a mature scientific document, the culmination of a long period of anterior development. Here are the first anatomical descriptions presented in a systematic way . . . [It is also] "the record of a scientific vocabulary in evolution". What is strange is that it is only one-third of the original manuscript. It deals exclusively with the skeletal and soft tissue parts of the head and neck. The surgeon who copied it in the 18th dynasty broke off at the 48th case, covering only the upper third of the body—the head and neck.

Finch makes a close analysis of the cases, selecting those most worthy of comment. His conclusions are startling. The early Egyptians had accurately mapped the internal anatomy of the head, identified and mapped the location and function of certain important cortical centers of the brain, a feat not to be achieved again until the 19th century. They mapped the sites of the brain where sounds are processed to give hearing. What is even more remarkable is that case descriptions of certain conditions with their clinical consequences are given that are almost impossible to detect or describe fully without modern X-rays. No longer can it be claimed that it is with the Greek begins the clinical approach and that these early books are just rambling collections or unsystematized observations. The clinical method begins here. It involves a method identical to our own involving an examination, a diagnosis, a prognosis and a treatment (where indicated). All of this, thousands of years before Hippocrates.

* * *

Karenga's essay "Towards a Sociology of Maatian Ethics" is a major contribution to the sociology of Egyptian religion and ethics. For many readers Maat is a new concept but it would be wrong to try and define it in an easy word or two. Karenga enters into all of its implications—cosmic, social and personal. I turn to Theophile Obenga, the distinguished African linguist and philosopher, to suggest with a lucid, poetic and evocative brevity the range of its meanings on all of these planes.

"Maat is the primordial principle which gives order to all values . . . it is, indeed, part of the cosmic order, part of the Truth-and-Justice that allows the Pharaoh (for all that he is and symbolizes) to protect the country from disorder, from chaos, from famine, from misery. In addition, all men living in society must conform to Justice and Truth, to Maat, the supreme Virtue, guide and measure of all human activity . . . Seen as a kind of preestablished harmony in the cosmos, Maat is order, Truth-and-Justice, Felicity supreme, inviting man in society to do and speak, think and act, to live and die according to what is true, normal, harmonious; according to virtue, with all the hieratic, traditional, transcendental, imperative and absolute implications that that word "virtue" takes on in the Black-Egyptian mentality." (see Obenga in this issue).

What Karenga is attempting (and this is just a preliminary to a larger, full-length treatise) is a comprehensive study of Egyptian ethical literature. These texts are the oldest treatises on social order in the world.

Why have they been neglected when they provided much of the basis for later moral orders, like the Judeo-Christian? Max Weber, the famous sociologist, points to the contributions of Maat to Ancient Judaism. Breasted in *The Dawn of Conscience* goes further, tracing the evolution of human conscience and ethics in Egypt and demonstrating Israel's great debt to Kemet. Breasted's comment on this matter, quoted by Karenga, is worth reiterating.

"The ripe social and moral development of mankind in the Nile valley, which is three thousand years older than that of the Hebrews, contributed essentially to the formation of the Hebrew literature which we call the Old Testament . . . Our moral heritage, therefore, derives from a wider human past enormously older than the Hebrews, and it has come to us rather *through* the Hebrews than *from* them."

What were the main reasons then for the academic and intellectual mistreatment and neglect of Maat?

Maat suffered from the fact, Karenga tells us, that its last centuries coincided with the first centuries of the Christian religion which not only supplanted it but at times systematically attacked it. It was actually outlawed by Theodosius in the fourth century and again by Justinian in the sixth. Egyptian symbolic use of animals in religious expression was not understood by European invaders and seen by them as zoolatry without any serious attempt on their part to understand the theology and ethics which embraced and explained it.

A study of Egyptian ethics makes us realize, for example, how the use of slaves to build the pyramids would have been repulsive and abhorrent to the values of a pharaoh or an Egyptian bureaucracy. What was usual then but is unusual today is the conception of the bureaucrat or government executive as the embodiment of moral virtue. The idea of the man or woman in power as a source of purity and righteousness rather than as a source of tyranny or corruption would rouse a chuckle of impious skepticism among many today. But the concept and practice of righteous leadership started with the Pharaoh himself, the king, whom Jacob Carruthers calls "the temporal embodiment and agent of Maat". There is an emphasis in the sacred teachings—the Sebait—on government by moral example and on leaders as moral exemplars. Ethical philosophy, in fact, evolved first as a philosophical portrait of the king and later diffused through society, becoming a paradigm for human behavior in general.

Karenga also touches on the concept of person-in-community in Egypt, not person as an individual, alone and alienated, but "a moral agent who derives and develops his/her identity, purpose and direction from and through his/her community", a concept summed up beautifully in the African dictum "I am because we are and because we are therefore I am" A basic assumption of Maatian philosophy is that the self-actualization of humans is only achieved in relation to others. "The perfectability and authenticity of the human being lies in his/her sociality. Righteousness is only real in personal and social practice." Karenga contends that the moral teachings of Kemet introduce and sustain a strong communitarian conception of the human personality.

This essay, on which the section ends, is illustrated by line-drawings of the scribes (seshu), some of whom were prime ministers and priests. Their writings restated, reinforced and elaborated the ethic of Maat.

THEOPHILE OBENGA: AT THE FOREFRONT OF EGYPTO-NUBIAN AND BLACK AFRICAN RENAISSANCE IN PHILOSOPHY

Jacques Habib Sy

Theophile Obenga's recent contribution on "African Philosophy in Pharaonic Times: 2780-330 Before Our Era"[1] is a milepost in the history of African philosophy. Indeed, for the first time in Africa's modern history, and thanks to the pioneering efforts of Cheikh Anta Diop, G.G.M. James, and before them all the lineage of great African thinkers, a fundamental breakthrough, a new decipherment of African philosophy is undertaken with a view to demonstrating two major truths.

The first truth is that Egypto-Nubian philosophical texts belong to Black Africa's intellectual and cultural tradition and should not be seen any more, particularly by African philosophers, as "religious" or "ethno-philosophical" endeavours. World opinion has been misled by centuries of eurocentric and manipulative reading of Black pharaonic philosophical legacy. This heritage had reached mankind's highest stage of intellectual speculation in ancient times. It is through this African philosophical tradition that emerged for the first time in history "a systematic reflection on the world, nature and man himself"[2], thus, creating the conditions for the birth of Greek philosophy.

The second truth submitted to our historical consciousness by Obenga is that the philosophical systems, literature and orature of Black Africa and pharaonic Egypt are identical and belong to the same cosmogonal and mythological matrix. Obenga argues that the primary material on which such systems are based "must be read and interpreted as African philosophy's historical sites and theoretical foundations"[3].

Following G.G.M. James[4] and Cheikh Anta Diop's[5] brilliant essays on Africa's impact on the Indo-European, on the Hindu, Chinese and Oriental philosphical world views, Obenga has translated and re-interpreted major hieroglyphical, Greek and Latin texts of the Old World. The Egyptian texts represent our ancestors' original and authentic philosophical speculations on Life and Death, Truth and Justice, social order and chaos, happiness in eternity, the Beyond and sidereal immensity, the emergence of matter, the absolute beginning and its relationship to primordial waters, *Nun* and *Maat*, created and uncreated beings, existence and existing, being and nothingness, astronomy, sciences, medicine, ethics and cosmogenesis, etc.

This enormous patch of mankind's first interrogation on being and matter, on the struggle between life and death,and the ultimate reason for being is unveiled by Obenga not only through pharaonic civilization's sacred texts (hieroglyphics means in ancient Greek "sacred scripture") but also through original texts written by the first Greek and Roman philosophers and Black Africa's orature, the ancient wisdom surviving in oral tradition and mythology, written into philosophical texts.

A first-hand reading of the ancient African and Greek texts is necessary to demonstrate the anteriority of African philosophy and to show how the so-called "Greek miracle" can only be explained by reference to the thought of the early Egyptian. The cast and character of early Egyptian thought itself can only be understood within an African psycho-cultural context for it springs essentially from what may be called "an African personality."[6]

In his quest for an objective understanding of the beginning of beginnings in philosophy, Theophile Obenga has translated and commented upon twenty seven hieroglyphical texts or fragments of texts—some of which were translated for the first time by a Black African scholar—and seventy seven original texts used in his demonstration as "complementary material". This long voyage through time and space enables the reader to understand the hidden meaning and secret codes contained in the Texts of the Pyramids (2,780 to 2,260 B.C.E.—Old Kingdom), the so-called Book of the Dead (2,300 to 1,700 B.C.E. between the First Intermediary Period and the Middle Kingdom), the Bremmer Rhind papyrus (dated 400 B.C.E., but already existing in all likehood several centuries before), the Shabaka Inscription (2,780 to 2,260 B.C.E.), the Amenophis IV Hymn to Atum (1,372 to 1,354 B.C.E.—18th Dynasty), the Coffin Texts (2,060 to 1,785 B.C.E. Middle Kingdom), etc. The testimonies of ancient Egyptian themselves—pharaohs, architects, scribes, Nubian masters in ethics, literature, history and philosophy—and the statements of Greek travellers and historians, Roman rulers and legislators, all direct witnesses to the Nile Valley's achievements, are skillfully presented by Obenga as factual and irrefutable evidence of Black Africa's preeminence in philosophy.

In his introductory remarks, Obenga suggests the following major periods in the history of African philosophy:

1. *The Egypto-nubian pharaonic period* (2,780 to - 2,260 B.C.E.: Old Kingdom). The beginnings of philosophy were then attested by the texts of the Old Kingdom, the *Maxims* or *Teachings* by Kagemni and Ptahhotep.

2. *The patristic period* (1st to 5th centuries). The schools of thought created in Alexandria, particularly under the Ptolemais and the Roman Empire, in Cyrene, Carthage and Hippone were all under the leadership of Egypto-Nubian priests relying on thousands of years of philosophical, ethical and scientific traditions. All the major Greek, Maghrebin and Roman philosophers of this period (Demetrius of Phalere, Diodorus Cronos, Hegesias, Euclid, Manethon, Aristarchus of Samos, Archimedes, Sextus, Plutarchus, Socrates, Plato, Aristippus, Erathostene, Claudius Maximus, Saint Augustine, etc) were, either directly through long periods of apprenticeship or indirectly through thousands of books copied from the Nubian temples, initiated by the Black priests, keepers of their forefathers' secret teachings.
3. *The Maghrebin Muslim period* (7th-14th centuries) is best represented by Ibn Badjdja's *Treaty of the Soul* (XIIth century, Fez, Morocco), Ibn Battuta's ethnographical and geographical studies (14th century, Tangiers, Morocco) and the great Ibn Khaldun's *Muggaddima* (14th century, Tunis).
4. *The medieval Black Muslim period* (15th-17th centuries). During this period universities (Sankore, Timbuctu), schools and centers of higher learning (Gao, Djene) were created when the great Sudanese empires were at the peak of their glory. Mohammed Bagayogo and Ahmed Baba (16th century) kept alive among the West African intelligentsia the Islamic schools of thought.
5. *The modern and contemporaneous Black African period* (18th century to present time) emerged with thinkers like the Ghanaian Anton Wilhelm Amo who taught during the 18th century in German universities and Edward Wilmot Blyden (19th century). There are also the more recent schools of thought among continental and diasporan Black African philosophers.[7]

Focusing his vast erudition on the pharaonic period, the Congolese scientist has translated and commented on major ancient texts that were wrongly classified as part of the "religious" wisdom of the Nile Valley civilization.

Texts of the Pyramids (par. 1040, 1230, 1466 and 2063)

Obenga suggests that 45 centuries ago, pharaonic Egyptians sought to speculate on "the question of questions", that is "the question of origins, the question of knowledge of the world, the cosmos and its advent".[8]

In paragraph 1040 and 1230, it is said that before the birth of Pharaoh himself and before the Universe came into being there was Nun (*Nnw*). Nun was neither God-the-Creator nor Nothingness nor Chaos: it was the primeval, absolute and abyssal water in the depths of which already existed matter, a matter which would come into being through and by itself, a matter conscious of itself and ready to create.[9] Here the Egyptian Nun precedes and gives birth to the *demiourgos*, the supreme architect of the world. Unlike the idea of creation as suggested by the Platonians or the Sumerians, with suffering immanent to the origin of being, the ancient Egyptians held that Primordial Idea came out of the Nun with intrinsic power and creativity, thus generating the gods themselves and all forms of life. Therefore, the origin of origins, matter, under the form of inaugural water, was seen by Black Egyptians as a vital principle, the principle of principles, the matrix of the Universe, the pre-existing, the already existing and that which would come into being.(hprt)

Obenga suggests that this text represents the first attempt ever undertaken during the long history of *homo sapiens sapiens* to speculate on the origin of matter and to explain life on earth and primordial phenomena in Nature as a distinct part and at the same time the innermost being of matter. Consequently, the pharaonic Nun (2500 B.C.) predated the notions of the stoics on substance/water and substance/"seminal reason" (300 B.C.). In all likelihood, those late systems of thought were borrowed from the philosophers of the Nile Valley. One is astonished by the sophistication of the dialectical approach already present in the Texts of the Pyramids.

Paragraph 1466 of this Text is seen by Obenga as the living proof that Egyptian thought was dominated at the outset by the "idea of a universe before the present universe, another universe before the demiurge himself and all his creation".[10] Here "the universe and god are distinct, the universe being anterior to the demiurge, but a universe most different from the one that we are able to know or that we presently know".[11] Drawing a parallel between this text and Plato's *Timaeus*, Obenga observes that the Greek author foresaw the creation of the cosmos by God. But in Plato's speculation God created only fleshes, the secondary material, not the primary material. Recognizing that before the existence of God there was matter, Plato and Aristotle ("Before the birth of the world always existed the constitution that was anterior to it", *On The Sky*, I, 10, 280 a) were echoing 2000 years later the brilliant premonition of the Ancient Egyptian.

Obenga suggests that the most outstanding fact that deserves attention is the emergence, in the Nile Valley, three thousand years before our era, of a radical thought on not-being, thought conscious of itself and projecting itself at the vanguard of a truly beautiful philosophy of the beginning of beginnings.[12]

Paragraph 2063 a-b deals with fundamental elements in the cosmos: water, fire and air. Obenga argues that these elements were seen by ancient Egyptians as concrete substance like the earth and a symbiosis of matter and spirit, a copulation between objective and subjective or between positive and negative as prescribed by the law of the diagram of opposites. Thus 2000 years later Thales, Anaximander, Anaximenes and Heraclitus merely re-initiated a philosophical speech almost identical to the one transmitted to them by the Egypto-Nubian priests, based on metaphysical speculations on Nature's constitutive elements. The Nile Valley civilization had already offered to the world a philosophical vision recognizing the harmony between matter and spirit.

Book of the Dead (chapters XVII & LIV)

Commenting on the beginning of Chapter XVII, Obenga suggests that the concepts of Nun (*Nnw*), "primeval Chaos" and "primeval waters", all point to the idea that "all dimensions of human existence had a beginning, a genesis, except absolute water taken as such in its very absoluteness, that is to say the humid, aqueous, fertilizing, creative abyssal depths".[13] This emphasis on *water* is of the same order as the cult of water omnipresent in Black African cosmogonies. The publication by Marcel Griaule of his "Conversations with Ogotemmeli", a Dogon sage, revealed to the world the complexity of African philosophical speech recorded and stored for centuries in the powerfully trained memories of elders and priests, with extremely rigid codes to guarantee its authenticity. When the French explorer Griaule asked Ogotemmeli "what life is there in earth", the latter answered: "Earth's vital force is water". Among the Bambara, water is the sacred seat for the *Nommo*, the primordial Verb. The Akan as well as the Bantu-Venda show a similar reverence for water as the place for the first act of creation and the primary receptacle for primeval waters, these guarantors of the vital force contained in animal, vegetal and human reigns.

Obenga holds that such world views are rooted in the same African ecosystems dominated by rivers (the Nile, Niger, Senegal, Congo and Zambezi rivers), water rains and water sources, the power and generosity of which fertilize the earth and give cadence to the rites of daily life in African agrarian societies.

Theophile Obenga further points out that all these waters represent the Nun, symbol and source of life, supreme landmark for progress and Creation's eternal re-beginnings. They are the living expression of human copulation with the cosmos and the forces governing its evolution. The same principle on primeval waters is omnipresent in Greek mythology, suggests Obenga. This is another indicator of Black Africa's and Black pharaonic Egypt's impact on the very foundations of the Indo-European world view.

Chapter LIV entitled *The Initial Egg* is seen by Obenga as evidence of the profound cultural unity between Africa and ancient Egypt. Indeed, in ancient Egypt where it was called *swht* ( ) as well as among the Bambara in Mali, the Fali in Northern Cameroon or the Abure in Ivory Coast, the reference to the primordial or cosmic egg belongs to the same cultural substratum.

Papyrus Bremmer Rhind (pp. 69-70)

This papyrus dated -400 is described by Obenga as an "eminently philosophical" text with strong recipes on logic and dialectics, the means *par excellence* for reasoning. The theoretical notions on existing (*hpri*), existence (*hprw*), to exist/to be (*hpr*) were the object of philosophical speculations on being, the relationship of man to himself and cosmos (a Greek word meaning the world and derived by Aristotle from the same principles that he learnt himself during his long journey in Egypt). That which existed brought Being into existence. The Existing presupposed Being. The Existing was self-generated by its own energy, its own vital force (*ba*) in a cosmic movement whereby it was the only and unique one to exist "during the anterior era" (*m p3wt t3*). Unicity and multiplicity belonged to the same matrix, existing and reason. The phenomenon of creation was seen by ancient Egyptians as a demonstration for the existence of existing. At the origin was Reason followed by primeval Verb (the Nommo). Ra was a god-creator whose existence came from *Nun*, the radical principle of all principles, the unfounded foundation for all foundations. Before the "mystery" of origins, the ancient Egyptians set the question of questions in philosophy, that is "what is?", "Why being rather than nothingness?".

Obenga's original interpretation of the Bremmer Rhind Papyrus leads him to the conclusion that *philosophy* as it is known today was practised by ancient Egypt who passed it on to its most notorious Greek students. The notions of unicity, origin and primeval Receptacle as developed by the ancient Greeks originated from the Nile Valley. Interpreting ancient Egyptian philosophy as a religious discourse is a relatively recent attempt to downgrade the validity of the world's oldest philosophical thought. Before such a dangerous ideological abuse, Obenga suggests that African Egyptologists should read the ancient Egyptians texts from a different perspective, rejecting Western mainstream ideological interpretation of the Nile Valley philosophical texts as religious thought. Obenga shows that the notion of Maweja Nanjila (the Oldest Spirit) among the Luba in Zaire, the use of the sacred scarab with ontological and metaphysical meaning in many parts of Black Africa as well as the presence of lizard (*asha* in ancient Egyptian language), falcon (*bik*; Horus), buffalo (*ka*), leopard (*aby*), hippopotamus (*khab*), crocodile (*meset*), etc, in Black Africa's philosophical and cosmological world view correspond in ancient Egypt to the same symbols, notions and philosophy on existence and being.

Inscription of Shabaka (Old Empire, -2780 to -2260)

This ancient text was translated by the author for the first time in his book *L'Afrique dans l'Antiquite* in 1973. The exercise was then seen by the late Professor Cheikh Anta Diop as "a decisive turning point" in Nile Valley studies. Obenga's skillful translation and interpretation of the Shabaka hieroglyphic text (Sudanese period) shows the conceptions of creation by African priests in Memphis more than four thousand years ago. The initial principle of genesis, creation and their relationship to primeval intelligence and the supreme order that regulates the universe were the target of a national effort aimed at apprehending the birth of the cosmos and human condition in the sidereal abyss. Thanks to the Egyptian philosophers in Memphis, this effort led to man's first design of a model of thought integrating the mineral, vegetal, animal and human realms. Obenga shows how and why the African philosophers of the Nile Valley had been affected in their vision of the cosmos by the discovery of the laws regulating and guaranteeing a certain equilibrium between human, vegetal and animal beings. The relationship between these distinct beings or elements was seen by ancient Egypt as a harmonious symbiosis. There prevailed over all a rational eternity, policing itself, and an awesome power radiated through each being, each creature, even the gods, by *Nun*, the Principle of principles.

The vital principle present in each phenomenon was also a reflection of *Ra*'s transmutation into the *Ba*, the souls, seats of the vital force present in every being. Obenga compares this supreme architecture of the universe and its laws of motion to the cosmogonal order sought by the Dogon through the concept of *Amma* (or *Amon, Amon-Ra* in ancient Egypt and *Imana* in Rwanda), the Supreme Builder and Creator of men, plants and animals, Creator of *Nommo* ("the master of water") and *Yeban* (master of the earth, guarantor of the principle of humidity in the earth). The Dogon texts as transcribed by Dieterlen and Ganay in 1942 are identical to the Shabaka Inscriptions. In both of these speculations Ptah and Amma represent more than a religious revelation, they symbolize the rational initial principle, that is to say, an ordering of the universe, indeed of the world, that transcends the narrow perception of a world governed by gods in full competition with human beings and nature.

It is through this grand reflection on the principle of the unicity/multiplicity of God that mankind discovered the principle of monotheism symbolized in ancient Egypt and Black Africa by Amon, Atom, Khepri and Ra (sun-God). These efforts must be seen as man's first attempt at a systematic philosophy. The same symbolic artifacts (water, fire, universal energy, infinite, one and multiple, etc) were used by Thales, Anaximenes and Anaximander when thousands of years later they were initiated by Egyptian wisdom into the art of philosophy. The origin of the principle of Logos must be found not in Greece but in ancient Egypt through the doctrine of sovereign speech as a source for energizing and ordering reality.

The *Hymn to Atum* written by Amenophis IV—Akhnaten (1372 B.C.E. to 1354 B.C.E) and transcribed by Obenga is another strong indication that David's famous Psalm #104 in the Bible was directly inspired by Akhnaten's poetry and philosophical efforts. Obenga suggests that the *Hymn to Atum* reveals that pharaonic Egyptian thought was a solar thought. It tried "to understand the Sun as life, eternal strength and duration inseparable from man's destiny on this planet."

It would be tedious to explore with Obenga the vast body of ancient African philosophical literature unearthed through written texts as well as oral tradition. The innovation in Obenga's massive work lies in his definition of philosophy. Through a critical scrutiny of ancient systems of belief, moral precepts, hymns to the glory of beauty and power, metaphysical interrogations on the true meaning of life, Obenga suggests that the existence of philosophy supposes "any conquest of the unknown, an impact on destiny". Philosophy is certainly "intellectual certitude" and the need for "moral perfection" but it is also "knowledge and action hereafter", "abstract imagination", "creation of new ideas" and "a permanent concern for knowing man, time, space, number, the nature of things, etc".

Obenga suggests after Cheikh Anta Diop[14] that the study of philosophy should be historically dated. But Obenga goes beyond the traditional definition of philosophy (a thought conscious of itself and able to separate myth from concept) accepted by Diop.[15] While recognizing the genetic relationship between ancient Egyptian and Black African systems of thoughts, Obenga asserts that most of the ancient hieroglyphical texts should not be seen simply as religious thought since they represent a philosophical speech of a high order. Not only had ancient Egypt conceptualized a complete world view, he contends, but it built also the first body of philosophical literature in antiquity. When Cheikh Anta rejects the contention that the later African and Egypto-Nubian cosmogonies should be considered as "a philosophical thought conscious of itself",[16] Obenga invites Africans to understand that the Nile Valley is the foundation, the primordial source of Greek and hence Western philosophy.

By deciding to write a history of the origins of philosophy, Obenga shatters the notion that "African thinkers do not do conceptual analysis" and that therefore they "do not do philosophy"[17]. With a wealth of detail, he shows from primary and secondary evidence that a definition of African philosophy should necessarily take into account the scientific discourse of ancient Africans. Astronomy, geography, medicine, ethics, metaphysics, dialectics, belong to the same cultural substratum.

Obenga shows, as did Cheikh Anta in his mathematical inquiries on Black African and ancient Egyptian scientific apparatus,[18] that culture, science and philosophy belong to the same matrix. This reality is well expressed by Henry Olela who recognizes the fact that "philosophy was not and is not immune to the universal human process of sharing and assimilating of cultural traits, (and that) philosophy was not, is not, culture free"[19]

Obenga claims, after G.G.M. James, but with the help of original hieroglyphical texts freshly interpreted, that the roots of ancient Greek philosophy lie in the philosophical, cultural and religious thoughts of the Nile Valley which antedated it by thousands of years. A genetic appraisal of African and Egypto-Nubian philosophies cannot be performed in isolation from what has been inadequately termed as "Greek philosophy". The philosophical body of ancient Greek literature should rather be seen as a Greek interpretation of Egypto-Nubian philosophy and as a Greek apprenticeship in African philosophy.

Using "complementary sources", that is, testimonies of ancient Greek scholars themselves, Obenga shows that the source of philosophical knowledge must be found in Black Africa's philosophical thought, still showing important conceptual vestiges in texts of the oral tradition.

When Theophile Obenga's entire work is published, it will generate a new basis for the discussion of African philosophy, its historical premises and future status. It will indeed force historians of African philosophy to evaluate Cheikh Anta's claim that in pre-colonial times African cosmogonies had reached a point where they were close to a thought conscious of itself but that they "became degraded and fossilized". The book will surely compel African scholars to weigh Cheikh Anta's basic position on the history of philosophy, which is that "it would be excessive to take (the African cosmogonies) today as philosophical systems. Likewise, it would be a mistake to launch a false debate on them".[20]

The foundation for such a reappraisal on the evolution of African philosophy must of necessity be based on the points of convergence between Diop and Obenga. Both of these great African thinkers recognize the genetic relationship between African, ancient Egyptian and ancient "Greek" philosophies. They both agree that African philosophers should stop this senseless debate about the existence or non-existence of an African philosophy and focus their attention on the cultural and philosophical meaning of hieroglyphical and original Greek and Latin texts. Without this they may not be able to decipher the philosophical enigmas present in African thought since remotest antiquity.

Biographical Notes

1. Unpublished manuscript, Libreville, 1988.
2. Op.cit., p. 5.
3. *Ibid.*, p.5.
4. James, George. *Stolen Legacy.* N.Y.: Philosophical Library,
5. Diop, Cheikh Anta. *Nations negres et culture.* Paris: Presence Africaine, 1954.
6. Obenga, Th., *Op.cit.*, p. 7.
7. *Ibid.*, pp. 1-4.
8. *Ibid.*, p. 21.
9. *Ibid.*, pp. 21-22.
10. *Ibid.*, p. 26.
11. *Ibid.*, p. 28.
12. *Ibid.*, p. 12.
13. *Ibid.*, p. 33
14. Diop, Cheikh Anta. *Civilisation ou Barbarie.* Paris: Presence Africaine, 1981, p. 13.
15. *Ibid.*, p. 387.
16. *Ibid.*, p. 405.
17. See: Wright, Richard A. *African Philosophy: An Introduction.* University Press of America, p. 21.
18. *Cf. Civilisation ou Barbarie* and "Comment enraciner la science en Afrique: exemples walaf (Senegal)" in *Bulletin de l'I.F.A.N.*, T. 37, ser. B, #1, 1975
19. Olela, Henry, "The African Foundations of Greek Philosophy" in Richard Wright, *op.cit*, p. 56
20. See, *Civilisation ou Barbarie, op. cit.*, p. 405.

AFRICAN PHILOSOPHY OF THE PHARAONIC PERIOD (2780–330 B.C.) (Excerpts from a work in translation)

Théophile Obenga

INTRODUCTION

The history of African philosophy follows quite clearly the framework of the general history of the African continent. Chronologically, we are able to distinguish these periods:

1. Pharaonic *Egyptian* philosophy. This is the time of the Old Kingdom (2780—2260 B.C.), with the *Pyramid Texts*, the *Shabaka Inscription*, the *Maxims*, or *Instructions* of Kagemni and of Ptahhotep;

2. *The Thinkers and Philosophers of Alexandria, Cyrene, Carthage and Hippo*. The Alexandrian School, which existed for more than six centuries under the Greek kings of the family of Ptolemy and under the Roman Empire, attained its greatest glory between 323 and 221 B.C., with such men as Demetrius of Phalereus, the sophist Diodorus Cronus, Hegesias (who philosophized extensively on death and was, ironically, called an apologist for suicide), Euclid (who found in Egypt, cradle of geometry, works that would serve in the composition of his own works—his *Elements* is considered a geometry text par excellence), and Manetho, the Egyptian historian. Aristarchus, the Alexandrian scientist, affirmed the movement of Earth on its own axis and around the Sun, and attempted to measure the distances from the Earth to the Moon and the Sun (see the treatise *On the Magnitude and Distance from the Sun to the Moon*). Another philosopher of this period was Archimedes who created the statics of solids and fluids. There were also Sexte the Empiricist, a philosopher and physician, and Plutarch, a priest at Delphi who travelled in Egypt and visited several times in Rome, who preserved the principal ideas of Aristarchus' system.

The Cyrenaic school, founded by Aristippus (a student of Socrates), played a great role in the development of Greek thought with its very free thinkers such as Theodorus, nicknamed "the Atheist", and Aristippus the Younger, grandson of the founder of the school. Aristippus' ideas exercised their influence on men like Bion of Borsthenes, and Euhemerus, who died at the end of the third century

B.C., and whose philosophical radicalism was considered scandalous (he taught that the gods of mythology were nothing more than kings of some distant epoch, deified by the fear or admiration of people). The Cyrenaic school (Libya) made happiness the goal of philosophical contemplation, advising that all action be measured in the same way intellectual pleasure is; it recommended, on the one hand, respect for laws and development of the mind (disinterested speculation), while, on the other, insisting upon the practical applications of science. Aristippus and his disciples were "intellectuals" in a sense of the word very near that of modern times.

Eratosthenes, a mathematician, astronomer and philosopher of the Alexandrian school, was from Cyrenaica (Libya). In Mediterranean antiquity, only one true measurement of the Earth was known, that of Eratosthenes. This Cyrenian's measure of the circumference of the Earth is an achievement of "classical" ancient history. For Eratosthenes the measurement of the Earth's circumference is the result of three distinct operations: establishing and placing a fairly short arch in relation to the total meridian; making an actual measurement on the ground of the corresponding length of this arch; and, finally, making the calculation which is a comparison of these two elements.[1]

In the 1st century A.D., a philosopher came out of Carthage, Claudius Maximus (he once presided over a witch trial). Others who illustrated first century thought and letters are Javolenus Priscus, Apuleius, Lollianus Avitus, Fronton, Pertinax. In the third century there are Balbin and Grodien; in the fourth century, Avienus, Symmachus, Vindicianus; in the early fifth century, Macrobius, Symmachus the Younger, and Volusianus, friend of Augustine, as was Rutilius Numatianus.[2]

Saint Augustine (Thagaste [Souk-Ahras] in Algeria), November 13, 354—Hippo (Annaba, ancient Bone, in eastern Algeria), August 28, 430) mediated at length upon time as experienced by man, and its relation to the divine, the absolute, the Eternal which gives meaning to the ephemeral.

3. *Maghribian Philosophy*. Examples include Ibn Badjdja (died in Fez in 1138), author of the *Traité de l'âme* [Treatise on the Soul]; Ibn Battuta (1304-1377), the ingenious Moroccan ethnographer and geographer; and, above all, the great Ibn Khaldun (Tunis, 1332-Cairo, 1406), the historian, sociologist and philosopher. He revealed his philosophy of history in the *Prolegomena* (the *Muqaddima*), an imposing discourse on the history of the universe which is, in reality, a veritable encyclopedia of the sciences;[3]

4. *The Medieval Philosophical Schools of Timbuktu (University of Sankoré), Gao and Jenne*. These were bastions of black Muslim culture at the time of the great Sudanese empires (Ghana, Mali, Gao, Songhay) where the Islamized peripatetic tradition was perpetuated. The University of Sankoré was represented by Professor Mohammed Bagayogo, who taught the eminent Ahmed Bada. Numerous direct accounts report that the learned Ahmed Bada had close to 1600

volumes in his library, and that "he was celebrated in Maghrib and his renown spread far and wide".[4]

5. *Modern and Contemporary African Philosophy*. Some of the important names of this period are Anton Wilhelm Amo,[5] Ghanaian philosopher of the eighteenth century who studied and taught both philosophy and the "liberal arts" (non-theological sciences), from 1727 to 1747, in the three great German universities at Halle, Wittenberg and Iena; G.W. Leibniz whose thoughts prevailed through his disciple Christian Wolff (1679-1754), a philosopher and mathematician; and Edward Wilmot Blyden,[6] black thinker of the late nineteenth century.

Contemporary African philosophy has already shown several streams of thought which have been well delineated, for example, in Zaire:[7] the "culturalist" stream which undertakes a philosophical approach to African realities; the hermeneutic stream which exploits African language, art and symbols through means recently developed in the West; the diachronic stream which attempts to elaborate the history of African philosophy as a subject area for research and instruction; and, lastly, what is called the "functional" stream which contemplates the inclusion of science and technology in Africa's social, economic and cultural realities, at the same time attempting to establish the fundamental perspectives of a new epistemology. Professor Kwasi Wiredu,[8] a contemporary Ghanaian philosopher, believes the comparison between African philosophy and Western philosophy to be "a great existential urgency." He is addressing a requirement formulated long ago by Marcel Griaule: "It is becoming increasingly necessary to begin, from this day on, to place Bambara thought, Dogon thought and those of Asia on the same level of importance as that of classical antiquity."[9]

The present investigation will address Pharaonic Egyptian philosophy as it is taken from the original, authenticated texts, translated and with brief commentary. It is imperative that both their language and pharaonic texts themselves be taken seriously; they will themselves speak, for themselves and for us, as *Tradition*, henceforth to be blended—as is an accepted heritage—into our contemporary philosophical practice.

The texts selected and explicated over the course of this work have to do with man, society, the world, the universe, the absolute. They represent an historical reconstruction of African thought—part of our Black African tradition—which must have a place in the whole of philosophy and the future of the principles, languages, and methods of world philosophy. The texts bear witness to an exacting thought which is itself aware of its importance, a kind of heightened vigilance at the "centermost" heart of a culture and environment. It is a living thought, for more than twenty centuries in search of truth and justice, social order, internal human equilibrium, cosmic intelligence, and true well-being—lasting, unalterable and eternal. The Pharaonic Egyptians began early on—at the very beginnings of their nation's history—to contemplate their destiny. To their technical know-how and their feats in construction, they added from the outset an organized and systematic thought, a moral consciousness, an ethic.

These are the materials which our research and teaching must now cultivate, read and interpret for what they have been: the historical bases and theoretical foundations of African philosophy thousands of years before the birth and flower of ancient Greek philosophy. In fact, Greek philosophy enjoyed at its origins an "eastern contribution", specifically Chaldean and Pharaonic. "The first Hellenics to philosophize on things divine and celestial—Pherecydes, Pythagorus and Thales, for example—were all agreed that they were the students of the Egyptians and the Chaldeans, and that they [themselves] wrote very little."[10]

The rediscovery of Ancient Egypt since the early efforts to decipher hieroglyphics by Champollion (1790-1832) has furnished additional justification for asserting that "Egypt was the cradle of philosophical speculation as we know it."[11]

Indeed Champollion, former professor at the Universities of Bristol and London, alludes to the Shabaka Inscription which, thirty centuries before the Greeks, speaks of an ordered concept of life in a language which suggests a tradition already several centuries old.[12]

The African philosohical tradition which briliantly initiated a systematic reflection on the world, nature and man himself, constitutes at the same time and in the same motion the foundations of Greek Philosophy.[13]

An Egyptologist of the stature of Serge Sauneron would not write the following absent-mindedly or complacently: "Also, the revelations of Ogotemmôli, or the 'Bantu philosophy' carry precious elements which aid us to better understand certain aspects of Egyptian religious thought; but we can expect no help in this domain, or precious little, from a reading of Plato . . ."[14]

The Pharaonic Egyptian world is, in effect, intrinsically African: "Black worship is the latest expression of the dogmas of Ethiopia and Egypt."[15]

In the proceedings of the celebrated international symposium organized by UNESCO in Cairo in 1974, we can extract these two passages characteristic in their convergent pertinence and accuracy:

> "Professor Vercoutter remarked that, in his view, Egypt was African in its way of writing, in its culture and in its way of thinking."
>
> "Professor Leclant recognized the same African character in the Egyptian temperament and way of thinking."[16]

We know all what the Institut de Papyrologie et d'Egyptologie of the Université de Lille III owes to Prof. Jean Vercoutter, director of the French archaeological mission in the Sudan (Isle of Saï, Mirgissa). professor at the Collège de France, Jean Leclant is now a member of the Institut de France and Permanent Secretary of the Académie des Inscriptions et Belles-Lettres. The acknowledgment and assessment of such scholars of Egyptology can only be a matter of reality, of science, and not, as is often the case, of ideology.

It is, therefore, legitimate to read Black African thoughts and cosmogonies with an orientation toward the Nile Valley; reciprocally, Egyptology can only arrive at a real understanding of Pharaonic civilization—its deepest "soul", its "mysteries", its human specificity, its originality, its true face and all its "strangeness"—the day it encompasses Ancient Egypt in its native and original context, the Black African world. Because "the psychology and culture revealed by the Egyptian texts identify themselves with the Black personality."[17]

In summary, a history of African philosophy is possible. But such an elaboration is very demanding. It requires, in fact, a perfect knowledge of Ancient Egyptian, of Greek, Latin and Arabic over and above the techniques and methodologies unique to the history of philosophy. Without Greek, there can be no true understanding of Western philosophy; without Ancient Egyptian, it is not possible to reconstruct the authentic Black African philosophical tradition in its most ancient, most fundamental temporal dimension.

The work of our generation, therefore, must not be articulated exclusively around "ethno-philosophy" and Tempels' work. On the contrary, it is a difficult and complex effort which must explore all the cultural centers of the Black African world, examine the unifying ties of all these centers, re-establish the African philosophical tradition itself within itself. This effort must, therefore, renovate the teaching of philosophy in black Africa, develop a philosophy favorable to freedom and progress in Africa, and take an active part in the great philosophical and scientific problems of the contemporary world.

Philosophical monographs and journals are being produced in Black Africa alongside purely literary works. The breach thus opened by the contemporary Black African intelligentsia has created a "situation" on the philosophical front. We want to contribute here to the enormous need for growth in this philosophical endeavor by examining for a moment the long history of African philosophy, specifically the beginnings of this history with Pharaonic philosophy.

CHAPTER ONE

I. THE UNIVERSE BEFORE THE PRESENT UNIVERSE

Translation

> Before the birth of the world there already existed the constitution which was anterior to it.
>
> Aristotle, *On the Heavens*, I, 10, 280a.

A. The Non-created Beginning

Translation

> [W]hen I was born in *Nun* before the sky existed, before the earth existed, before that which was to be made firm existed, before turmoil existed, before that fear which arose on account of the Eye of Horus existed.
>
> *The Ancient Egyptian Pyramid Texts* §1040

Commentary

The great pyramids of Giza were built between 2700 and 2600 B.C. Their construction presupposes the existence of solid mathematical and astronomical foundations. (An in-depth treatment of the great pyramids can be found in the painstaking work of Jean-Phillipe Lauer.)[1]

These temple-tombs honor the dead god-king.The pyramids are, therefore, the center of a cult. The famous texts known as the "Pyramid Texts" appear for the first time in the tomb of Unas at the end of the Fifth Dynasty. The same texts, with some variations, additions or omissions, are found again in the pyramids of the principal successors of Unas: Teti, Pepi the First, Merenre and Neferkare-Pepi II.

Professor Jean Leclant, member of the Institut de France and a professor at the Collège de France, foresees—along with many of his collaborators—a truly complete version of the *Pyramid Texts*. At our request, Prof. Leclant was kind enough to forward copies from K. Sethe, the German Egyptologist, as well as his own texts from the French Archaeological Mission in Saqqarah led by Leclant himself.

The text in translation which is briefly cited here is a gripping mythological description of the genesis, but, of even greater interest, it is a description of the world before creation. The time of myths, of course, is the pre-history of philosophy, a time when the substance of mythology is not yet recognized as such. "Myth is linked to the first knowledge man acquires of himself and his environment; to an even greater extent, it is the structure of that knowledge."[2]

More than 2500 years before Christ, the Pharaonic Egyptians had grappled with the question of questions: the question of origins, of understanding the world, the cosmos and their advents. Their thinking was exceptionally radical. *Before* the birth of the Pharaoh himself and of all the Universe (gods, sky, earth, death and its meaning), there was neither Creator-God nor Nothingness nor Chaos, but *Nun*. There was that which resembles nothing now known or made. An abyssal water, absolute, *already* containing all the raw materials which would be assembled by the demiurge, a kind of latent consciousness at the heart of this primordial water. At its origins, then, the ancient Egyptians posited matter as abyssal water. This matter would become conscious of itself, and manifest itself as creation, that multiform figure of all which is, all which exists or will come into being.

Beginnings are very difficult to image, most especially the creation or advent of the world. For Plato, in the *Timaeus*, the demiurge pre-exists the birth of the world, and he creates it out of his goodness. Well before the platonic creation, in Sumer, Enki is the organizer of the world, the Creator of life, but he acts upon a world already formed, the origin of which is not explained. We know by heart the creation story of the Bible: "In the beginning, God created the heaven and the earth. And the earth was without form and void; and darkness was upon the face of the deep. And the Spirit of God moved upon the face of the waters." [KJV, Genesis 1:1-2] Out of India we read in Chapter 1 of the *Laws of Manou*:

> There was That, made of darkness, indistinguishable, without characteristic, indefinable, unknowable and entirely inert./Then appeared Lord Swayambhu (the Autonomous), the unevolved which evolved That from raw elements. He it is who, harnessing his energy, dissipated the darkness.

The *Popol-Vuh* (Chapter 2) of the Maya-Quiche puts darkness, silence, and stillness with light pouring forth at the beginning; "there was nothing."

So we see the Demiurge (Plato), Enki the Ordainer (Sumer), God or Elohim (the creator-gods of the Bible), and the Lord Swayambhu—all of these are born or appear independent of their own creations, above and before all of their work. In Egypt, the demiurge comes out of *Nun* and sets about creating. There is no independence of the Creator (the Demiurge) in relation to the creation or birth of the world. In Ancient Egypt it could be said that the Idea came forth, endowed with power, out of the primal matter. In the beginning there was matter—

water—which, though weak, obscure, and abyssal, was powerful, dynamic, capable of creation and innovation, begetter of the gods themselves and the rest of creation. All manner and all forms of Life are the issue of the initiating, non-created water, the originator. in fact, of all subsequent development.

The Pharaonic explication for the origin of all that is—the Universe and all that exists in it—is strangely current in that it places from the outset not God or the darkness but matter in the form of the inaugural water.

In our times, one of the fundamental explications of the origins of the Universe is this: A diffuse electromagnetic field, a vestige of the beginnings of the Universe, indicated that the Universe began with a state of infinite density made up of free elemental particles. There was no gravitation in the beginning of the Universe, only a matter which in its nature is quite different from that of our present universe. It is the purely radiative period of the Universe dominated by radiation. The Universe was truly opaque. Thermal balance between radiation and matter is upset at a temperature approaching 3000 degrees K. Then comes the period dominated by matter which is a by-product of radiation; the Universe expands and, one after the other, the galaxies distance themselves one from another.

At 5000 degrees K there can be no solids or even liquids. Thus, there was no "primordial water", no "primitive ocean". Only free atoms—or still smaller particles, electrons, protons—can exist.

The Ancient Egyptians had the enormous advantage over Sumerian mythology, the platonic creation, and the biblical genesis of not positing a creator-demiurge distinct from the creation and preceding it. Quite the contrary, they placed matter at the very beginning, a matter in its nature quite different from that which was to follow from it. However, the weakness of their understandings was to image this abyssal matter at this very earliest point, at the beginning of beginnings, to be "liquid". The essential, however, remains: matter before all other things, before the demiurge and the other gods created by it and after it; before the sky and the earth, before living beings and their evolution, before the totality of the Universe, before the cosmic All.

According to these pyramid texts, everything is, therefore, issued from matter (a primordial matter difficult to know) and—immediately and quite naturally—the image of water came to these thinkers on the banks of the Nile, vital axes of Upper and Lower Egypt, from the time of their pre-dynastic ancestors.[3]

Nun (2500 B.C.) brings to mind on a number of points the *seminal reason* of the Stoics (c. 300 B.C.).

For the Stoics the substance at the outset is itself without quality; it is the primordial matter which later becomes water through the intervention of air. The "seminal reason" of the world remains in that which is liquid; it renders matter able to receive its capacity for the generation of other beings.[4]

The following demonstrates these similarities:

Ancient Egypt	Stoicism
1. 2500 B.C.	C. 300 B.C.
2. *Nun*, primal matter, abyssal, primordial water	*Substance* without quality, becomes *water* through air
3. *Atum* or *Ra* alone in the Nun: the demiurge is creative reason and is itself issue of the abyssal matter; the development of all creation follows (gods, earthly and heavenly worlds,etc.)	*Seminal reason of the world* the mutation of the substance without quality into water (through air) begets in the very makeup of the liquid the creative reason which thus renders matter capable of generation

* * *

B. The Universe Before the Present Universe

Translation

> The King's mother was pregnant with him, (even he) who was in the Lower Sky, the king was fashioned by his father Atum before the sky existed, before earth existed, before men existed, before the gods were born, before death existed . . .
> *The Ancient Egyptian Pyramid Texts §1466*

Commentary

The present Universe, the Whole of what is, consists of just that—all that is in the world and in nature: the dwelling place of the dead, the upper sky, the habitable earth, the oekoumene, man and the planet Earth, the ancestral gods and the deified ancestors themselves, and death.

As a rule, the human spirit endeavors to understand how all this came to be. Often enough, a demiurge—a creator—is imagined at the very origins of the Universe. The creation or advent of the world and all it encompasses is the work of a demiurge. This is a recurring pattern throughout the world's mythologies.[5]

Egypt's idea of a universe before the present universe, another universe before the demiurge itself and all of its creation is really quite novel. Here we move into an area in which our familiar quest for "genesis" and "origin" does not exist. There is simply "matter", as yet without a theme, absolute in its sovereignty, before it is implicated by the demiurge in a process of becoming. It is a kind of "spatial milieu" before time and space, beyond time and space. All that is perceptible will express itself out of and within this "milieu" in the begetting of the Universe, such as it is today perceived, known, explored, and exploited by human ingenuity.

The Ancient Egyptians imagined and thought about an origin ("presence", "matter", "spatial milieu still incapable of expressing what is real, what is perceptible") *antecedent* to the origins of the Universe. It is really quite extraordinary to think that this idea emerged in the Old Kingdom, 2780-2260 B.C.

In the *Timaeus*,[6] God did not create the matter of bodies, that is, that undetermined substance. This primal matter of the world, undeterminable though it is, had always existed. Did Plato consider God the author of the primal matter? In the text we see only that chaos precedes the world. Yet the activity of God was absent from chaos and, therefore, God was not its author. The divine operation which produced the world (cosmos) takes place the moment God separates the four elements (that jumbled group of constitutive elements of corporal matter existing for all time in the primordial substance) and then reunited them harmoniously. God separates these elements, he then reunites them, but he does not make them.

It is important to note that Plato (428 or 427-348 or 347 B.C.) does not put forth the existence of the cause—errant and unreasonable—when he wants to explain that which is before the divine acts of the demiurge, and he does not for a reason.

God only produced the secondary matter of the elements. He is not the author of their primal matter.

Well before the Greek philosopher, the Ancient Egyptians conceived of a matter preceding the origin of the world, uncreated but uniquely capable of becoming the material of creation: the spatial milieu of all existence.

This must be emphasized: Pharaonic Egypt conceived of a universe before the demiurge itself and all its universal progeny, all its creative activity. The universe and the creator-god are distinct, the universe being anterior to the demiurge; but it is a universe which is very different from the universe we can know or now know. That is a truly original thought.

This highly philosophical thought of something which is not born and which existed before the birth of the world was also noted, long after the Egyptian philosophers, by the always penetrating Aristotle: "Before the birth of the world there existed the constitution which preceded it."[7]

Before generation and decomposition, there is the unbegotten, the uncreated; that which is not begotten and which the Egyptians referred to by the word *Nun*, substratum without face or form, the amorphous.

To Cicero (106-43 B.C.), as another example, the world and god were merged. The world is an animate being endowed with consciousness, intelligence and reason. It is a wise and reasoning being. The world is god: "The world is god and the whole power of the world is contained in that divine element."[8] Egyptian thought in placing a world apart from god before all advent (all genesis, all birth, all generation, all creation) is much more "materialistic" than the Stoic explication which is taken up again by the Latin writer.

Saint Augustine (354-430), the most celebrated of priests of the Latin Church and who greatly influenced Western theology, does not, of course, place uncreated matter before the creator. For this philosopher and theologian, God created matter at the same time he created his other works.

Everything which exists (*universa mundi moles*) is the work of God: all that is the world's mass, the sun, the moon, the stars, the sky, the earth, the birds, the land-animals, man. But the Creator-God did not create his works (*opera*) from nothing (*ex nihilo*), nor from a matter which was unknown to him or which would have been created before the Creator-God himself. The matter out of which came the cosmic All is a *concreated matter*, that is, a matter created by God simultaneously with the work he created out of this same matter. Original matter and the creatures issued forth from it by the creative power of God are, in fact, one and the same thing. Original matter became diversified in forming the cosmic All through the work of God. This is how Saint Augustine expresses it:

> For they were made of nothing, by Thee, not of Thee; not of any matter not thine, or that was before, but of matter concreated, (that is, at the same time created by Thee) . . .[9]

The ancient Egyptians, on the other hand, posited a material state before God and all his creation. What is more, God the Creator and Engineer himself came out of this primordial, *uncreated* matter. The ancient Egyptians affirm the *uncreated* before the god-demiurge, and Saint Augustine the *concreated*, that which is created by God at the same time as the creatures. The concept of the uncreated or non-created is more materialistic than that of the concreated.

Somewhere around 3000 B.C., with [the pharaoh] Menes, there emerged the Pharaonic institution which unified the country from North to South. This was the organized program for draining and controlling the waters of the Nile by a systematic irrigation plan; the writing which served to regulate the rites and the calendar, and to transmit to distant parts the messages of Pharaoh. At about this same time the Egyptians created a most impressive architectual grouping—the Pyramid and its prodigious monument complex—moving from the use of sun-dried brick and wood to quarried stone.

In this same period, the Old Kingdom, the first philosophy was born, as vigorous as the geometry of the pyramids, as precise as the Pharaonic ritual, from the outset, a thoroughly dynamic system. At the beginning of that which is as we now perceive it (according to the demiurge creation), they said, there was the non-created.

The Egyptians organized their explication of the world around this idea, a notion which is inherently philosophical. This is an extraordinary stroke of inspiration dating from the earliest moments of Egyptian thought: "From this uncreated come the forms of the creation."[10]

It is thus that Egyptian thought supports the architecture of the temple, presides decisively over the construction of the pyramids, imposes an almost absolute rigor in the conduct of essential rites—it is, to be sure, an idea of an uncreated aware of its potential which makes of the pharaonic system a *dynamic* system, in the largest and strongest sense of the word.

C. Nun, Primeval Water

Translation

> I am Atum (*ink Itm*) when I am the One to exist (*m w^c m wn*) being alone in *Nun (w^c r.k m Nnw)*, and I am Râ when he rises in glory (*ink R^c m h^{c}i.f*), when he commands and governs what he made (*m s^3 hk^3 ir.n.f s^3*).
> Who is this?—It is Râ (*n·R^c*).
> I am the great god who came into existence out of himself (ink nṯr c^3 hpr *ds*.f), the water (*mw nw*, "the waters"), *Nun (Nnw nw)*, father of the gods (it.f nṯrw).
> Others say (ky dd, "other to say"): It is Râ (*R^c nw*).
> He composed the names of his limbs (km^3 rnw nw h^{c}w.f); then came to exist the gods who follow him (hpr my nn nṯrw imyw smswt).
> Others say: It is Râ in his rising in the eastern horizon of heaven (ky *d*d R^c nw m wbn.f m ^{3}ht i^{3}btty nt nwt).
> I know yesterday (iw.i rh.kwi sf) and I know tomorrow (rh.kwi dw^{3}t).
> Yesterday is Osiris (*ir sf Wsir*) and tomorrow is Râ (*ir dw^3 w R^c nw*).
> The enemies of the master of the Universe were destroyed (htm.tw hftyw nw nb-r-*dr*).
> There he reigns with his son Horus (im.f hn^c nw s^3.f Hr).
> *The Book of the Dead*, Beginning of Chapter 17.

Commentary

The Book of the Dead[11] is the oldest illustrated book in the world. It contains texts of differing lengths, written nearly always on papyrus, bearing the name and the titles of the deceased. These texts are the prayers which accompanied the dead to the tomb.

A fair number of the texts date back to the First Intermediary period of the Middle Kingdom, covering the period from apprxoimately 2300 to 1700 B.C.: they are *The Egyptian Coffin Texts* and the *Books of Two Paths*, gathered by the great Dutch Egyptologist Adriaan A. de Buck.[12]

The beginning of all beginnings is *Nun*, the absolute waters which contain the seeds of creative power; the ocean anterior to every manifestation of life and movement; the "prior world" which holds within it already matter; the "chaotic" milieu of forms-inwaiting; the pre-temporal, unformed form of the creator-god.

The genesis will then be the placement of the cosmos out of this primordial water which precedes the god-creator who, itself, emerges from this same water origin. The demiurge will gain consciousness of itself in this "primordial Chaos" before coming into being, by and of itself, and will then set to work.

Thus, in Pharaonic thought all components of the present world—the gods and the stars, the earth and the sky, the world of the living and the dwelling place of the dead—all the dimensions of human existence had a beginning, a genesis, a commencement. The one exception is the absolute water, placed in its own absoluteness in the abyssal depths, humid, aqueous, inseminating, creative.

What does all this mean in the context of a rural, agrarian society? We know how central a role *water* plays in the Black African cosmogonies of the Dogon of Mali, for example, or the Bambara, the Akan, or the Bantu-speaking peoples of Central, Eastern and Southern Africa. There are precise accounts of these revelations:

1. *"Water" and "Nummo" Among the Dogon*

"Ogotemmêli used the terms 'Water' and 'Nummo' indiscriminately.

'Without Nummo,' he said, 'it was not even possible to create the earth, for the earth was moulded clay and it is from water (that is, from Nummo) that its life is derived.'

'What life is there in the earth?' asked the European.

'The life-force of the earth is water.'"[13]

2. *The Central "Waters" of the Heavens Among the Bambara*

In the beginning, the waters which came from the "well-springs of heaven" and flowed upon the earth were pure, clear, generous and graceful . . . Now, only the falling rainwater has conserved its character, especially the first rain of the rainy season. Thought to be an excellent purifier, it is called *dane sandyi*, "inseminating water", because it brings their souls, *ni*, to the grains; the earth, sterile and "empty", becomes full and fecund, plants are reborn, animals and insects reproduce[14] The Bambara believe that before taking on its corporal being, *Faro* was a "voice". It was the Reorganizing Word of the Universe. Where is it? In the water. "When he sent the running waters down to earth, he had long been manifest solely by his voice. He had no embodiment at all and, as he was in need of an appropriate matter from which to carry out his accomplishment, he waited for his moment in the waters of the sea."[15]

3. *Tano, Water God of the Akan of Ghana and the Ivory Coast*

"The great river god of the Gold Coast (Ghana) and of the Ivory Coast is *Tano* or *Ta Kora*. In the north of Dahomey (Benin), the Niger is called *Kora* and signifies 'the Immense'.

"Like other gods of the earth, *Tano* is said to be a creator. This can be seen in an excerpt taken from the inscriptions on a drum:

> 'The current (of the river) has its origin in the creator.
> 'He created all things,
> 'Pure, pure Tano.'"[16]

4. *Vortex, Site of the First Creation Among the Bantu-Venda*

> "According to the Venda (and most other Bantu people) the site of the first creation is a great vortex situated to the east."[17]

Here again we see the East and water as the place of the first creation, the creation of water itself and the great river god, the waters of origin, the life-force of the earth. Water—always water, the Great Waters, primordial creative energy, ultimately deified by all of Black Africa since Pharaonic antiquity.

This fascination with water is tied to the fertility of the fields and the fecundity of beings and of things. Hence, the myths and ideas must, of necessity, be found in their living context which is why they are given flesh and blood, they become incarnate.

From Pharaonic Egypt up to the present day, Black African thought has explained the origins of existence through the concept of primeval waters. We have seen *Nun, Tano, Nummo*, "the father of the gods" (*it ntrw*, as the Egyptian text said). All are explained by images of water in the environment: streams and rain, seas and lakes, the water of great rivers. All these waters emerge from the cosmic water to their force and their soul to all things. Water exists and brings to existence.

The waters of the Nile, the Niger, the Senegal, the Congo, and the Zambezi (with its rainbow and its eternal falls) come from *Nun*, from within it. Agrarian Black African societies since their highest Antiquity have lived at the cosmic level, by the plan of the Great Waters which, tirelessly, from season to season, day to day, permit them to live out their lives and rituals. Thus the life-giving flood of the Great Waters is *Nun* reclaiming and recreating, reclaiming and recreating. We are in a world of Repetition, a world of Continuous Creation. Rituals, essential gestures, assure that man is in time with the cosmos and an agrarian rite can only be efficient if it is at once both technical and spiritual.

Nun is a structure, a progression. It gives ontological consistency to the primitive world of the creator-gods. *Nun* puts in human terms the principal requirements of being in the world, all the while "residing" in the distance and in its own mystery (outside time), a numberless number, truly transcendent, indeterminable. It is, in short, Matter; the Matter before movement. *Nun* is the mind of the Absolute.

So, a Black African cosmogony exists. The facts here examined underscore in some detail deep historical relations across all regions of the African continent from the time of Pharaoh's Egypt. This cosmogony makes of the primeval water a creative principle, and perhaps Black Africa tradition in some small way influenced Thales whose thinking also finds roots deep in the "Homeric" myths of the East.[18]

D. The First Egg

Translation

> O Atum (*i Itm*), grant me the sweet breath which is in thy nostrils (imi n.i t^3w n*d*m imy fn*d*.k)! I am the Egg (ink swht *t*y) which was in the Great Cackler (*imyt Gn-gn Wr*); and I guard (*iw(.1) s^3wt*) this mighty thing with which Geb has opened the earth (hprt *t*wy ᶜ3t wipt Gb r t^3): if I live, it lives (ᶜnh.i ᶜnh.s). O to be young and live (nhh.i ᶜnh.i), and breathe the air (ssn.i t^3w)!
>
> I am he who separated that which was united (ink w*d*ᶜ i'ᶜbt.1); I circle (to protect) her Egg (phr.n.i h^3 swht.f). I am the morning of times (*bk^3.i n ^3t*) and of great power (wr phty). Seth (St*h*).
>
> *The Book of the Dead*, Chapter 54.

Commentary

The First Egg, the Mother Egg (the word "egg" has the feminine gender in Ancient Egyptian), contains the Breath of Life at the dawn of the world. This cosmic Egg so mysterious is the morning of the world being born, becoming.

We see again the notion of a cosmic egg in the great cosmogonic rituals of deepest Black Africa several examples of which follow:

According to the Bambara (Mali, West Africa), the earth has the form of an egg. Candidates for initiation are grouped in the round, bringing to mind the configuration, the geometry of the first egg.[19]

This is a matter of integrating man and the cosmos through rites and initiation gestures. Which means that no symbol, no geometric figure can be introduced gratuitously in such a context the mental outlines of which were put in place hundreds, even thousands of years ago.

Among the Fali of northern Cameroon a dwelling is the authentic reproduction, at the human scale, of a vast myth of origin—specifically, the primordial egg: "The single room of the main residence represents the primeval egg out of which came men's earth, square, a form which is represented by the rectangular courtyard; by its roundness, the edifice itself suggests the equilibrium of the world, just beginning but already organized."[20]

Reference to the origin myth of the cosmic egg is clear. The house, for the Fali, constitutes a total representation of the life of the Universe, following the complex symbolism of the First Egg. It is an incarnate, living philosophy, traced upon the ground: the African hut ties man to the absolute. Architecture becomes thought and thought architecture.

The separation of sky (*Nut*) and earth (*Geb*) by air (*Shu*) is again linked to the primordial egg myth. But the celestial vault always maintains relations with the earth and the activities of men, its inhabitants.

Among the Aboure of the Ivory Coast the egg of *Vlohue* (the temple cock) was used to determine the hour: "It is told that the egg of this bird, while full as it moves toward 6 and 7 o'clock, empties its substance a bit at a time as the sun rises in the firmament and is completely empty by noon. The egg becomes very light. This is the hour to interrupt the day's work to eat. In the afternoon, the egg fills anew with the setting of the sun to be full again toward 6 o'clock. This is the time to cease the work of the fields to return home."[21]

The egg, a beautiful symbol, is forever tied to the movement of the cosmos, particularly that of the sun which is everything for life on earth. Rural societies still bear evidence of the importance of the sun brought down through the centuries to the rhythm of life's cycles, natural and social.

The egg expresses here the idea of a wholeness, of perfection, of integrity, purity, of youth and of life. The egg points to the future, the world it will bring to life.

E. The Fundamental Elements: Earth, Fire and Air

Translation

> The waters of life which are in the sky come,
> the waters of life which are in the earth
> come, the sky is aflame for you, the earth
> quakes at you before the god's birth; . . .
> *The Ancient Egyptian Pyramid Texts*, §2063

Commentary

For most of Western Europe speculation was born in Greece out of the contemplation of nature.

Nature (the world) was thought of as a unity. Hence, the naturalism of speculation.

This is the age of the first Ionian philosopher, Miletus. In this period, the ultimate principle of the world is no longer found in either Chaos or the Ocean or the Night. The Milesian school sets forth a One which for Thales is *Water*, the thing out of which the world was formed; for Anaximenes it is *Air*; for Heraclitus, *Fire*; for Anaximander it is the Indefinite infinite (*aperion*)—not water, not air, not anything finite but matter nonetheless and, thus, still part of nature.[22]

These fundamental elements of the first Greek speculation had already been posited thousands of years before by the Egyptians:

Water (the waters of life which are in the earth and sky)

Fire ("the sky is aflame")

Air ("the earth shakes")

Chronologically, we see this:

a. 2780-2260 B.C., *The Ancient Egyptian Pyramid Texts* dating to the Old Kingdom of Egypt

b. Late 7th Century—Early 6th Century B.C., *Thales*

c. c. 610—547 B.C., *Anaximander*

d. 6th Century B.C., *Anaximenes*

e. c. 540—c. 480 B.C., *Heraclitus*

The Anteriority of Egypt is clear. It is also accepted as historical fact that Thales drew from the well of the Egyptians.[23]

Earth brings to mind concrete substance or "matter" (as do water, sky, fire and air), wheras god brings to mind "spirit". This opposition between "matter" and "spirit" does not exist in Ancient Egypt where nature forms a whole, matter anc consciousness intermingled. Water is a thing, it is living water, germinative, (water has the male gender in Egyptian); it is a force, a power, a divinity. Spirit and Matter are both modes of being part of Reality. The "object" ("the objective") is not separable, in Egyptian thought, from the "subject" ("the subjective"). The knowledge of what *is* is affirmed by the human spirit itself. Life is in matter. Organization is the general tendency of the universe which encompasses the totality of that which is, "spirit" and "matter".

It is Cartesian reductionism which irreconcilably and irreducibly placed matter in opposition to spirit: "The "matter-spirit" opposition is much more recent. It came along with the notion of matter as purely mechanical and geometric which dates back perhaps to Galileo, certainly to Descartes . . . This notion of matter purified of all spiritual element developed for the most part in France and in Great Britain."[24]

Today, the Real may be approached within a framework other than that of classical Physics, which has no experience with the time-space continuum and which treats phenomena "mechanically". Today, the duality of subject/object is no longer as much in circulation—the object has become inseparable from the subject, and the Universe is but representation, a Reality of spiritual essence. It is our spirit which reasons as it looks upon the world.

The Cartesian West has come back to these more inclusive approaches which have been advocated by Egypt and eastern thought for millenniums.[25]

Frequently, by virtue of its living character, Egyptian philosophy is confused with its religion. The gods are evoked, praised, and it is they who speak: "Thus spoke the Lord of the Universe", "Thus spoke Ptah", "I am Atum", etc.

But is Plato's philosophy in the *Timaeus*, for example, religion when it evokes the gods and goddesses before expatiating on the Universe, the birth of the world and the nature of man?

The text of this invocation of the divinities is as follows: "We must invoke the Gods and Goddesses with the prayer that our discourse throughout may be above all pleasing to them and in consequence satisfactory to us."[26]

To come back to the fundamental elements—these appear in the thought system of the Bambara of Mali apropos of the creation.

The ethnologist Germaine Dieterlen gives this commentary on the creation of the Universe as it was related to her by Bambara informants: "In the bosom of *yereyereti* (creative vibration) there was a spirit, *miri*; in that spirit, there was execution, *wali*: in execution there was the coming of things, *nati*; and in this latter, the going of things, *tali*. These four terms define as well the four fundamental elements of the creation, respectively, air, earth, fire, and water. Air and fire are male, earth and water are female."[27]

Hence the following table of correspondences:

Yereyereti/Creative Vibration

The Universe

miri, spirit	air	male principle
wali, execution	earth	male principle
nati, the coming	fire	female principle of things
tali, the going of things	water	female principle of things

* * *

II. ONTOLOGY AND COSMO-GENESIS

Translation

What all fundamental principles have in common is that they are the primordial source of either being, becoming or knowledge.

Aristotle, *Metaphysics*, 1, 1013a, 17 sq

A. How the Existing Came to Exist

Translation

The Book of knowing (m*d*3t nt rh) the forms of existence (hprw) of Ra (nw R^c) and of (thus) killing Apopi the snake (shr ^{c}3pp).

Thus spoke the Lord of the Universe (*d*d mdw Nb-r'*dr-d*d.f):

When I manifested myself to existence, existence began to exist (hpr.i hpr. hprw). I came to existence in the shape of the Existing who came to existence for the First Time (hprw.kwi m hprw n(w) hpri hpn ms sp tpy). Since I came to existence as the existence of the Existing, I therefore existed (hpr. kwi m hprw n hpri hpi.i). And it was thus that I came to existence (hpr hprw), because I was anterior to the Anterior Gods that I had created (pw n p3.n.i iw n*t*r p3wtyw irw. *n.i*), because I was anterior to these gods (p3.n.i. m m*t*rw *p3wtyw*), because my name was anterior to theirs (p3 rn.i), because I made the anterior era as well as the Anterior Gods (isw iri.i sp p3wt n*t*rw p3wtyw). I made all the things I wished to make in this world (irry.i mrwty nbt m t3 pn) and I expanded in it (wsh.n.i im.f). I tied my own hand (*t*s.n.i *d*rt.i), alone (w^{c}i.kwi), before they were born (önn msi.snò), before I spat out Shu and coughed up Tefnet (n iss.n.i m Sw nn df.n.i m Tfnwt). I used my mouth (*ini.n.i* r.i *d*s.i) and Magic was my name (rn.i pw Hk3w). I am the one who came to existence in (my) form of existence (ink hpr.n.i m hprw) when I came to existence as the existence of the Existing (*hpr.kwi m hprw nw Hpri*). I thus came to existence in the anterior era (*hpr.n.i. m p3wt t3*) and a multitude of forms of existence came to exist from (this) beginning (*hpr^{c}š3 hprw m tp^c*), (because before then) no form of existence had come to exist in this world (nn hpr hprw nbt m t3 pn). I made every thing (*iri.n.i irryy nbt*) alone (w^{c}i.kwi), before any being (other than myself) manifested itself to existence (nn hpr ky) to act with me in these places (*iriw.n.f hn^c .i m bw pwy*). There, I made forms of existence from the force (which is in me) (*iri.i hprw im m b3 pwy*). There, I created Abyss (*ts.n.i im m Nnw*) being (still) dormant (m nni) and not having found a place to stand up yet (*nn gmi.n.i* bw ^{c}h ^{c}.n.i. im). (Then), my heart proved efficient (3ht n.i ib.i), the plan for the creation came before me (sntt n.i m hr.i) and I made everything I desired to make, alone (*iri.n.i irry nbt w^c i.kwi*). I conceived the design in my heart (sntt n.i m ib.i) and I created another form of existence (*km3.n.i ky hprwx*0, and the modes of existence deriving from the Existing were many (^{c}š3 hprw nw Hpri).

Bremmer Rhind Papyrus, pp. 68-70

Commentary

The manuscript dates from the fourth century B.C., but it must have been written several centuries earlier.

The text is eminently philosophical, filled with great virtues and comprehension formulas which are nothing but logic and dialectics and constitute the tools of Reason *par excellence*.

As a close reading of the text shows, the author subjected himself to a strict "conceptual rigor":

hpr, kheper, intransitive verb which means: "to come to existence," "to become," "to change," "to transform," "to be in actuality," "to exist," "to be."

hpr-ds.f, kheper-djes.ef, "he who comes to existence by himself;" it is the epithet qualifying Ra, the sun-god;

hprw, kheperu, "shape," "configuration," "modes of being," "modes of existence," "existence" (*hpr hprw, kheper kheperu*, "existence came to be," "existence began to exist");

Hpri, Khepri or *Kheperi*, the Existing: the young sun-god in the form of a sacred scarab beetle;

Nb-r-dr, Neb-er-djer, "lord of the Whole," "Master of the Totality," "Lord or Master of the Universe;"

t3, *ta*, Coptic tŏ, "earth," "country," "world"; *m t3 pn, em ta pen*, "in this world;" literally: "in world this," (the demonstrative after what is being demonstrated). This is a recurrent semantic form found in Bantu languages:

Ancient Egyptian : m t3 pn
Bantu-Mbochi : mo tse *pha* (*t3, tŏ, tse, se*, si, same word)
French : dans ce monde
English : in this world
The Egyptian and the Mbochi are identical : *m/mo*,
tŏ/tse, pn/pha.

*w*ᶜ *i, wuâyi*, "alone", "unique." This must not be understood as "solitude" or "solitary isolation," but as the unique characteristic of the One Being, the absolute oneness of the One Demiurge. In many Bantu languages we have: *wo, wo-si*, means: "one," "alone," "unique" with the following dialectal variants: *poo, mo, m , i-mo-si, chi-m fi-m , f , mb , -m :p⟩f; p⟩b⟩w ; p⟩b⟩w ;*

p3(w), pa(u), "to have done in the past," is to be linked with *p3t* (*pat*), "antiquity." And we have : *p3.n.i, pa.en.i*, "I was anterior," "I had anteriority;" *p3 rn.i, pa ren.i*, "my name was anterior" (*rn*, "name"; in Coptic: *ran, rĕn, lĕn*; in Bantu: *rina, lina, dina, ina, zina*, "name");

n*t*rw p3twtyw (*nut, nuti*, "god" in Coptic,) the anterior gods," that is, the most ancient gods who exist from the beginning;

p3wt tpt, "the beginning of all time;" *p3wt*, the primordial time;" *p3wty, pauty*, "The Anterior God;"

m sp tpy, em sep tepy, "the First Time," "On the Occasion that came first," "the very First Time;" *sp tpy, sep tepy*, "the First Occasion," "the Creation;"

sntt, senett, "plan," "foundation," "design;"

km3, kema, "to create," "to generate."

As soon as it exists, the Existing brings existence into existence. It is immediate, a kind of sudden epiphany of being in its very manifestation. For the Existing, to be is to exist in actuality. It is through its own force (*ba*), its own energy, its own movement that the Existing comes to existence. The Existing is self-begetting.

He is the Absolute, the one who exists of itself, from the beginning, being "alone" in being, existing before the gods of the beginning themselves, before creation, before the things wished or desired by the One itself. It alone is able to exist "in the antecedent era" (*m p3wt t3*), that time anterior to the anterior gods (*ntrw p3wtyw*).

Out of oneness, the multitude will come forth. This represents a dialectic of the One and the Multiple: "The modes of existence derived from the Existing were numerous" (*âsha kheperu nu Khepri*). The Existing brings into being other forms of existence through love (*meruty; irry.i mrwty nbt m t3 pn*) and through his own will (öirio, "to make," "to want," "to act;" *iri.n.i irry nbt*) and, being alone (*wʿi.kwi*), through his own power. He is the absolute being; he is also love and will.

The being is also, and above all, reason: he conceives designs in his heart (*ib*), that is to say, in all consciousness and in all lucidity. And when reason has conceived everything, the plan for creation presents itself before the One, before the Creator, before his face (*m hr.i*, "before my face"), in all clarity, without confusion. Creation is an idea which is clear, neat, distinct, consistent with the creator, for he is the absolute, he is love, will and reason, and acting force, he is master of the totality, efficiency *par excellence*.

The ancient Egyptians call creation "the first Occasion" (*sp tpy*). It is an event which comes before all others. It is a primal event, but also a radical event, unique, brought forth by the love and will of the Existing himself, who pre exists everything, absolutely, who, in other words, is the eldest of the eldest. Through creation, the existence of the Existing becomes multiple, abundant, diverse. Creation is a general event which produces everything that is. But creation does not create the demiurge which is anterior to creation's action, that is to say, anterior to creation itself, anterior to designs and plans coming from its heart, its kindness, its reason.

An inaugural act, creation also serves as proof, as demonstration of the Existing's existence: "I exist, therefore existence exists." For the Existing, to manifest oneself to existence is to bring (*iri*) other forms of existence into being, it is to create, to make (*km3*). Thus, human beings imagine the demiurge with senses: it (the demiurge) uses its mouth (*rŏ*), its hands (*drt*), its heart (*ib*). what is conceived in the heart (which, for the Ancient Egyptians is the seat of intelligence, reason, intellectual perception) is uttered by the mouth. Thus, at the beginning there was Reason, and only later came the Word. Even before bringing into being, concretely, by uttering the name (*rn, ran, lĕn*) of what is about to be, the demiurge first conceives what will be through the power of the word, the efficiency of creative speech.

The first point of departure is the Egyptian *Nun*, the foundation and the *raison d'être* of all that comes later. It is at once the material and formal cause, the efficient and the final cause of everything, of all gods and all their creatures. Abyss is not a receptacle with a contents like that of the *Timaeus* (52d 53c): it is the absolute indifferentiation, having no form that could be described or known, but Abyss gives being to Ra, existence, and existence exists from the moment of the manifested existence of Ra. It can be said that Ra is a creator god. But little is known of the Abyss from which Ra emerges and manifests itself. The Abyss is the fundamental principle among all principles, the foundation of all foundations but is itself without foundation, a kind of somnolent darkness (it is necessary, after all, to find an image for the Abyss), hence Ra (the deified Sun) emerges to act, to bring into being all forms of existence.

Thus, in the fourth century B.C., the Pharaonic Egyptians had thought through, felicitiously and with finesse, the primordial question underlying all philosophy: "What is?" "Why is there being (Abyss) rather than nothingness?" "What about the absolute being?" These questions are at the very center of philosophical preoccupations.

Thus, *philosophy* in the strictest sense of the word, was practiced in Ancient Egypt. Texts such as the preceding sufficiently prove this fact. The exegetes are mistaken to interpret all the important Egyptian texts as religious documents left behind by their authors to make their religion understood. When discussing Ancient Egypt it is always "religion" and never "philosophy" which is mentioned. This fault can only be attributed to the interpreters of the Egyptian texts. African Egyptologists must react against this generalized tendency which may well be the result of an unadmitted and yet dangerous bias. Ancient Egyptians thought about being, life, and death. Let us not reduce their important writings to the single dimension of the "sacred," the "religious." Let us exercise enough critical judgement to see them in another light from now on.

Such highly abstract thought is not exclusive to the Nile Valley, it is also found in the heart of Black Africa.

It is a prodigious thought which, in Black Africa, has been perpetuated only in secret societies, true centers of philosophy for a thoroughly initiated few.

As the Pharaonic text puts it, the Existing comes into existence of its own will, all at once. The Existing is the first to exist, the eldest god, anterior to the Anterior Gods and who, alone, makes everything he desires to make. So it is that all the multi-shaped forms of existence derive from the Existing.

This extraordinary event of creation is found word for word in an initiatory (philosophical) text collected from among the Luba of Zaire: "In the beginning of All Things (in the Universe), Maweja Nangila—the Eldest Spirit, the first one, the eldest and great lord of all Spirits which appeared later—manifested himself, all alone and by himself.

"Then, he first created the Spirits.

"He created them, not in the same way as he created the other things, but through a metamorphosis of his own being, by dividing himself magically and without losing anything of himself."(1) Mawega Nangila is the first to exist, he is of himself. Alone, of his own force, he creates all the other gods (spirits) who will later exist. The creation of these "secondary spirits" is a metamorphosis of Maweja Nangila himself, and is reminiscent of the Existing who spat out Shu and coughed up Tefnet, he who by using his mouth created all these; Magic ("*hekau*") was his name.

The similarity between how the Existing making itself manifest to existence in Ancient Egyptian thought and that of the Luba of Zaire is fundamental, profound, indeed, unassailable. They follow the same intellectual and metaphysical pattern. And it is no coincidence; such kinship demonstrates that matters of great importance to a people survive, they are perpetuated in those elements of a culture which become innate and are not destroyed by either time or space.

Let us add to this commentary an observation which is of paramount importance. As far as symbolism is concerned, the Egyptian scarab beetle, which is so distinctive, performs a role in the creation of being and beings: *kheper*, "to be, to exist;" *kheper-djes-ef*, "the one who comes to existence of himself;" *kheperu*, "modes of being"; *kheperi*, "the being, the existing."

The Egyptian sacred scarab is found elsewhere on the African continent with the same symbolic value and in an identical cultural and metaphysical context.

Here is a pertinent testimony of two ethnologists who are well-known for their intellectual patience: "A well sculptured box shows a bulge having the shape of a scarab, the insect which was created first and engendered all the others. . . . There may be a relationship between the importance that both the Egyptians and other African peoples gave the scarab.(2)

Here, the ethnologists refer to practices and beliefs associated with the scarab in central Zaire, among the Kuba (Bushongo) who are known the world over for the finesse and greatness of their ancestral civilization. Indeed they had an extremely well organized, powerful kingdom, high quality sculptures in wood and ivory, luxurious velvet cloth with patterns and colors of exquisite taste.

Many other creatures of the African fauna receive a similar symbolic, metaphysical, religious, trancendental, cosmogonic treatment in other Black African civilizations beyond the Egypto-Nubian Nile Valley: the lizard (*âsha*, in Egyptian), the cobra (*djet*), the falcon (*bik; Horus*), the bull (*ka*), the leopard (*aby*) whose skin was used as a sacerdotal garment, the hippopotamus (*khab*), the crocodile (*meseh*), the horned viper (*ef*), the vulture (*a*), the ibis (*akh*, "spirit": symbol of Thot), the owl (*em*), the bee (*bit*; heraldic sign of Lower Egypt), the jabiru (*Ephippiorynchus senegalensis*) whose Egyptian name is *b3*, *ba*, (*ba*, "soul, the most vital part of human beings in their deepest, divine essence; *bau*, "spirits," "power").

In other words, the same cultural and psychological macrostructure constitutes, as it were, the historical foundation of all civilizations in the Black African world.

Here is an example of a Black African cosmogony which utilizes many of the same elements: "In the beginning there was only darkness and except for water, nothing existed on earth. In this chaos, Bumba, the Chembe, reigned all alone. . . . He first threw up the sun, then the moon and later the stars. That is how light was born. . . . And Bumba threw up again and this time, he gave birth to the leopard, Koy Bumba; the crested eagle, Pongo Bumba; the crocodile, Ganda Bumba, the little fish, Yo Bumba; the tortoise, Kona Bumba; the white heron, Nyanyi Bumba, the scarab and the goat, Budi Bumba in this order. He then vomited human beings. . . . The animals he had created in this way started to people the world. . . . Another son, Choganda, threw up a plant from which all vegetation originated. . . ."(3)

Nothing was established or erected in the beginning of beginnings. There was only water (Abyss). The demiurge (Ra, Atum, Chembe), reigns *alone*, unique in the primordial non-created. Coming to existence by itself of itself, the Demiurge starts making all the creatures that will thus enter a full evolutionary cycle by engendering in turn, other forms of creatures, through time and space, until the end of time. Therefore, there is an incessantly changing universe, incessantly in mutation, a universe which is always active, always creating. However, all elements, all beings, all things necessarily derive from unique anterior forms. Creation continues for the universe in an immense creative saga.

* * *

B. How the World Came to be According to the Memphis Philosophers

The Shabaka Inscription

[Editor's Note: Here follows the original hieroglyphic inscription. In the absence of the accepted English translation of this text, we present the transliteration provided by the author with the translator's English version.]

The text dates to the Old Kingdom (2780-2260 B.C.); it was copied on a large granite tablet (1.37 by 0.92 meters) by order of the Pharaoh Shabaka (around 710 B.C.). The tablet, which is somewhat damaged, is now located in the British Museum, No. 498 ("Shabaka Stone"). Cf. Théophile Obenga, *L'Afrique dans l'Antiquite*, [Africa in Antiquity], (Paris: Présence Africaineò, 1973), Chapter VI: "Creation of beings according to the Shabaka Inscription", pp. 129-161.

Translation

The gods who came into existence through Ptah (nṭrw ḫprw m Ptḥ)

—Ptah who is on the Great Throne (Pth hr st wrt)

—Ptah-Nun, the father who begat Atum (Pth-Nnw it iri *Itm*)

—Ptah-Naunet, the mother who gave birth to Atum (Pth-Nnwt mwt *msi Itm*)

—Ptah the Ancient (literally "The Great",) is the heart and the tongue of the Ennead (Pth Wr h3ty ns pw n Ps*d*t)

—. . . . gave birth to the gods (. . . msi n*t*rw)

—. . . . gave birth to the gods (. . . msi n*t*rw)

—Ptah, ...Nefer tem, who is put before Ra each day (....... *r srt Rʿ rʿ nb*)

—It is by means of the heart that he came into existence

—It is by means of the tongue (a thought) that he came into existence in the form of Atum. The great and powerful Ptah, who has transmitted (his force) to all (gods) and their *kau* (plural of *ka*) truly,

by means of | this heart | means by which Horus came
| this tongue | means by which Thot came
| into existence as Ptah

Transliteration

hpr m h3ty |
| m tit Itm iw wr ʿ3 Pth sw*d*3 phty.f n
hpr m ns |

| h3ty pn hpr.n Hr im.f
n*t*rw nb w |
k3w.sn isk m | m Pth
| ns pn hpr.n *D*hwty im.f

—It happened that the heart and the tongue had power over (all) other parts to teach (hpr.n sm3 ib ns m ʿwt (nbwt) hr *sb3*): he (Ptah) exists (as heart) in every body (wnt.f m-hnt ht *nb (t)*) and as (tongue) in every mouth (m-hnt r nb) of all human beings (rm*t* nb (t), of all animals (ʿwt nbt; *ʿwt*, "little cattle",) of all vermicules (hf3t nb (t); hf3t, "intestinal worm"), and of (all) living beings (ʿmht; *ankhet*) to think (hr k33t) (as heart) and to order (hr w*d*-mdw) (as tongue) all the things (ht nbr) he (Ptah) wishes (*mrrt.f*) to think or order.

—His Ennead (Ptah's) is before him (Ps*d*t.f m-b3h.f) as teeth (m ibhw) and as lips (*m spty*): they are Atum's (Itm) seeds (*mtwt*) and hands (drty). And so, Atum's Ennead came into existence by means of his seeds and his fingers (m mtwt.f m *d*bʿ w.f Ps*d*t). The Ennead (Ptah's) is certainly (hm pw) constituted by the teeth and lips in the mouth that proclaims the name of all things (ibhw spty m r pn m3*t* rn n ht nbt; m3*t* rn, "Proclaim the name") and from which (*im.f*) Shu and Tefnet came out (*pri.n Sw Tfnwt*).

—The Ennead created (msi.n Ps*d*t, "The Ennead gave birth to") what the eyes see (*m33 irty*), what the ears hear (s*d*m ms*d*rwy), what the nose smells (ssn fn*d*: lit.: "the seeing of the eyes, the hearing of the ears, the smelling of the nose) so they can inform (sʿ r.n) the heart (hr *ib*; lit.: "so they can relay information to the heart.") Because *it* (the heart) is what makes it possible for every conceived thing to come out (*ntf ddi pri ᶜrkyt nbt*), and it is the tongue which repeats what has been thought in the heart (in ns whm k33t h3ty; lit.: "through the tongue is repeated what the heart has thought").

—Thus all the gods, Atum and his Ennead (sw msi nötòrw nbw Itm Ps*d*t,f) were created (given birth to). For all divine speech came forth through what the heart thought and what the tongue ordered (commanded) sk hpr.n is mdw nb k33t w*d*t ns).

—Thus the *Kau spirits* were created as well as *hemesut*, the (female) spirits who make all foods and all meals (htpt, "offerings") by means of speech (sw ir k3w mtnw hmswt irr *d*f3w nb(w) htpt nb(t) m mdt *t*n (for *t*n). (Thus is rewarded) the one who loves (irr mrr.t(i)) and (is punished) the one who hates (m*d*i.t(i)). And so, life is given (di.(n) ᶜnh) to (*n*) the one who is peace-loving (hry htp) and death (*m(w)t*) is given to the one who is criminal (hry hbnt).

—Thus (*sw*), all tasks are made (*ir k3t nb (t)*) and all arts (hmt nb (t)), the actions of the hands (*ir.t wy*), the motion of the legs (*sm.(t) rdwy*) and the functioning (*nmnm*) of all limbs (ᶜt nb(t)) in accordance with (hft) the order (w*d*t-mdw tn) which was thought within the heart (*k33t ob*) and which came out through the tongue (*pri.t ns*), and which gives meaning to all things (irrt im3h ht nb(t)) [im3h, "*Bedeutung*" as Sethe puts it and "*Wesen*" as Junker puts it. This must be understood as follows: "according to the order conceived in the heart, expressed by the tongue and from then on, visible in all things."]

—And so it was said (*hpr.n dd*) that: "Atum was begotten, the gods were brought to existence by Ptah" (*ir 'Itm shpr ntrw r Pth*). It is precisely he, To-Tenen, who gave birth to the gods (*T3-tnn is pw msi ntrw*). It is (also) from him that all things came out, such as foods and meals (pri.n ht nb(t) im.f m htp *d*f³w), such as offerings for the gods (m htpt n*t*rw) and such as all good and beautiful things (m ht nbt nfrt). Thus it has been found and recognized (out of wisdom) that his power is greater than that of (other) gods (sw gm s33 ᶜ3 phty.f r n*t*rw). Thus, Ptah was happy (sw htp Pth) after he made all things and all divine words, assuredly (m-ht irt.f ht nbt mdw n*t*r nb (i)sk).

—He (Ptah) gave birth to the gods (msi.n.f n*t*rw),
He made the cities (*ir.n.f niwwt*),
He founded the nomes (*grg.n.f sp3wt*),
He placed the gods in their temples (di.n.f n*t*rw hr hm (w.sn),
He strengthened their sacrifices (srw*d*.n.f p3wt.sn),
He founded their temples (grg.n.f hmw.sn)
He fashioned their bodies according to their wishes (stwt.n.f *d*t.sn r hpt-ib.sn).
And thus the gods entered their bodies (sw ᶜk n*t*rw *d*t.sn)
of wood (m ht nb(t); lit.: "of all kinds of wood"), of stone (m ᶜ3t nb(t)), of clay (*m im nb*),

Of all kinds of other things which grow due to his authority (ht nb(t) rd hr-htw.f [for hr-htf, see Gradiner, paragraph 178],

And in which they took shape (hpr.n.sn im).

—Thus were united within him (i^cb, transitive verb: "to be united") all the gods and their *ka*, content and united with the Master of the Double Country (sw i^cb n.f ntrw nbw k3w.sn is htpy hnmy m nb T3wy); *T3wy*, "the double Country," is Egypt: the High Country and the Low Country represent Upper and Lower Egypt).

Commentary

The philosopher-priests of Memphis show here the mechanism of creation. The heart (*h3ty*) and the tongue (*ns*) are mere images used to express abstractions: reason and speech, the Spirit and the Word.

It is through thought and the spoken word that Atum (The All-in All), all the other gods, and all of their creations are given life.

The authors of the text were searching for the initiating principle of creation, of genesis, of intelligence and of the order that underlies the universe. It is a commendable exercise in contemplation, to understand the design behind the birth of the cosmos, behind human existence. This more than two thousand years before the Greek and Hebrew civilizations.

It is clear from this text that the Egyptian philosophers of Memphis had conceived the idea of a universe made up of numerous phenomena, filled with diverse beings (humans, animals, plants, minerals); celestial beings, aquatic beings, terrestrial and luminous beings, etc.), different one from the other but all regulated by a rational order, a rational principle.

An eminent egyptologist came to the same conclusion after a close and critical reading of the same Memphian text: "This concept of the existence of a rational principle at the origin of the world is very close to the concept of the Logos."[4]

And he finishes his reading by stressing the fact that this philosophical text of Ancient Egypt "reveals one of the highest marks of pre-Hellenic thought, a pinnacle that, throughout her history, Egypt has never surpassed. This shows that Ancient Egypt had produced the best she could at the very dawn of her formation, at a time when she was still groping for her national identity." (5)

The construction of the pyramids, the invention of the three hundred, sixty five and a quarter day calendar, the code of values inscribed in books of wisdom and of instruction, the determined move toward finding access to abstract thought in order to comprehend the Whole, such is the extraordinary prowess that the first dynasties of Pharaonic Egypt must be given credit for. From the very beginning, they acquired fundamental knowledge, made extraordinary inventions, achieved works of wisdom of great moral value and posed fundamental questions. What miracle made it possible for the Ancient Egyptians to perform such spectacular wonders from the beginnings of their national history? This will always remain an open question.

We have earlier stressed the fact that the texts of the African oral traditions dealing with the origin of the world are strikingly similar to the Pharaonic speculation. What follows is a startling example from Dogon thought which shows the order in which all things and all beings were created: *Oral text recorded by G. Dieterlen and G. Ganay* (6):

> Yara gyina lapora yara tunyo boy
> laporo igiru yarabire tunyo boy
> laporo nandaru yarabire tunyo boy
> laporo wada yarabire tunyo boy
> wada pigere yarabire tunyo boy
> nandaru wada igiru gyu maraga boy
> boro dyenunu boy.

Translation:

> All things are Amma's things
> Amma (created) the earth and he did good
> Amma (created) the sky and he did good
> Amma (created) water and he did good
> Amma (created) Nummo and he did good
> The sky water fell onto the earth
> And entered the holes.

Amma (in the Nile Valley: *Amon, Amon-Ra;* in Rwanda: *Imana;* there is everywhere the same consonantal frame: *m-n*) has created the spirit *Nummo*, "master of the waters." He then created the *Yeban* spirits who own the earth which will remain wet for a long time. After them, *Amma* created animals, plants and man.

One would think this a Pharaonic text, so much is it like the one inscribed on the Shabaka stone. The parallels are quite remarkable:

I. Pharaonic Egyptians (P.E.) : "Thus were created the gods,
Atum and his Ennead"
The Dogon of Mali (M.D.) : "Thus Amma created Nummo,"
Master of the world.

II. P.E. : "The Kau spirits"
M.D. : "The Yeban spirits"

III. P.E. : "Ptah created all gods, all humans, all animals, all vermicules and every living thing," and all the creation partakes in Ptah's essence."
M.D. : "Amma created animals, plants and

humans. All things live because of Amma"
IV. P.E. : "And So Ptah was happy"
M.D. : "And so Amma did good."

In neither case do we see any religious revelation whatsoever. Ptah and Amma are but images to name the creator—god, the one who puts order in the world, the initiating rational principle. Beyond the mythical story, it is this initiating principle which is fundamentally at issue, it is this they seek. The Dogon do use images of the "heart" and the "tongue", at least not in the text cited above by the ethnologists.

In sum, there is between Pharaonic Egypt and the rest of Africa an unquestionable cultural kinship, a common speculative universe, a deep similarity of thought.

Paul Masson-Oursel, the French philosopher and distinguished scholar (open to philosophical endeavors for all humankind, regardless of their cultural, biological, historical or geographic diversity) was correct to note that "the Black African world view" was "the backdrop of the pharaonic civilization." (7)

Indeed, the Pharaonic speculations are identical to Black African ideas of genesis and markedly different from those of pre Socratic Greek philosophers who also sought to discover the primordial element or groups of elements from which the universe originated.

Thales affirmed that, in the final analysis, the world came from water. Anaximenes argued that the universe came out of a kind of fog. For Anaximander, something even more vague called "the infinite" was the basic principle of all things.

If the object of philosophy remains the human effort to discover ordered thought, if civilization can only be understood as a societal system dominated by a coherent concept of life, then it is irrefutable that Pharaonic Egypt was the very cradle of philosophical speculation as we know it. Furthermore, she reached such a speculation in the absence of all religious revelation. Shabaka, who lived in the eighth century B.C., was a contemporary of Isaiah. However, the text that he had copied on stone for posterity dates back from the historical origins of Pharaonic civilization. Thus, more than 2000 years before Thales, Pharaonic Egypt was involved in deep philosophy and had invented a concept of ordered life embedded in a language that suggests a tradition which was several centuries old.

All things taken in isolation are but manifestations of a Unity, of a Whole, an eternal and infinite world-force with a unique universal energy: the names given to this energy which makes all beings are only images: Amon, Atum, Khepri, Ra (sun-god).

We turn now to a review of the terms having deep philosophical content:

h3ty, "heart;" pl. *h3tyw*, "thoughts."

ib, "heart;" "mind," "understanding," "intelligence," "will," "desire,';' "wish," "attention." In the Memphian text, "heart" is synonymous with "comprehension."

ns, "tongue;" *ns*, "speech." Speech is the concrete expression of the creator-demiurge's thoughts. This reflects the absolute efficiency of the potency of speech. The Word is creator of discourse and the Pharaonic Egyptians firmly believed in the efficacy of ritual or magical speech. The heart conceives the idea of the universe and the tongue concretely makes the idea real by giving orders.

k3, "soul," "spirit" "essence of a being," personality," "fortune" (royal will). This is an approximate translation, as it is with the substantive *b3, ba*. The concepts of *ka* and *ba* are widespread all over Black Africa with the same essential and almost metaphysical meaning. Among the Mbochi of the Congo, *o-kaa* designates the essence of an individual's clan, and *ba*, his moral or physical integrity, his personal vital force.

m3t, "proclaim," "to say loud and intelligibly in order to bring to existence." What is proclaimed comes out of indifferentiation, out of non existence and takes shape or has effect at the very moment of utterance.

ʿrk, "to know," "to perceive," "to conceive" (intellectually), "to have the full knowledge of."

We have here a corpus of precise philosophical vocabulary highlighting the intimate liaison between language and the coming into being of the world and of man. Speech, as it is used here, has a clear ontological meaning, and this ontological speech, uttered by the demiurge, calls the world into existence. The way in which the demiurge speaks is sovereign, transcendental.

Well before the Bible and the Koran, well before the teachings of the Greek philosophers, Ancient Egypt had clearly conceived a doctrine of the Word, of the Logos, in the enactment of reality: "In Ancient Egypt, the demiurge created the world by pronouncing the names of things and beings. Sovereign speech is powerful enough to enact all reality through the utterance of the name."[8]

Also, the hieroglyphs themselves were clearly essential and ontological signs endowed with a deep meaning, a consistent order of discourse which involves nature as human value in the overall movement of existence. To the intitiated eye, the Egyptian hieroglyphics constituted a world-view. They were living beings, essential forms running through all things to make their presence felt.

Plotinus who was born in Egypt around 203 or 207 B.C. was correct to perceive hieroglyphics as a "science," "a wisdom," an essential form of being: "Hieroglyphs, as seen by Plotinus are organic wholes" effortlessly attaining perfection.[9]

This, then, is the measure of the ontological potency of a word written in hieroglyphics; it gives to thought the extraordinary capacity to mobilize itself and all of reality.

It is hardly necessary to stress the enormous power of the spoken word in Black Africa, it is enough to note that Maweja Nangila made creatures, each according to their nature, by using one or the other of his powers: pronunciation of the word or the call (by gesture). The text specifies: "Furthermore, he named them. To name something is to qualify it for reality."[10] Later the passage is truly gripping: "Denomination has (among other things) the power of metamorphisis because in giving names to things at the same time he created them, Maweja Nangila conferred upon them their forms, their virtues and their individual modes of behavior."[11]

In Black Africa, to call someone by name is to reveal a "human being", that is, a human being from this village or that ethnic group, from this family having these ancestors. The aim is to situate the individual in space and time and, at the same time, to give that person being "in its entirety." To name is to beget, to call up a genealogy, and evolution. To call an unknown person, you simply hail him without naming him; to call someone you hardly know, you look at him without speaking to him and simply thrust your lips forward; to call someone you've known for a few days, you call him by pointing your index finger or by a motion of your right hand; to call someone you know very well, you call him by pronouncing his name and his titles. "It is in that manner that Maweja Nangila called forth man who, at the time of creation, bore an exact resemblance to him."

From the time of Pharaonic Egypt, the spoken word has been sovereign in Black Africa. From time immemorial, there have been not oral civilizations (as ethnologists and foreign anthropologists call them) but civilizations of the powerful, creative Word. Orality is but a secondary phenomenon, whether or not it can be associated with the existence of writing. That is precisely the point: with all her hieroglyphs, it is clear that Ancient Egypt was also a high civilizaiton of the mighty and magical Word!

General Conclusions

[Editor's Note: The conclusions presented here do not follow directly after the preceding chapters in the longer, more exhaustive manuscript from which these passages are excerpted.]

If, in order to reach the essential, all philosophy presupposes conquering the unknown, having a hold over destiny: if the love for intellectual certitude and the craving for moral perfection also characterize all philosophy; if, in this world, knowledge and action fall into the province of philosophy in its effort to fashion an image of the abstract, to create new ideas (always anxious to know the essence of human existence, time, space, and the nature and number of things), then Ancient Egypt was certainly engaged in philosophy. At the same time, Egypt produced a mythology and a solar religion—quite apart from its philosophy—along with other purely literary achievements.

There was a distinctive philosophical activity in Pharaonic Egypt. This effort of the radical questioning of stark reality lasted more than twenty-five centuries—which is to say throughout the splendid Pharaonic civilization.

In the very beginning, before all the fundamental elements, before the Demiurge or the Creator himself, there was *Nun*, posited as an abyssal matter, aqueous and vital, the Unique Substratum, the singular place of the plural emergence of the elements that form the universe, tha totality of knowable reality. What is created comes out of what is uncreated, out of the agitation of an almost impalpable water. *Nun*, which is the ideogram of no anterior fate whatsoever, has no beginning. It is that in which matter and spirit move together toward their own identity. But *Nun* is not itself consumed by what it will beget. In the innermost center of its mysterious geometry, it silently fashions all of duration without itself partaking of any temporality.

If intelligence works its abstract way in an attempt to understand and explain the Universe, it is because, in the final analysis, man and the Universe share the same pattern of becoming without Nun. Here, we are obviously dealing with a speculative order of thought.

Beyond the genealogical character of this theoretical view of all that is and exists, as such, one must be sensitive to the fundamenal unity of all the elements in the Universe. Nun is the seed of being and of thought, as it is the seed of our concept of what is. That is why the Africans of Pharaonic Egypt thought Nature to be a cosmic order, constantly renewing itself, as does the sun which rises and sets each day, and why the world is habitable in spite of the night.

Thus, the theory of *Nun*, which makes it possible for life to pre-exist in matter but only reveal itself as a creative force in intelligence (*Ra, Atum*)—a complex and superior form taken by *Nun* itself in its structural mutation—implies another theory, that of *Maat*. *Maat* is the primordial principle which gives order to all values, including, for example, the waging of war by the Pharaoh himself. It is, indeed, part of the cosmic order, part of the Truth-and-Justice that allows the Pharaoh (for all that he is and symbolizes) to protect the country from disorder, from chaos, from famine, from misery. Besides, all men living in society must conform to Justice and Truth, to *Maat*, the supreme Virtue, guide and measure of all human activity.

Maat belongs to the order of "that which must be" whereas *Nun* belongs to the order of "that out of which came" the world, such as it is; the primordial structure of the cosmos and the invention of the knowledge of self go hand in hand with duty. This is the basis upon which rests Pharaonic philosophy: *Nun* represents the notion of functioning matter and *Maat* represents, in perfect hieroglyphics, the elevated notion of moral perfection. Dynamic and living matter, *Nun* is the essence of all things and creates of itself the passage from non-being to being, from "before" to "after", the passage from somnolence of consciousness to the awakening of reason which, through the word, names, designates, classifies, orders, commands—in short, brings into being. Seen as a kind of preestablished harmony in the cosmos, Maat is Order, Truth-and Justice, Felicity supreme, inviting man in society to do and speak, to think and act, to live and die according to what is true, normal, harmonious; according to virtue with all the hieratic, traditional, transcendental, imperative and absolute implications that that word (virtue) takes on in the Black-Egyptian mentality.

The notion of death is secondary in Ancient Egypt. It is the notion of living, of acting in accordance with justice and truth which is of primary importance, essential, motivating and justifying all rituals, all codes. It is important to preserve life, always, in this world and beyond. Purity of the heart is an invaluable possession. The tomb, decorated and embellished, and the funeral rites however close to death they may be, all this is merely secondary in the land of the Pharaohs. It is stellar destiny which, in death, gives man happy and eternal life in the everlasting heavens. This glorious fate is reserved for just and upright souls and cannot be dissociated from the moral philosophy of *Maat*.

The Egyptian temple and all places of worship (lakes, sanctuaries, pyramids, obelisks, palaces) must belong to the cosmic order of *Maat*. That is why all the axes of sacred edifices are obedient to the energizing lines of the Universe itself. Here again we see the thirst, the desire, vivid and renewed, for integration into the cosmic whole. Moreover, the decorations on the walls and ceilings of temples always celebrate the starry Universe in a state of constant and perpetual creation. Festivals which renew human and cosmic forces have always existed in Black Pharaonic Egypt. If the stars and constellations were at the center of the Egyptian philosophers' and priests' preoccupations (so much so that they became astronomers admired in Ancient Greece, by Aristole, in fact) it was because the intellectual impulse of Black Pharaonic Egypt, an impulse rare to find in those distant times, sought to identify itself with the force and power of the sun which enables everything to live on earth.

Therefore, the underlying concept of King Akhnaton's *Great Hymn to the Sun* contains a philosophy which identifies itself with natural sciences as does Pharaonic mathematics (as the very little of the *Rhind Papyrus* shows). In both, one can see the same basic concept: All "things" have a status, a category; but close, dynamic and sometimes unsuspected relationships and interconnections exist among them. On what may be called the ontological level, the Akhnaton text provides this explication; on the epistemological level, Ahmes' mathematical text invites consideration of the world and all reality as mathematically fathomable through the power of numbers. In the history of thought, those Egyptian philosophical concepts have had a long and rich odyssey due to their historical passage from Egypt to Ancient Greece.

Also because of *Maat*, sickness is seen as a cosmo-biological phenomenon in Ancient Egypt. The human body coupled with human susceptability make of him a complex being in which are united the human and the divine, the terrestrial and the cosmic, the ephemeral and the immortal. The Ancient Egyptians thought that it was important to preserve everything in man through magic, amulets, ointments and sacred oils, powders and ritual words, medicines of all kinds, prayers, incantations, scientific experiments, chemistry, surgery, mummification, offerings (flowers, breads, beer, geese, etc.) to the dead, appeal to the living, security of the tomb. A total medical treatment was required for the patient's moral, social and physical health. Cosmic and psychosomatic medicine were in use in Egypt before all forms of medicine in the Ancient Middle East. Theirs was a medicine whose philosophy was ever so transparent, precisely because it was linked to the cosmic theory of *Maat*. The Egyptian scribe does not only copy. He is scholar who is concerned for the immortality of his name. The life of the mind is of paramount importance in the land of the Pharaohs. To write is to write in accordance with the precepts of *Maat*, of Truth-and-Justice.

To affirm that Pharaonic art is "ordered" and "beautiful" is to say far too little. Because of this same *Maat* philosophy, Egyptian art—each individual work—is a tension of numerous essential qualities, moral, philosophical and aesthetic. The pyramid architects were certainly well-versed in all the sciences, in history, geography, physics, acoustics, geology, mechanics, astronomy, mathematics. As they, too, were initiated, they had to respect the divine laws of the national cannon which was itself from *Maat*. They had to possess an impressive number of moral qualities to lead so many people, for so many years on such difficult building sites. In describing Pharaonic art (which cannot be dissociated from truth) one can justifiably speak of "artistic cosmology", to use the expression of Etienne Souriau. And it is no doubt knowingly that Plato praises instrumental and vocal music, dance, rites and ceremonies which formed what may be called a total art on the banks of the Nile.

Cheikh Anta Diop never forgot to think and to say that Black African culture—from as far back as Pharaonic Egypt—is to be found in every manifestation of humanity. The cultural whitewash performed throughout the modern world by the technological West must drive the elite of each affected people to resist their total destruction. We now know how vain such colonial qualifiers as "exotic", "savage", "primitive", "uncivilized", and "pre-logical" are.

It will therefore be necessary to take some risks so that modern Africa, which is building itself up in an implacable world, does not repudiate her specific culture which belongs as well to universal man. Racially and culturally, Pharaonic Egypt and Black Africa are intrinsically related. Thus, Pharaonic philosophy constitutes the first moment in contemporary Africa's long philosophical tradition.

Perhaps the modern world has no need for this historical and philosophical understanding to build itself up or to continue its progress in both science and technology. But history is the salt of human existence. Indeed, history is our reason for living and the reason we ourselves give ourselves, by whatever name: Creator or Nature, or, in our time, Biology, Society or Culture.

To bring precision to this important question, one can say in emcompassing this philosophy as a whole that happiness is one possible aim of human action (hence the contemporary African problematic of "a philosophy of development"). Theories of personhood and self, of pain and pleasure, of desire, anxiety, of consciousness and unconsciousness, of thought, of rationality, of knowledge, memory, language, social relations, ideas and concepts of freedom, of being, action, values, ethics—all of these can be traced as they have evolved in the history of Western philosophies. They can be fond at the beginning of Greek philosophy, in stoicism, epicurism, among the eighteenth and nineteenth century philosophers, in marxism, psychoanalysis, existentialism, in analytical philosophy and in phenominology.

More and more, we are being forced to fashion a planetary culture. Everything leads us in that direction.

The Orient (India, Asia) will contribute its share because of its great and precious heritage in consciousness, its knowledge of and techniques for introspection. Buddhism will certainly play a role as we become much more aware of the extreme complexity of psychic reality. Contemporary physics is actively interested in oriental wisdom to give its work a new and broader conceptual framework. We are witnessing another expansion of the mind, to paraphrase Hegel, who is quite penetrating when he does not concern himself with the historical evolution of humanity.

It is also obvious that the Islamic thinkers and philosophers who understand the notion of freedom and who have already exhibited moments of extraordinary energy, intelligence, consciousness and effort, will also contribute to this new endeavor of the human race—to build, today, consciously and rationally, the knowledge and will necessary for the survival and happiness of humanity.

The modern world is here, massive, total, all-encompassing and abundant. It often turns its back on human behavior, on human needs. But humanity, with its richness of cultural diversity, will rediscover its two lost dimensions: transcendence and community. And it will do so without forsaking its forges, anvils and hammers, even though, at the close of the twentieth century, science and technology are thrusting us toward future millenia.

The absolute—at once physical and spiritual, as were *Nun* and *Maat* to the Ancient Africans of Pharaonic Egypt—will, of necessity, intervene in the present struggle, and will extol the transcendence of man over all determinism of nature and society. I believe that man once knew happiness in the full philosophical sense of the word. His task must not be—each day, unrelentingly—to re-invent that bliss. It is still attainable.

Notes to the Introduction

1. A. Thalamas, *La Géographie d'Eratosthène* ['The Geography of Erastosthenes], Versailles, Ch. Barbier, 1921. 10 fig., 256 p.

2. Paul Monceaux, *Les Africans. Etude sur la littérature latine d'Afrique. Les païens* [The Africans: A Study of Latin Literature in Africa. The Pagans], Paris, Lecène, Oudin et Cie., 1984, 500 p.

3. Ibn Khal,dün, *Discours sur l'histopire universelle (al-Muqaddima)* [Discourse on Universal History], new translation, preface and notes by Vincent Beyrouth, 1967-1968, 3 vol.
This "Maghribian philosophy" is itself well within the general framework of the history of Muslim philosophy, a subject which has been throughouly treated in the remarkable work edited and with introduction by Sharif of the Philosophical Symposium of Pakistan. M.M. Sharif, *A History of Muslim Philosophy. With short accounts of other disciplines and the modern renaissance in Muslim lands*, Karachi, Royal Book Company, 2 vols., 1983 reprint; the two volumes together form 1972 pages.
Cf. A. Badawi, *Histoire de la Philosophie en Islam* [History of Philosophy in Islam], Paris, J. Vrin, 1972.
Aldo Mieli, *La Science arabe et son röle dans l'évolution scientifique mondiale* [Arab Science and its Role in World Scientific Evolution], Leiden, E.J. Brill, 1966, reprint, enlarged with bibliography and analytical index by A. Mazahéri.
Ahmed Y. al-Hassan, *L'Islam et la science* [Islam and Science], in "La Recherche" (Paris), No. 134, June 1982, vol. 13, pp. 720-728, illust.

4. Abderrahman Es-Sa'di, *Tarikh es-Soudin*, translated by O. Houdas, Paris, Adrien-Maisonneuve, 1964 ed., pp. 57-58.

5. Burchard Brentjes, *Anton Wilhelm Amo. Der schwarze Philosoph in Halle* [Anton Wilhelm Amo. The Black Philosopher of Halle], Leipzig, Koehler & Ameland, 1976, 25 illustr., 116 p.

6. E.W. Blyden, *Christianity, Islam and the Negro Race* (1887), Edinburgh, At the University Press, 1967 ed., collect.: "African Heritage Books", No. 1.

7. Cf. the *Review philosophique de Kinshasa* [Kinshasa Philosophy Review], vol. I, no. I, Janvier-Juin 1983, Kinshasa (Zaire). This No. I bears the stamp of the writing or knowledge of the college of Zaire philosophers who have laid firm research foundations. The works of this time period are, therefore, not reducible to a "simple" attitude (critical or polemical) vis-à-vis *La Philosophie bantoue* [Bantu Philosophy] (1945) of R.P. Placide Tempels!

8. K. Wiredu, *Philosophy and an AFrican Culture*, Cambridge, Cambridge University Press, 1980, pp. 37-50.

9. M. Griaule, *Philkosophie et religions des Noirs* [Philosophy and Black Relgions] in a collection entitled *Le Monde noir* [The Black World], special edition 8-9 of "Présence Africaine" edited by Theodore Monod, Paris, Présence Africaine, 1950, pp. 307-321; for this quotation, p. 321.

10. Flavius Josephus (Jewish general and historian, born in Jerusalem in 37, died in 100), *Contr. Ap.*, I, 2.
Also, this reminder from a specialist of the greco-roman world: "We must also remember that Egypt and Babylonia influenced Greece by way of numerous civilizations derived from the eastern Mediterranean." Benjamin Farrington, *La science dans l'Antiquité. Grèce-Rome* [Science in Antiquity: Greece-Rome], translated from the English by Henri Chéret, Paris, Payot, 1967, p. 11.

11. Frederic Tomlin, *Les grands philosophes de l'Orient* [Great Philosophers of the East], translation, Paris, Payot, 1952, p. 19.

12. Lancinay Keita, *The African Philosophical Tradition*, pp. 35-54, in Richard A. Wright, *African Philosophy: An Introduction*, Washington, University Press of America, 1979.

13. Henry Olela, *The African Foundations of Greek Philosophy*, pp. 55-69, in Richard A. Wright, editor, op cit. (1979).

14. S. Sauneron, *Les Prètres de l'ancienne Egypte* [Priests of Ancient Egypt], Paris, Editions du Seuil, 1957, p. 4, Collect.: "Le Temps Qui Court", No. 6.

15. Frédéric Portal, *Des Couleurs symboliques dans l'Antiquité, le Moyen-Age et le Temps modernes* [Symbolic Colors in Antiquity, the Middle Ages, and Modern Times], Paris, Editions de la Maisnie, 1979, p. 4.

16. *Le Peuplement de l'Egypte ancienne et le déchiffrement de l'écriture méroitique* [Thge Peopling of Ancient Egypt and the Deciphering of Meroitic Script], Paris, UNESCO, 1978, p. 87.

17. Cheikh Anta Diop, *Antériorité des civilisations nègres: mythe ou verité historique?* [Anteriority of Black Civilizations; Myth or Historical Fact?], Paris, Présence Africaine, 1967, p. 12. A great specialist in Egyptian "religion" is of a similar mind when he writes: "The Egyptian cosmogonies are, in large part, legends which fairly closely resemble those of Uganda. Yet one senses that the Egyptians tried to discern the indiscernible and that they wished to know the ultimate reason for things. . . . The Egyptian notions are deeply ancient, so much so that no people can grasp a time so far removed." E. Amélineau, *Prolégomènes à l'étude de la religion égyptienne* [Prolègomèna Considers Egyptian Religion], Deuxième partie, Paris, Ernest Leroux, 1916, p. 106.

Notes to Chapter I

1. J.Ph. Lauer, *Le Mystère des Pyramides* [The Mystery of the Pyramids], Paris, Presses de la Cité, 1974, with diagrams and plates, biblio., 378 pp.

2. Georges Gusdorf, *Mythe et Métaphysique. Introduction à la Philosophie* [Myth and Metaphysics. Introduction to Philosophy], Paris, Flammarion, 1953, p. 11.

3. Michael A. Hoffman, *Egypt Before the Pharaohs. The Prehistoric Foundations of Egyptian Civilization*, New York, Alfred A. Knopf, 1984, tables, 84 plates, XXi-391 pages, biblio., (pp. 357-376).

4. *Les Stoïciens* [The Stoics], Paris, Gallimard, texts translated by Emile Bréhier, 1962, p. 59. Collection: "Bibliothèque de la Pléiade".

5. Cf. Pierre Mabille, *Le Miroir du Merveilleux* [The Mirror of Wonders], Paris, les Editions de Minuit, 1962, pp. 73-109: "La création", 1st edit., Le Sagittaire, 1940.

6. Th. Henri Martin, *Etudes sur le Timée de Platon* [Essays on the *Timaeus* of Plato], Paris, J. Vrin, 1981, reprint of the 1941 edition.

7. Aristotle, *On the Heavens*, I, 10, 280a.

8. Cicero, *On the Nature of the Gods*, Book II, XI, 20.

9. St. Augustine, *Confessions*, Book XIII, 48: "De nihilo enim a te, non de te facta sunt, non de aliqua non tua vel quae antea fuerit, sed de concreata, id est simul a te creata materia."
[Translator's Note: E.B. Pusey, Tr., *The Confessions of St. Augustine*, New York, E.P. Duttin, 1950]

10. Jean Leclant, *Le monde égyptian. Les Pharaons. Vol. I-Le temps des Pyramides. De la Préhistoire aux Hyksos (1560 B.C.)* [The Egyptian World. The Pharaohs. Vol. I-The time of the Pyramids. From Pre-History to the Hyksos (1560 B.C.)], Paris, Gallimard, 1978, p. 17.

11. Paul Barguet, *Le livre des morts des Anciens Egyptiens* [The Book of the Dead of the Ancient Egyptians], intro., trans., comment., Paris, les Editions du Cerf, 1967, 307 pp. Collection: "Littératures anciennes du Proche-Orient", No. 1.
E.A. Wallis Budge, *The Book of the Dead. The Papyrus of Ani*, New York, Dover Publications, 1967; 1st edit., British Museum, London, 1985. Introduction, Egyptian text, transliteration, biblio.

12. Adriaan A. Buck, *The Egyptian Coffin Texts*, Chicago, 1935-1961, 7 vols.

13. Marcel Griaule, *Dieu d'eau. Entretiens avec Ogotemmêli* [The God of the Waters. Conversations with Ogotemmêli], Paris, Les Editions du Chêne, 1948, p. 25.

14. Germaine Dieterlen, *Essai sur la religion bambara* [Essay on the Religion of the Bambara], preface by Marcel Griaule, Paris, P.U.F., 1951, pp. 44-45.

15. Germaine Dieterlen, *op. cit., p. 41.*

16. Geoffrey Parrinder, *La religion en Afrique occidentale illystrée par les coryances et pratiques des Yorouba, des Ewe, des Akan et peuples apparentés* [Religion in west Africa Illustrated by the Beliefs and Practices of the Yoruba, the Ewe, the Akan and Related Peoples], Paris, payot 1950, p. 6.

17. Jacqueline Roumeguère-Eberhardt, *Pensée et Société africaines. Essais sur une dialectique de complémentarité antagoniste chex les Bantu de Sud-Est* [African Thought and Society. Essays on a

Dialectic of Antagonistic Complementariness Among the Bantu of the Southeast], Paris, La Haye, Mouton et Cie., 1963, p. 57.

18. Jean Rudhardt, *Le Thème de l'eau primordiale dans la mythologie grecque* [The Theme of the Primordial Water in Greek Mythology], Berne, Editions Francke, 1971, pp. 110-116: "Thalgès et la tradition mythique". Collect.: "Travaux Publiés sous les Auspices de la Société Suisse des Sciences humaines", No. 12.

19. Dominique Zahan, *Sociétés d'initiation bambara. Le N'Domo et le Koré* [Bambara Initiation Societies, The N'Domo and the Kore], Paris, La Haye, Mouton et Cie., 1960, 10 figs., XXIV pl., map, 438 pp.

20. Jean-Paul Lebeuf. *L'Habitation des Fali* [Fali Dwellings], Paris, Hachette, 1961, p. 584.

21. Georges Niangouran Bouah, *La division du temps et le calendrier rituel des peuples lagunaires de Côte d'Ivoire* [The Division of Time and the Ritual calendar of the Lagoon-dwelling Peoples of the Ivory Coast], Paris, Institut d'Ethnologie, Musée de l'Homme, 1964, p. 36.

22. Aristotle, summarizing the ancient theories, points out that it has to do with a body more substantial than water and more dense than air (*oi d'udatos men leptoteron, aeros de puknoteron*) which envelopes the heavens entirely because of its infiniteness (*o periechein pantas tous ouranous apeiron on*). Aristotle, *On the Heavens*, III, 4, 303a, 12-13.
An ancient Black African thought noted: "Water and Fire are the elder brothers of all things." *Une Bible Noire* [A Black Bible], Bruexelles, 1973, p. 36.

23. Th. Hopfner, *Orient und griechische Philosophi [Eastern and Greek Philosophy], Leipzig, 1925.*

E. Amélineau, *La cosmogonie de Thalè et les doctrines de l'Egypte* [The Cosmogony of Thales and the Doctrines of Egypt], in "Revue de l'Histoire des Religions" ["Journal of the History of Religions], 1919, vol. 62.

Gérard Legrand, *La pensée des Présocratiques* [Pre-Socratic Thought], Paris, Bordas, 1970. Vigorous study of all the Pre-Socratic philosophers.

24. Marcel mauss, *Conceptions qui ont précédé la notion de matière* [Concepts which Preceded the Notion of Matter], in the collective work: *Qu'est-ce que la matière? Histoire du concept et conception actuelle* [What is Matter? History of the Concept and Present Conception], Paris, P.U.F., 1945, p. 778.

25. See for example:

Jean E. Charon, *L'esprit et la relativité complexe. Introducton à la psychophysique* [The Mind and Complex Relativity. Introduction to Psychophysics], Paris, Albin Michael, 1983, 239 pp.

Bernard d'Espagnat, *A la recherche duy éel. Le regard d'un physicien* [In Search of What is Real. A Physicists View], 2nd ed. revised and expanded, Paris, Gauthier-Villars, 1981, p. 168: "The association between the observation of nature and a conscious activity of the mind has the good fortune of providing results which, mysteriously and quite imperfectly, open to us perspectives on being."

26. Plato,, *Timaeus*, 27c.

[Translator's Note: Francis M. Cornford, *Plato's Cosmology: The Timaeus*, New York, Humanities Press]

Lucretius (c. 95-55 B.C.), by contrast solicits the aid of the goddess Venus (*dea Venus*) to write his poem on Nature: "Te sopciam studeo scribendis versibus esse/Quos ego de rerum natura pangere conor." ["I pray to you {Venus} be with me as I write these verses/That I compose about the world of nature."] *De rarum natura*, Book I, 24-25. This invocation by Lucretius never stopped the Latin poet, himself close to Epicurus, from considering the latter a materialist writer in the purest sense of the term. Because matter, for Lucretius is the germinal seed of all things, every thing owes its origin to the *corpora prima*—materials—which are just that, generating bodies (*genitalia corpora*), the germinal seeds of all things (*semina rerum*).

27. Germaine Dieterlen, *Essai sur la religion bambara* [Essay on Bambara Religion], Paris, P.U.F., 1951, preface by Marcel Griaule, p. 10. the *miri* is also the "egg of the world in which Nature was enclosed." (p. 10)

Notes to the General Conclusions

1. T. Fourche and H. Morlighem, *Une Bible Noire* [A Black Bible], Brussels, Max Arnold, p. 15.
2. E. Torday and T.A. Joyce, *Notes ethnographiques sur les peuples communement appelés Bakuba,ainsi que sur les peuplades apparentées, les Bushongo*[Ethnographic Notes on the Bakuba and the Bushongo], Brussels, Annals of the Belgian Congo Museum, 10:213.
3. Torday and Joyce, *Notes ethnographiques*, p. 20.
4. John A. Wilson, *L'Egypte. Vie et mort d'une civilisationé* [Egypt. Life and Death of a Civilization], Paris, Arthaud, 1961, with a preface by George Posener, p. 59. Collection "Signes des Temps", No. 9.
5. Ibid., p. 60.
6. G. Dieterelen and G. Ganay, *Genie des Eaux chez les Dogons* [The Water Genie Among the Dogons], Paris, Paus Geuthner, 1942, p. 3.
7. Paul Masson—Oursel, *Histoire de la Philosophie. Premier fascicule supplementaire. La Philosophie en Orient*, Collection Histoire de la Philosophie [History of Philosophy. First Supplement], Collection Edited by Emile Brehier, Paris, PUF, 1957, p. 42.
8. Georges Gusdord, *La Parole* [Speech], Paris, PUF, 1977, p. 16. (First Edition, 1952).
9. Pierre Hadot, *Plotin ou la simplicité du regard* [Plotinus or the simplicity of sight], Paris, Etudes Autustiniennes, 1972, p. 50. (First ed. published by Plon).
10. T. Fourche and Morlighem, *Une Bible noire* [A Black Bible]. Brussels, Max Arnold, 1973, p. 39.
11. Ibid., p. 42.

EDITOR'S NOTE

These are excerpts from a larger work, still awaiting publication. They were selected for translation from the French by Habib Sy. The translation was done by Elizabeth Clement and Irene d'Almeida.

Because they are excerpts, the notes relate to specific chapters of the work and are not in a regular sequence.

SCIENCE AND SYMBOL IN EGYPTIAN MEDICINE: COMMENTARIES ON THE EDWIN SMITH PAPYRUS

Charles S. Finch III, M.D.

In our time, we are accustomed to attributing the beginnings of scientific medicine to the Greek physician Hippocrates who lived in the 5th century B.C. It is said that the foundation of a purely clinical approach to illness exemplified by techniques of history-taking, examination, diagnosis, prognosis, and empirical therapy begins with Hippocrates and his School, reaching its greatest development in classical times with Galen. Thus Hippocrates has been styled the "Father of Medicine" and physicians all over the world take the semi-sacred Hippocratic Oath upon completion of their medical studies. But who was Hippocrates really? He has excercised an immense influence on medicine for nearly 25 centuries and we would think that he was a clear-cut historical figure. However, on closer inspection, he is rather dim and shadowy. We know that he was born on the island of Cos, the descendant of a line of priests of Asclepios, that he became a physician of renown, and that he was revered enough as a physician that eventually an entire school sprung up around his teachings. But we don't know much more than that:

> Practically nothing is known of his life but many legends have sprung up about this great doctor and teacher.
>
> Even two hundred years after his death, no one knew anything definite about Hippocrates' life.[1]

Only a fraction of the large Hippocratic written corpus can be directly attributed to him and he cannot even claim authorship of the fabled Hippocratic Oath. In all fairness to him, however, he never gave himself the title of "Father of Medicine" nor is there any reason to doubt that he was a physician of unusual gifts. Moreover, it becomes glaringly evident through a study of the Egyptian medical papyri that Hippocrates and his followers drew heavily upon the theory and practice of ancient Egyptian medicine.[2] So heavy was this indebtedness that had Hippocrates ever had the question of priority put to him he might well have echoed the dictum of Homer who in the *Odyssey* stated, "In medical knowledge,

Egypt leaves the rest of the world behind." In fact in some ways, Hippocrates had not even advanced as far as the ancient Egyptians before him. He never mentions pulse-taking and considered the brain to have been a gland.[3] To cite but two examples in therapeutics, the Hippocratic methods of setting clavicular fractures and reducing a dislocated mandible are almost exactly as described in the Edwin Smith Papyrus.[4] See Fig. 1. There are many more examples that could be cited of the pronounced similarity of important facets of Hippocratic medicine to ancient Egyptian medicine and, based on the historically verifiable pattern of cultural borrowing of Greece from Egypt, this indicates that much of Hippocratic medicine was Egyptian medicine in Greek form.

Hippocratic method for reducing a dislocation of the jaw, first described in the Edwin Smith papyrus

This idea is given greater weight when we examine the Alexandrian school of Greek medicine, of which Galen was the greatest exponent. In fact, the Alexandrian period represents the Golden Age of Greek Medicine in which startling discoveries in anatomy and physiology were made. This rather sudden efflorescence of Greek medicine at Alexandria can be attributed to one major cause: the collection of all available Egyptian scientific papyri by the early Ptolemies under the roof of the Library of Alexandria. This justly-famous library at its height contained over 700,000 volumes and made the city the intellectual center of the classical world. The scientific renaissance of the Alexandrian period was therefore due to the Greek world's unlimited access to the learning of ancient Egypt. The famous "discoveries" by the Greek sceintists of that time were, for the most part, "re-descoveries" of ancient Egyptian learning and thought. Herophilus, an Alexandrian Greek of the 4th century B.C., is ordinarily credited with the discovery of the diagnostic applications of pulse-taking though we now know that this was described in both the Ebers and Smith medical papyri 35 centuries before his time. It seems likely that Herophilus had access to the ancient Egyptian *Book of the Heart and Vessels*, the same source of information used by the ancient Egyptian authors of the Ebers and Smith papyri. Moreover, Herophilus and his Alexandrian contemporary, Erasistratus, are usually credited with first delineating the relations between the peripheral nerves and the central nervous system. But a modern medical historian says about the Edwin Smith Papyrus:

> It is difficult to escape the conclusion that the author clearly realized the relationship between the nervous system and voluntary movements and the fact that the side and localization of the paralysis depend on the situation of the nervous lesion.[5]

He goes on to say,

> It is, therefore, interesting to point out again that these two learned physicians (Herophilus and Erasistratus) practiced in Alexandria in Egypt . . . while five centuries later Greek physicians were still visiting Egypt to consult the library at Memphis.[6]

Galen, himself, though a member of the Hippocratic School, spent many years in Alexandria furthering his medical education. Nor did Galen and his physician contemporaries limit themselves to Alexandria, also traveling to the famous healing temples and libraries of Sais and Memphis in search of medical knowledge. It is therefore in vain that we look to Greece for the origins of modern medicine; we can only do so in ancient Egypt, the teacher of the Greeks.

In an earlier article, the present author provided an introduction to an African medical science that began in Egypt but continued its development, in often remarkable ways, elsewhere in Africa.[7] In this article we will examine Egyptian medical science more closely, through the agency of the Edwin Smith Papyrus, to understand better its impace on the history of medicine.

Before proceeding with a discussion on Egyptian medicine, a short space must be devoted to the question of Egyptian chronology. Since the beginning of Egyptology as a scholarly discipline, there have been running debates about Egyptian chronology which, broadly speaking, have divided into two camps: the "long" chronology vs. the "short" chronology. The long chronology, propounded by scholars such as Lepsius, Petrie, and Budge, dates the beginning of the Egyptian dynastic period—that is the unification of the Two Lands under Menes—somewhere between 5,000 and 4,000 B.C. This was the dominant view until the early part of this century when Meyer proposed a date of 3400 B.C. for the beginning of the last dynasty. Since then Egyptologists have, by convention, adopted modifications of Meyer's scheme so that now the dominant opinion dates the beginning of Egyptian history around 3100 B.C. The argument turns around three important elements used to reconstruct Egyptian chronology: 1) the history of Manetho which divides Egyptian history into 30 dynasties of 330 kings, covering a space of more than 5,000 years, 2) surviving fragments of king lists that appear on the Turin Papyrus, the Palermo Stone, etc., and 3) the 1460-year Sothic cycle is determined by the gradual backward slippage of the Egyptian civil year of 365 days in relation to the Sothic year of 365¼ days. This Sothic year of 365¼ days was determined by the heliacal rising of the star Sirius, the brightest of the stars seen from Earth, co-incident with the beginning of the annual Nile Flood which marked the beginning of the Egyptian New Year. Because there is a discrepancy of ¼ day between the two years, it takes 1460 years ($1460 \times ¼ = 365$) for the two calendars to coincide again. The short chronology rests on two assumptions: 1) a revision of Manetho in which numerous dynasties in the two Intermediate Periods are conflated, thereby reducing the length of time attested to by Manetho by 2,000 years and 2) that the Egyptians did *not* begin using the Sothic year until the beginning of a new cycle about 2780 B.C. The first rationale is dubious and the second is simply inadmissable. Surviving inscriptions from the 1st dynasty, that is *prior* to 2780 B.C., refer to the relationship between the heliacal rising of Sirius, the beginning of the flood, and the New Year.[8] This means that the Egyptians *had* to have known of the sothic cycle before 2780 B.C. which, by referring to the date of the beginning of the previous cycle, goes back to 4240 B.C., the first identifiable calendar date in history. The existence of a highly sophisticated calendar at such a remote period means that there had to have been a civilization in place advanced enough to have acquired and recorded the astronomical knowledge necessary for the creation of such a calendar. The lopping off of great segments of time from Manetho's history, in the scheme of the short chronology, is therefore not entirely defensible. There is reason to believe, after Budge, that the first dynasty of Menes actually begins around 4400 B.C.—or shortly thereafter—instead of the received date of 3100 B.C., pushing Egyptian history back 1200 years or so.

What does this have to do with our subject? Breasted, the translator and commentator of the Edwin Smith Papyrus, has demonstrated by linguistic analysis that the extant manuscript, though written during the 18th dynasty (circa 1500 B.C.), is actually a late copy of an original first produced early in the Old Kingdom, perhaps as early as the 1st Dynasty. But if we date the beginning of the Old Kingdom sometime between 4400-4200 B.C., i.e., close to the earliest calendar date, then the Edwin Smith Papyrus reflects medical knowledge that existed in northeast Africa 6,000 years ago. Moreover, it is a mature scientific document, the culmination of a long period of anterior development. This means that the true beginnings of what we think of as scientific medicine are so remote as to be lost to the gaze of history.

The level of medical science revealed in the Edwin Smith Papyrus makes it the most remarkable medical document to survive from antiquity. The present translation is the fruit of the marvelous scholarship of James Henry Breasted who, after 10 years of work, published his version in 1930. Breasted included an extensive commentary and was immensely aided in his labors by physician colleagues. His translation has stood the test of time and remains the standard one for the Edwin Smith Papyrus.

It is in Egypt, as exemplified by the Edwin Smith Papyrus, that the first anatomical descriptions appear in a systematic way. More than two hundred different anatomical parts have been described in the extant Egyptian medical literature.[9] Many of these terms appear in the Edwin Smith Papyrus and Breasted is entirely correct when he asserts that one reason why this document is so valuable is that it preserves for us a record of a scientific vocabulary in evolution. The first treatise writer(s) not only inherited but modified and created terms to describe the anatomy and pathological conditons giving us a medical vocabulary that is 6,000 years old. The language of these early medical terms was very archaic so that by the time the redaction of the original manuscript occurred around 1500 B.C., it was necessary for the editor to append glosses to explain the otherwise impenetrable meanings.

In the present article, there are provided lists and illustrations depicting the various anatomical and medical terms gleaned from the surviving medical papyri.[10] See Figures 2-6; Tables 1-2. It is to be noted that the anatomical terms derived from the Edwin Smith Papyrus focus almost exclusively on the skeletal and soft tissue parts of the head and neck. It was originally a treatise dealing systematically with traumatic injuries from the head down. Unfortunately, the 18th dynasty copyist broke off after the 48th case which meant that only the upper third of the body, i.e., the head and neck, were covered in this edition. Though the original was undoubtedly a complete manual of traumatic surgery, the Edwin Smith Papyrus represents only one-third of it.

Breasted is of the opinion that the original author was probably a military

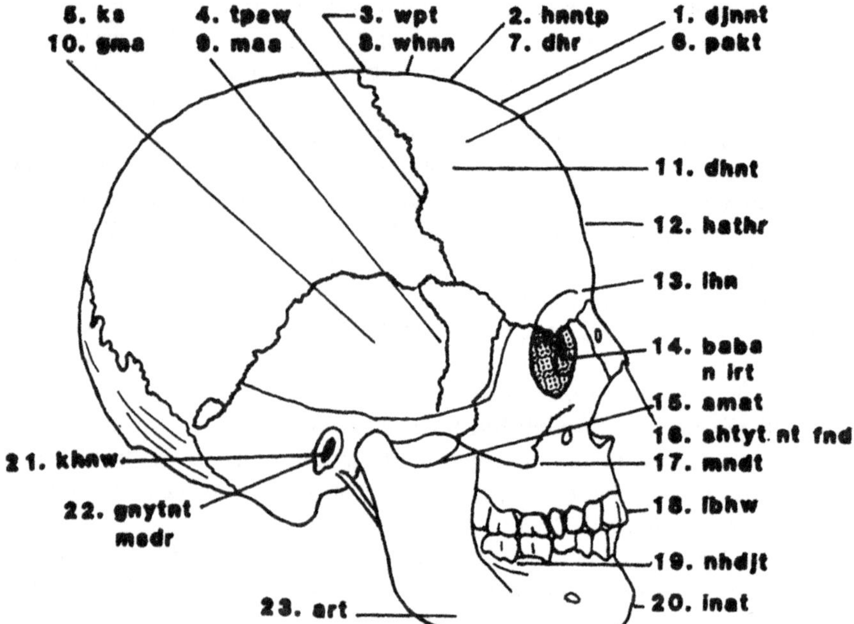

Figure II
Some Anatomical Terms of the Cranium

Egyptian	*English*	*Egyptian*	*English*
1. djnnt	cranium	13. ihn	superciliary arch (eyebrow)
2. hn n tp	cranial vault	14. baba n irt	orbit
3. wpt	vertex	15. amât	mandibular notch
4. tpaw	cranial suture	16. shtyt nt fnd	bony nasal chamber
5. ks	bone	17. mndt	cheek bone
6. pakt	cranial bone	18. ibhw	teeth
7. dhr	suture membrane	19. nhdjt	molars(?)
8. whnn	bregma*	20. inât	chin
9. maâ	temporal region	21. khnw	internal auditory canal
10. gma	temporal bone	22. gnyt nt msdjr	external auditory canal
11. dhnt	frontal bone		
12. hat hr	forehead	23. ârt	body of the mandible

*journal of coronal & sagittal sutures

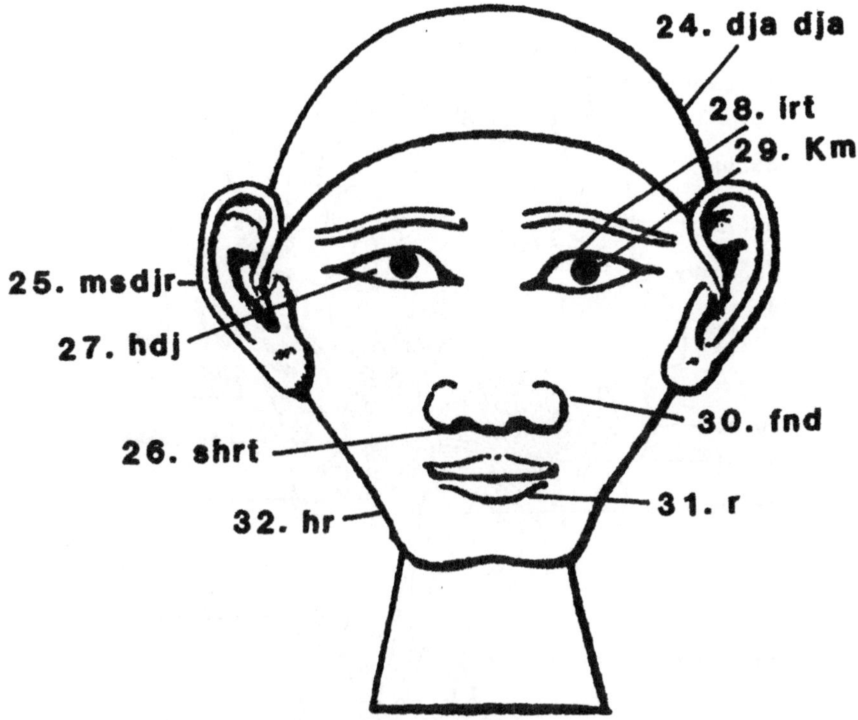

Figure III
Some Anatomical Terms of the Face

Egyptian	*English*
24. djadja	head (entire)
25. msdjr	ear
26. shrt	nostril
27. hdj	sclera (white of the eye)
28. irt	eye
29. km	pupil ("black" of the eye)
30. fnd	nose
31. r	mouth
32. hr	face

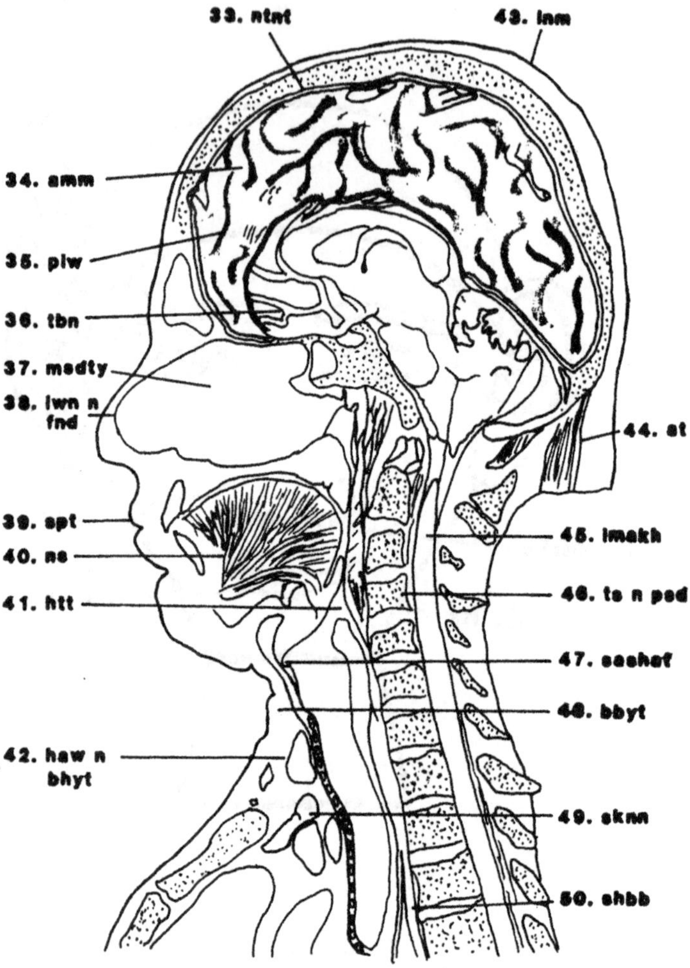

Figure IV
Some Soft Tissue Terms of the Head & Neck

Egyptian	*English*	*Egyptian*	*English*
33. ntnt	meninges	42. hâw n bbyt	thyroid(?)
34. âmm	cerebrum, brain	43. inm	skin
35. piw	convolutions (of brain)	44. ât	muscle
36. tbn	brain	45. imakh	spinal cord
37. msdty	nasal fossa	46. ts n psd	dorsal (cervical) vertebra
38. iwn n fnd	nasal cartilage	47. sashat	larynx
39. spt	lip	48. bbyt	supra-clavicular region
40. ns	tongue	49. sknn	thymus(?)
41. htt	pharynx	50. shbb	esophagus

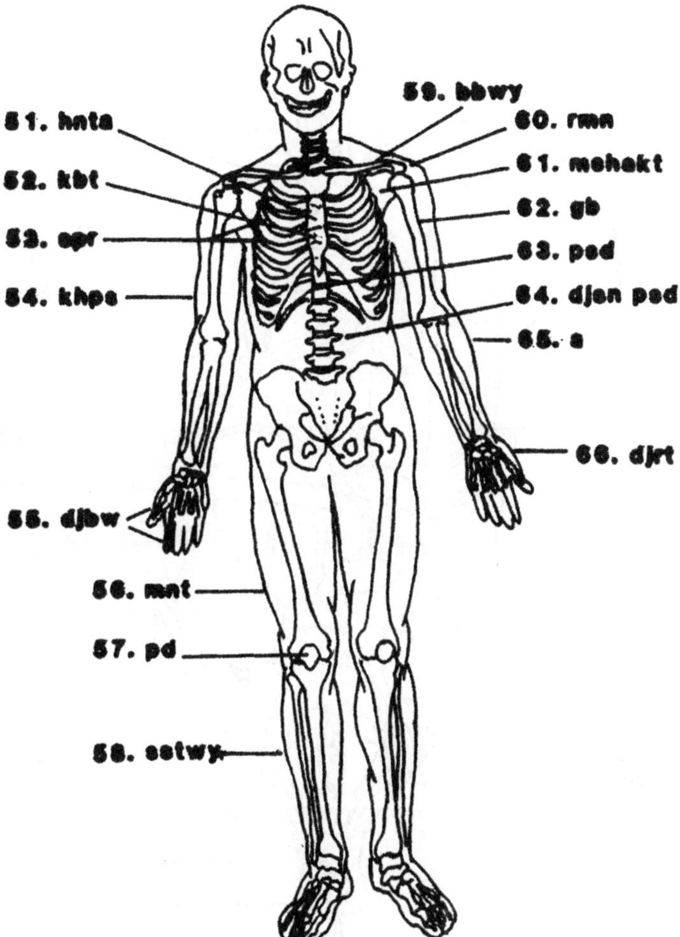

Figure V
Some Anatomical Terms of the Skeleton

Egyptian	*English*	*Egyptian*	*English*
51. hnta	manubrium	59. bbwy	clavicles
52. kbt	sternum	60. rmn	shoulder
53. spr	ribs	61. mshâkt	scapula
54. khps	arm	62. gb	humerus
55. djbw	fingers	63. psd	back
56. mnt	thigh	64. djs n psd	thoracic vertebra
57. pd	patella	65. â	forearm
58. sstwy	calves	66. djrt	hand

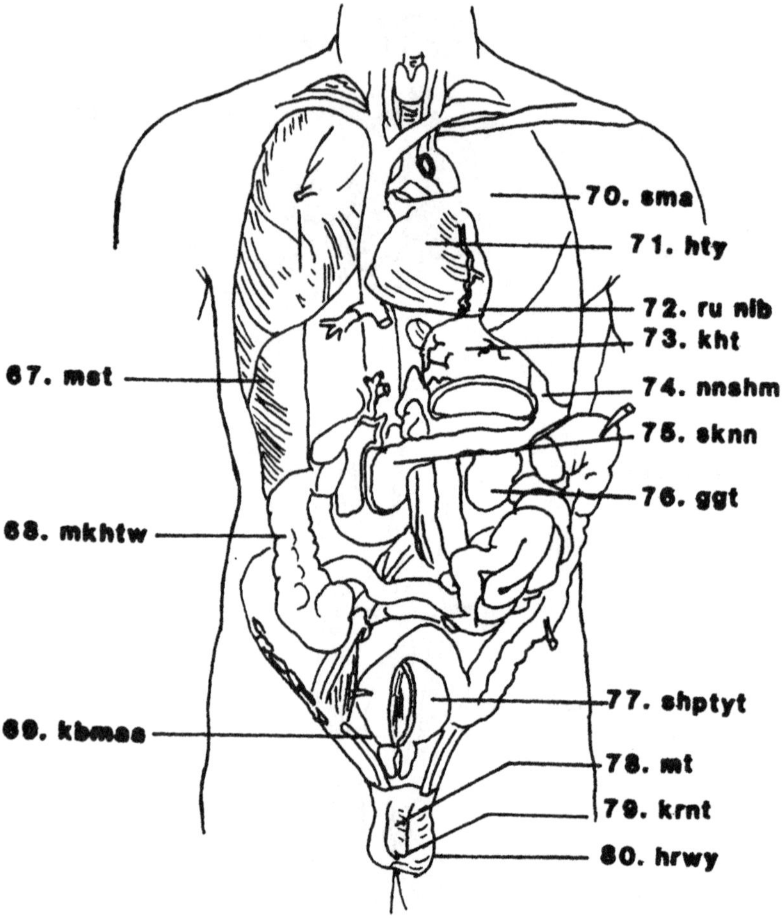

Figure VI
Some Anatomical Terms of the Viscera*

Egyptian	*English*	*Egyptian*	*English*
67. mst	liver	74. nnshm	spleen
68. mkhtw	intestine	75. sknn	pancreas
69. kbmaâ	rectum	76. ggt	kidney
70. sma	lung	77. shptyt	bladder
71. hty	heart (pericardium)	78. mt	phallus
72. ru n ib	cardia	79. krnt	prepuce
73. kht	stomach	80. hrwy	testicle

*Figure shows overlying organs cut away to reveal interior organs.

surgeon since the majority of the cases involve the kind of trauma most likely sustained in combat. Other medical historians are of the opinion that the original complier of this surgical manual actually drew upon his experiences treating traumatic injuries incurred during the construction of the Great Pyramid.[11] Yet the traumatic injuries described in the Edwin Smith Papyrus are much more easily reconciled to the assumption that they were received in combat. The nature and location of the wounds and injuries depicted are best understood as being delivered by hand-held weapons. According to Breasted, the original author was a battlefield surgeon who wrote this treatise as a capstone to a career full of varied surgical experience in the field. This is undoubtedly true as far as it goes but the Edwin Smith Papyrus conveys the distinct impression that the author was also drawing upon a reservoir of past knowledge. It is hard not to believe that, while writing this manual, he immersed himself in the medical literature written by his predecessors and amplified this "book" research with his own direct experience. The author does actually cite *The Book of What Pertains to the Embalmer* and *The Book of What Pertains to His Wounds* as references.[12] Our author was questionably a brilliant scholar, clinician, and writer, unifying these gifts to a degree rare in any age.

TABLE I
Additional List of Ancient Egyptian Anatomical Terms[10]

	Egyptian	English		Egyptian	English
1.	wgyt	ramus of the mandible	20.	tp n mndjwy	nipple
2.	ths n :nhbt	cervical vertebra	21.	wfa	lung
3.	wab n irt	"root of the eye"	22.	wpt nt kht	epigastrum
4.	khâm	anterior cervix (neck)	23.	khry	hypogastrum
5.	ish	saliva	24.	khpa	navel
6.	aîs n djnnt	cerebro-spinal organs	25.	bnf	bile
7.	nkh	cerebro-spinal fluid	26.	wdd	bile
8.	wrmw	convolutions of the brain	27.	phwyt	anus
9.	mtw	vessels, canals, channels	28.	khpdwy	buttocks
10.	snf	blood	29.	mwyt	urine
11.	shrtyw	blood vessel network	30.	bh	sperm
12.	wat	masseter muscle (jaw)	31.	mtwt	sperm
13.	hâwt	body	32.	hmt	uterus
14.	iwf	flesh	33.	shd	vulva
15.	bksw	spinal cord	34.	sptyshd	labia
16.	ts n psd	spinal vertebra	35.	kt	vagina
17.	mdw	skeleton; backbone(?)	36.	ânt	fingernail
18.	djefed	pupil	37.	inst	thigh
19.	mndj	breast	38.	rd	posterior thigh; hamstring

TABLE II
Some General Medical Terms From The Edwin Smith Papyrus[10]

	Egyptian	English
1.	wbnw	wound
2.	âr	penetrating
3.	djâr	to probe, to palpate
4.	kft	gash, cut, wound
5.	wbnw n kft	gaping wound
6.	khat	to examine, to observe
7.	st ib	"action of the heart;" pulse
8.	âd	heart muscle(?)
9.	thm	to perforate
10.	pshn	to split, to crack
11.	nha	disorder, disturbance
12.	ishw-w	to ooze, to exude
13.	tkhb	any fetid bodily excretion; pus, serum, etc.
14.	wr	exceedingly, massive
15.	shfwt	swelling, edema, tumor, pustule
16.	sd	fracture
17.	tia	convulsions(?)
18.	skr	injury, blow
19.	si	shuffle
20.	rwty	external, peripheral
21.	ih	pain, injury, affliction
22.	mdjd	pressure, compress
23.	djaw	disease, attack, ailment
24.	hr pwy	at the end of, distal
25.	ahd	weak, feeble, infirm
26.	dgmy	speechless, comatose(?)
27.	gr	silent, aphasic(?)
28.	gmw	sadness, obtundation(?)
29.	mdt	to speak
30.	nrwt	sprain
31.	wnkh	dislocation
32.	nswt	displacement, subluxation
33.	shm	crushing

Of the more than 200 anatomical terms identified in the Egyptian medical literaure, nearly 100 are found in the Edwin Smith Papyrus. However, this was a surgical treatise, and though filled with anatomical terms, we cannot assume that it or any of the other surviving medical papyri necessarily exhaust Egyptian anatomical terminology or contain the sum total of Egyptian anatomical knowledge. In our time, only in a modern textbook of anatomy could be found all of the thousands of anatomical terms used in modern medicine. Manetho informs us that Athothis, the second pharoah of the 1st dynasty, was a physician who wrote a textbook of anatomy and it is tempting to speculate that such a treatise—which would have been more or less contemporaneous with the Edwin Smith Papyrus—would have contained many more than have survived to the present and thus been more revealing of the true extent of Egyptian anatomical knowledge. Reading through the Edwin Smith Papyrus there is the sense that Egyptians had more knowledge of anatomy and surgery than we are accustomed to giving them credit for. Moreover, we assume that whatever anatomical knowledge they did come by was serendipitously acquired from the purely ritualistic dissections that accompanied the funerary ceremonies. We know that elsewhere in Africa, bodies were dissected on quasi-clinical grounds[13] but nothing of the sort is documented in the literature of ancient Egypt prior to the Alexandrian period when the ban against clinical dissection was lifted by the Ptolemies. Yet in reading through the Edwin Smith Papyrus, one cannot escape the conclusion that the Egyptian priest-physicians either used the thousands of funerary dissections for scientific instruction or found a way to perform purely clinical dissections.

There is a body of opinion, now somewhat diminished, that assumes that the ancient Egyptians had no knowledge of the mental functions of the human brain. Probably this is due to the Egyptians' habit of locating the anatomical seat of the soul, conscience, and feeling in the heart.[14] One of their reasons for doing so may be related to the keen sensitivity of the heart to mental and emotional states but there is simply no basis for assuming that the Egyptians did not know that the brain was the seat of all mental functioning. In fact the topmost part of the cranium, the vertex, is of tremendous importance in the pharoaonic mythos. It supports the crown which is fronted by the raised uraeus serpent, the symbol of divine and royal power. This raised serpent is positioned in such a way that the very top of the serpent's head, as it juts out from the pharoah's forehead, is exactly on a level with the vertex of the cranium. See Figure 7. The body of this "cranial" serpent extends backward in a sinuous fashion exactly down the middle of the cranium, attaching to the circular band that surrounds the head. This

The head of the raised serpent is exactly level with the vertex on both crowns of this royal pair.

body of the serpent effectively divides the cranium into two equal halves, or hemispheres, and symbolically serves the same purpose as the sagittgal suture of the cranium. See Figure 8. This serpent is therefore emblematic of that which divides while it unifies. See Figure 9. What is of further interest is that the Egyptian name for the cranial vertex is "wpt" which means "to open;" also "to discern" or "to judge," a clear reference to the cerebrum as the seat of judgement. But the symbolism inherent in the term "wpt" also signifies the "opening" of the higher cortical centers that correspond to the "awakened"state, in this way identical to the rising of the Kundalini Serpent of Tantric Yoga that climbs from the base of the spine to the top of the head during the course of spiritual excercises. The opening of the transcendental eye of spiritual vision occurs when this serpent energy reaches the vertex. It is significant that among the ritual kings and traditional priests of Africa, their power is said to reside in their heads; even in the rural South of the United States, the successful Voodoo doctor is said to be "strong in his head."[15]

Another datum that refutes the opinion that the Egyptians were unaware of the thinking functions of the brain comes from a linguistic analysis of an Egyptian word for "cerebrum" which is "âmm." This work also means "to know" and

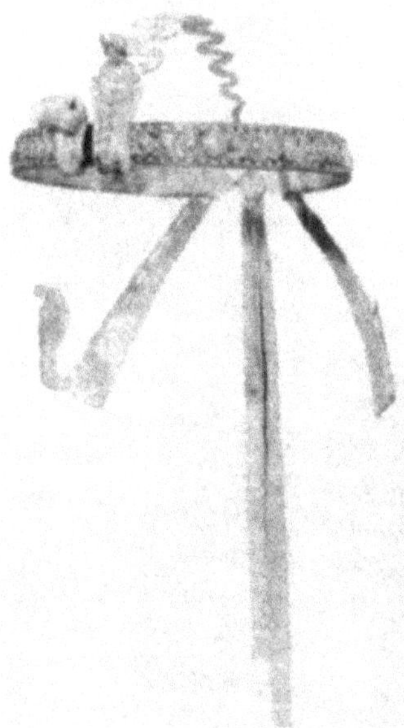

Uraeus Crown. The serpentine body recapitulates the sagittal suture of the cranium

The mummified crown of Tutankhamen in which the double uraeus serpent conjoins the two hemispheres of the brain.

"to understand," which defines, therefore, the anatomical cerebrum *and* its mental function.[16]

As revealed in the Edwin Smith Papyrus, the Egyptians not only designated the gross anatomy of the brain but also defined certain specific portions of it and their functions. One of their words for the temporal region of the skull was "maâ" and it is in the temporal region that the centers for hearing and speaking are situated. Thus one of the Egyptian locutions for "to listen" was "to give the maâ" in the same way we might say "lend an ear."[17] This locution for "to listen" does not, therefore, refer to the anatomical ear but to the sites in the brain where sounds are processed to give hearing. This is but one indication in the Edwin Smith Papyrus that the ancient Egyptians had identified and localized this important cortical center.

That the Egyptians had accurately mapped the internal anatomy of the head may be revealed in the anatomical phrase "wab n irt," which means literally "the root of the eye." According to Schwaller de Libicz, this idea of "the root of the eye" related to the nourishing functions of the vessels and nerves (mtw) and conforms to an actual anatomical reality. He points out that as the optic nerve enters the posterior aspect of the eye, it contains in its sheath the retinal artery which in truth does "nourish" the posterior portion of the eye.[18] He further tells us,

> "Root of the eye" cannot signify the orbtial cavity, but really does mean "root" which is designated by its determinative, a small plant. But the root is what nourishes the plant and it is therefore certain that the text, by "root," means to connote all of the nerve and blood channels . . .
>
> . . . the authors of this old papyrus knew very well the internal anatomy of the cranium.[19]

One of the most salient anatomical descriptions in the Edwin Smith Papyrus is that of the brain along with its convolutions and meningeal covering. Though we will comment on the brain's gross anatomy later, it is worthwhile here to explore the Egyptians' concept of the meninges and their functions. The Latin name that we use for the meninges is "mater," meaning "mother," and they consist of three layers: 1) the dura mater ("hard mother"), the tough, fibrous, outer layer that is directly apposite to the interior of the bony cranium; 2) the pia mater ("soft mother"), the soft, pliable inner meningeal layer that adheres closely to the outer substance of the brain itself; 3) the arachnoid ("spider-like"), a fine, reticulated, web-like membrane situated between the outer layer of the dura mater and the inner layer of the pia mater. The Egyptian word for meninges is "netnet," suggesting by the doubling of the word "net," the apparent two-fold nature of the meninges on gross inspection.[20] This term "net" is quite interesting: it is the Egyptian word for "weaving" and for "water."[21] It is also the

Egyptian name for Neith, the Virgin Mother goddess and the goddess of weaving, whose inscription on the entrance to her temple at Sais bore these words:

> I am all that has been, that is, or shall be. No mortal shall lift my veil.

The meninges symbolically are the woven "veil"which encloses the brain and spinal cord. The meninges also enclose the cerebrospinal fluid in which the entire brain and spinal cord structures are bathed, and we have seen how the root word "net" can also mean "water" or "fluid." Our Latin terminology "mater," or "mother," for the meninges is allusive to the most important aspect of Neith as one of the earliest Egyptian forms of the Great Mother. In this guise she is connected to water in her manifestation as the sky-goddess Nut, Mistress of the Celestial Waters. This simple root "net," by giving us in its duplicative form the Egyptian word for "meninges," contains an ensemble of meanings which resonate between the science and symbol of ancient Egypt.

The Egyptian word for cerebrospinal fluid—which bathes the brain and the spinal cord—is "nkh." We have already called attention to the special significance of our Latin terminology for the meninges, "mater" or "mother," and it should be no less interesting to us that the Egyptian word "nkh" can also signify "child" or "babe."[22] Taking the meninges, the cerebrospinal fluid, and the brain together, this ensemble forms a direct analogy to the enclosed, fluid-filled pregnant womb. To further this analogy, it is interesting to note than an older name for the anterior foramen of the brain's third ventricle is "the vulva" and the quadrigeminal cistern used to be called "the testes."[23] A key to understanding the genesis of the symbolic analogy between the cranium and its contents and the reproductive system might be discovered in the more primitive typology of the Melanesian Trobriand Islanders who have lived in their isolated South Sea habitat for more than 30,000 years. In their explanation of pregnancy, a spirit child comes to rest on the top of a woman's head and when conception occurs, the spirit child flows down through the head in the blood into the womb.[24] If, as the present author believes, these ideas had their genesis in the original African homeland of these people, then this would have been the earliest source of the imagery that connected the brain to the womb. These ideas represent a stage in the progress toward a physiologic conception of pregnancy and though the historic Egyptians were well acquainted with the physiologic nature of conception, they still preserved the earlier ideas as part of their scientific symbolism.

One last point of interest will demonstrate the continuing hold of the ancient symbolism on modern medical science. One of the names of the hippocampus, which is part of the brain's limbic system, is the "Horn of Ammon."[25] The hippocampus is a center of memory and "Ammon" is the Egyptian Amen, the ram-headed deity of Thebes. The root of the word "amen" is "men" and this latter, among several meanings, signifies "to be established, to be made firm, to

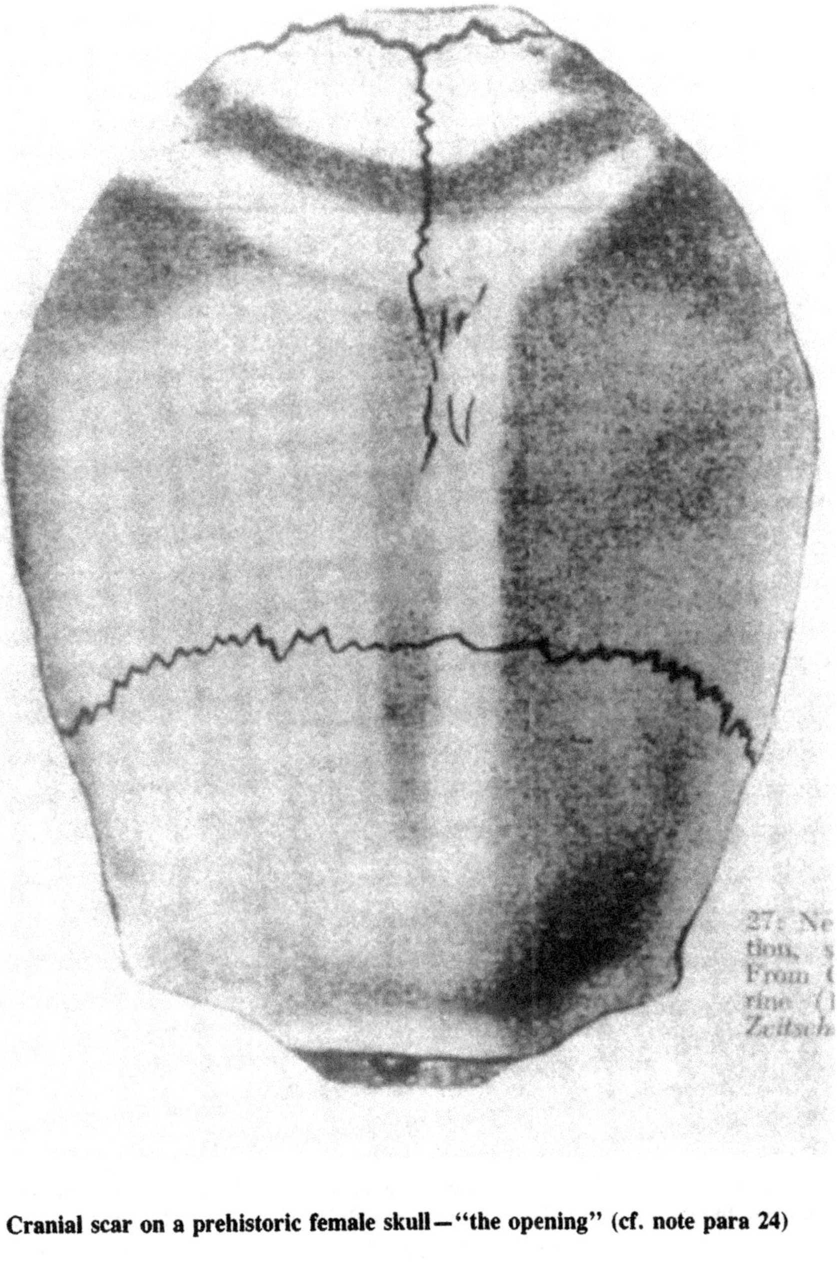

Cranial scar on a prehistoric female skull—"the opening" (cf. note para 24)

be made permanent," very appropriate meanings for a name denoting the part of the brain that is the memory center.

A few selected cases of the 48 recorded in the Edwin Smith Papyrus can now be considered to illustrate the scope of Egyptian medical knowledge.[26] It will be noted, as we proceed through this discussion, that this ancient physician adopts a clinical method almost identical to our own involving an examination, a diagnosis, a prognosis, and a treatment (if indicated); all of this some 35 centuries before Hippocrates.

The first case under consideration is Case 6. The reader will note that the case description is written in a characteristically concise, though figurative, style which is nonetheless clinical in tone. It is in this case that are first met the terms for "meninges" and "cerebrospinal fluid" as well as a description of the external appearance of the brain. The glosses are the explanatory notes, appended by the 18th dynasty editor, necessary to properly understand the archaic language.

CASE SIX: *A Gaping Wound In The Head With Compound Comminuted Fracture Of The Skull And Rupture Of The Meningeal Membranes.*

Examination: *If thou examinest a man having a gaping wound in his head, penetrating to the bone, smashing his skull, and rending open the brain of his skull, thou shouldst palpate his wound. Shouldst thou find that smash which is in his skull like those corrugations which form in molten copper, and something therein throbbing and fluttering under thy fingers, like the weak place of an infant's crown before it becomes whole—when it has happened there is no throbbing and fluttering under thy fingers until the brain of his skull is rent open—and he discharges blood from both his nostrils, and he suffers with stiffness in his neck,*

Diagnosis: *Thou shouldst say concerning him: "An ailment not to be treated."*

Treatment: *Thou shouldst anoint that wound with grease. Thou shalt not bind it; thou shalt not apply two strips upon it; until thou knowest he has reached a decisive point.*

Gloss A: *As for—"Smashing his skull, and rending open the brain of his skull," it means the smash is large, opening to the interior of his skull, to the membrane enveloping his brain, so that it breaks open his fluid into the interior of his head.*

Gloss B: *As for—"Those corrugations which form on molten copper," it means copper which the coppersmith pours off before it is forced into the mold, because of something foreign upon it like wrinkles. It is said: "It is like ripples of pus."*

Gloss A shows us conclusively that the author is denoting the meninges when he speaks of the "membrane" ('netnet') enveloping his brain." Moreover, he establishes their relation to the cerebrospinal fluid when he writes, "it breaks open the fluid into the interior of his head," meaning that the rupture of the meninges caused by the blow causes the fluid within it to flow into the cranial

Sword cut on an ancient Egyptian skull. The Edwin Smith papyrus describes such injuries.

cavity. Gloss B gives us an unmistakable description of the convolutons of the brain which in fact do resemble "corrugations which form on molten copper." The Examination, describing the hemmorhage through the nostrils with stiffness of the neck, is clinically on target. Any skull fracture due to penetrating trauma can very readily result in bleeding through the nose. The stiffness of the neck can be the result of two possible complications: 1) meningeal inflammation (meningitis) due to the invasion of the cerebrospinal structures by external microorganisms or 2) bleeding into the nuchal (posterior neck) segment of the spinal cord. As the surgeon notes here when he concluded that this is "An ailment not to be treated," these are both prognostically grave signs.

The next case, Case 8, presents a fascinating discussion of a rather rare neurosurgical condition, the "contre-coup" cranial injury. To understand this properly it must be pointed out that the motor and sensory fibers that control most voluntary movement and sensation actually arise on the side of the brain opposite to the side they control. This means that the movement and feeling on the left side of the body is controlled by the right side of the brain and that of the right side of the body by the left side of the brain. The term "contre-coup" means that the force of a blow on one side of the skull is transmitted and causes injury to the opposite side of the brain. The effects of this injury will be felt on the side of the skull to which the blow was delivered rather than, as might be expected, the opposite side. We might note here, by the way, that this description of a contre-coup injury makes it almost certain that we are dealing here with work of a battlefield surgeon since this is precisely the kind of injury that would be caused by a club striking the side of the head.

CASE EIGHT: *Compound Comminuted Fracture Of The Skull Displaying No Visible External Injury.*

Examination: *If thou examinest a man having a smash of his skull, under the skin of his head, while there is nothing at all upon it, thou sholuldst palpate his wound. Shouldst thou find that there is a swelling protruding on the outside of that smash which is in his skull, while his eye is askew because of it, on the side of him having that injury which is in his skull; and he walks shuffling with his sole, on the side of him having that injury is in his skull,*

Diagnosis: *Thou shouldst account him one who something entering from outside has smitten, as one who does not release the head of his shoulder fork, and one who does not fall with his nails in the middle of his palm; while he discharges blood from both his nostrils and from both his ears, and he suffers with stiffness in his neck. An ailment not to be treated.*

Treatment: *His treatment is sitting, until he gains color, and until thou knowest he has reached the decisive point.*

Second Examination: *Now as soon as thou findest that smash which is in his skull like those corrugations which form on molten copper, and something therein throbbing and fluttering under thy fingers like the weak place of an infant's crown before it knits together—when it has happened there is no throbbing and fluttering under thy fingers, until the brain of his skull is rent open—and he discharges blood from both his nostrils and both his ears, and he suffers with stiffness in his neck.*

Second Diagnosis: *Thou shouldst say concerning him: "An ailment not to be treated."*

Gloss A: *As for—"A smash in his skull under the skin of his head, there being no wound at all upon it," it means a smash of the shell of his skull, the flesh of his head being injured.*

Gloss B: *As for—"He walks with shuffling with his sole," he (the surgeon) is speaking about his walking with his sole dragging, so that it is not easy for him to walk when the sole is feeble and turned over, while the tips of his toes are contracted to the ball of his sole, and the toes walking fumbling the ground. The surgeon says: "He shuffles," concerning it.*

Gloss C: *As for—"One whom something entering from outside has smitten," on the side of him having this injury, it means one whom something entering from outside presses, on the side of him having this injury.*

This modern clinician can only read these case presentations with amazement and admiration. The ability to relate a specific trauma to a complex set of neurological signs and symptoms as we see here is the mark of a physician whose clinical acumen has been developed to the highest degree. The physician was well aware than an illness had a natural history which underwent excerbations and remissions before the final outcome became conclusive. This is indicated in this case by virtue of the second examination. In fact in Case 7, the surgeon records his findings and opinions which are derived from yet a third examination. In the Second Examination of this case we seem to have the only known Egyptian reference to the procedure of trephination when the patient's skull is said to be "rent open." Trephination, practiced extensively throughout Africa since prehistoric times, is a method in which an instrument is used to bore through the skull to remove bony fragments from a fracture or to relieve cranial pressure. Many have doubted that the Egyptians actually used this technique but Paul Ghalioungui has reproduced photos of two trephined skulls from an Egyptian gravesite.[27] If we are correct is assuming, after Breasted,[28] that it is trephining being referred to in this case, then it is additional proof that this technique was a part of the therapeutic armamentarium of ancient Egyptian physicians.

Gloss B gives a lucid and painstaking description of the shuffling gait with contractures of the toes, indicative of a hemi-paresis or severe motor weakness, caused by this contre-coup injury. Then, as now, the mainstay of care was supportive treatment.

Finally it must be pointed out that when the surgeon says, "his eye is askew," as a result of this injury he seems to be referring to damage to the oculomotor nerve, one of three controlling eye movements.[29] Again, the remarkable thing to

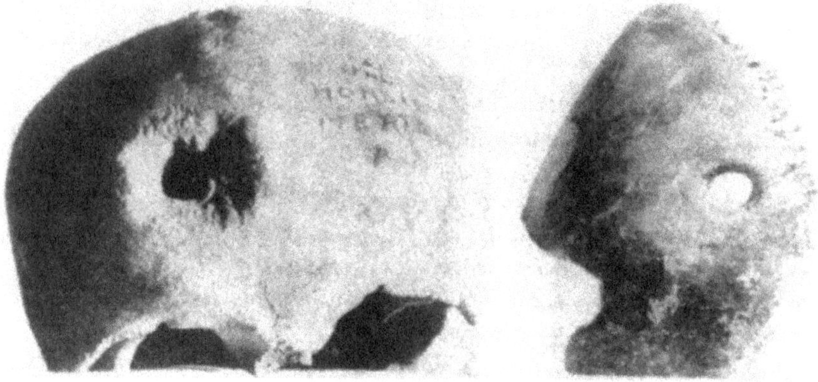

Two trephined skulls from ancient Egypt

note is the way in which the surgeon correctly relates a specific event (head trauma) to a neurological outcome.

Case 20 is one of four in which the surgeon demonstrates his knowledge of the relationship between injuries to the temporal portion of the brain and the faculty of speaking. In the anterior portion of the temporal region of the brain lies Broca's area which is the motor center of speech. An injury or lesion here affects the patient's ability to properly articulate words, though he will understand what is being said. Behind Broca's area is Wernicke's area which is the receptive center of speech; a lesion here affects the patient's ability to understand the spoken word though the purely mechanical ability to form words remains untouched. Persons affected in Wernicke's area will speak coherently but in meaningless, non-sensical phrases. A speech problem affecting Broca's area is known as "expressive asphasia" and that in Wernicke's area as "receptive aphasia." Not uncommonly, a temporal lesion will affect both areas causing a "mixed" or "total" aphasia.

CASE TWENTY: *A Wound In The Temple Perforating The Bone.*

Examination: *If thou examinest a man having a wound in his temple, penetrating to the bone, and perforating his temporal bone, while his two eyes are blood-shot, he discharges blood from both his nostrils, and a little drops; if thou puttest thy finger on the mouth of that wound he shudders exceedingly; if thou ask of him concerning his malady and he speaketh not to thee; while copious tears fall from both his eyes, so that he thrusts his hand often to his face that he may wipe both his eyes with the back of his hand as a child does, and does not know that he does so.*

Diagnosis: *Thou shouldst say concerning him: "One having a wound in his temple, penetrating to the bone, and perforating his temporal bone; while he discharges blood from both his nostrils, he suffers with stiffness in his neck, and he is speechless. An ailment not to be treated,"*

The patient is unable to verbally respond to the surgeon's interrogation which shows that the surgeon recognizes this as an expressive aphasia caused by an injury to the temporal portion of the brain. The tearing of the eyes is a very interesting sign. Trauma to the temple can result in a facial nerve injury causing increased tearing in the eye on the involved side. But our ancient surgeon is very explicit about the presence of *bilateral* tearing. Individuals suffering from an expressive aphasia will often become so frustrated at their inability to speak properly that they will burst into tears.[30] As for the repetitious movements of the hand to the eyes, Schwaller de Lubicz considers this an example of an "apraxia," a neurological sign characterized by meaningless, unconscious movements.[31]

Case 22 is very similar to Case 20 and seems to describe a total aphasia. In the Examination, the surgeon says concerning the patient, "If thou callest to him and he is speechless and cannot speak . . .," which may indicate an absolute incapacity for speech such as would be true of total aphasia. However, Schwaller de Lubicz gives another possible interpretation of this locution. Looking at Gloss C, it states: "As for—'He is speechless,' it means that he is silent in sadness, without speaking, like one suffering with feebleness (prostration?) because of something that has entered from outside." The combination of speechlessness and "silent in sadness"may refer to a king of mental obtundation that would justify us in thinking, as Schwaller de Lubicz believes, that this patient is in a coma.[32] Whatever the case, it is difficult not to believe that the ancient Egyptian physicians, on the basis of the evidence presented here, identified and possibly even mapped the location and function of certain important cortical centers of the brain, a feat not to be achieved again until the 19th century.

Case 31 is one of a group (Cases 29-33) which demonstrates further the uncommon level of clinical expertise achieved by this ancient surgeon. He describes in accurate detail the catastrophic clinical consequences of a certain type of spinal cord injury.

CASE THIRTY-ONE: *Dislocation Of A Cervical Vertebra.*

Examination: *If thou examinest a man having a dislocation in a vertebra of his neck, shouldst thou find him unconscious of his two arms and his two legs on account of it, while his phallus is erected on account of it, and urine drops from his member without his knowing it; his flesh has received wind; his two eyes are blood-shot; it is a dislocation of a vertebra of his neck extending to his backbone which causes him to be unconscious of his two arms and his two legs. If, however, the middle vertebra of his neck is dislocated, it is an "emissio seminis" which befalls his phallus.*

Diagnosis: *Thou shouldst say concerning him: "One having a dislocation in a vertebra of his neck, while he is unconscious of his two legs and his two arms, and his urine dribbles. An ailment not to be treated."*

Gloss A: *As for—"A dislocation in a vertebra of his neck," he is speaking of a separation of one vertebra of his neck from another, the flesh which is over it bleeding uninjured; as one says, "It is wnkh," concerning things which had been joined together, when one has been severed from another.*

Gloss B: *As for—"It is an 'emissio seminis' which befalls his phallus," it means that his phallus is erected and has a discharge from the end of his phallus. It is said: "It remains stationary" (mn saw), when it cannot sink downward and it cannot lift upward.*

Gloss C: *As for—" While his urine dribbles," it means that urine drops from his phallus and cannot hold back for him.*

Figure XIII

Vertebral Dislocation (see Case 31)

The language is so simple and concise that it may not be easy to appreciate the mine of clinical information contained in this case description. First there is a completely accurate description of quadriplegia ("unconscious of his two arms and his two legs") resulting from a compression injury to the cervical spinal cord due to a spinal dislocation. Though not specified, it is thought that this compression occurs below the 4th cervical vertebra because breathing remains intact.[33] The descriptions of the genitourinary complications are very striking for our surgeon delineates priapism, spermatorrhea, and bladder incontinence as complications of this condition. Can it not be assumed that he knew that the physiological sexual response and the urinary functions are mediated through the spinal cord?[34] Such things did not become known to modern medicine until the last century. One other phrase from this Case begs explanation and that is the reference in the Examination to the fact that "his flesh has received wind." If a quadriplegic patient experiences a prolonged survival, his body becomes thick and soft. Schwaller de Lubicz is of the opinion that this phrase "his flesh has received wind" refers to the "insufflation" effect that occurs in the quadriplegic body.[35]

Cases 29-33 all represent additional case descriptions of vertebral dislocations and sub-luxations and their clinical consequences. At present, some of these conditons are almost impossible to detect or describe fully without X-ray studies. The question then arises is how did our ancient surgeon, living nad practicing 6,000 years ago, manage to diagnose and describe these problems *without* benefit of X-rays?

A tour through the Edwin Smith Papyrus puts us in the rather incongruous position of having to assert that as history dawns in the Nile Valley at the end of the 5th millenium B.C., medicine is already at a very advanced state and that in fact, it underwent a decline in later ages which was not reversed until the scientific breakthroughs of the 18th and 19th centuries. It is the conceit of modern historiography that human culture has evolved in linear fashion from the simple to the complex, from the primitive to the advanced, from the lower to the higher, reaching its pinnacle in the post-Renaissance civilization of Western Europe. A more clear-sighted perception of history would show us that this flies in the face of the true facts; the progression of human civilization might be more accurately described as a sinusoidal wave, in which the ebb and flow of civilized progress is represented by peaks and valleys. From every pinnacle there is a regression and every succeeding civilization is faced with having to re-discover old truths. The Greek "miracle" is but the detritus of ancient Egyptian thought and many of the "marvels" of the modern age are the fruit of recovering older ideas. But this recovery is only partial. Schwaller de Lubicz calls modern science "a science without illumination" because it has consciously forfeited the dynamic interplay between science and symbol which made Egyptian wisdom proverbial throughout the ancient world.

Notes

1. Bogdnoff, M.D., et al, editors, "Introduction" to *The Aphorisms of Hippocrates*, Birmingham, The Classics of Medicine Library, 1982, p. 3.
2. Ghalioungui, P., *The House of Life: Magic and Medical Science in Ancient Egypt*, Amsterdam, B.M. Israel, 1973, p. 31.
3. Ibid., p. 41.
4. Ibid., p. 42.
5. Ibid., p. 40-41.
6. Ibid.
7. Finch, C., "The African Background of Medical Science," *Blacks in Science: Ancient and Modern*, I. Van Sertima, editor, New Brunswick: Journal of African Civilizations, Ltd., 1983, pp. 148-55.
8. See Lamy, L. *Egyptian Mysteries*, New York: Crossroad, 1981, p. 6, for a reproduction of an ivory tablet from the 1st dynasty on which is inscribed the words "Sirius, Opener of the Year, Inundation 1."

9. Ghalioungui, op. cit., p. 48.

10. See Leca, A.P., *La Medécine Egyptienne*, Paris: Les Editions Roger DaCosta, 1983 and Schwaller de Lubicz, R.A., *Le Temple De L'Homme*, Volume 1, Paris: Caracteres, 1960 for lists of Egyptian medical and anatomical terms.

11. Ghalioungui, op. cit., p. 44.

12. Breasted, J.H., *The Edwin Smyth Papyrus*, Brimingham: The Classics of Medicine Library, 1984, pp. 434, 446. The titles that the ancient author refers to in Breasted's translation are rendered respectively as "Treatise on What Pertains to His Wounds" and "Treatise on What Pertains to the Embalmer."

13. See Finch, op. cit., p. 149.

14. The Egyptian word for "heart" in this usage is "ib." Today we still used terms such as "hard-hearted," "tender-hearted," or "stout-hearted" to describe emotional states or character types.

15. Puckett, N.N., *The Magic and Folk Beliefs of the Southern Negro*, New York: Dover Publications, Inc., 1969, p. 189.

16. Budge, E.A.W., *An Egyptian Hieroglyphic Dictionary*, New York: Dover Publications, Inc., 1978, pp. 120-21.

17. See Schwaller de Lubicz, op. cit., p. 568.

18. Ibid., p. 572.

19. Ibid., p. 573.

20. Ibid., p. 583. In gross appearance, the meninges are a two-fold membrane; the third layer of the meninges, the arachnoid, is not readily observable on external inspection because it is "sandwiched" between the dura mater and the pia mater.

21. See Budge, op. cit., pp. 399-400.

22. Ibid., p. 386.

23. Bell, C., *Engravings of the Brain and Nerves*, Birmingham, The Classics of Medicine Library, 1982, pp. 30, 45.

24. Malinowski, B., *The Sexual Life of Savages in Northwestern Melanesia*, London: Routledge & Kegan Paul, 1982, p. 149. The Trobriand Islanders claim that in order for conception to occur, the woman has to "be opened" which is the function of sexual intercourse. This sexual opening is in some way connected to the "opening" (wpt) that occurs on the top of the head which allows the spirit-child to descend to the womb. This relationship is confirmed in a remarkable way by H.E. Sigerist who, on page 113 of his *Primitive and Archaic Medicine*, refers to the discovery in 1895 of a number of *female* skeletons from prehistoric France whose skulls bore "a T-shaped scar beginning on the frontal bone, running all along the sagittal suture, and branching into two parts along the posterior edge of the parietal bones." This would have been a primitive type of "opening" (wpt) of the head as a mode of conception.

25. Bell, op. cit., p. 17; also, *Dorland's Medical Dictionary*, Philadelphia: W.B. Saunders, 1974, p. 724.

26. All of the following case cited are taken from the Classics of Medicine Library edited of Breasted's translation. See Note #12.

27. See Ghalioungui, op. cit., plates #15 a and b, after p. 122.

28. Breasted, op. cit., pp. 56, 208.

29. The three cranial nerves controlling eye movements are the oculomotor (III), the trochlear (IV), and the abducens (VI). According to my neurologist informant, Dr. Patrick Griffith, the oculomotor and the trochlear are the most likely to be affected by blunt trauma to the temporal region, causing the eye to skew.

30. The author would like to express his gratitude to Dr. Patrick Griffith for his comments on this material.

31. Schwaller de Lubicz, op. cit., p. 622.

32. Ibid., pp. 623-24.

33. Ibid., p. 588.

34. One of the errors for which Greek medicine is repeatedly called to task is the idea that male sperm is formed in the spinal cord. This idea was very likely due to a misinterpretation of the Egyptians' clinical description of "emissio seminis" that results from a spinal injury.

35. Schwaller de Lubicz, op. cit., p. 589.

Additional References

Majno. G., *The Healing Hand*, Cambridge: Harvard University Press, 1975.

Sigerist, H.E., *Primitive and Archaic Medicine*, New York: Oxford University Press, 1972.

TOWARDS A SOCIOLOGY OF MAATIAN ETHICS: LITERATURE AND CONTEXT

Maulana Karenga

I. Introduction

A critical sociological study of ancient Egyptian or Maatian ethics provides both intellectual promise and challenge for several reasons. First, there is a clear quantitative and qualitative poverty of critical studies on ancient Egyptian religion and ethics. There is in fact no serious work on ancient Egypt with ethics in its title and only a few titles which give ethics more than a perfunctory and per forma treatment in the course of discussions on other subjects. F.W. Read's (1925) *Egyptian Religion and Ethics* succeeds in yielding little of either. Instead, it is an unscholarly compendium of uninsightful assertions, factual and interpretative errors and undisguised bias. Easily the best early works on Egyptian religion and ethics are Renouf (1880), Petrie (1898), Breasted (1934), and Frankfort (1961) in spite of their anticipatable problems of interpretation and focus. More currently Morenze (1978) especially, and Hornung (1985) stand out as having evolved beyond the essentially biased and intellectually impoverished early treatment of Egyptian religion.

One might wonder, as a matter of intellectual curiosity, why in comparison with an established and developing literature on religions of other great classical civilizations, i.e., China and India, that the systematic and critical study of Maat is a neglected or ill-treated field in the sociology, phenomenology and history of religion. In fact, it is usually relegated to the less-than-academically-respectable area of the occult where one may use its literature to achieve numinous experiences but not for intellectual inquiry into the varied evolution and meaning of the religious experience of humankind. There are perhaps three main reasons for this academic and intellectual mistreatment and neglect of Maat. First, as Renouf (1880:1ff) points out, Maat suffered from the fact that "its last centuries coincide with the first centuries of the Christian religion which gradually supplanted it." The category "supplant" is clearly a euphemism, for what transpired was a systematic attack on Maat by early "Christian apologists" (Renouf's appellation) and the eventual outlawing of Maat through edict by Theodosius in the 4th century and again by Justinian in the 6th century (James, 1954:154). Christian antagonists like Clement of Alexandria and Origen mocked and reductively translated Maat as essentially zoolatry without attempting to understand its animal and natural symbolism and the theology and ethics which embraced and explained it (Renouf, 1880:2ff). It was as if the Christians in Spain who had been conquered by the Moors were attacked for ritualistic cannibalism for practicing communion and symbolically eating the body and drinking the blood of Jesus.

Secondly, Renouf attributes the intellectual and religious hostility to reports of the Greeks whose weighty influence in European culture is well established. Although the Greeks admired the Egyptians for their wisdom, science, art, etc., and even borrowed from them and studied under them as Herodotus, Strabo, Plato, Diodorus Siculus and others report (James, 1954), they are also on record as finding the Egyptians' symbolic use of animals in religious expression distasteful and confusing. Finally, classical European scholars like Junvenal ridiculed this about Egyptian religion and thus left a legacy which tended to contribute to intellectual disappreciation and disinterest in the critical study of Egyptian religion.

Thirdly, Egyptian religion suffers from the severe biblical criticism of Egypt and its alleged "polytheism" and "idolatry" (Weber, 1925:200-201). Egypt is at once the mythic "land of bondage" and a spiritually corruptive context for biblical Israel, struggling to establish and keep its covenant with Yahweh. Scholars influenced by this Judeo-Christian interpretation are also less likely to find value or interest in the critical study of Egypt's "questionable" religion. Given all this negative data from both Western religious and cultural sources, then Renouf (1880:4) rightly observes that it is no wonder that "many writers should at present speak of Egyptian religion as one of the lowest and grossest forms of nature-worship, as consisting in what is commonly called African fetishism, or at least being based on it." He (1880:5) concludes by observing that one, however, should be wary of mistaking symbol for substance and remember as a sobering fact that caricaturization of Judaism and Christianity by the Romans and others and the ambiguous symbolism in Christianity with its "Lamb of God", and Apocalypse Lamb with seven horns and seven eyes who is the Lord of Lords and King of Kings—being worshipped by four beasts as well as other similar imagery. It is at this point one recognizes most clearly the value of Weber's "interpretive" or "understanding" sociology which calls for the interpretation and understanding of motives and conduct of others "in terms of their professed or ascribed intentions" and their own framework, if one is to claim an adequate understanding of the object of study (Gerth and Mills, 1958:56).

A second reason that the sociological study of Maatian ethics offers such intellectual promise and challenge is its ethical and religious parallels to Judeo-Christian religion and ethics—and the speculation and inquiry this suggests concerning origins, influence and interactions. Even Max Weber (1925) in his *Ancient Judaism* points to both Judaism's contributions from and affinities with

Maat. Among those he lists and discusses are prescriptions of the Decalog and the charity ethic. The "strong similarities" to the Decalog prescriptions which are found in the Maatian Book of Coming Forth By Day (commonly called the Book of the Dead), he (1925:250ff) notes, predate the Decalog, being "available in complete form even before the Israelite confederacy was formed." A central theme in the charity ethic reads like a passage from the Christian New Testament. It is a prescriptive to give "bread to the hungry, water to the thirsty, clothes to the naked and a boat to those without one" (Karenga, 1984:111). It is these similarities and othes that leads Weber (1925:250) to state that "In substance these commandments anticipate largely the charity of the Gospels." And that "presumably the development of old Israelite charity was influenced by Egypt, directly or by way of Phoenicia."

But the scholar who did the most to establish and explicate this link is undoubtdly James Breasted, America's pioneer orientalist, who in his seminal work, *The Dawn of Conscience*, traced the evolution of human conscience and ethics in Egypt and showed Israel's debt to Egypt. "It is now quite evident," he (1934:xv) wrote in this work, "that the ripe social and moral development of mankind in the Nile Valley, which is three thousand years older than that of the Hebrews, contributed essentially to the formation of the Hebrew literature which we call the Old Testament." One must conclude then that "Our moral heritage, therefore, derives from a wider *human* past enormously older than the Hebrews, and it has come to us rather *through* the Hebrews than *from* them." He goes on to say that "the rise of man to social idealism," then, "took place long before the traditional theologians' 'age of revelation' began." And what is equally important to him "(i)t was a result of the social experience of *man himself* and was not projected into the world outside." This, of course, is a contention which Weber, Durkheim and Marx would have little trouble accepting and which likewise fits well within the conceptual arc and thrust of the sociology of religion and ethics.

Finally, Breasted (1934:Chapter XVII) details the Egyptian contribution stressing conceptual data, narrative imagery and textual borrowing. Especially, stressed is the literal and verbatim borrowing in the Book of Proverbs from the Book of Amenomope, written three hundred years before Solomon. Weber (1925:6) is correct in his contention that "Egyptian influences rested on trade relations between the Old Kingdom and the Phoenician coast, on Egyptian mining in the Sinai peninsula, and on geographic nearness." But as I (Karenga, 1982:171) have argued elsewhere, it was also because Egypt was a cultural paradigm for the surrounding world—even for Greece at one point (James, 1954). And thus as F. Ll. Griffith, an eminent Egyptologist, argues, the borrowing was not abnormal, for "when the Hebrews were becoming civilized under Solomon and his successors, they looked especially to Egypt and Babylonia for instruction in the arts of life . . ." (quoted in Karenga, 1982:171). However, although such contentions are intellectually provocative to some, to others they are emotionally disconcerting and one could make a case for the proposition that this too is one of the reasons Egypt has not been treated with more intellectual objectivity and appreciation. For what is at stake is no the simple revision of historical data, but the complex challenge to the priority and uniqueness of a major religious tradition and the authenticity of various claims associated with the above assumptions. Nevertheless, the intellectual promise and challenge remain and deserve an honest and objective pursuit.

Finally, a sociological study of Maatian ethics provides an intellectual challenge and promise because of the poverty of work done on the sociology of ethics as distinct from the sociology of religion. As Gill (1975:7) notes, "There is a small but growing interest amongst sociologists in the social determinants of moral ideas—though this has traditionally been a pursuit of anthropologists rather than sociologists." Among those pursuing such work are: Alasdair MacIntyre, *A Short History of Ethics* (1966); Maria Ossowska, *Social Determinants of Moral Ideas* (1970); and John Barnsley, *The Social Reality of Ethics* (1972). Still the poverty of works done in the general area of the sociology of religion remains.

Barnsley (1972:17ff) states that there are at least four reasons why "this aspect of sociology has received little attention relative to its importance." These are 1) the fact that "the subject straddles several disciplines" and thus require greater intellectual effort and competence; 2) the "current tendency to disguise moral decisions as technical decisions" given the "cult of objectivity" and the peril and problematic ethical studies pose to the pursuit and maintenance of scientific status in one's work; 3)the "lack of a common moral vocabulary for discussing, and potentially reconciling (the) diverse opinions" which populate and challenge our common culture; and 4) "the intrinsic difficulties of the field" of the sociology of ethics which pose problems of conceptual clarity usually assigned to philosophy, more specifically, more philosophy. Given these problems and the difficulties they pose, a critical contribution to the sociology of ethics becomes both an intellectual challenge and promise and a much-needed addition to the field.

II. The Socio-Historical Context of Maatian Ethics

The socio-historical setting for Maatian ethics reaches back to a period between 4000 and 3500 B.C.E when the Egyptian state was established out of two opposing kingdoms, Upper and Lower Egypt, in two successive unions. "These two unions, the earliest great national organizations of men in history, brought before the minds of men an imposing fabric of the *state* which at length made a profound impression upon religion" (Breasted, 1934:19). At the same time, however, as argued below, religion was always a critical force in the organization and shaping of the state, for it gave the state both its moral and political paradigm

(Carruthers, 1984: Chapter 3). This is reflected in both the *Shabaka Text* (Memphite Theology), discussed below, which is an intellectual legitimation of divine kingship and the divine mandate to rule, and in the *Sebait*, the *Instructions*, which offer an implicit and explicit theory and view of leadership and society based on Maat, the Eyptian moral and spiritual way.

Maatian ethics evolved in a period of consolidation and growth, and peace and security with Menes' conquest of Lower Egypt and the uniting of it with Upper Egypt circa 3500 B.C.E., which laid the basis for the establishment of the First Dynasty and the expansion and growth of the Egyptian state. This in turn led to the growth of a bureaucracy, similar to the Chinese bureaucracy with its emphasis on meritocracy and righteous leadership (leadership and appropriate comparisons will be made below). This rising bureaucracy is key to the formulation and evolution of Maatian ethics. For they were both indispensable, capable and socially conscious. In fact, "Egypt was a land which by its very geographical form demanded careful administration" (James, 1984:51). It was "six hundred miles of Nile Valley from Memphis, approximately at the apex of the Delta, south to Aswan." Historically, weak administration produced and/or contributed to internal chaos, as in the Intermediate Periods (circa 2475-2160 and 1788-1580 B.C.E.), and strong administration as in the Old Kingdom (2980-2475 B.C.E.) insured order and security and led to great achievement. This was Egypt's Pyramid Age and the time of great intellectual, architectural, and scientific achievements and organization of its vast human and material resources was essential.

The bureaucracy was essentially a civil service, as scholars have noted. And "the practice of official authority was inspired by disinterested service and justice on the part of the bureaucrats in the interests of the king and his subjects" (James, 1984:52). The chief executive officer of the bureaucrats was the prime minister and those under him in the greatest numbers bore the title "sesh" literally scribe, but with the extended meaning of civil servant and intellectual. Thus, sesh became synonomous with civil service and the scribal profession was "the principal repository of literacy and learning in the land." Moreover, "the mastery of reading and writing were essential for proper exercise of administration, and the scribal schools, . . . were undoubtedly academies for the bureaucracy.

The prime minister's office and tradition was significant, however, not only for its administrative role but also for: 1) the formal royal instructions by which the prime minister carried out his duties, and 2) the tradition among prime ministers of setting down *Instructions* (*Sebait*) for those who succeeded them and which became one of the main sources of Maatian ethics. In fact, the oldest complete book of *Instructions* is by Ptah-Hotep, vizier or prime minister of King Isesi of the Fifth Dynasty (c. 2350-2310 B.C.E.) (Lichtheim, 1975:61ff; Simpson, 1973:159ff). It became the model for all other *Sebait*.

Another aspect of socio-historical setting in which Maatian ethics were shaped, was Egypt's secure and peaceful context. As James (1984:71) notes, the settled, peaceful and tradition-oriented life "encouraged a more placid and benevolent attitude to humanity than might be found in countries afflected by endemic warfare and poor living conditions." In other words, "In Egypt where society was nurtured in such relatively comfortable conditions, the virtues of moderation and justice were more easily practiced and sustained than in lands torn by conflict," such as Palestine and Mesopotamia. Thus, the model person is not the warrior or even priest, but the gentle person—who serves and is responsible. Sheltered by a strong central government, a self-sufficient economy and by a capable army and a difficult geography which discouraged invaders, Egypt up to the 11th Dynasty enjoyed an unparalleled era of peace, development and great achievement (Wilson, 1956:13). And even afterwards in the Middle Kingdom when order and a strong central government were restored, art, architecture and ethical and creative literature flourished and expressed a self-confidence, optimism and humanity reflective of the socio-political state of things.

In summary, then, Maatian ethics evolve in a context of social order and development, and key to their emergence is the *sesh* (scholar, scribe or bureaucrat). It is from these that the formulation of the ethical vision emerges and it is they who advocate and attempt to bring into being the just society. Moreover, as discussed below, the *Seba* (moral teachers), i.e., scribes as teachers of ethics, pose a philosophical paradigm of righteous leadership supported by a moral culture as key to the achievement of the just society. And it is this paradigm which offers a philosophical framework and grounding for the conceptualization and development of the ethics of large-scale organizations and the central role righteous (Maatian) leadership plays in this.

The economy of Egypt rested on a solid agricultural base, urban commerce, and maritime trade. It was managed, as mentioned above, by a large professional civil service which produced its laws, rules and ethics as well as "collected taxes in kind throughout the country, stored these goods in government warehouses and supervised their distribution . . ." (Trigger et al, 1983:58). They, of course, ruled in the name and at the pleasure of the king, but were effectively in control of the daily operation of the government. Within the "class" or "stratum" structure of Egyptian society, the royal family in its extended sense was at the apex, followed by land-holding nobles, civil servants, merchants, peasants and domestic servants.

In spite of the erroneous biblical charges levelled against Egypt and the uncritical scholarship which supported these contentions, many scholars now concede there was no large-scale slavery in early Egypt in the modern sense or even Greek sense of the word, that essentially "domestic servant" is a more accurate category, and that temporary conscription not slavery was the nature of labor recruitment for building the pyramids (Ruffle, 1977:36; James, 1972:37-38; Bierbrier, 1984:12-13). James (1972:37) contends that "Herodotus may have been chiefly responsible for the belief that the pyramids were built by slave labour." But as mentioned above, the myth also was advocated and reinforced by Judeo-Christian literature.

Bierbrier (1984:12) states that "it cannot be emphasized too strongly that these men (who worked on the pyramids) were not slaves but temporary conscripts." In fact, what one has here is a mandatory national service on national building projects similar to mandatory military service. "Every Egyptian citizen was in theory required to lend a hand in this effort and had to provide the state with a certain number of days of labor" (Bierbrier, 1984:10, 12). Bierbrier tells us that "The organization of manpower would have been straightforward. During the time of the Nile flood when land would have been covered with water and unfit for agriculture, the farmers could be conscripted to work on the royal pyramid complex."

In addidtion, to these regular workers, professional craftsmen were also employed. It was again, however, the civil service administrator who organized this huge labor force, ostensibly based on experience gained in irrigation works and projects for the Nile. Some scholars, including Weber, speculate that this was the origin of the bureaucracy. But regardless of the class or stratum structure, it is the bureaucracy, as mentioned above, that proved key to the development of Maatian ethics. In fact, the *Sebait* (which are the central treatises on ethics) were written, at least at first, essentially to establish the ethical grounds for a Maatian leader or civil servant. It was through teaching, tradition and development that it became the collective moral focus and legacy of the entire Egyptian people. Given their origin and early stress, as Frankfort (1961:62) notes, many scholars make "a pragmatic misinterpretation" of the Books of Wise Instruction (*Sebait*). But when Ptah-Hotep gives advice for leadership, it is both practical and moral. For in the final analysis, all African morality requires proof in practice and *akh*, a key category in Maatian ethics, means both moral and practical good. Thus, in the phrase "Maat is good and its worth is lasting," good is both of moral and practical value. It is, in a word, not only righteous, but right, not only morally good but effective, advantageous, and beneficial.

For Ptah-Hotep, then, Maat is not only morally right, it is effective, it works and yields benefit. Thus, Ptah-Hotep (5:1-4) teaches the incoming civil servant: "If you are a leader and command many, strive for excellence in all you do so that no fault can be found in your character. For Maat (the way of Truth, Justice and Righteousness) is great; its value is lasting and it has remained unequalled and unchanged since the time of its Creator. It lies as a plain path before even the ignorant and those who violate its laws are punished." Answering the age old question of the evil which prospers, he counsels that "Although wickedness may gain wealth, wrongdoing has never brought its wares to (a safe) port. In the end it is Maat that endures and enables the upright to say 'it is the legacy of my father and mother'." Again, the Egyptian understanding is that righteousness causes one to endure and prosper. As Ptah-Hotep (19:4) maintains, "Established are those whose standard is righteousness who walk according to its ways. They shall surely prosper thereby but the greedy will not have even a grave."

Weber (1925:252ff) in his discussion of bureaucracy in Egypt discovers what he calls the "economic ethic" of Egypt and contends that it is "distinguished by its strong evaluation of dutiful vocational work and punctuality." "This was," he says, "a natural result of the liturgy—organized, bureaucratically-managed, and half-state-socialist economy." He also notes "a strong vocational pride" in Egypt. But, he continues, "the great instability of Egyptian wealth, the quite frequent ascent of plebians into the bureaucracy (especially of the New Kingdom) at an early time pushed the conceptions of gentility of the landed nobles in the background." Although he concedes that "Education alone determined rank and station of the notable (*sar*), he maintained that "the absolute hierarchical subordination of the bureaucracy *determined man's ideals* (italics mine). Finally, he reductively translates Maat saying "the crown of perfection was *ma*, thus loyalty, meaning at once propriety and 'dutiful devotion'." In a word, he continues, " 'to bow for the rest of one's life' was considered to be man's fate" and thus "the vocation conception accordingly remained strictly traditionalist."

These contentions are obviously ill-informed and incorrect historically, linguisically and conceptually. Weber's pejorative description of the Egyptian state is neither accurate nor informative. What Weber eventually admits is that there was a "charity ethic" in Egypt expressed in ethical teachings and practice. In fact, the Declarations of Virtues and Innocence command, as ideal and example, giving "bread to the hungry, water to the thirsty, clothes to the naked and a boat to those without one." Moreover, one is to be "a father for the orphan and a husband to the widow." Likewise in the *Sebait*, Amenomope (28:1-3) teaches respect and concession for the widow who harvests from the field saying, "Do not expose a widow if you catch her in the field nor fail to be understanding of her reply." Also, "Do not refuse your oil jar to a stranger to double it for your friends and family." For "God loves those who respect the poor more than those who revere the rich."

The commitment to social welfare is a strong part of the economic ethics of Egypt and even in the Late Period, in the Book of Phebhor (Chapter 17), we read:

> Those who give food generously when they have money are the ones to whom fate gives fortune. For wealth goes to those who give food to others by means of it. The heart of God is satisfied when the poor stand provided for before Him. Thus, if you acquire property, give a portion to God by giving a portion to the poor. If you acquire property, spend it on your town so that there will be no turmoil in it. If it is in your power, invite those far away as well as those near you. For those who invite those from afar, their name will be great when they go afar. Those who love their neighbors will

The scribe's equipment. Middle Kingdom

> find a family around them. God allows one to acquire wealth in return for doing good. And those who give food to the poor, God takes them to Himself in mercy without measure.

Thus, social welfare is a fundamental and continuing component of Maat.

Also key to Maatian economic ethics is communal sharing with others whether poor or not. It is again a clear case of Maat as rightness and effectiveness. For to do Maat is to create a context which is both righteous and mutually beneficial, in a word, it creates a moral culture in which individual and organizational prachas roots and reinforcement. The classic concept here is expressed in the passage from Phebor quoted above, i.e., "Those who love their neighbors will find a family around them." Also, Ptah-Hotep (33:1) teaches "Be generous as long as you live. What goes into the storehouse should come out. For bread it made to be shared. Generosity is a memorial for those who show it long after they have departed." And again he says, "Share with your friends that which you have, for that which is yours is a gift of God. Those who fail to share with their friends are shunned for having a selfish soul." He concludes saying it is not goods "but righteousness by which people are sustained" (22:1-2)—.

The corollary to this aspect of the ethic was prohibitions against greed. Thus, Ptah-Hotep (19:1,3) says, "If you wish your conduct to be perfect, to be free from all that is evil, guard against the vice of greed for material things. It is a bundle of all kinds of evil and a bag containing vices of every kind." Also, Amenomope (6:10-13) taught "Better is a bushel which God gives you than five thousand wrongfully gotten," and "better is bread with a happy heart than riches with much worry." And "Better is praise with the love of others than wealth in the storehouse." Finally, Phebhor (Chapter 15) says, "Do not be greedy lest your name sends forth an offensive odor. Greed brings conflict and fighting . . . and takes all sense of shame, mercy and trust. There is no end to the wrong done when money and greed are together."

Weber's contention that the entrance of common people into the merit-based civil service "pushed the conceptions of gentility of the landed nobles in the background" is at best incorrect and at worst both incorrect and class-biased. If we take the period he refers to and review the literature, we will find no supportive evidence for his contention. On the contrary, what one finds is continuation and expansion of the tradition, not its diminution or reversal. In fact, this entrance of the common people showed the stress on and practice of a merit-based civil service. The two Books of Instruction during the New Kingdom where Weber claims greatest proof for his contention are the Books of Ani and Amenomope written in the 18th and 20th Dynasties respectively. As Lichtheim (1976:135) introducing Ani asserts, "It combines traditional themes with a certain amount of innovation." The traditional are themes of parental honor and love, respect for and assistance to the poor, love for wife and children, respect

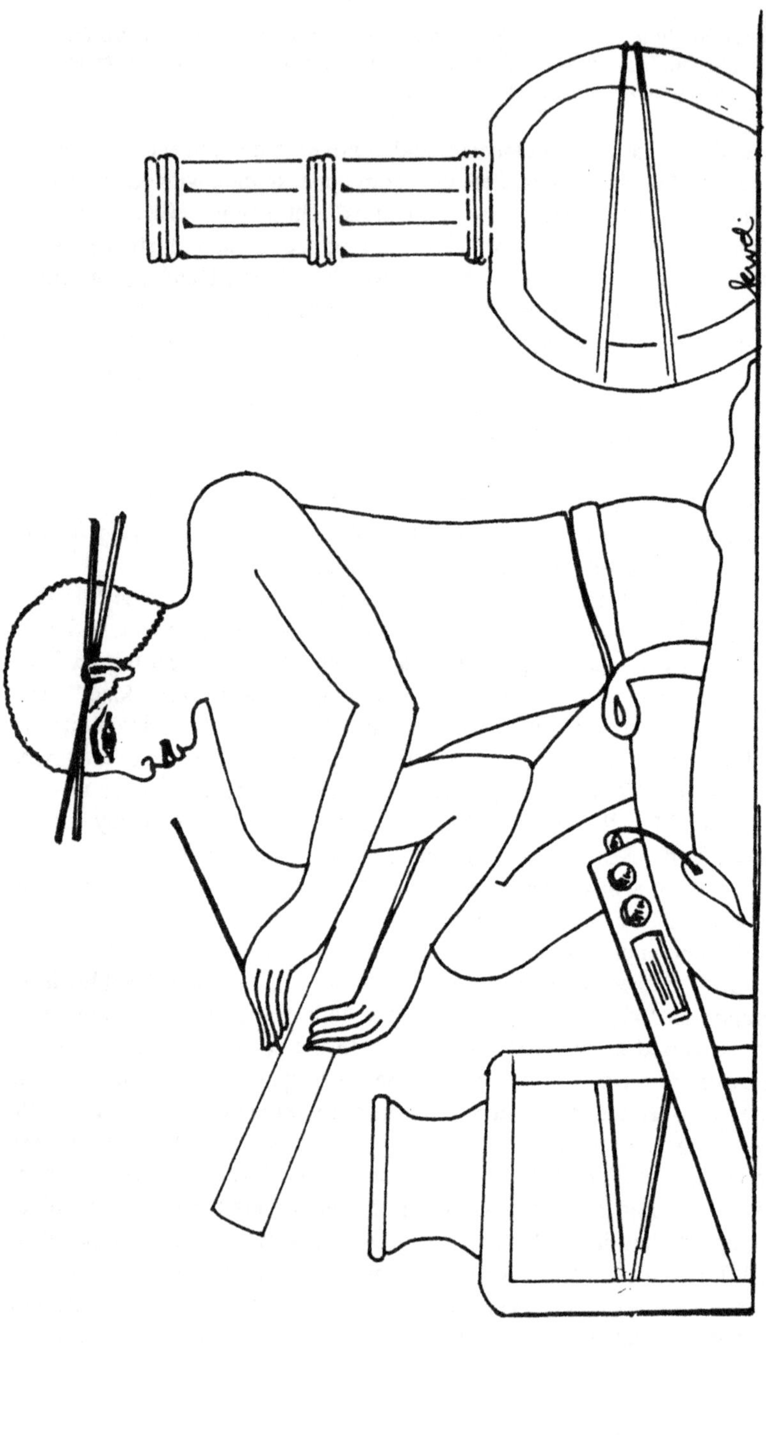

Scribe with writing equipment, Old Kingdom

for elders, cultivation of balanced and righteous friendships, respect for work, etc. For example, Ani teaches "One who is idle amounts to nothing, but one who is diligent is honored." "Walk each day in the way of righteousness and you will reach the place you're going." "If you are learned in the writings and have delved deeply in them, set their contents in your heart so that all will be of great value." "Stay away from the aggressive man and take him not as a companion. Take then for a friend one who is true and just, one whose actions you have observed. And if your righteousness equals his or hers, your friendship will be balanced." The innovation is the son responding to his father in the *Instruction*, something that occurs in no other *Instruction*.

In Amenomope, Lichtheim (1976:146) contends "the genre Instruction reaches its culmination" rather than declines as Weber argues. According to her, there is an increase in "gentility", if gentility refers to elevated tastes and ideas. For there is a "shift of emphasis away from action and success and toward contemplation and endurance." This in turn "leads to a redefinition of the ideal man." But the redefinition is not a total one; it builds on and adds to the original one. For "as nearly as Ptah-Hotep he ideal man lacked all martial values; . . . was a man of peace who strove for advancement and was generous with his wealth." And one finds similar values in Amenomope. But Amenomope's ideal man, Licktheim points out, "is content with a humble position and a minimal amount of material possessions. His chief characteristic is modesty. He is self-controlled, quiet, kind toward people and he is humble toward God." And he "is indeed not a perfect man, for perfection belongs only to God."

Lichtheim is correct only in terms of value stress, not value newness, for as quotes of Amenomope above show, he fits well within the ethical conceptual framework of all the other Seba (moral teachers) from Ptah-Hotep to Phebhor. For the virtues of modesty, self-control, reverence to God, kindness toward people, and disappreciation for materialism are present at varying levels of emphasis in the other Books of the *Sebait*. In the Book of Kagemni (Old Kingdom), one reads "The modest person is strong and one who is true in word and just in deed is praised. Houses are opened to the humble and a wide seat given to one who is gentle in speech and conduct." And "Be not arrogant among your peers because of your strength. And beware of acting in such a way to encourage opposition." And in Ptah-Hotep the very first verse counsels modesty saying, "Be not arrogant because of your knowledge. Take counsel with the unlearned as well as with the wise. For the limits of knowledge in any field have never been set and no one has ever reached them. Wisdom is rarer than emeralds, and yet it is found among the women who gather at the grindstones." He also says, "If you are a leader, be courteous and listen carefully to the presentations of petitioners." Moreover, "If you are a powerful person gain respect through knowledge and gentleness of speech and conduct. Give commands only where necessary and fitting. Those who abuse their authority provoke resistance and those

The King's Scribe, Re'-hotep. Fifth Dynasty.

who place themselves above others are brought low" (Lichtheim, 1975, 1976; Karenga, 1984; Simpson, 1973).

Weber's claim that "the absolute hierarchical subordination of the bureaucracy determined man's ideals" is an inaccurate assumption and assertion on two levels. First, the claim that only one factor, even if the factor were real, "determined man's (the Egyptian people's or the bureaucracy's) ideals is more deterministic than one would expect from Weber and wrong in any case. Causality tends to be multidimensional in all cases and in the case of Egyptian ideals—ethical and otherwise—there were several causal factors which, of course, is the focus and motivating assumption of this paper. Secondly, the hierarchical subordination was not "absolute" in the sense Weber implies but was undoubtedly strong in respect for levels of authority which of course tends to be the nature of all bureaucracies. Still there was latitide in judgment with a stress on propriety and procedure. Ptah-Hotep (25:3) counsels, "Be not silent when it is your duty to speak," and "Speak even if you offend or are opposed" (25:1). Thus moral and political duty, which as argued throughout the text, are inextricably linked in Maatian ethics. Moreover, he advises that "If you are one of worth and wisdom who sits on a council of governance, apply your heart (and) mind toward that which is wise. Speak only when you know you can assist in the solution of a difficulty. For silence is better than useless chatter. There is an art to giving sound advice in council. Surely, it is more difficult than all duties. Those who grasp this can make it serve them well" (24:1-3).

If Weber perceives in this "excessive" reluctance for initiative, it is because he forgets his own principles of bureaucracy which are based on rationality and rule observance, and because he forgets or overlooks the Egyptian emphasis on "gentleness in speech and conduct" which paves the way, reflects Maat and is *akh* (good, effective, right). AsWilson (1956:92), who misunderstands this also, nevertheless concedes, one succeeds but "That is achieved by following the roles, but rules themselves provide for individual initiative." The rules are both moral and political, ethical and procedural and compel knowledge and due deliberation as Ptah-Hotep counsels above. For as Wilson notes, "the world order has provided a place for the initiative of the "wise" man who is constantly set in contrast with the 'ignorant' man" or fool.

Wisdom in Egypt is moral wisdom in the service of social and human good. Therefore, wisdom is the wisdom of Maat in the spiritual, ethical and social sense. But it requires listening, learning and doing what is right. Thus, Ptah-Hotep teaches, "Respected are those who listen well; they will excel and their deeds will distinguish them. But failure will follow those who hear not. Defining the moral and social significance of wisdom, Ptah-Hotep says, "if right exists in the heart of those who have been set in authority, they will be beneficient always and their wisdom shall endure forever." For "the wise are known for their wisdom and the great by their good actions." Thus, as Wilson concludes, "the

Scribe, New Empire, made from alabaster.

text combines an insistence upon obedience to the precepts of the past and an encouragement of personal endeavor, because the precepts of the past allow for a degree of individualism."

Certainly, "individualism" is not a correct category for the philosophical anthropology of Egyptian or any African society. But what Wilson means is personal initiative, and in this he is correct. Nevertheless, it is important to stress that as the texts and history show, in African society a person is not an individual alone and alienated, but a *person-in-community*, a moral agent who derives and develops his/her identity, purpose and direction from and through his/her community. As John Mbiti has observed in his *African Religions and Philosophy* (1970), the classic conception of this is the statement, "I am because we are and because we are therefore I am." This is nowhere clearer than in the Egyptian texts which introduce and sustain a strong communitarian conception of the human personality. Furthermore, it is important to recall the *Book of Khun-Anup* cited above which sanctions and encourages criticism of leadership *by the standard of Maat*—even by a peasant. It is thus only logical to assume as much, if not more, for the leaders themselves.

Weber's assertion about "the great instability of Egypt's wealth" begs proof, which unfortunately Weber does not provide. In fact, it was the overall stability—economic and political—of Egypt which provided the fundamental basis, as argued above, for its high level of development and elevated ethical consciousness and practice. Also, Weber's note that the "vocation conception" remained "strictly traditionalist" contradicts his prior claim that it had lost its "gentility" conceptions with the influx of "plebians". As I argued above, these standard Maatian values were all part of tradition, and far from changing or losing these values, the incoming officials built on and expanded them. It was not subservience, then, which made the vocational concept and practice traditionalist, but the Egyptian reverence for tradition and the wisdom of governance distilled from long and studied experience. This is the meaning of King Kheti's commentary on the wise man when he says, "Truth comes to him in its essential form, shaped in the sayings of the ancestors" (3:6). One final note, however, on Weber. He made no critical study of Egypt and therefore is not to be taken seriously on his major contentions and attempts at comparative analysis. But as this discussion shows, his incorrect and unsubstantiated assertions serve as a conceptual and a contentional backdrop for a more critical and definitive analysis.

Finally, the socio-historical setting of Maatian ethics is marked by its strong and profound reverence for tradition and the past. This was expressed in terms of both ancestor and elder veneration and a profound respect for ancient knowledge and achievement. In Maatian sacred literature, there are abundant models of virtue from the past used to instruct. Gardiner (1964:56) makes the point that "one of the most characteristic traits of the Egyptian habit of mind" is the "extraordinary attachment to the traditional as opposed to the actual." In fact, he

Unknown scribe, Fifth Dynasty (25th-24th century B.C.E.). From Saqqara.

continues, "no other people has shown a greater reverence for what was by them termed 'the time of the ancestors', . . ." especially the Old Kingdom, the classic period. These periods were ideal points of reference and it is from and by these that their concepts of morality, the just society, the will of God, etc., evolve and are justified. Thus, Kheti writes "Follow in the footsteps of the ancestors, for the mind is trained through knowledge. Behold their words endure in books. Open and read them and follow their wise counsel" (Karenga, 1984:50). In the *Instructions* to the prime minister, discussed below, the past and tradition are appealed to and consulted. And the solution to moral, technical, and other kinds of problems were ultimately solved by reference to and building on the past.

It is at this point that one sees the moral imperative to restore the ideals and achievements of the past as in Confucian ethics. In fact, restoration, although often conceived of by some authors as simple and artistic or architectural restoration of temples and pyramids is more definitively a moral obligation and an act of ritual. Therefore, king and priest alike demonstrate the strong grip of the past in both the moral and historical sense and seek to preserve it by constantly restoring it and making it even better. In the *Shabaka Text*, which King Shabaka restored, we read "His Majesty had found it as a work of the ancestors . . . (in ruins) and His Majesty wrote it out anew so that it was more beautiful than it was before" (Lichtheim, 1975:51ff). Ram Roy, High Priest of Amen, in a commemorative inscription recounts how he restored the Temple of Amen after it was in ruins, "making it more spacious, raising it and make it more excellent."

Also, Queen Hatshepsut after having restored what the Aamu invaders who ruled Egypt in its chaos had destroyed, writes, "I have restored that which was in ruins; I have raised up that which was destroyed when the Aamu were in the midst of Kemet, overthrowing that which had been made as *they ruled in ignorance of Ra*" "italics mine). It is here that the religious and moral implications begin to appear. For Hatshepsut is not simply restoring temples, books, cities, etc.,; she is in a larger sense restoring order in society and the cosmos and thus, Maat. For one of the most fundamental understandings of Maat, as stated above, is cosmic and social order which are inextricably linked. This becomes clearer in the passage, "Tutankhamun drove out disorder (Isfet) from Egypt, and Maat (order, justice, righteousness) is firmly established in its place." Finally, on another level, restoration as a moral and ritual act is a reenactment of Ra's creation at the first time. It is pushing back chaos and disorder, and establishing order and rightness in the cosmos and society. It is, in a word, acting like Ra, i.e., creatively and righteously, which, as will be discussed below, is a fundamental concept in the philosophical anthropology of Maat.

It is important to stress here that the Maatian commitment to tradition is not a reactionary desire to return to and/or restore some past regime. For there is no historical evidence of this. It is rather a constant thrust to be in harmony with the mytho-historical and ethical paradigm of the Maatian society. Also, here Chan's

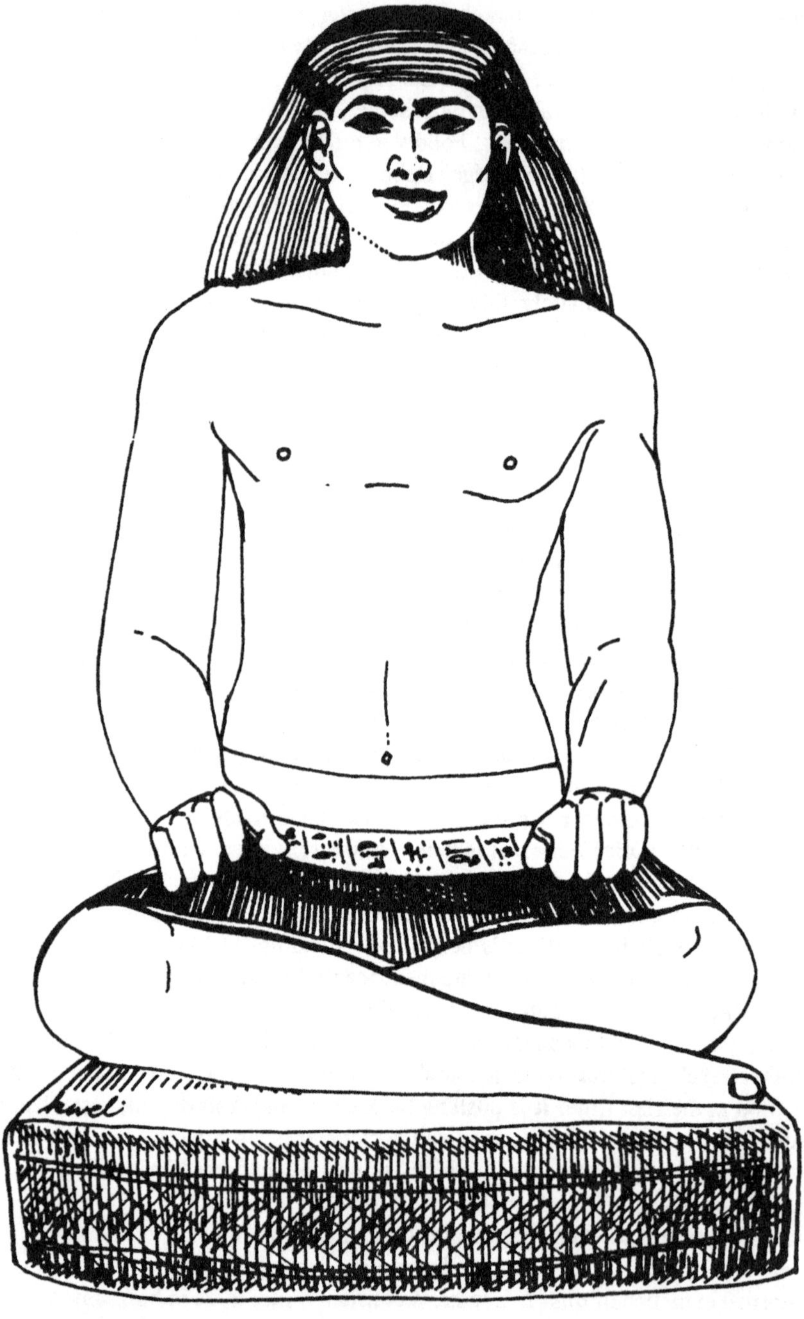

Scribe, New Kingdom, 25th Dynasty.

(1984) observations in this regard on Chinese respect for paradigms of the past are instructive. Chan (1984:424ff), building on Hans-Gorg Gadamer's hermeneutics on tradition, argues that the concept of tradition can be either a "form of authority" or a "source of truth". "Tradition as a form of authority," he notes, is "seen to be diametrically opposed to freedom and reason." But what he argues, along with Gadamer, is that "there is no intrinsic opposition between reason and tradition." In fact tradition, rightly conceived, "serves to povide a horizon from which we may view the world." Given this, "the past, then, is not the 'no-longer'; it is not some 'thing' we can reconstruct methodologically or experience in a flight of fancy." On the contrary, "the past and present are constantly merged in the experience of understanding." And thus, tradition becomes "the ground of understanding". This, he concludes, "is what Gadamer means by the principle of 'effective history'," and it is this effective history and respect for it that Chan sees in the *Analects* of Confucius. For it is an appreciation of tradition which not only yields knowledge but requires an understanding which involves initiative and interpretation. As Confucius observed, "A man who reviews the old so as to find out the new is qualified to teach others" (*Analects*, II:2). And the *Sebait* teach the past as a source of wisdom and practical example.

What both Maatian and Confucian ethics seeks to do is not to overthrow the established order but to rectify it by restoring the Maat or Tao exemplified in a paradigmatic age. Thus, the Maatian moral vision, like the Confucian moral vision, as stated above, is an attempt to come to grips with the "problem of how one humanizes the exercise of authority and inequalities of social power" which to this day "remains with us whatever we may think of his solutions" (Schwartz, 1985:70). This, of course, is no apologia for either Confucianism or Maatian ethics, which need none either in terms of their own internal logic or in critical comparison with Western religions which themselves shelter race, class and sexual biases. It is rather an attempt to understand these ethics in their own terms and contexts, rather than reductively translate them as simply class-supporting or myth-sheltering enterprises—a charge of course one can and has raised against the "revealed religions".

III. The Normative Paradigm: Literature and Virtues

There are several conceptual and practical pillars in the complex architecture of Maatian ethics. Chief among these are: 1) the concept and practice of Maat itself; 2) the early and evolved concept and practice of righteous (Maatian) leadership rooted in service; 3) social justice; 4) a philosophical anthropology informed by concepts of **imago dei** and **imitatio dei** and the essentiality of learning and practice; and 5) the seven cardinal virtues which inspire and sustain that practice.

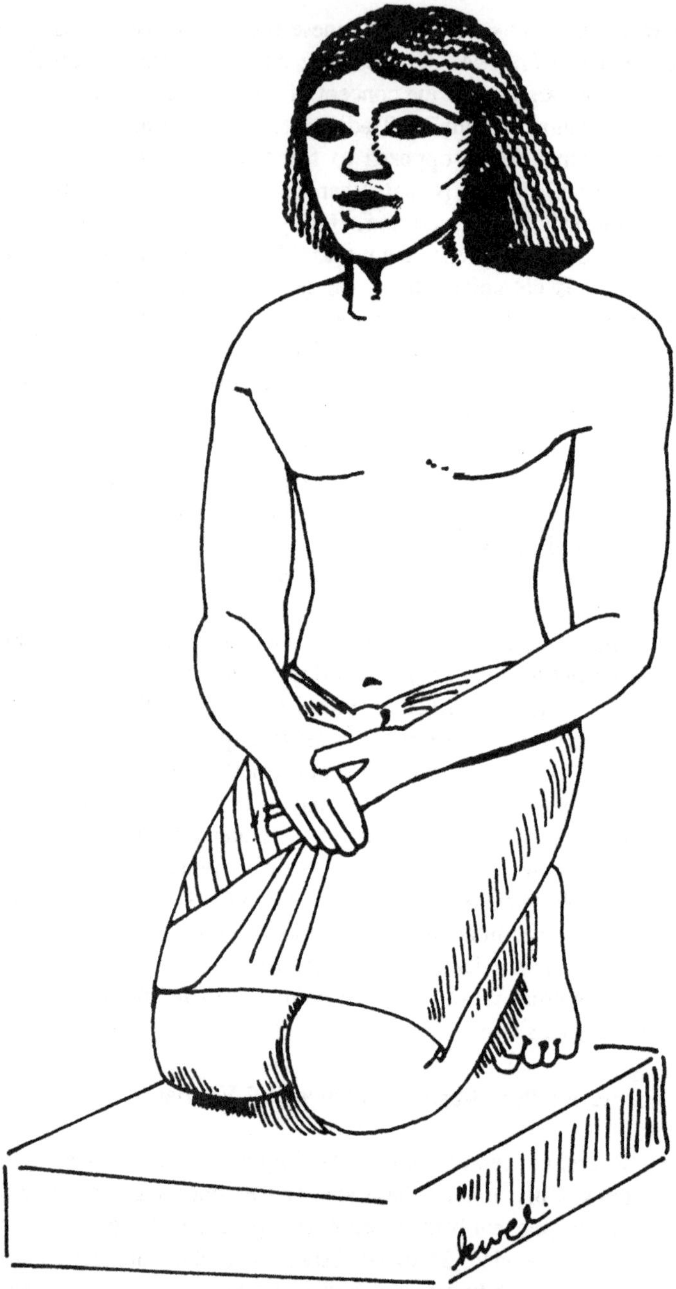

The Kneeling Scribe, Fifth Dynasty, from the tomb of Prince Ur-irni at Sakkara. (25th-24th century B.C.E.) Funerary priest Ka-em-ked.

The Concept and Practice of Maat

Maat has interrelated meanings. It is the right way, or path of righteousness. In addition to being the Right and true way, early in the Old Kingdom (2750-2180 B.C.E.), Maat acquired the sense of being the cosmic, natural and social order, established by Ra, God, at the time of creation. As Frankfort (1961:63) states, "The Egyptians recognized a divine order established at the time of creation; this order is manifest in nature in the normalcy of phenomena; it is manifest in society as justice; and it is manifest in an individual's life as truth. Maat is this order, the essence of existence. . . ." Morenz (1978:113) agrees, stating that "Maat is right order in nature and society, as established by the act of creation and hence means according to context, what is right, what is correct, law, order, justice and truth." Continuing, he maintains that "This state of righteousness needs to be preserved or established, in great matters as in small." Thus, "Maat is . . . not only right order but also the object of human activity." Given this "Maat is both the task which man sets for himself and also as righteousness, the promise and reward which await him on fulfilling it." It is in recognition and pursuit of this that a moral ecology of shared commitments in the cognitive and affective sense is established and sustained.

The *Sebait*, as all Egyptian religious and ethical literature, then, pose Maat as the indispensible goal and standard for a righteous person and society. For as Breasted (1934:145) notes, "having arisen as an individual and personal matter, as a designation of right conduct in the family or immediate community, Maat . . . then gradually passed into a larger arena as the spirit and method of *national* guidance and control of human affairs, a control in which orderly administration is suffused with moral conviction." Therefore, Ptah-Hotep tells the sesh, "If you are a leader and command many, strive for excellence in all you do so that no fault can be found in your character. For Maat—the way of Truth, Justice and Righteousness—is great; its value is lasting." Also, he says, "if respect for Maat exists in the heart of those who have been set in authority, they will be beneficient always and their wisdom shall endure forever" (Karenga, 1984:31, 48). Such stress on righteous leadership is typical of the *Sebait* and again reflects their roots in the emerging and established sesh stratum.

Like Tao, Maat is the only true way and its opposite, *isfet*, is untruth, falsehood and disorder. As the *Sebait* teach, isfet is "the abomination of God" and "that which is perennially defeated in the order of the universe" (Frankfort, 1961:75). Therefore, "it is fatal for a man to identify himself with it." For being out of harmony with the order of heaven, earth and sociey, i.e., Maat, is to invite destruction. On the other hand, "a man's success in life appears as proof of his frictionless integration in that order" (Frankfort, 1961:70). Therefore, Ptah-Hotep (14:4) states that "those of great heart (the righteous) are the chosen of God, but those who obey base desires, become the possession of the enemy."

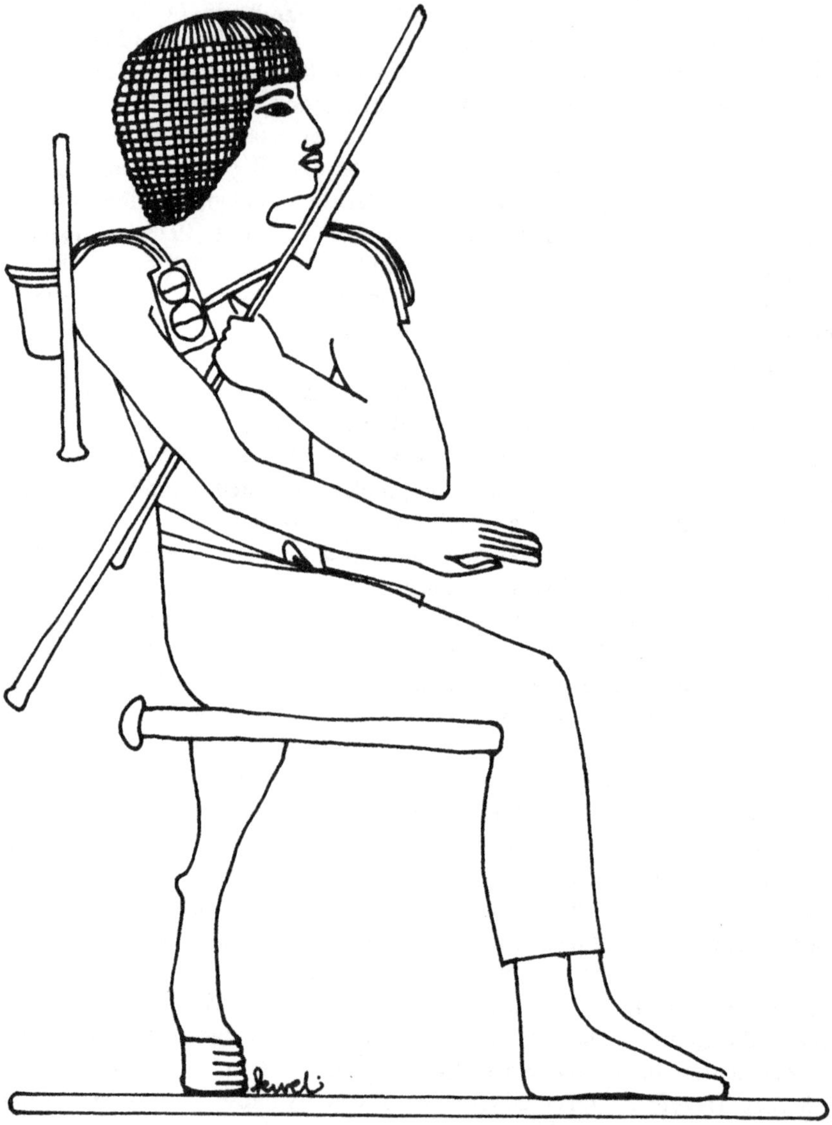

Prime Minister/Scribe Hesy-ra, Third Dynasty, Tomb near Saqqara.

Likewise, Khun-Anup teaches that "Maat is for eternity. It goes to the grave with those who do it. When they are buried and the earth envelops them, their name is not erased from the face of the earth. They are remembered because of their goodness. For this is a principle established by the word of God" (Lichtheim, 1975:181).

The Concept and Practice of Maatian (Righteous) Leadership

The concept and practice of righteous leadership is central to Maatian ethics. Within this context, a discussion of the *Shabaka Text* is important. For it is a souce of both the paradigmatic age of God and the ancestors and the theory of the divine kingship, i.e., righteous rulership, which is so essential to Maatian ethics and which expanded to include a theory of civil service.

The *Shabaka Text*, as Breasted (1934:19) observes, is the "earliest known discussion of right and wrong in the history of man." Commonly called the Memphite Theology, the *Text* dates from the middle of the Fourth Millenium B.C.E. In this document are both a religious drama of creation and a religio-political drama of the founding of Egypt, the inauguration of divine kingship, and the triumph of right over might—all concepts central to the ethical evolution of ancient Egypt (Frankfort, 1969: Chapter 3).

The *Shabaka Text* is notable and relevant for several reasons. First, it is both cosmology and a theory of kingship which "describes the order of creation and makes the land of Egypt, as organized by Menes (The Uniter) an indissoluble part of that order" (Frankfort, 1969:24). The monarchy becomes then a part of a divine plan and the social order becomes a reflection and part of the cosmic order. Second, it offers a principle of the triumph of might over right in the narrative of the struggle between Horus, the righteous, and his uncle, Setekh (Seth), the coercive, and the decision of the netchers (gods) in favor of Horus (Carruthers, 1984:85).

Thirdly, the principle by which the cosmic order and the social order are established is Maat, and the king becomes what Carruthers calls the temporal embodiment and agent of Maat. Maat, then, is both a cosmic and social principle which sets the standard for both God and human. Carruthers (1984:54-55) stressing this, states that "Maat is more often encountered in its ethical context, but as a conceptualization it transcends the bounds of human interaction and becomes the foundation for cosmic direction." Also, as I (1984:11) have argued elsewhere, Maat "is a divine concept, power and practice which not only informed and aided (the Creator, Ra's) action, but was established as the fundamental concept, power and practice for the organization, maintenance and development of human society also." It is a link and dialectic we have discussed above and points to the Maat concept of total moral context for thought, affection, practice and evaluation.

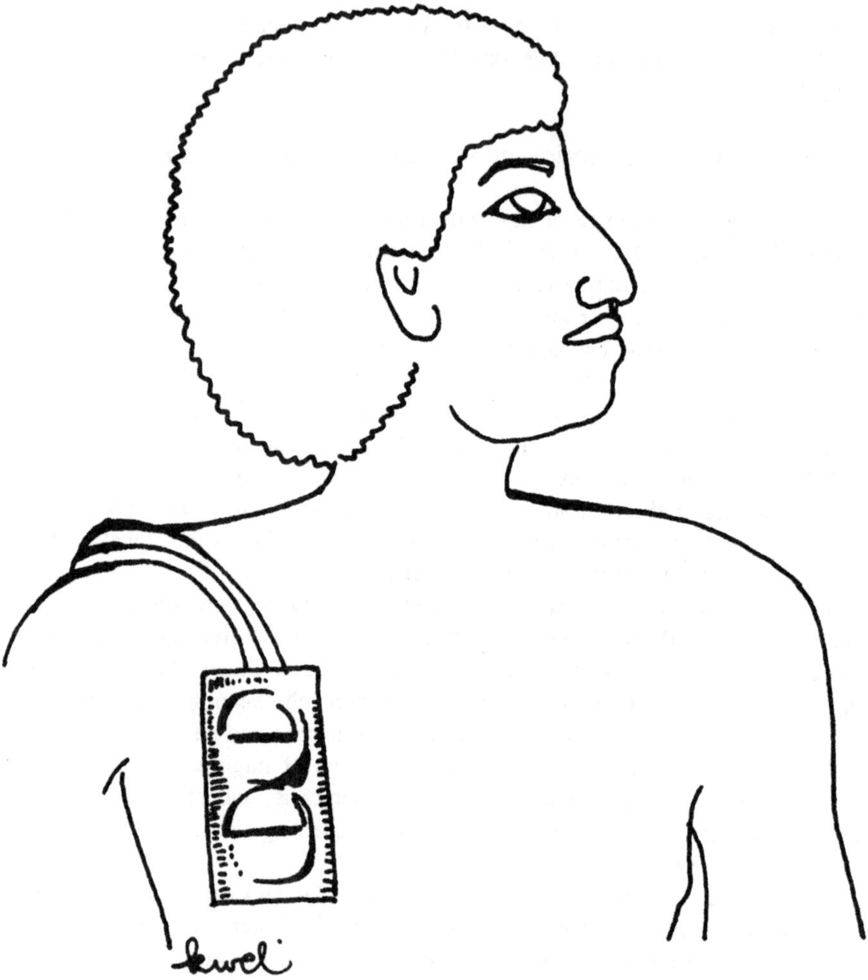

Prime Minister/Scribe Hesy-ra, Third Dynasty, Tomb near Saqqaara. Close up of details.

Given this, the fourth significant aspect of this doctrine of united cosmology and divine kingship is that it places an ethical obligation on king, the civil service and community to do Maat, to uphold it and live it. Thus, Carruthers (1984:86) maintains that a "pharaoh, having been entrusted with the office of divine pharaohship, had to adhere to the inseparability of governance from Maat in the oversight of the citizens' affairs." This, Carruthers notes, in the context of ancient Egyptian governance "is referred to as *wedj sekheru* (the command of those who govern or counsel)." Comparatively speaking, it parallels the Confucian concept of the Mandate of Heaven (T'ien-ming). But it also points to a shared responsibility of those who in daily operation of government must emulate and insure the righteousness demanded of the king.

Maat, then, is the order established by Ra, the Creator, and king and community are called upon by the sacred texts to preserve it, restore and enrich it. This is the call for and establishment of a Maatian or moral culture in which Maatian thought and practice take root and thrive. The king was morally compelled to drive out isfet, Maat's opposite, and establish Maat in its proper place so that one may say "the land is as it was at the first time" (quoted in Morenz, 1978:114). For as Frankfort (1969:149) notes, "the order established at the beginning of the world was considered to be normative for all times." This meant that Ra was creator and king of the world and the pharaoh was in his likeness, i.e., creator, king, law-giver, etc. Thus, it was said of him (her) at the coronation, "You are the living likeness of your father . . . for Authoritative Utterance is in your mouth, Understanding is in your heart and your speech is the shrine of Truth (Maat)" (quoted in Frankfort, 1969:149). Again, at the coronation, Queen Hatshepsut is acknowledged and welcomed by the powers of heaven with the words, "Welcome, O daughter (of Amon-Ra). Behold your law and order in the land. You arrange it, you set right that which is faulty in it. We acknowledge the descendant of him (Amon-Ra) who created us" (see also Frankfort, 1969:105). In Maatian ethics, then, *wedj sekheru* (the command of those who govern or counsel) is both an *obligation* and *right* to rule. The obligation is to rule in righteousness and the right is derivative from and based on the successful execution of the obligation. This is also the concept of *imitatio dei*—assimilation and imitation of God through righteousness.

Therefore, Seti I was praised at Abydos as follows: "You have fixed Maat in Egypt; it has become united with everyone" (Morenz, 1978:121). This is both sacred duty and honor. It is this concept from which the concept of social welfare evolves which is so prevalent in the sacred literature, especially in the Declarations of Innocence and Virtue as well as the *Sebait*. It is in the context of this commitment that King Kheti in the *Book of Kheti* (Chapter 15) teaches both the concept of *imago dei* and *imitatio dei* for humans and the granting by God of earth and sky and all therein for humankind. Ra, he says, "has built His shrine around them and when they weep he hears." And equally important, Kheti

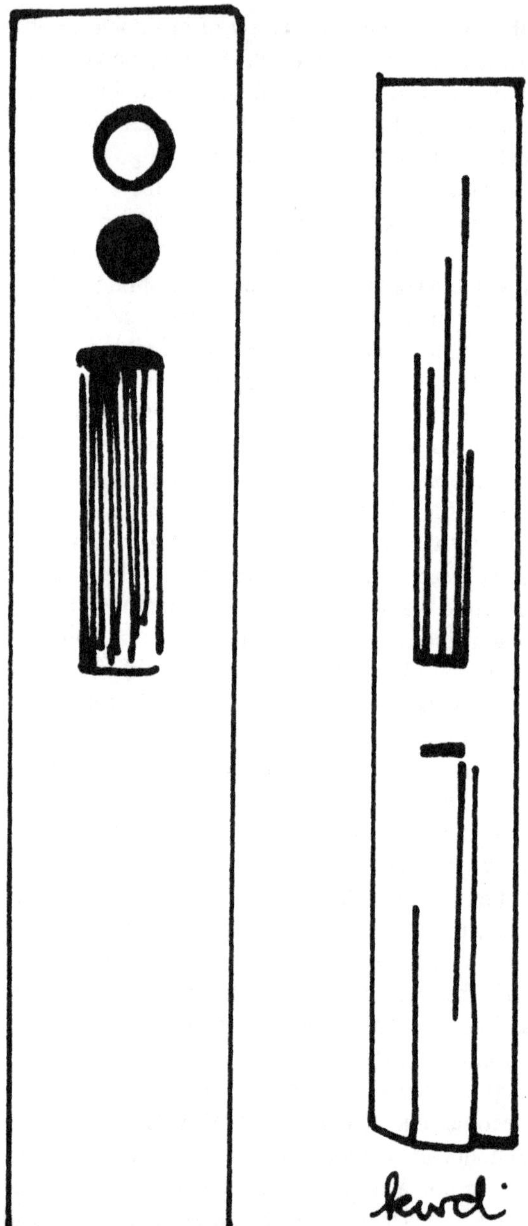

Scribes' Palettes, New Kingdom, made of wood and schist.

recognizes his moral obligation to the people and his need to imitate Ra, by asserting that Ra "made for them rulers even from the egg, leaders to lift the load from the back of the weak." This does not mean that declaration and deed always coincided, but what one has is an ideal which serves as moral standard and inspiration for political leadership and community, and a yardstick by which rulers and other leaders were measured and could measure themselves as Kheti does in this text.

Also central to the ethical corpus of Maatian literature is *The Instructions of the Prime Minister* (James, 1984:60ff). This text was possibly developed in the Twelfth or Thirteenth Dynasty, as a standard for bureaucratic ethics which are reflected, reinforced and expanded in the general ethics of the *Sebait* and other ethical sources. It shelters ethical values which are central to the Maatian concept of righteous rulership. First, it calls for one process, seeing "that everything is done in accordance with what is specified by law," "letting a man plead his innocence," and not dismissing "a petitioner before you have considered his words." For the petitioner prefers "consideration of his petition to judgment in the matter." Secondly, there is a command to avoid bias for "God hates biased behavior,". "Treat equally the one you know and the one you do not know, the one who is near and the one who is far away." Thirdly, the prime minister is commanded to avoid arrogance." Finally, one is commanded to do justice. For "the worth of a magistrate is that he behaves justly." "You will succeed in fulfilling your office by acting justly," it concludes. For "What is wanted is that justice be done."

This, in fact, is a call for Maat, for Maat is both the moral and linguistic equivalent of truth, justice and righteousness. What one has here, as James (1984:73) observes, is an estabished ethical code which was taken seriously by the rulers of Egypt and the people. For Maat and its command for jusice and impartiality "embodied a long-established, and much-cherished aspiration which formed one of the principal tenets of behavior in public and private life in ancient Egypt." Thus, it was also the foundation and motivating principle for the paradigmatic just and harmonious society.

This same ethic of Maat is restated, reinforced and elaborated in the *Sebait*, literary products of pime ministers, seshu (scribes) and priests. Maat required justice, personal and social, and the departure point was respect for the human personality, both as an image of God (Book of Kheti) and a fellow equal human as in the Book of Knowing the Creations in which the Creator, Ra, establishes the principle of equality in his "making every person like his or her fellow," and creating wind, water and earth "so that the humble might benefit from (them) like the great" (Karenga, 1984:7).

Social Justice

This theme and thrust of social justice with preferential commitment to the

Amenhotep, son of Hapu as a young man, 18th Dynasty, reign of Amenophis III, (1403-1365 B.C.E.), Karnak.

common person is nowhere more evident than in the Book of Khun-Anup, commonly called "The Story of the Eloquent Peasant". It essentially is a text on social justice, a moral narrative, in which Khun-Anup, a peasant, pursues a grievance against a rich person and wins. In the process of the narrative, Khun-Anup not only gets justice but delivers a treatise on justice and the obligations of leadership which frames and reflects the social expectations even from the masses (Lichtheim, 1975:169ff). Here Khun-Anup urges leaders to "speak justice and do justice for justice is mighty. It is great, it endures. Its worth is real and it leads one to blessedness." The leader is instructed that "Doing justice is breath to the nose" and it is by doing justice that one achieves eternity. The Maatian leader, Khun-Anup says, is "the father of the orphan, the husband of the widow, the brother of the divorced woman and a protective garment for the motherless." Moreover, he instructs the leaders that "The balancing of the land lies in Maat (Truth, Justice, Righteousness). Do not speak falsely for you are great; do not act lightly for you have weight; be not untrue for you are the balance (scales of justice) and do not swerve for you are the standard (Karenga, 1984:31ff; Lichtheim, 1975:169ff).

This moral narrative ostensibly used as a text in Egyptian schools is significant in the study of Maatian ethics for at least five reasons. First, it is a critique of leadership by a simple peasant and carries implicitly within it a recognition of the right—whether formal or customary—to engage in such a critique. Secondly, its popularity and use in schools could also imply an active tradition of critique and redress of grievance as well as right. Thirdly, the fact that the peasant, Khun-Anup, wins over an upper class person reinforces the concept and practice of a justice without class bias. Fourthly, it is, as Breasted (1934:183ff) suggests a definition and boast by the officials of a just society with honest officials committed to Maat, an open and .able process for redress of grievances and the triumph of Maat regardless of class. Finally, the text is important because of the valuable contribution it makes to the corpus of Maatian ethical literature on the question of the nature and value of justice.

In the text, Khun-Anup delineates five criteria for a just leader and thereby gives us an important insight into the Maatian concept of social justice. He defines the just leader as: 1) one "without greed"; 2) one without baseness; 3) "a destroyer of falsehood"; 4) "a creator of righteousness; and 5) "one who comes at the voice of the caller" (Lichtheim, 1975:172). The meaning of the second and third criterion is worthy of note for it moves beyond internal righteousness to suggest a need not simply not to lie oneself but to destroy falsehood in society; not simply to destroy evil but also to create rightness and by extension to create the conditions for its coming into being. Again, we see the essentiality of self-conscious practice to create the just society. Finally, the fourth criterion is out of the ethic of care and responsibility which is based both on imitatio dei in his justice. For it is Ra who is "prime minister of the poor", who listens and

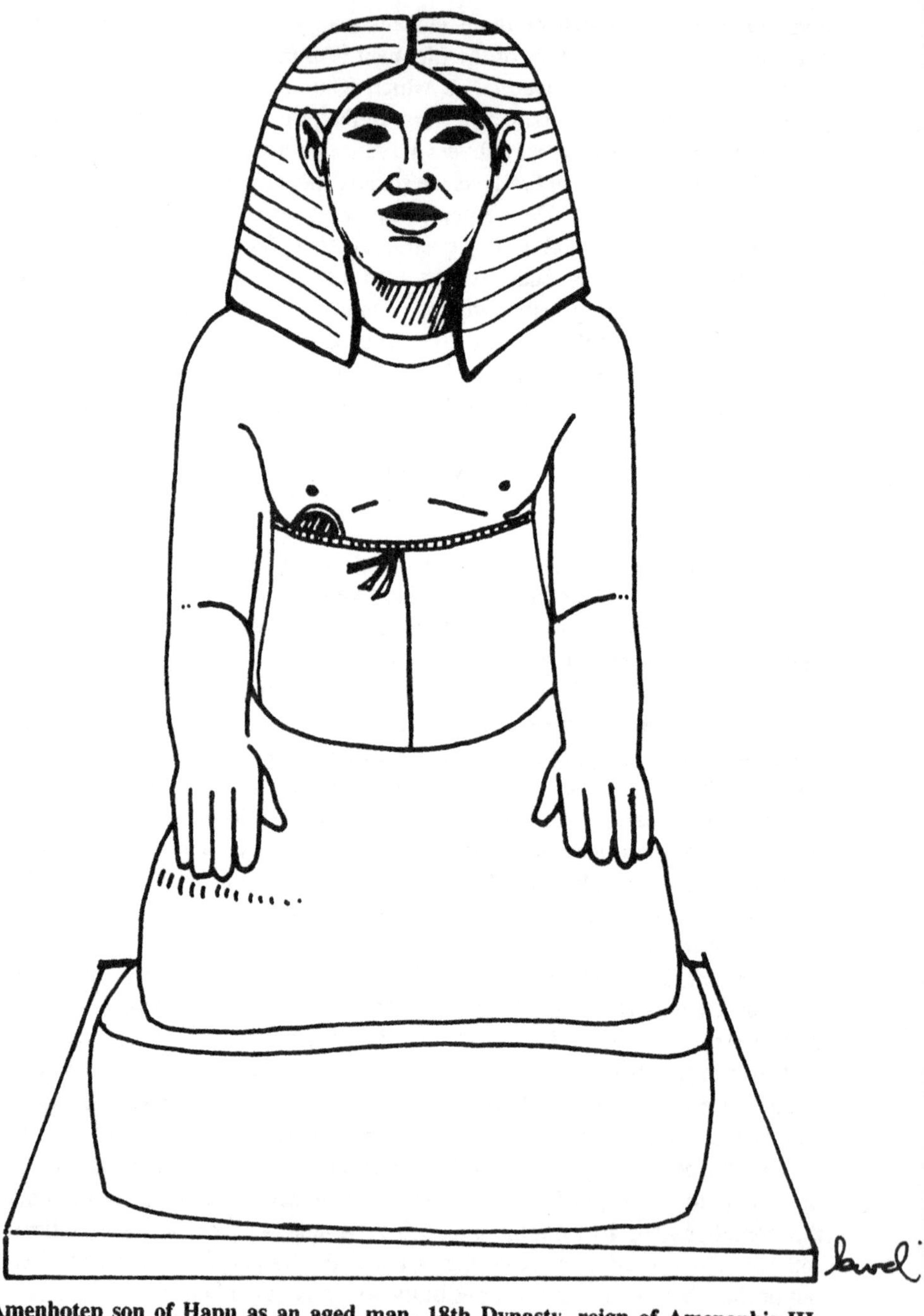

Amenhotep son of Hapu as an aged man, 18th Dynasty, reign of Amenophis III, (1403-1365 B.C.E.), Karnak.

"hears the prayers of one who calls on him," who "comes at the call of the humble and needy." Truly "Amen Ra is He who knows compassion and hearkens to those who call him," and he "rescues the oppressed from the oppressor." Thus, the just leader is morally compelled to imitate divine activity, which in turn is reflective of divine character. And compassion and empathetic understanding and loving kindness which translates in assisting, strengthening and delivering the poor and vulnerable.

Maatian Philosophical Anthropology

The philosophical anthropology of Maatian ethical philosophy evolved first as a philosophical portrait of the king but later diffused throughout society, becoming a paradigmatic definition of humans in general. Beginning in Maatian theology, the anthropological paradigm was reinforced and expanded by the awesome achievements of the Egyptian people which, as Breasted (1934:44) notes, expanded human vision and the concept of human possibility. Maatian philosophical anthropology is grounded in several fundamental assumptions. The first of these is that humans are in the image of God. This again is the basic *imago dei* concept. As Seba Kheti stated, "They are in his image and came from his body" (15:5). Inherent in this assertion is the assumption that human nature is endowed by Ra and is essentially good, being in his likeness. Like Confucian philosophical anthropology, Maatian philosophical anthropology posits no need for an ontological transformation (conversion, salvation, moksa, etc.), nor for any external intervention for redemption. On the contrary, being in the image of God, gives one the ontological potential for perfectability. This perfectability which forms a second philosophical pillar in Maatian anthropology is affirmed in Ptah-Hotep's urging one to "strive for excellence (or perfection) in all you do so that no fault can be found in your character" (5:1). Again, Ptah-Hotep (19:1) teaches those civil servants and persons who "wish your conduct to be perfect . . ." which is another expression of the assumption of ontological potential of the human personality.

In the early period of Maatian theology and ethics, the king is the paradigmatic human and his onotlogical potential is even greater, for he is a god, and after death becomes one with Ra. The ontological grounds for this is Maat which is defined not only as a cosmic, natural and social order but also, as the essential substance and sustenance of God and king. As Frankfort says, "it is by means of the concept of Maat that the essential affinity of god and king is expressed" (1969:157-58). He then cites Queen Hatshepsut's statement: "I have made bright Maat which he (Ra) loves. I know that he lives by it. It is my bread; I eat of its brightness. I am a likeness from his limbs, one with him." Maat, then, is the grounds for the ontological unity between God and humans. And thus no ontological gap exists between them, as it does in Western religious anthropologies.

Priest/Scribe Ankhpakhered, Scribe of the offering table in the Temple of Amon; Late Period, 25th Dynasty, cir. 680 B.C.E.

As in Confucian anthropology, then, no mediating process of salvation or redemption is needed.

Thirdly, if Maat, i.e., the spiritual/ethical dimension of humans, is the crucial constitutive element of being human, then Maat must be cultivated by righteous thought, emotion and behavior in order for each human to realize his/her potential fully. The end point of this for the king, as mentioned above, was godhood, and that of ordinary humans was perfectability. Thus, in the *Book of Vindication* (so-called Coffin Texts) when the righteous dead rise and stand vindicated, "maa-kheru", before history and heaven, s/he says, now "the length of the sky belongs to my strides and the width of the earth belongs to my domain." For "I am he/she who is one with God. I have become He." This in Maatian theology is an expression of the concept of spiritual assimilation through righteousness, in a word, by becoming the embodiment of Maat, i.e., the essence of God.

A final basic assumption of Maatian philosophical anthropology is that Maat, the self-actualization of humans, is only achieved in relations with others. As in Confucian anthropology, the perfectability and authenticity of the human being lies in his/her socialty. Maatian ethics, like African ethics in general, have and stress a practical dimension. Righteousness, in Maatian ethics, is only real in personal and social practice. Therefore, Maat is a social and personal task, a "lived concreteness". Linked to this concept of practical social ethics as opposed to contemplative personal ethics is the Maatian imperative to create and maintain the just society. This expresses a fundamental reciprocal relationship between the philosophical conception of a just or Maatian society and the practical ethics designed to achieve it. For one presupposes and facilitates the other in an ongoing dialectic of thought and practice.

This is also the point at which the ethic of care and responsibility as distinct from simple justice reveal itself, for relationships are the particular context in which humans realize themselves and assist others in self-realization and growth. The operative ethic here is service (wenut) and love (merut). Ankhsheshonqi (1:1-12) teaches that one begins by serving God, mother and father, sister and brother, "one who serves you", but ends by serving anyone, for it will benefit you. Moreover, he asserts that you should "let your good deed reach one who needs it." For "There is no good deed done except for one who needs it." Moreover, he cautions against the moral dilemma of being disappointed at not being recognized for doing good deeds. Thus, he says, :Do not say 'I did a good deed to this person, but he (she) did not acknowledge it to me'." For, he says, "if you do good by a hundred persons and just one of them acknowledges it, no part of it is lost." However, expressing optimism born of the virtue of relational reciprocity, he counsels that you should "Do a good deed and throw it in the water and when the (water) dries up you will find it." The lesson here is that service is for the person serving as much as if not more than, the person served. Thus, he (Ankhsheshonqi, 3:2) says, "Sweeter is the water of one who has given than the wine of one who has received."

Goddess of Records, Seshat; from mortuary temple of King Sen-Wosret I.

Relations are also shaped and informed by the concern for loving and being loved. Love (merut) appears both as a family and friendship concern but equally important as a social concern. In the *Book of Prayers and Sacred Praises*, the constant prayer is "May Ra put the love of me in the hearts of the people so that all may be fond of me." In the *Sebait*, Ptah-Hotep says, the great of heart are loved while the base hearted is held in contempt; and Kheti (4:6-8) tells his son, the prince, "Make the memory of you last through love of you. Multiply the people whom the city shelters, then God will be praised for your donations. And the people will give thanks for your goodness and pray for your health." Finally, Amenomope counsels just and compassionate treatment for the poor, and truth and justice for all concluding that one will find the Maatian behavior "a path of life". For "Better is praise and love of others than wealth in the storehouse."

As in Confucian ethical philosophy, learning in Maatian philosophy is essential, even indispensible. The living of Maat presupposes and necessitates a learning of Maat. And in the *Sebait*, learning is a fundamental virtue. Lichtheim (1975:6) notes that the *Sebait* "at all times . . . was inspired by the optimistic belief in the teachability of Man." Likewise, Frankfort (1961:60) writes that "the great popularity of the 'teachings' (Sebait) is in itself revealing. The Egyptians were evidently convinced that the good life could be taught." It is, he concludes, "a conviction (which) betrays a surprising confidence in the efficacy of man's understanding" and above all his transformability. "This as he notes differs from Mesopotamia and Palestine where anxiety and doubts about the transformability of humans and their fate reigned. It is because of their serene belief in the human capacity for transformation and progressive perfection, Frankfort believes, that the *Sebait* "are viewed so rarely in the religious context where they belong." Instead, "they are usually interpreted as secular guides of conduct." This means that not only is there a failure to see that in African and other Third World cultures "the contrast between the secular and sacred is difficult to draw", but also such uncritical treatment "obscures their true significance and their particularly Egyptian character."

It is also important to note that learning is directed toward wisdom and that wisdom in ancient Egypt is *moral wisdom in the service of social and human good*. It thus is the wisdom of Maat in the spiritual, ethical and social sense. It requires listening, learning and doing what is right. Therefore, Ptah-Hotep (40:3) teaches "Respected are those who listen well; they will excel and their deeds will distinguish them. But failure will follow those who hear not." Defining the moral and social significance of wisdom, Ptah-Hotep (42:2-5) says, "the parents are compelled to teach the moral and social lessons to their children which they themselves were taught so that the children may walk in the "ways of the ancestors", i.e., the way of Maat. Moreover, they are to be examples of righteous living for practice is the concrete lesson. Therefore, Ptah-Hotep (42:5) says "Let your life be an example and live justly for if justice remains a firm foundation, your children will prosper."

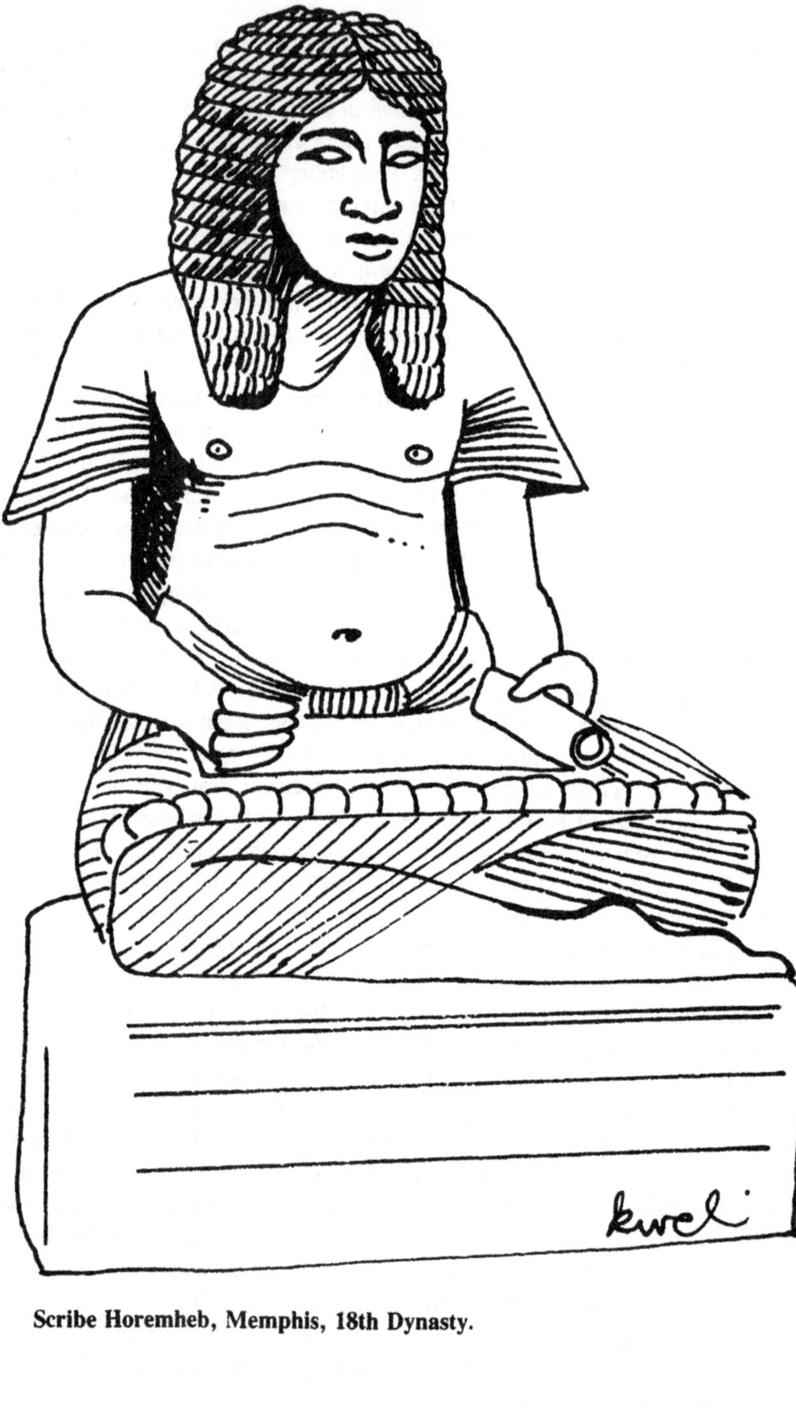

Scribe Horemheb, Memphis, 18th Dynasty.

As in Confucian anthropology, Maatian anthropology posits a paradigmatic person—the *geru-maa*, the truly self-mastered "whose whole character is infused with Maat" (Morenz, 1978:118). The word is composed of "geru", which means silent, self-mastered, self-controlled, and of "maa" (true, righteous) and thus means the truly self-mastered or the righteous self-mastered person. Budge (1924:98) makes the mistake of translating it as "the man who is truly resigned to God's guiding hand" and equates it with "submission" as the cardinal virtue in Islam. Frankfort (1961:66) is more correct in expanding the meaning from the simple root meaning, silent, to concepts of self-control, self-discipline and self-mastery. "We are," he says, "apt to misunderstand the ideal of the silent man." For "it does not exalt submissiveness, meekness, or any kind of otherworldliness. The silent man is pre-eminently the successful man." But here Frankfort falls into the vulgar pragmatic interpretation he criticizes in others, calling the *geru-maa* essentially a "go-getter". It is not material things that the *geru-maa* primarily pursues, but righteousness. And it is because of this that he prospers. In some places, Frankfort seems to realize this by his stress on the concept of "success as attunement" with the cosmic, natural and social order, but in other places he seems to lapse into the vulgar pragmatic interpretation.

The *geru-maa* is posed as the ideal person throughout the evolution of Maatian ethics, but it gets its more definitive expression in the *Book of Amenomope*, a book of *Sebait*, written in the 20th Dynasty (c. 1195-1080 B.C.E.). In defining the *geru-maa*, Amenomope distinguishes him/her from the hot-tempered or unrestrained man, a distinction which is apparent in the Old Kingdm from the Book of Ptah-Hotep onward. He (4:1-9) says:

> Now, the unrestrained man or woman in the temple is like a tree grown in unfertile ground. Its leaves wither quickly and its unripe fruit falls to the earth. It reaches its end in the lumber yard or it is floated far from its place. And its burial cloth becomes a flame of fire.
>
> But the self-mastered man or woman sets him or herself apart. He or she is like a tree grown in fertile ground. It grows green and doubles its yield of fruit. It has its place in the eye of its owner. Its fruit is sweet, its shade is pleasant and its end is reached in the garden.

Here one finds the self-mastered person strong, productive and durable. S/he is "shade" and fruit to those around and thus her/his end is in the garden (i.e. context) where s/he belongs.

In summary then, Maatian philosophical anthropology poses human nature as essentially good as a result of the assumption of a shared nature with God ontologically and morally through Maat. Secondly, Maatian anthropology posits an ontological potential of perfectability for the human person through pursuit of fundamental values. Maatian anthropology does not require a mediating process to establish unity with God, such as salvation, redemption, etc. Also, self-

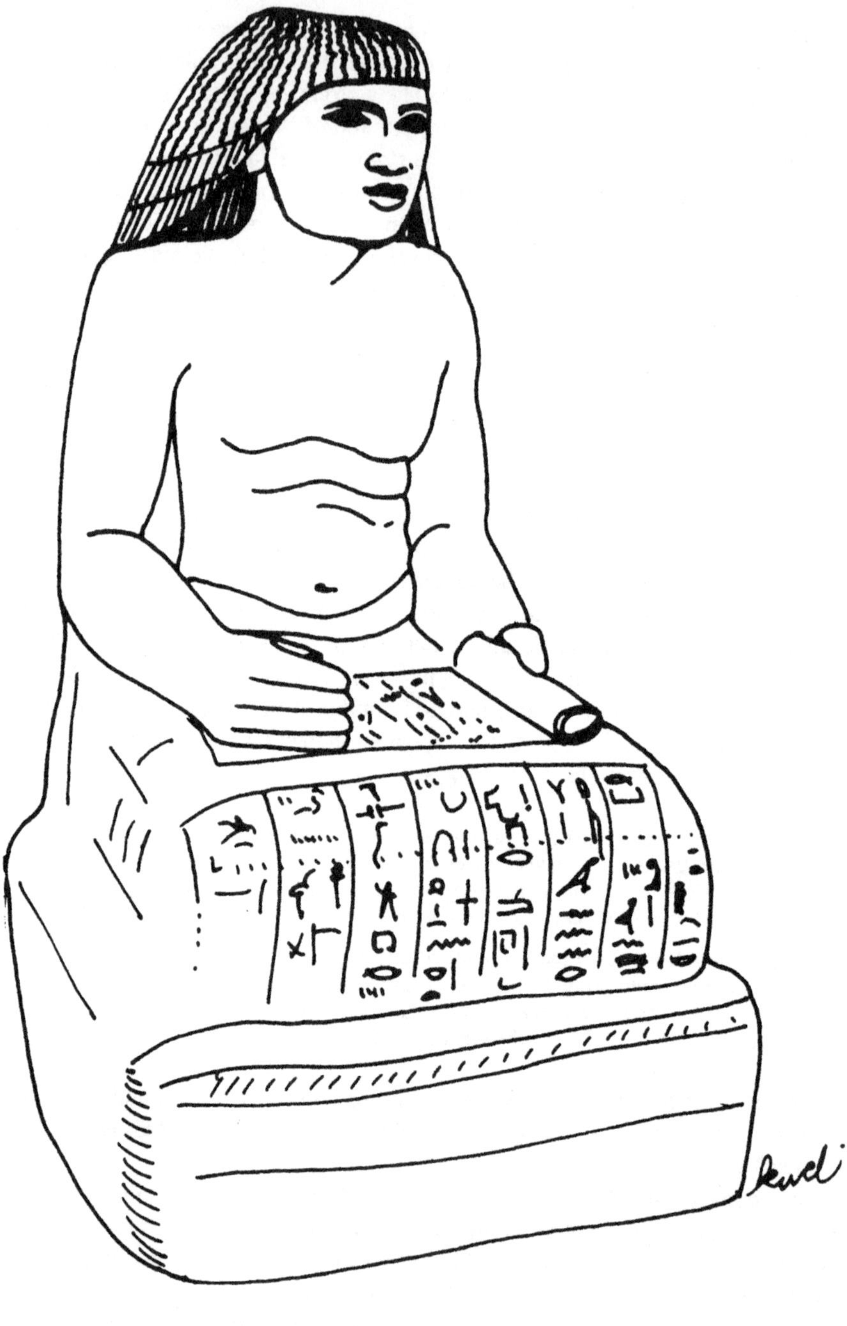

Scribe Pes-shu-per; 25th Dynasty.

cultivation through righteous behavior is the ultimate goal and therefore is achieved in relations with others. That is to say one becomes a person-in-community. For in Maatian moral philosophy, sociality and social practice are the sine qua non of being human and self-realization. Finally, Maatian ethics pose learning as essential, even indispensable, to the self-cultivation and self-authentication of the ultimate person, i.e., *geru-maa*. And this process occurs within a value framework and discipline of cardinal virtues to which we now turn.

The Seven Cardinal Virtues

Virtues are at the heart of Maatian ethics as noted above. They are excellences of human character which sustain practices which enable persons to achieve various desirable goods, but also sustain them in their quest for the good (MacIntyre, 1982:204). They are anchor and adze for the shaping of character, grounding and instrument for development of the higher self, society and world posed by Maat, i.e., the imago dei and imitatio dei. As noted above, central to Maatian ethics and the virtues they contain is the imperative of practice. The centrality, even indispensability of practice is based on four factors. First, practice is essential to learning. By practice of Maatian values one absorbs and understands them. Equally, practice refines and validates learning. Secondly, it's the logical conclusion to learning. In Maatian ethics, learning is for a practical end—that is to say, one learns to practice and achieve self-cultivation in community. As Ankhsheshonqi (6:4) says, "It is in the development of character that instruction succeeds." Thirdly, practice is central to Maatian ethics because there is no way to achieve one's self-cultivation and prove one's commitment except in relations with others. As argued above, sociality is basic to being human and sociality is grounded in and expressed by relations with others, i.e., practice of the values. Thus, the imperative is not simply to speak truth and justice but also *to do* truth and justice.

Finally, the imperative of sociality leads to and requires the creation and maintenance of the just society which in the final analysis is central to the dialectic of producing and sustaining the good life. For, as argued above, a good person requires and produces a good society and vice versa. The just or good society is by definition, the Maatian society, and it in turn is informed and inspired by seven cardinal virtues: 1) truth, 2) justice, 3) propriety, 4) harmony, 5) balance, 6) reciprocity, and 7) order. These are cardinal in that all of these categories can be and are translated in the sacred texts as *Maat*. Thus, to speak and do truth is to speak and do Maat and the same with the other virtues. Maat, then, is not only a transcendent principle, but a spiritual and social task and a promise and reward for achieving it. For by learning and practicing Maat, one can create a social context in which "all one wishes will be granted," i.e., the just or Maatian society. One last point on this: In spite of the many meanings and expressions of Maat, its translation as *righteousness* allows for and suggests a subsuming of all the virtues under it. For righteousness is required for the ethical practice of any and all of them.

The virtue of truth or truthfulness is central to Maatian ethics and appear throughout the *Sebait* and other ethical literature. King Khei (7:103) tells his son, Merikare, "Speak the truth in your house that the princes of the earth may respect you. Righteousness is fitting for a ruler. For it is the front of the house that inspires the back." (Note also here the emphasis again of government by moral example and leaders as moral exemplars.) And Ankhsheshonqi (6:24) says, "Speak truth to everyone, let it cling to your speech." Finally, Ptah-Hotep poses truth as central not only to leadership, but also to self-cultivation and self-mastery. "If you move among people, gain respect and truth through speaking openly and truthfully. Those who are trusted and speak truthfully will become leaders and masters of themselves," he (14:1) counsels.

A second cardinal virue of Maat is justice—justice on both the personal and social level. As stated above, some scholars consider justice the key social virtue of Maat and truth the key personal virtue (Frankfort, 1961:63). Justice is urged both in the formal setting of court and in the daily relations of family and society as a fundamental imperative. Speaking of justice in court, Ptah-Hotep (21:1-2) says, "If you are chosen to maintain order among the people, handle matters with a strict sense of justice. Do not lean to one side or the other. Take care that no one claims that you are unfair and your actions results in a judgment against you." Also, Amenomope (20:2,3,5) argues against class-biased justice saying, "Do not give consideration to those in clean clothes and reject those who appear in rags." Moreover, "Accept not the gift of the strong man nor oppress the weak because of him." Reflecting the principle of assimilation with God through righteousness and imitatio dei, he concludes, "Surely the strength of one who is like God saves the wretched from their oppressor." In social justice, Kheti (10:1-2) argues for a non-class selection of workers in pursuit of the meritocratic bureaucracy discussed above, saying, "Make no distinction in your behavior between those of rank and the common people. Rather choose a person because of his or her skills so that every craft may be carried on."

Finally, great stress is placed on giving. Social justice to the poor and vulnerable is taught. The classical formula for this is "Give bread to the hungry, water to the thirsty, clothes to the naked and a boat to those without one." (This latter imperative reflects the essentiality of travel on the Nile.) Moreover, the ethics urges one to be a husband for the widow, a father for the orphan and to never abuse the physically or mentally disadvantaged. Also, one is commanded to protect the weak from the strong as much as is in their power.

Although the emphasis on justice is in both the *Sebait* and the *Instructions of the Prime Minister*, the locus classicus of this virtue, as noted above, is in the *Book of Khun-Anup*, which is the oldest treatise on social justice in the world. It upholds justice as a primary social virtue and a duty of the Maatian leader. It is justice, Khun-Anup says, that the Maatian leader "should be a model for all men" (Lichtheim, 1975:179). Especially should the Maatian leader give justice to the poor and not deprive them of their sustenance. In fact, one who practices this injustice is called by Khun-Anup "a hawk to the little people, one who lives on the poorest of birds" and "a butcher whose joy is slaughter."

A third cardinal virtue of Maat is propriety. This is similar to propriety in Confucian ethics except it seems less rigid. Still there is definite deference to the ruler and parents and rules for relations with others. Instructive of all the relations is family relations. Carruthers (1984), however, has divided the relations into three types: relations with those in higher authority, with peers and with the general public. Petrie (1898) had also divided the relations into three kinds: superior, peer and inferior. But Carruthers' categories are more true to the ethical spirit of the classifications. However, I would identify four basic relations: those with family, higher authorities, subordinates and peers. Carruthers collapsed family and peers into one category, but I think because of the strong deference to parents and elders, that could prove problematic.

The deference to the leader and parents is loyalty and service, but, as in Confucian tradition, there are limits imposed by the demands of righteousness. Thus Ptah-Hotep (25:3) says, "be cautious in your speech lest you offend." but "be not silent when it is your duty to speak. And when giving advice in counsel to those who employ you speak the truth even if it offends" (15:1). Propriety is also expressed by filial piety. In terms of this, Ani states that one should do good for parents even after they are dead, for not only is it right, but also because it is *"akh"*, effective in building a context in which moral practice is the norm and tradition. Thus, he (9:3) says, "As you do for your parents your children will do for you also." This is both in support of the concepts of moral exemplar and reciprocity. For peers, especially friends, one should be honest, truthful and loyal. And to subordinates, one should avoid abuses of position and practice justice. For as Ptah-Hotep (25:2) says, "those who abuse authority provoke resistance. And those who place themselves above others are brought low."

A fourth cardinal virtue is harmony, which is a fundamental value not only for society but for the family. Phebhor urges use of wealth and practice of generosity and righteousnes in one's community "so that there will be no turmoil in it." And Ankhsheshonqi posits an ethical desire that "the heart of a wife and husband be one so that they may be free from contention." For "if a woman and man are at peace, they will never fare badly." Likewise, if they are at odds, they will never fare well (4:6-7). The fifth cardinal virtue is balance, which is similar to the Confucian value for moderation. Confucius said, "to exceed is as bad as not to reach" (*Analects*, XI:15). Phebhor (4:16) said, "Those who apply the right measure in all good things are not blamed." He suggests that excess is fatal in some cases and counterproductive in others. "If a beam is larger than its right measure, the excess is cut off. (And) if the wind blows beyond its right measure, it wrecks the ships" (4:14-15). Moreover, he says "(excessive) pride and arrogance are the destruction of their owner" (4:22). But "those who are gentle in character create their own fate" (5:1).

Reciprocity is the sixth cardinal virtue of Maat. It is expressed in terms of duty to others as in the Confucian *shu* (altruism). In terms of altruismn, Ankhsheshonqi (1:16) teaches, "Do not do to a person what you dislike and thus cause another to do it to you." This is what one calls the negative side of altruism. The positive side is found in the Book of Khun-Anup which says, "Do to the doer that he/she may also do" (Karenga, 1984:32). This has two meanings. First, it suggests an empathetic reciprocity, doing to others what one wants others to do to him/her. Secondly, however, it is an initiatory reciprocity by which one provokes good actions as a way for all to follow. This is an expression of the moral exemplar whose action, as Khun-Anup says, can be equated with "thanking one for what one may do and blocking a blow before it strikes." In a word, it is creating a model and environment conducive to others' moral growth. Again, we have the stress on the moral culture and community.

Finally, the seventh cardinal virtue of Maat is order. By order is meant lawful or anticipated regularity. It is both a framework for social and self-cultivation and an end result expressed in the Maatian society. It presupposes the other six virtues in a context which duplicates the cosmic and natural order which, as argued above, are ontologically and ethically linked to humanity in reciprocal relations. Nowhere is this reciprocity and relationship better expressed than in the sacred wishes of Ankhsheshonqi (16:19-25) who says, "May the floodwaters never fail to come. May the fields never fail to flourish. May children do honor to their father and mother. May the moon follow the sun and not fail to rise. May I recognize my friends that I may share goods with them. May I recognize my brother and sister that I may open my heart to them and may life always follow death." Here one has clear anticipation of lawful and expected regularity on the cosmic, natural and social level and it becomes a model for social and personal life. Thus, the call is for order in one's personal life expressed as internal discipline and development; order in one's family life based on filial, sibling and spousal love and mutual respect; and order in society based on justice. This justice, as mentioned above, is geared toward the most vulnerable members and holds even the pharaoh accountable. For as argued above, the command to rule in Maat is at the same time a right and an obligation; an obligation to push back isfet (chaos, disorder and evil) so that Maat (order, harmony and righteousness) can reign in the land in the image and imitation of the highest ideal, i.e., God and/or an idealized "first time (sep-tepy) of the past."

References

Barnsley, John (1972) *The Social Reality of Ethics: The Comparative Analysis of Moral Codes*,

London: Routledge & Kegan Paul.
Bierbrier, Morris. (1984) *The Tomb Builders of the Pharaohs*, New York: Charles Scribner's Sons.
Breasted, James H. (1934) *The Dawn of Conscience*, New York: Charles Scribner's Sons.
Budge, E. Wallis. (1924) *The Teaching of Amen-em-apt, Soh of Kanekht*, Martin Hopkinson and Co., Ltd.
Carruthers, Jacob H. (1984) *Essays in Ancient Egyptian Studies*, Los Angeles: University of Sankore Press.
Chan, Alan. (1984) "Philosophical Hermeneutics and the Analects: The Paradigm of 'Tradition'", *Philosophy East & West*, 34, 4 (October) 421-436.
Frankfort, Henri. (1961) *Ancient Egyptian Religion: An Interpretation*, New York: Harper & Row.
______. (1969) *Kingship and the Gods: A Study of Ancient Near Eastern Religion as the Integration of Society and Nature*, Chicago: University of Chicago Press.
Gardiner, Alan. (1964) *Egypt of the Pharaohs: An Introduciton*, London: Oxford University Press.
Gerth, H.H. and C. Wright Mills, (eds.) (1958) *From Max Weber: Essays in Sociology*, New York: Oxford University Press.
Gill, Robin. (1975) *The Social Context of Theology*, London: Mowbrays.
Hornung, Erik. (1985) *Conceptions of God in Ancient Egypt: The One and the Many*, Ithaca, NY: Cornell University Press.
James, George G.M. (1954) *Stolen Legacy*, San Francisco: Julian Richardson Associates.
James. T.G.H. (1972) *The Archaeology of Ancient Egypt*, New York: Henry Z. Walck, Inc.
______. *Pharaoh's People*, Chicago: University of Chicago Press, 1984.
Karenga, Maulana. (1982) *Introduciton to Black Studies*, Los Angeles: University of Sankore Press.
______. (1984) *Selections From The Husia: Sacred Wisdom of Ancient Egypt*, Los Angeles: University of Sankore Press.
Lichtheim, Miriam. (1975) *Ancient Egyptian Literature: A Book of Readings*, Volume I—1975; Volume II-1976; Volume III-1980, Berkeley: University of California Press.
MacIntyre, Alasdair, (1966) *A Short History of Ethics*, New York: Macmillian.
______. (1982) *After Virtue: A Study in Moral Theory*, Notre Dame: University of Notre Dame Press.
Mbiti, John. (1970) *African Religions and Philosophy*, Garden City, New York: Anchor Books.
Morenz, Siegfried. (1978) *Egyptian Religion*, Ithaca, NY: Cornell University Press.
Ossowska, Maria. (1970) *Social Determinants of Moral Ideas*, Philadelphia: University Press.
Petrie, W.M. Flinders. (1898) *Religion and Conscience in Ancient Egypt*, London: Methuen & Co.
Read, F.W. (1925) *Egyptian Religion and Ethics*, London: Watts & Company.
Renouf, P. LePage. (1880) *The Hibbert Lectures, 1879: Lectures on the Origin and Growth as Illustrated by the Religion of Ancient Egypt*, London: Williams and Norgate.
Ruffle, John. (1977) *The Egyptians: An Introduction to Egyptian Archaeology*, Ithaca, New York: Cornell University Press.
Schwartz, Benjamin. (1985) *The World of Thought in Ancient China*, Cambridge, MA: Harvard University Press.
Simpson, William K. (ed.) (1973) *The Literature of Ancient Egypt: An Anthology of Stories, Instruciton and Poetry*, New Haven: Yale University Press.
Trigger, B.G. et al. (1983) *Ancient Egypt: A Social History*, New York: Cambridge University Press.
Weber, Max. (1925) *Ancient Judaism*, Glencoe, Ill.: The Free Press.
Wilson, John. (1956) *The Culture of Ancient Egypt*, Chicago: Chicago University Press.

MISCELLANEOUS ESSAYS

MISCELLANEOUS ESSAYS

Introduced by Ivan Van Sertima

We close with a number of miscellaneous essays. Charles Finch introduces us to the work of one of the great Egyptologists of the nineteenth century—Gerald Massey—who fought singlehandedly against the racist versions of Egyptian history. Massey amassed more evidence than anyone in his time to prove that the roots of Egypt lay in Africa. Even the word "Africa" can be traced to "Af-rui-ka," which, in the Egyptian language, means "birthplace". Massey traces to Africa the origin of the first images to fashion mental concepts and make the world comprehensible, concrete mental stages and images that were never abandoned by the Egyptians because "the plasticity and richness of the types were such that they could embody more and more complex and abstract ideas and symbols".

Finch has taken on a formidable task, because Massey's books are a series of steps, and it took 36 years for him to make those steps until he reached the summit of critical understanding and obtained a full grasp of his multidimensional subject. It is to Finch's credit that he can show so clearly how his thinking broadened, evolved, and finally focused as he matured from book to book.

Larry Williams introduces us to a list of Black women in the study of Kemet, several of whom have made significant contributions to the field. We must make special mention of those who have written for the Journal over the last ten years—Rosalind Jeffries, Eloise McKinney Johnson, Danita Redd, Sonia Sanchez, Virginia Simon and Diedre (Rekhety) Wimby. We have also published Druscilla Dundee Houston posthumously.

Equally important in this section is Beatrice Lumpkin's essay for children. In the many states in which I speak there is hardly an audience that does not raise the question: How do you get this new information out to the children?

Legacies Inc.—the audio arm of the Journal of African Civilizations created by Jacqueline Van Sertima—provides an answer to this urgent need. She has selected the most eloquent and lucid of the oral presentations done on the themes of the journals, which she so brilliantly designs. Parents and teachers have found these tapes extremely valuable since the journals cannot easily be digested until readers reach their late teens. But there are children's books on Egypt. Alas, most of these tales are told and illustrated in such a way as to create the impression that early Egypt had nothing to do with Black or African people. Beatrice Lumpkin's essay comes, therefore, as a welcome guide. She sorts out the facts, fictions and lies in these tales and advises parents and teachers what would be best to fascinate and inform the young reader.

The glossary at the end of the book (compiled by Runoko Rashidi with the help of Regina Blackburn) is intended to simplify technical terms or terms of mixed linguistic origin. A miniature dictionary such as this may be elementary to an academic but it can prove useful to the layman or to a student entering the fascinating but bewildering rooms of Egyptian history for the first time.

THE WORKS OF GERALD MASSEY: STUDIES IN KAMITE ORIGINS

By Charles S. Finch, M.D.

At present, peoples of African descent are faced with the epochal task of reviving African culture, in its widest sense, and it becomes ever clearer that such a rebirth can only proceed as the values that evolved out of the African high cultures of the past are rediscovered. To renew the potential for cultural flowering, the wellspring of one's history must be retapped. The land of Kam, "the black land" which we know as "Egypt", was renewed yearly by its wellsprings at the source of the Nile in Africa's heartland so that it might live and tell Africa's story. In the works of Gerald Massey, *Book of Beginnings, Natural Genesis,* and *Ancient Egypt,* written in six volumes we have a titanic attempt to repossess that story from the neglect and obfuscation of the centuries. In these works there is an inexhaustible mine of information and scholarly understanding of which this review can only provide the barest sample but from this it is hoped that there can begin a serious reappraisal of the labor of this monumental scholar.

If there is a unifying theme that runs through these six volumes it is this: that Africa was the source of the world's people, languages, religions, myths, and symbols and Egypt Africa's mouthpiece. In Massey's view, Egypt brought the African genius to its highest and finest expression and then proceeded to instruct the world in Africa's wisdom. Inner Africa was the mother, the great Nile the father, and Egypt the brilliant son and fulfiller.

Gerald Massey was born in extremely humble circumstances, the son of a destitute canal boatman, in Hertfordshire, England, in 1828. He received a very scanty early education in the "penny" schools of his home and by the time he was eight was working 12-hour days, first in a silk factory then as a straw plaiter. At age 15, he was able to find employment as an errand boy and it was at this time that his truly prodigious efforts to educate himself began. His position gave him mobility and he spent spare moments browsing through book stalls reading everything he could get his hands on. Massey recounted heart-rending tales of having to stop in the middle of a book to run errands only to find it gone upon returning. His wages often went to book purchases in lieu of the day's meals. Not much more is known of his early life though by the time he was a young man, he had acquired enough learning to turn his hand to poetry. Until his early forties he was able to carve out a modest living as a lecturer, poet, and literary critic. He is still known in England as a poet and an authority on Shakespearean sonnets. Also during this period he turned to radical causes, becoming such a well-known socialist that it is said that he became the model for George Sand's novel, *Felix Holt: Radical*. He was attuned to the leading intellectual currents of his day and became a fervent adherent of the Darwin-Wallace theory of evolution. His deep idealism led him to strong stands against vivisection, a practice increasingly common with the advance of biology.

Massey, during the middle period of his life, was drawn increasingly to spiritualism. He knew many of the prominent mediums, participated in seances, and maintained a lifelong interest in spiritualism. Though he was a rigorous empiricist, an exacting scholar, and a believer in natural science, this did not lead him into a narrow positivism. It is a mark of the man that he could embrace Darwinian evolution, spiritualism, socialism, and anti-vivisectionism seemingly without conflict. However, it was his associations in spiritualist circles that brought him into contact with the Egyptian hieroglyphics and gradually this interest became so consuming that in 1871, he abandoned all his other pursuits to devote himself to a general study of Egyptology, with particular emphasis on the hieroglyphics.

The first product of this intensive research, conducted mostly in the British Museum, was *Book of Beginnings*, first published in 1881. In the course of his studies, he was befriended by Samuel Birch, the leading British Egyptologist of the time and the translator of a version of the "Book of the Dead," one which was to figure prominently in Massey's own work. Birch evidently gave Massey invaluable assistance and guidance and it was a debt that Massey readily acknowledged through the remainder of his life. But in spite of Birch's patronage, the intellectual climate of the time was ill-disposed toward this rather astounding work. Some relatively unbiased souls such as Massey's hero Alfred Russell Wallace, the eminent evolutionist, and Richard Burton, the famous explorer, did read the two volumes of *Book of Beginnings* and pronounced favorably upon them but Wallace made the telling remark that "there might not be a score of people in England who were prepared by their previous education to understand the book."[1] Aside from a handful of other relatively unbiased reviews in publications like *Nature, The Guardian*, and *The Theosophist*, the general reaction was hostile and disbelieving. In an era when the search for evidence of man's origins was concentrated entirely in Asia, that Africa could have instead been man's birthplace was considered preposterous.

In the first volume of *Book of Beginnings*, Massey staked out his position boldly and without equivocation. For him, "the starting point of the human family"

> . . . has now to be sought for in Africa, the birthplace of the black race, the land of the oldest known human types, and of those which preceded and most nearly approached the human . . . *Aethiopia and Egypt produced the earliest civilization in the world and it was indigenous.* (emphasis mine) So far as the records of language and mythology can offer us guidance, there is nothing beyond Egypt and Aethiopia but Africa . . .[2]

In the first chapter, Massey established that premise and disposed of the established theories, particularly those of Bunsen and Brugsch, postulating an Asian origin to Egyptian civilization. Here, Massey asked why, if the dynastic Egyptians were originally Asians, they knew nothing of the camel, an Asian animal, until very late in their history? Why is it that the Egyptians themselves looked southward to Africa as their birthplace and referred to it as "the land of the gods?" Even the word "Africa" can be traced to "Af-rui-ka" which in the Egyptian language signifies birthplace.[3] Moreover, numerous Egyptian customs were unmistakably African in character from the practice of tracing ancestry through the maternal line to the ceremonial anointing of bodies. Massey also points out that the deep reddish-brown color of the Egyptians pictured on the monuments is also characteristic of a number of other African peoples like the Masai of East Africa.[4] Even late in their history, when there had been significant admixtures from non-African peoples, the Egyptians retained the coloring and facial type that clearly marked their African origins. Nonetheless, orthodox Egyptologists devised ingenious arguments for obscuring the plain facts. James Henry Breasted, in his *A History of Ancient Egypt*, claimed to have refuted the contention that the ancient Egyptians were "Negroes" by tracing them instead to the Galla of Ethiopia. The Galla are a people whose color ranges from a deep brown to Black, with woolly hair, and with full-features who in the recent past have been classed by anthropologists as "Hamites" and therefore "not Negroes." It is by such foolish sophistries that men like Breasted have sought to circumvent the issue of the African origins of the Egyptians. The classical historians, Herodotus and Diodorus, who wrote eye-witness accounts stated categorically that the Egyptians and Ethiopians shared the same color, culture, and origins. In any case, for Massey the issue was plain and the cultural identity between Africa and Egypt provided the scaffolding for his study into human beginnings.

In Massey's view no authority in philology, mythology, comparative religion, or Egyptology could ever really understand his business until he delved into the phenomenology of types, i.e., "typology." Typology was the foundation of all human symbolism, myth, language, and religion. Despite Massey's seminal studies in typology, there was no other serious investigation into this area until the advent of the Jungian school of psychoanalytic theory almost 40 years later. Despite the massive accumulation of data in archeology, anthropology, and philology during the 19th century, the *essential quality* of ancient religion, myth, and language eluded the grasp of most authorities. Massey, through typology, plumbed to depths that revealed to him a record of human development hidden to all else.[5] His discovery of the ancient typology anticipated the Jungian "archetypes" of the collective unconscious by several decades.[6] The types originated in natural phenomena, the first teachers of man, and became the means by which the human mental and psychic world was gradually pieced together.

The primal type was that of the "Great Mother" and all she came to represent.

The mental world of primeval man was a concrete world and its profoundest mystery was that of production of new life. Everywhere in nature it was observed that this was the prerogative of the female of the species. According to Massey, and this has been documented in anthropological studies, early men made no connection between sexual congress and reproduction, e.g., there was no fatherhood. The cessation of the female cycle, followed by the swelling and bulging of the female body, culminating in the bursting forth of new life was an awesome, transcendant mystery and the female, in her exclusive motherhood, became the paradigm for the first images of the deity. God, in the first advent, was female, not necessarily in a human image because the surrounding fauna and flora provided examples of superhuman types of females, i.e., the great, obese hippopotamus, the long-lived tortoise, the terrifying crocodile, the ferocious lioness, the grand, over-spreading sycamore tree—all of these embodied powers at once non-human and superhuman. These provided the earliest divine images; only much later was the deity personated in the image of the human female. But as the human counterpart of the female mystery, it was around the human mother that early society first congealed. J.J. Bachofen, one of the first to postulate the primacy of the matriarchy, held that agriculture, the first laws regulating social conduct, the earliest arts and crafts, indeed all those things which first discreted humankind from its animal beginnings, evolved under the matriarchal structure, with the mother supreme as procreator, nourisher, and preserver.[7] This primeval African Mother was the prototype of the "virgin mother," the mother whose children, in Massey's words, "were born but not begotten." This is but one example of how the typology of primordial man in Africa gave rise to the symbolic and eschatological figures of the later "revealed" religion.

The Great Mother was the primal type and from her emanated other related types, figured as her children and originally numbering seven, a number whose mystic significance is with us still. These children of the Mother embodied and typified the powers of nature: darkness, light, air or breath, water or moisture, earth, fire, and blood. These powers were not "worshipped" out of fear and ignorance, as commonly asserted. The golden hawk, for example, became an emblem of Horus the sun because of its color and because of its ability to soar to such heights as to seem like the sun. The immense water cow or hippopotamus was an image in nature of the pregnant female and thus of the Great Mother. The creeping, death-dealing serpent could in one aspect represent darkness and death but when figured with its tail in its mouth would be a symbol of eternity. With its ability to exchange old skin for new, the serpent would also be an image of renewal and resurrection. The ibis, giving itself an enema with its long, curved beak, would be an early ideograph of Thoth, the physician. The leopard and other cats, with their nocturnal habits and preternatural sight, would be symbols of the night sun, i.e., the sun that passed beneath the earth from west to east during the night-time hours. Thus, the powers of nature, whether animal, vegetative, or elemental, were not "worshipped" but provided images to fashion mental concepts and make the world comprehensible. Though the dynastic Egyptians had advanced far beyond the primitive and concrete mental stage of the first imagers in Africa, they never dispensed with the types. The hieroglyphics show this clearly and the plasticity and richness of the types were such that they could embody more and more complex and abstract ideas and symbols. The golden hawk, the first image of the sun, could in time also come to represent the human soul.

The first volume of *Book of Beginnings* was devoted primarily to tracing the origins of the culture, language, and religion of the British Celts to Egypt and Africa, i.e. Kam. Today Massey would be labeled a "hyper-diffusionist" because of his assertion that the cultures of the world were Kamite in origin. With respect to the aboriginal Britons, the Celts, he carefully dissected their language, religion, and customs to prove their Kamite origins. He reproduced an extensive comparative glossary showing the identity of hundreds of Egyptian and Celtic-English words. His derivation of the English word "mother" is instructive:

> Our word Mother is not derived from the Sanskrit Ma, to fashion, but from the Egyptian name of the mother as MUT. Mut means the mother, the Emaner, the mouth . . . Mut the chamber, place, abode, womb . . . AR (Eg.) is the child, or the likeness, the type of a fulfilled period, the thing made. Thus MUT-AR is the place, the gestator, the founder and emaner of the child.[8]

Massey applied the same method to thousands of words in languages from Hebrew to Maori.

In the second volume, Massey conducted a searching examination of the Hebrew legends of the Old Testament and in revealing their Afro-Egyptian or Kamite origins, revolutionized forever Hebraic and Old Testament studies. Of particular consequence is a remarkable chapter entitled "The Egyptian Origin of the Jews Traced from the Monuments." His research had convinced him that the five books of Moses represented Egyptian astronomical allegories which had been literalized, historicized and humanized. The Book of Exodus especially seemed to abound with Egyptian astronomical types that were recreated to form Jewish "history." As he stated:

> The Hebrew Books of the Genesis, Exodus, Numbers, Joshua, and Judges are invaluable as a virgin mine of mythology; they are of utmost importance as an aid in recovering the primeval types of Egyptian thought . . . For the Hebrews, who collected and preserved so much, have explained nothing. There is evidence enough to prove the types are Egyptian and the people who brought them out of Egypt must have been more or less Egyptian in race, and of a religion that was Egyptian of the earliest and oldest kind.
>
> Undoubtedly there is some very slight historic nucleus in the Hebrew narrative, but it has been so mixed with myth that it is far easier to recover the celestial allegory with the aid of its correlatives than it is to restore the human history.[9]

Massey proceeded to show the connection between the Egyptian astronomical and mythological types and all the important Old Testament prophets and patriarchs. There *was* an exodus from Egypt. In fact there were three alluded to in historical testimony, but none of these had anything to do with a *foreign* race of shepherds enslaved for 400 years in Kam and then led out of it by a messianic prophet. The latter years of the great 18th dynasty were years of religious ferment between the worshippers of the Mother and her Son and those of the great paternal deity, Amen-Ra. This ferment led to several exodes out of Egypt by the worshippers of the Mother. The Egyptians, faithful recounters of the events of their history, never mentioned a group or nation that could remotely be identified with the Jews of Exodus. Moses was a type of the Egyptian lion-god "Ma-Shu" and the only apparent historical parallel is with Osarsiph, a Egyptian priest of Ra at On, who led one of the above-mentioned dissents against the established patriarchal religion and subsequently fled with some followers out of Egypt. The worshippers of the Mother's Son were worshippers of Iu which means "he who comes" and who was the Mother's first male consort, before "the fatherhood became known." Iu is identical to the Hebrew Iah, the Gnostic Iao, and the Celtic Hu. His worshippers were "Ius." In one aspect he was "Iu-su" or "he who comes as the son" and in another "Iu-em-hept" or "he who comes in peace" both being antetypes of the later Jesus. Sigmund Freud, himself a Jew, in *Moses and Monotheism* agreed that Moses must have been an Egyptian priest who took the part of the downtrodden, led them into the Sinai, and taught them the worship of one god. Space does not permit further discussion of this vast and complex subject but Massey showed convincingly that the Jews, originally worshippers of the Mother and Son who later renounced them for the all-exclusive Father, brought their religion and language out of Africa, their original home.

In *Natural Genesis*, published in 1883 two years later than *Book of Beginnings* and considered to be a continuation of the earlier book, Massey most fully expounded the system of typology that had enabled him to pierce the mists of human beginnings. By his reckoning, Egypt's greatest legacy to the world was not her temples and monuments, but her hieroglyphics because they faithfully preserved as ideographs the earliest types, thus providing the key to unraveling the mystery of man's origins. Reading through *Natural Genesis* it becomes clear that Massey's typology corresponds more or less directly to the "archetypes" of Carl Jung and had the latter ever examined Massey's work, he might have been non-plussed to find intact the basic framework of his system of archetypes.

In *Natural Genesis*, Massey showed how the early evolution of human consciousness depended on the development of types. Along the lines of descent from an early ape-like ancestor, man's first semi-articulate utterings patterned closely after that of the baboon, the "clicking cynocephalic ape" met with in the Egyptian ideographs who was the "announcer and adorer" of the sun and associated with Thoth. The sole remnants of this primordial speech can be found in the click languages of the present-day Hottentots and Bushmen of southern Africa.

This primitive speech would have been onomatopeic, that is similar in sound to the thing represented, and later speech would to a large extent be abraded and worn down from the original onomatopeia:

> TA . . . is the female Mama . . . "Tat-Tat" is a sound that may have originated with the child in sucking.[10]

Here we have the later Egyptian word "Ta" devolving and wearing down from a much earlier onomatopeic word "Tat-Tat." To illustrate further:

> . . . (the) Puff-Adder became the letter F; which was a syllabic Fu and an Ideographic Fuf, our Puff. Fu (Eg.) denotes puffing, swelling . . . extended with breath. The Snake distended and "fu-fu'd" and thus made the sound that constitutes its name.[11]

Perhaps even the word "ma"—mother in scores of languages—arose from the sound of an infant crying.

Massey painstakingly explored the important primeval types that passed in various forms into every religion. The tree and serpent were two such types forming a dyad that constantly reappeared in the mythic symbolism of different lands and which were incomparably older than when met with in the Genesis story. The conjunction of these two types must have arisen from the association of the tree and arboreal python found throughout Africa. Now at the astronomical stage of myth, the tree was figured as a type of the pole and the serpent as a type of the string of seven circumpolar stars that encircle or "coil" around the pole.[12] The caduceus of Hermes and the Hindu kundalini serpent coiled around the spinal column are two later applications of these types. The constellation of the Great Bear—the "Thigh" to the Egyptians—was the astronomical Great Mother and the seven circumpolar stars her children. In the later myth, typified by Genesis, the Great Bear was dragged down from the heavens as it were and humanized as the woman who was associated with her co-types, the tree and the serpent. There were many feminine and maternal types: the mount or rock, the tree, the cave, the dove, the well, the ark, the cow are but a few examples. Compare this to Jung's Mother Archetype:

> The archetype is often associated with things and places standing for fertility and fruitfulness: the cornucopia, a ploughed field, a garden. It can be attached to a rock, a cave, a tree . . ., a deep well . . ., or to vessel-shaped flowers like the rose or the lotus.[13]

Jung went on to say that in its negative or dark aspect, the archetype could be represented by any devouring animal such as a dragon, a large fish, or serpent. Had Jung copied verbatim from *Natural Genesis* he could have hardly echoed Massey more closely.

In his elaboration of the typological system, Massey's chapter in the second volume, "Typology of Time," is especially important because the determination and recording of cycles and their periodicity became ever more significant to Kamite man as he formed settled communities that depended on seasonal agriculture for sustenance. The earliest modes of time reckoning were to be found in nature, and the female because of her more or less regular monthly periodicity, became the earliest time-keeper:

> . . . coming of age applies to both sexes, but, as may be seen by the Kaffir festival of female puberty, it was the woman-nature that made the primaeval revelation, and was the first teller of time; the demonstrator of periodicity in its most attractive and most mystical aspect.[14]

At a later stage, the heavenly bodies with their regular and cyclic movements became the chief tellers of time but nature was man's first teacher before the heavens were mapped. Jung's most important disciple, Erich Neumann, wrote an extraordinary book entitled *The Great Mother: An Analysis of an Archetype* which seems to further confirm Massey's typology. Neumann had this to say about time and woman:

> Since she governs growth, the Great Mother is the goddess of time. From menstruation, with its supposed relation to the moon, pregnancy, and beyond, the woman is regulated by and dependent on time; so *it is she who determines time . . .*[15] (emphasis mine)

The culmination of Massey's long labor of 36 years was *Ancient Egypt*, published in the year of his death, 1907. In summing up his feelings about the importance of the work he said:

> Comparatively speaking, "A Book of Beginnings" was written in the dark, "The Natural Genesis" was written in the twilight, whereas "Ancient Egypt" has been written in the light of day.[16]

In this book, Massey appeared to have obtained a full grasp of this multidimensional subject. In these two volumes, we see unfolding a tripartite scheme of Kamite religion: typology, mythology, and eschatology. He had reached a summit of critical understanding.

In *Ancient Egypt*, Massey delved into an area untouched in his previous writings: totemism. He demonstrated how the evolutionary pattern led man from primordial sign-language to totemism and thence to spiritism. The totemic phase, overshadowed by the Great Mother, was a harbinger of the elements that came to constitute what is now understood as religion. This was the time when humans were discreted out of the primal, promiscuous horde into matriarchal lineages determined by the natural totemic types, whether figured as plants or animals. The totem imparted (1) lineage identification by relation to a common maternal ancestor, (2) a mode of inter-lineage food distribution, and (3) a means for promoting exogamy or out-marriage, thereby imposing the first taboos against indiscriminate sexual intercourse. This was the time when the post-menopausal mother, her life's purpose fulfilled, voluntarily offered herself up to her children to be eaten as a sacramental meal to (1) preserve her from the the ravages of old age and (2) to keep her blood within the totem group. It was the blood of the mother that determined descent and blood was (and is) the most potent image of life. Blood was the seventh elemental figure among the first seven children of the Mother and its image was later exchanged for that of the son in human form, i.e., he who became the Mother's first consort. This then is the original eucharist, i.e., the consumption of the body and blood of the saviour to infuse the communicant with new life and potency. As Massey attested, the first saviour was the Mother. She was the earth who germinated life, the tree whose fruit sustained life, the water which renewed life. In these aspects and more, she was man's saviour.

In an extraordinary chapter entitled "Elemental and Ancestral Spirits," Massey entered into a discussion of the Kamite interconnection with the spirit world. Massey, the spiritualist, did not find this incongruous:

> The colossal conceit of obtuse modern ignorance notwithstanding the ghost and the faculty for seeing the ghost are realities in the domain of natural fact. The seers may be comparatively rare, although the clairvoyant and seer of spirits is by no means so scarce as either a great painter or great poet. The abnormal faculties are human, and they can be increased by cultivation.[17]

Massey, though somewhat clairvoyant himself, would never have claimed to be a mystic. He was a careful empiricist, believed in rational science, and refused to countenance "miraculous" happenings that contravened the laws of nature. Still, he considered that the "mesmeric" forces of spiritualism were well within the domain of nature and strongly affirmed the ability of the ancient sages of Egypt and Africa to manipulate such forces.

In the prefatory to *Ancient Egypt*, Massey wrote that his earlier books "were met in England with the truly orthodox conspiracy of silence." Considering that his writings completely overturned the accepted theories on the birth of civilization as well as the very foundations of orthodox Christianity, it isn't any wonder. As shown in *Ancient Egypt*, the highest and last phase of the Egyptian science of the soul—a science slowly fashioned over many milleniums from its inner African beginnings—was the eschatological one. The drama of Osiris with its interwoven themes of life, death, and resurrection was the most perfect expression of this and gave rise to the later Mediteranean cults like those of Tammuz, Adonis, and Dionysus. Even though the Osirian drama was Egyptian soul science in its most spiritualized form, it preserved and maintained the earlier typology and astronomical mythology. According to Massey, the Egyptian priests and their Ethiopian predecessors had maintained an unbroken continuity of star-gazing for 10,000 years and longer. Moreover, as has been previously shown, the types (and archetypes) were reconstituted in the heavens and thus to the ancient Kamites, the celestial world and terrestial world mirrored each other. The important stars and star-groupings were given names and histories and reflected directly the natural types. Examples of this are the constellations of the beetle or scarab (our crab), lion, ram, bull, fishes, etc. Astronomical mythology passed through stages: it was first stellar, then lunar, and lastly solar. The Osirian drama was of the solar type but incorporated all of the previous astronomical mythos. Osiris was the night-time sun passing through the nether world of Amenta as a result of his murder by Set, the principle or darkness, who figured later as the Semitic Satan. At the dawning, Osiris is resurrected as his son Horus who fights and defeats the devouring dragon of darkness for light to triumph another day. Osiris, in his eschatological aspect, was also the soul of the deceased who after conquering the forces of evil and corruption in Amenta, is resurrected as the glorified, i.e., the spiritual sun of which Horus is the symbol. Everything in the Kamite world was of a piece, representing complete interpenetration of typology, mythology, and eschatology.

Massey capped his signature work with an elaborate and detailed investigation into the Kamite origins of Christianity. He was able to trace all the important Christian themes to Kamite typology and astronomical mythology. He asserted that the Gospels, like certain Old Testament accounts already alluded to, were just the humanized and historicized astronomical mythology of Egypt, instituted by the early Christian canonizers and confirmed at the Council of Nicea. The word Christ, which in Greek means "anointed," is equivalent to "karast," Egyptian for the embalmed and anointed mummy, a figure of resurrection and life after death. The karast is also the "messu," Egyptian for "anointed one," from which the word "messiah" comes. As an example of Christianity's astronomical antecedents, the birthdate of Christ, originally celebrated in early January, was purposefully moved back to December 25 to co-incide with the birthdate of the sun-god Horus (and all the sun gods of antiquity) at which time the constellation Virgo was on the eastern horizon; the sun as son, then, was truly born of the Virgin. Gospel episodes appear to have actually been lifted from the Egyptian originals and given a Palestinian dressing. In the Temple of Luxor, built in 1700 B.C., there are four scenes in a vignette which show the Annunciation, the Conception, the Birth, and the Adoration of the Child, here depicted as Horus, in later Christian iconography as Jesus. It is also of note that the Christian crucified figure was the Lamb until the 7th century. The Saviour, in one aspect, was the Lamb, the image of the sun in Aries during the time when the equinox occurred in Aries, between 2410 and 255 B.C. Christ as a crucified *man* was a relatively late figure in Christian iconography. In the appendix to *Ancient Egypt*, Massey listed more than 200 direct parallels between the Jesus legend and the Osiris-Horus cycle. The earthly Jesus is equivalent to Horus; Jesus the Christ corresponds to Osiris, the resurrected god.

There were a number of Christian and near-Christian cults struggling for existence in the first few centuries A.D. The Gnostics especially represented a type of Christianity in which the Egyptian originals were consciously preserved and which did not center around the false human history of a mythical saviour. The Gnostic Christ was a type of the Deified Man that lies dormant in every human and the attainment to which was the goal of the Egyptian soul science, typified by "The Book of the Dead." Outside the Gospels, there is no authentic reference to the man Jesus and his supposed history as portrayed in the Gospels by any contemporary commentator until the 2nd century. G.R.S. Mead, one of the most learned authorities in the field of Christian origins, categorically stated:

> It has always been an unfailing source of astonishment to the historical investigator of Christian beginnings, that there is not one single word from the pen of any Pagan writer of the first century of our era, which can in any fashion be referred to the marvellous story recounted by the Gospel writers. *The very existence of Jesus seems to be unknown.*[18] (emphasis mine)

A man named Joshua Ben Pandira (Jesus is Joshua in Greek) did live more than a century before the gospel Jesus was supposed to have been born. He was an Essene who learned "magic and wonder-working" in Egypt, traveled through and performed wonders in Palestine, and was tried and crucified by hanging on that account by Jewish magistrates in the city of Lydda on the eve of Passover (Christian Easter) in 70 B.C. If there was an historical Jesus, he was it. There was an almost universal expectation of the appearance of a savior in the world's religions of the time and perhaps the life and work of Joshua the Essene provided the germ around which the vast saviour mythology—in existence for thousands of years—coalesced. We know too, from the Dead Sea Scrolls and other revived documents, that Christianity evolved directly from Essenism and eventually supplanted it entirely.

The worship of Isis and Serapis (a form of Osiris) was lifted bodily out of Egypt and transplanted to Rome where for nearly four centuries the cult—particularly that of Isis—rivaled those of Jupiter and Mithra. Isis was especially popular in her aspect as mother with child, the infant Horus, and both she and Horus were pictured with Black coloring and Ethiopic features. Roman frescoes almost always show her priests to be Ethiopians and Roman legions carried her image and worship to the farthest reaches of savage Europe. When Christianity finally penetrated these regions, wherever the image of Isis holding the infant Horus was found she was turned into the Black Madonna with Child. For more than a millenium and a half, these Black Madonnas have been the holiest shrines of Catholic Europe and even today, millions of Europeans bow down to worship an African goddess and her child.

Massey had a jaundiced view of both Judaism and Christianity for what he considered their wilful perversion of the Kamite mysteries. To him, they were valid only insofar as they were, in some sense, true to their origins: the Jews as followers of Iu, "he who comes in peace" (as Iu-em-hept), and the Christians of the "karast" nature of Christ, i.e., the resurrected and perfected man, whose germ is in us all. One implication of Massey's work is that man's self-reconciliation lies in making his peace with the Mother, an object of his abuse over these recent millenia, and in effecting a reconciliation between the Mother and Father consciousness. In the Osirian legend, when Horus, light and sun, was about to achieve complete victory over Set, darkness and night, Thoth, the universal Mind and Balancer, stepped in, put a halt to the battle, and restored Set to his place. The universe was created in an equilibrium and it is the subtle and complex interplay between the light and dark that gives our universe its form and its reality. In the Deified Man, the paragon of Egyptian soul science, the opposites are united and transcended. This may be, in sum, the highest lesson of the opus of Gerald Massey.

Notes

1. Massey, Gerald, *Natural Genesis*, volume 1, London: Williams and Norgate, 1883, p. vii.
2. Massey, Gerald, *Book of Beginnings*, volume 2, London: Williams and Norgate, 1881, p. 599.
3. Ibid., vol. 1, p. 28
4. See Diop, C.A., *The African Origin of Civilization: Myth or Reality*, trans. by M. Cook, New York: Lawrence Hill and Co., 1974, for a fuller discussion of this.
5. One exception to this statement is the work of Godfrey Higgins, *Anacalypsis*, New Hyde Park: University Books, 1965, published almost 50 years before *Book of Beginnings*. The massive scholarship and penetrating understanding evident in this stupendous book seemed to prefigure Massey.
6. Jung defines his concept as follows: "In addition to our immediate consciousness, which is of a thoroughly personal nature . . ., there exists a second system of a collective, universal, and impersonal nature which is identical in all individuals. This collective unconscious does not develop individually but is inherited. It consists of pre-existent forms, the archetypes, which can only become conscious seconarily and which give definite form to certain psychic contents.

   . . . there is good reason for supposing that the archetypes are unconscious images of the instincts themselves . . . that they are patterns of instinctual behavior." Jung, C., *Archetypes and the Collective Unconscious*, trans. by R.F.C. Hull, Princeton: Princeton University Press, 1975, pp. 43-4.
7. See Bachofen, J.J., *Myth, Religion, and Mother Right*, trans. by R. Manheim, Princeton: Princeton University Press. See also Diop, C.A., *The Cultural Unity of Black Africa*, Chicago: Third World Press, 1978, for a critique of the Bachofen thesis of the universal primacy of the matriarcy.
8. Massey, op. cit., vol. 1, p. 245.
9. Ibid., vol. 2, p. 363.
10. Massey, *Natural Genesis*, vol. 1, p. 236.
11. Ibid. p. 250.
12. Our Christmas tree is also a figure of the pole, crowned on its apex with a star representing the pole star and its branches holding the lights that represent the stars that revolve around the pole.
13. Jung, op. cit., p. 81.
14. Massey, op. cit., vol. 2, p. 273.
15. Neumann, E., *The Great Mother: An Analysis of an Archetype*, trans. by R. Mannheim, Princeton: Princeton University Press, 1974, pp.226-7.
16. Massey Gerald, *Ancient Egypt: The Light of the World*, volume 1, New York: Samuel Weiser, 1970, Prefatory.
17. Ibid., p. 155.
18. Mead, G.R.S., *Did Jesus Live 100 B.C.?*, London: Theosophical Publishing Society, 1903, p. 48.

BLACK WOMEN IN SEARCH OF KEMET: A BIBLIOGRAPHY

By Larry Williams

Badham, Francis Leronia (1925) "Epitome Of Modern Exploration And Scientific Research In the Nilotic Regions Of Africa [An Outline Of the Principal Archaeological Explorations And Historical Researches Carried On In The Nile Valley And Especially In the Egyptian Sudan In The 18th, 19th And 20th Centuries]." A Paper Presented At The Cultures And Civilizations Of Negro Peoples In Africa: A Symposium, The African Civilizaion Section, Dept. of History, Howard University, June 2, 1925.

Bertram, Peggy Brooks (1988) "The 25th Dynasty: The Black Kings Of Kush", In Eye On History Column By Eva M. Doyle, *Buffalo Criterion*, Thursday, July 28 - August 2, 1988.

Bertram, Peggy Brooks (1988) "The Battles Of Taharka," Unpublished Poem, Buffalo, N.Y.

Bowles, Alice L. (1925) "Some Recent Archaeological Discoveries And Anthropological Studies Indicating An Apparently Central African Origin Of Some Outstanding burial, Religious And Social Practices Of The Ancient Egyptians." A Paper Presented At The Cultures And Civilizations Of Negro Peoples In Africa: A Symposium, The African Civilization Section, Dept. Of History, Howard University, June 3, 1925.

Brown, Addie (1987) "Ancient Kemetian Family Caring And Sharing Attitude And Patterns: Implications For Contemporary Black Families," A Paper Presented At The 4th Annual ASCAC Ancient Egyptian Studies Conference, July 8-10, Aswan, Kemet (Egypt).

Burwell, Etta Rebecca (1925) "A Digest Of the Origin And Evolution Of Some Outstanding Historical Opinions Regarding The Regional Beginnings And The Racial Affinities Of The Ancient Egyptians And Their Civilizations." A Paper Presented At The Cultures And Civilizations Of Negro Peoples In Africa: A Symposium, The African Civilization Sections, Dept. of History, Howard University, June 3, 1925.

Carruthers, Iva (1980) "Africanity And The Black Woman," *Black Books Bulletin*, Vol. 6, No. 4, pp. 14-20, 71.

Clark, Daima (1986) "Similarities Between Egyptian And Dogon Perceptions Of Man, God And Nature," In *Kemet And The African Worldview* (Eds.) Maulana Karenga And Jacob H. Carruthers. Los Angeles: University Of Sankore Press, pp. 119-130.

Clark, Daima (1985) "The Influence Of Egyptian Art On Southwestern Nigerian Art," A Paper Presented At The 2nd Annual Egyptian Studies Conference, 28 Feb.-March 3, 1985, Northeastern Illinois University, Chicago, Illinois.

Clegg, Legrand H. And Lisbeth Gant (1978) "The Black Roots Of King TUT," *The Black Collegian*, Vol. 8, No. 3, Jan./Feb., pp. 41, 44, 81.

Clegg, Legrand H. And Lisbeth Gant (1977) "The Big TUT Rip-Off: A National Insult To Blacks," *Sepia*, Vol. 26, No. 11, pp. 39-47.

Cobb, Dorothy Lee (1975) "The Cognitive Path," In *Understanding The African Philosophical Concert Behind The Diagram Of The Law Of Opposites*, Alkbulan Books, pp. 28-37.

Davis, Hilda Andrea (1925) "Some Recent Opinions Regarding The Ethiopian Or Central African Origin Of The Basic Features Of The Earliest Egyptian Civilizations," A Paper Presented At The Cultures And Civilizations Of Negro Peoples In Africa: A Symposium, The African Civilization Section, Dept. of History, Howard University, June 3, 1925.

Diggs, Irene (1983) *Black Chronology: From 4000 B.C. To The Abolition Of The Slave Trade*, Boston: G.K. Hall.

Gilbert, Gwen (1980) "Journey Into The Secret Life," *Black Books Bulletin*, Vol. 7, No. 1, pp. 8-12, 25.

Graves, Anna Melissa (1942) *Africa: The Wonder And the Glory* (1984 Reprint) Baltimore: Black Classic Press.

Hardiman, W. Joye (1987) "The Ancient Egyptian Frame Of Reference And Epistermological Value For The Liberation Of Black People," A Paper Presented At The 4th Annual ASCAC Conference, July 8-10, Aswan, Kemet (Egypt).

Hardiman, W. Joye (1986) "The Nature And Elegance Of Ancient Egyptian Literature," In *Kemet And The African Worldview* (Eds.) Maulana Karenga And Jacob H. Caruthers. Los Angeles: University Of Sankore Press, pp. 167-172.

Hardiman, W. Joye (1985) "Towards A Theory Of Ancient Egyptian Autobiographical Literature," A Paper Presented At The 2nd Annual Egyptian Studies Conference, 28 Feb.-March 3, 1985, Northeastern Illinois University, Chicago, Illinois.

Henry, Valarie (1986) "'Egyptian Origins Of Ballet," A Paper Presented At The Southern Regional ASCAC Conference, Atlanta, University, Sept, 26-28.

Houston, Drusilla D. (1926) *Wonderful Ethiopians Of The Ancient Cushite Empire*. Oklahoma: Universal Publishing Co.

Jeffries, Rosalind (1987) "The Foundation Of Symbols In The Art of Kemet And West And Central Africa "A Paper Presented At The 4th Annual ASCAC Conference, July 8-10, Aswan, Kemet.

Jogunosimi, Ife (1986) "The Role Of Royal Women In Ancient Egypt," in *Kemet And The African Worldview* (Eds.) Maulana Karenga And Jacob H. Carruthers, Los Angeles: University Of Sankore Press, pp. 31-42.

Johnson, Eloise McKinney (1984) "Egypt's Isis: The Original Black Madonna," In *Black Women In Antiquity:* Journal of African Civilizations, Vol. 6, No. 1, pp. 64-71.

Johnson, Pearl H. (1925) "A Resume Of The Classical Egyptian, Hebrew, Greek, And Roman Writings Treating Of The Traditions And Civilizations Of Ethiopia Presented At The Cultures And Civilizations Of Negro Peoples In Africa: A Symposium, The African Civilization Section, Dept. Of History, Howard University, June 3, 1925.

LaVille, Tamara (1985) "The Concept Of Initiation In Ancient Egypt", A Paper Presented At The 2nd Annual Ancient Egyptian Studies Conference, 28 Feb.-March 3, 1985, Northeastern Illinois University, Chicago, Illinois.

Madden, Sandra Ayana (1987) "Egypt's Lost Connection: An Analysis Of U.S. Social Studies Textbooks," Unpublished Manuscript.

McIntyre, Charshee (1986) "Ancient Egyptian Music And Its Influence On Music Throughout The World Particularly Greece, Assyria, Europe, And The Asiatic World Including The Hebrews," A Paper Prepared June 15, State University Of New York, College At Old Westbury.

Noble, Jeanne (1978) "What Is Africa To Me?" In *Beautiful, Also, Are The Souls Of My Black*

Sisters: A History Of The Black Woman In America. N.J.: Prentice-Hall, Inc. pp. 3-30.

Perrault, Gaylene (1987) "Creating A Bridge Between Radical Black Psychology, Radical Black Theology And Kemetic Studies," A Paper Prepared For the 6th Annual African Civilizations Conference, March 16-19, Atlanta, Georgia.

Ratabisha, Nzingha (1987) "Models Of African Womanhood: The Kemetic Experience," A Paper Presented At The 4th Annual ASCAC Ancient Egyptian Studies Conference, July 8-10, Aswan, Kemet (Egypt).

Redd, Danita (1987) "Hatshepsut: The Female Horus," In *Great Black Leaders: Ancient and Modern* (Ed.) Ivan Van Sertima, Journal Of African Civilizations, Vol. 9, December, pp. 166-204.

Redd, Danita (1985) "Black Madonnas Of Europe: Diffusion Of The African Isis," In *African Presence In Early Europe* (Ed.) Ivan Van Sertima, Journal Of African Civilizations, Vol;. 7, No. 2, pp. 108-133.

Sanchez, Sonia (1984) "Nefertiti: Queen To A Sacred Mission", In *Black Women In Antiquity* (Ed.) Ivan Van Sertima, Journal of African Civilizations, Vol. 6, No. 1, April, pp. 49-55.

Shane, Carrie Belle (1925) "The Question Of The Ethnic Affinities And The Territorial Origin Of the Proto-Dynastic Peoples Of The Nile Valley," A Paper Presented At The Cultures And Civilizations Of The Negro Peoples In Africa: A Symposium, The African Civilization Section, Dept. of History, Howard University, June 3, 1925.

Simon, Virginia S. (1984) "Tiye: Nubian Queen Of Egypt," In *Black Women In Antiquity* (Ed.) Ivan Van Sertima, Journal of African Civilizations, Vol. 6, No. 1, April, pp. 56-63.

Simon, Virginia S. (1983) "African King In Confedeate Capital," *Negro History Bulletin*, Jan./March.

Simon, Virginia S. (1983) "Christ Came To Nubia-Kush," *A.M.E. Zion Quarterly Review*, October Issue.

Walker, Evelyn (1975) "The Law Of Opposites: An Interpretation," In *Understanding The African Philosophical Concept Behind The Diagram Of The Law Of Opposites*, Yosef Ben-Jochannan Et. Al, Alkebulan Books, pp. 22-27.

Wallace, Janet (1987) "The Origin Of Beauty And Make Up: A Short Essay," *Bronner Bros. 41st International Beauty Show Program Book*, Atlanta, pp. 78-79.

Wimby, Rekhety Et Al. (1987) *Kemetic Name Book*, Kemetic Institute, Chicago, Illinois.

Wimby, Rekhety (1986) "The Unity Of African Languages," In *Kemet And The African Worldview (Eds.)* Maulana Karenga And Jacob H. Carruthers, Los Angeles, Un Of Sankore Name Bo Press, pp. 151-166.

Wimby, Rekhety (1985) "Ancient And Modern Cattle Cultures Of North And East Africa In Comparison," A Paper Presented At The 2nd Annual Egyptian Studies Conference, 28 Feb.-March 3, 1985, Northeastern Illinois University, Chicago, Illinois.

Wimby, Rekhety (1984) "The Female Horuses And Great Wives Of Kemet," In *Black Women In Antiquity* (Ed.) Ivan Van Sertima, Journal of African Civilizations, Vol. 6, No. 1, pp. 36-48.

Wimby, Rekhety (1980) "The Greco-Roman Tradition Concerning Ethiopia And Egypt", *Black Books Bulletin*, Vol. 7, No. 1, pp. 14-19, 25.

Young, Velma Thomas (1925) "Some Of The Recent Archaeological Discoveries And Studies, Indicating The Punite Or Central African Origin Of "Many Of The Great Gods Of The Egyptian Pantheon," A Paper Presented At The Cultures And Civilizations Of Negro Peoples In Africa: Section, Dept. of History, Howard University, June 3, 1925.

ANCIENT EGYPT FOR CHILDREN—FACTS, FICTION, AND LIES

Beatrice Lumpkin

"Those books don't stay on the self too long," the librarian told me, when I inquired about children's books on ancient Egypt. Young readers are fascinated by stories of pyramids and people who so enjoyed life that they mummified their dead in hopes of an afterlife.

But what are children learning about Egypt—facts, fiction, or lies?

How many of us know the facts—that the base of our entire Western civilization came from Africa? It was in ancient Egypt that the so-called Western philosophy, ethics, classical learning and science, even religion, originated. And European scholars acknowledged this gift, which they received via Greece from Egypt, until American slavery and the rise of imperialism changed the writing of history.

As a mathematics teacher I studied the ancient Egyptian contribution to mathematics. The first cipherization of numbers (using symbols instead of tally marks, for example, for ten), a system of fractions that was used up to modern times, geometric formulas including the volume of a truncated pyramid and the area of a curved surface, and formulas for the sum of arithematic series were among the earliest Egyptian discoveries.

In science, too, there were many Egyptian "firsts" including the first calendar, sun dial, water clock and steam engine, a 365-day year and 24-hour day, and the beginning of medicine as a science. The Egyptians were the teachers of the ancient Greeks. Little wonder, then, that the greatest center of "Hellenistic" science was in Egypt, at Alexandria, at a time when the population was native Egyptian and a few Greeks had immigrated to that great city.[1]

Western literature, architecture, religion and ethics were also greatly influenced by those of Egypt. In religion, the story of Moses as a baby in the bulrushes is a close analogue of the earlier Egyptian Horus story. (Isis hid Horus in a basket among the reeds of the Nile.) The Christian trinity was a later import from Egypt and is not found in the Old Testament.

Yet one after the other, the classical histories I consulted were negative in their evaluations of the Egyptian contribution. Just two examples suffice to show the extent of prejudice in the standard historiography:

Compared to the Greeks, wrote Morris Kline, "The mathematics of the Egyptians and Babylonians is the scrawling of children just learning how to write, as opposed to great literature."[2]

David E. Smith, whose *History of Mathematics* became a model for many later historians, said of Egyptian mathematics:

> So little was accomplished in the Orient from 1000 B.C. to 300 B.C. . . . the East has always been the East and the West has always been the West. . . . Even the ancients recognized the difference for Quintilian remarks, "From of old there has been the famous division of Attic and Asiatic writers, the former being reckoned succinct and vigorous, the latter inflated and empty."[3]

Although I was shocked, I should not have been surprised, because I had read W. E. B. Du Bois. He replied to Arnold Toynbee's claim that Egyptian civilization was "white" or European, and to other assertions that Egypt was in reality Asian, not African:

> There can be but one explanation for this vagary of nineteenth century science. It was due to the slave trade and Negro slavery. It was due to the fact that the rise and support of capitalism called for rationalization based upon degrading and discrediting the Negroid peoples. It is especially significant that the science of Egyptology arose and flourished at the very time that the cotton kingdom reached its greatest power on the foundation of American Negro slavery.[4]

We may continue to ask why both we and our children are fed such a racially biased story of the origin of our civilization. Why haven't we been taught that the base of our so-called Western civilization was created by the African peoples of Egypt? Why has the Egyptian contribution been downplayed, or if admitted, attributed to a mysterious non-African "white" race?

The reasons are economic and political. Racism is big business. In 1972 Victor Perlo estimated superprofits due to racist differentials in wages, rents, etc. as forty-nine billion dollars. Its political value in dividing working people and allowing the transnational companies to dictate American government policy is incalculable (*Economics of Racism USA*, New York: International, 1975).

Truthful literature on ancient Egypt can go a long way towards refuting racist premises by showing that modern civilization is based on the great achievements of the African people of Egypt. Good children's books could:

1. develop pride in the contributions of the African peoples of Egypt who laid the foundations for our own civilization;

2. build an understanding of historical development, an understanding which helps in all studies;

build the self-confidence of female students because many women rose to leadership in Egypt;

Unfortunately, of the thirty-two children's books in this survey, most did not live up to this potential. Many of the books contained excellent material but fell short in some crucial aspects, measured against the following checklist:

Does the book show the following?

1. Egypt is in Africa and the Egyptians are an African people.

2. The high civilization of ancient Egypt was initiated and developed by Egyptians and was not imported from any other continent.

3. Construction gangs for the pyramids, obelisks, and temples were not based on slave labor. Rather they consisted primarily of farmers who worked for an allowance, especially during the flood season when the fields could not be farmed. Farmers had legal rights and could, and did, enter the courts to enforce these rights.

4. The miracle of Egypt was not a passive "gift of the Nile"; rather it was the product of highly centralized, efficient administration and Egyptian science and technology.

5. Many of the first principles of science were developed in ancient Egypt.

6. The relationship of Egypt to Greece was that of teacher to student. Egyptian contributions to Western Civilization did not end with the Greek conquest but continued, on a higher level, at Alexandria and other Egyptian cities well into Roman times.

7. Women enjoyed far more equality in Ancient Egypt than in Europe or Asia. Some rights guaranteed ancient Egyptian women are not yet generally established, such as marriage contracts.

How did the books (twenty-three nonfiction and nine fiction) score in the survey? The books were those available on the shelves of the Oak Park, Illinois, Public Library, which had a larger collection on shelf than the Chicago Public Library Juvenile Division.

The African identity of ancient Egypt was specifically mentioned in only two of the books. A third book, of the twenty-three nonfiction books, does mention that Egypt is in Africa, but facial features in the illustrations do not show the people as African. Fully twenty of the twenty-three books omit mention of the African location and identity of Egypt.

In some cases the book illustrations suggest that the Egyptians were really Europeans. Right on the cover of *Gods and Pharaohs* by Geraldine Harris, there is a big spread of a rather Nordic looking, blue-eyed pharoah! One need only contrast this drawing with the statue of Tutankhamen, in the same pose of royal crook and flail crossed against his chest, to see the contrast between the clearly African features of Tut and the Europeanized version in this book.

The text of *Gods and Pharaohs* does indeed include valuable information. Perhaps the author had no control over the illustrations used by the publisher. Still the impact of art is much greater than the impact of copy for audiences of any age.[5]

Many books show the Egyptians as tanned Greeks, for example, *The Egyp-*

tians Knew, by Pine and Levine. There is not one word identifying Egyptians as Africans, or even locating Egypt in Africa in this otherwise useful book. That is especially unfortunate because this book is one of only three in this survey that was written for the lower grades.[6]

Wilbur Cross' book, *Enchantment of the World—Egypt*, has the opposite problem. Excellent photographs clearly show the African people of Egypt, but the text classifies Egyptians as non-African. Cross states, "Some people from Upper Egyptian areas are very dark skinned, the result of many generations of intermarriage with Nubians and other Africans." This implies that Egyptians are not Africans.[7]

In eight of these books, although nothing is said in the copy, good photographs are reproduced which clearly show the African features of ancient Egyptians. Does this reflect progress in books published since the late 1960s, when the fight to introduce Black Studies won many victories?

Of the eleven nonfiction books published before 1970, only three picture Egyptians as Africans, four as non-Africans, and four omit any reference to art on the identity of the Egyptian people. The figure is somewhat better for the twelve produced since 1970 with six picturing the Egyptians as Africans, two as non-African and four omitting such information.

The second survey question was on the indigenous character of the Egyptian civilization and is closely related to the first question.

The racist version of hisory, after asserting that the Egyptians were not African, then claims that the culture was imported. The implication is that the Egyptians were not capable of developing so high a civilization.

Ann Millard's *Egypt* repeats this version of history:

> Writing appears fully developed in Egypt, whereas in Mesopotamia a long history of experimentation in this art can be traced, and it has been suggested, therefore, that writing was introduced into Egypt from Mesopotamia.[8]

Millard did not have available the results of the Nubian Salvage Mission which uncovered further proof of the African origins of Egyptian writing and culture. This evidence includes very early hieroglyphs and the existence of generations of predynastic pharaohs in the South of Egypt.[9] Ancient Egyptian was an African language and the flora and fauna models used for hieroglyphs were also African. As Du Bois charged, the theory of an Asian origin of Egyptian language and writing was a racist, not a scientific construct.

T. G. H. James present the same theory of a foreign origin but also quotes an interesting alternative:

> As Egyptian civilization . . . seemed to appear as if from nowhere, it was proposed that some invading race must have arrived in Egypt. . . . Petrie in 1893 thought that the dynastic race came, not from Asia, but from further south in Africa.[10]

Unfortunately, the search for a source of Egyptian civilization farther south in Africa waited for seventy years, so deep was the prejudice that Africa could not be the source of high civilization. It follows that only five of the twenty-three books surveyed credit Africans for inventing this great African civilization.

How the pyramids were built was our next question. In Payne's *The Pharoahs of Ancient Egypt* we get the same picture, dramatized in some Hollywood spectaculars:

> He could hear the groans of the slaves who had labored under the lash of Cheops's brutal overseers to raise this mighty tomb skyward.[11]

Sondergaard in *My First Geography of the Suez Canal* is even more graphic, claiming the building of a canal cost the lives of 120,000 workers, a scare figure which has no basis in the historical record.[12]

A number of children's books have corrected this error. In *Gods and Pharaohs*, despite its blue-eyed pictures of pharaohs, Harris makes the following correction:

> It is wrong to think that the pyramids were built by gangs of slaves toiling under the lash. The main work force was the general population that had nothing to do for three-four months while the fields were flooded.[13]

It could be added that the work force was also paid, perhaps a form of work relief. Despite the growing realization that the slave-labor picture of ancient Egypt is false, this stereotype persists in children's books.

Was the ancient Egyptian civilization a passive "gift of the Nile"? Of the eight books which deal with Egypt "as the gift of the Nile," only two credit the ingenuity and intelligence of the Egyptian people for the development of this remarkable civilization. Silverberg's *Before the Sphinx* describes the heavy rains which "turned the Nile into a savage monster" requiring a great coordinated effort to turn the calamity of a flood into the blessing of irrigated agriculture.[14]

Payne speaks of the Egyptians being "forced to use their wits" given the challenge of partly predictable floods.[15] The other six which discuss the "gift of the Nile" continue to reverse cause and effect. In *The Nile*, for example, Warren writes, "Because of the river, Egypt became one of the great cradles of world civilization."[16]

The damage done by this viewpoint is often compounded by a belittling comparison to Mesopotamian civilization. Even in Boyer's valuable *History of Mathematics*, we read:

> Geometry may have been a gift of the Nile, as Herodotus believed, but the Egyptians did little with the gift. . . . For more progressive achievements one must look to the more turbulent river valley knwon as Mesopotamia.[17]

On the fifth survey question, we found that the outstamding contributions of ancient Egypt to mathematics and science were mentioned in only eight of the twenty-three nonfiction books surveyed. The Egyptian 365-day calendar was the forerunner of our calendar and was the invention most often mentioned in these eight books. It seems a pity that more wasn't done with the scientific aspects of mummification, since this feature of Egyptian culture has a universal appeal for young readers. The use of mathematics is also generally slighted.

On the relationship between Egypt and Greece, most Western authors claim that the classical Greek scholars were mistaken in writing that they had acquired their learning from Egypt. So it is to be expected that children's books published in the U.S. would also deny ancient Egyptians credit for achievements of the Alexandrian school which flourished in Egypt from about 300 B.C. for nearly a thousand years. In 415 A.D. a Christian mob brutally murdered an algebraist and philosopher, the Egyptian woman named Hupatia.

By omitting the achievements of the Alexandrian scholars, some of the most fascinating material in the history of Egypt is lost. Only by denying the Egyptian character of Alexandria, could the children's book, *Before the Sphinx*, say, ". . . in 1090 B.C. Egypt ceased forever to have major importance among nations."[18] In fact, Egyptian culture remained a leading force into the fifth century and came forward again, under Muslim rule, in the ninth century.

One of the pleasures of writing children's books on ancient Egypt is the opportunity to write about the advanced position of women. The equal rights of women to own, inherit, and retain their own property on the dissolution of marriage were all guaranteed by law. Women freely entered the Egyptian courts to enforce their rights. Many women gained wealth and power through their skill as traders. Women were among the most effective rulers of Egypt. The never-to-be-forgotten Hatshepsut even put on the two crowns of Egypt and declared herself King (not Queen)—Pharaoh of all Egypt.

This theme comes across strongly in *Ancient Egypt* by Charles Robinson, revised in 1984 by Lorna Greenberg. Marriage as a partnership with respect for the freedom of the wife and reverence for the mother was the Egyptian way.[19] But in all, only three of the books surveyed include the topic of women's rights.

In summary, of the nonfictional children's books on Egypt found on the shelves of the Oak Park, Illinois, Library, these books present a wide variety of facts on Ancient Egypt, but marred by omissions and distortions. Little is said about the African identity of Egypt. Hopefully, many children will look at the features of the pharaohs for themselves and will realize that Egyptians are Africans, even if these books say otherwise.

However, there is less of value in the fiction on Egypt which, incidentally, is almost all for "young adults." Only two of the nine books surveyed were below the junior high school level.[20]

Certainly the author of fiction has more leeway than the writer of nonfiction.

But both should respect the facts. Good historical fiction, especially for young readers, should not distort history. If the nine books surveyed are a representative sample of those recommended by the library journals, most novels for young readers fail the test as an instructional medium about Egypt.

Eight of these nine books portray ancient Egypt as a slave society. There is adventure without any insight into the culture of the time, as in *Treasure of Tenakertom.*[21] In this book and in *Honey of the Nile* there is a mistaken emphasis on Akhenaten as the "most important pharaoh" because he replaced the traditional religion with the supposedly monotheistic worship of the Aten.

In reality, Akhenaten did not play a key role in Egyptian history. Nor was his supposed monotheism a progressive development, rather it was a move towards less democracy and greater absolute power for Akhenaten. The fascination with Akhenaten proceeds from the viewpoint of modern, monotheistic Christianity, extrapolated into another time of many gods who were unified under the basic principle of Ma'at, truth, or the right way.

Four of the nine novels include some points of interest. *The Bright and Morning Star* opens with a family traveling to Kemi (Egypt) in the hope that the famous physicians of Egypt can save their sick child. Despite this promising beginning, the rest of the book deals with palace intrigue and provides little insight into ancient Egyptian culture.[22]

In *The Princess Runs Away* there is some description of Egyptian technology such as weaving and making papyrus.[23] *The Egypt Game* was especially interesting because the characters are modern kids who play that they're in Egypt. The hero of the book is a Black child and there is a sense of excitement about their fascination with ancient Egypt.[24]

Scarab for Luck by Meadowcraft is a good story for the middle grades with lots of adventure and lots of information. Unfortunately, it is marred by too many stereotypes. Huge statues are pulled by "four long lines of slaves," "Negroes" are referred to as different from Egyptians, doctors are shown practicing magic but not analyzing the disease scientifically (which Egyptian doctors did do within the limits of the knowledge of the time).

In the fiction surveyed here, my own two books, *Young Genius in Old Egypt* for grades four to six and *Senefer and Hatshepsut—A Novel of Egyptian Genius* for young adults[25] were omitted but not because of a false sense of modesty. These books were published noncommercially, with the DuSable Museum of African American History. To have included them in the survey would have skewed the results. They were written in the hope of meeting the above criteria but have reached only a relatively small number of readers. Thus, their impact remains limited.

There really is no shortcut to the goal of ridding our books of racism. The publishing monopolies will respond only to mass pressure and mass struggles by workers, parents, students, and faculty united to fight racism at all levels.

Notes

1. George Sarton, *A History of Science* (Cambridge: Harvard, 1959), p. ix.
2. Morris Kline, *Mathematics in Western Culture* (New York: 1953), pp. 9-10.
3. David E. Smith, *History of Mathematics* vol. 1 (New York: Dover, 1951), p. 93.
4. W. E. B. Du Bois, *The World and Africa* (New York: Viking, 1947), p. 99.
5. Geraldine Harris, *Gods and Pharaohs from Egyptian Mythology* (Vancouver: Schocken, 1983).
6. Tillie S. Pine and Joseph Levine, *The Egyptians Knew* (New York: McGraw-Hill, 1964).
7. Wilbur Cross, *Enchantment of the World—Egypt* (Chicago: Children's Press, 1982), p. 109.
8. Anne Millard, *Egypt—The Young Archaeologist* (New York: Putnam's Sons, 1971), p. 86.
9. Bruce Williams, "The Lost Pharaohs of Nubia" *Nile Valley Civilizations*, ed., Ivan Van Sertima (New Brunswick: Journal of African Civilizations, 1985), pp. 29-46.
10. T. G. H. James, *Archaeology of Ancient Egypt* (New York: Walck, 1972), p. 24.
11. Elizabeth Payne, *Pharaohs of Ancient Egypt* (New York: Random House, 1964), p. 44.
12. Arensa Sondergaard, *My First Geography of the Suez Canal*, (Boston: Little Brown, 1960), pp. 29-30.
13. Harris, *Gods and Pharaohs from Egyptian Mythology*, pp. 16-17.
14. Robert Silverberg, *Before the Sphinx* (New York: Thomas Nelson, 1971), p. 67.
15. Payne, *Pharaohs of Ancient Egypt*, p. 25.
16. Ruth Warren, *The Nile* (New York: McGraw Hill, 1968), p. 21.
17. Carl Boyer, *A History of Mathematics* (New York: Wiley, 1968), p. 23.
18. Robert Silverberg, *Before the Sphinx—Early Egypt*, p. 20.
19. Charles A. Robinson, *Ancient Egypt, a First Book*, revised by Lorna Greenberg (New York: Franklin Watts, 1984), pp. 18, 21.
20. Ruth F. Jones, *Boy of the Pyramids* (New York: Random House, 1950); Enid L. Meadowcroft, *Scarab for Luck* (New York: Crowell, 1964).
21. Robert E. Alter, *Treasure of Tenakertom* (New York: Putnam, 1964); Erick Berry, *Honey of the Nile* (New York: Oxford, 1938).
22. Rosemary Harris, *Bright and Morning Star* (New York: Macmillan, 1972).
23. Alice W. Howard, *The Princess Runs Away* (New York: Macmillan, 1934).
24. Zilpha K. Snyder, *The Egypt Game* (New York: Atheneum, 1965).
25. Beatrice Lumpkin, *Young Genius in Old Egypt* (Chicago: DuSable, 1979); *Senefer and Hatshepsut* (Chicago: Du Sable, 1983).

BOOKS SURVEYED BUT NOT CITED IN NOTES ABOVE

Nonfiction

Cottrell, Leonard. *The Secrets of Tutankhamen's Tomb* (Greenwich, Conn.: New York Graphic Society, 1964).

Fenton, H. Sophia. *Ancient Egypt—Book to Begin On* (New York: Holt, Reinhart and Winston, 1971).

Haag, Michael van. *Egypt, the Land and the People* (London: Silver Burdett, 1975-77).

Halliburton, Richard. *Second Book of Marvels—The Orient* (New York, Bobbs Merrill, 1938).

Hawkes, Jacquetta. *Pharaohs of Egypt* (New York: Harper & Row, 1965).

Henderson, Larry. *Egypt and the Sudan* (New York: Thomas Nelson, 1971).

Macauley, David. *Pyramid* (Boston: Houghton Mifflin, 1975).

Stuart, Dorothy M. *The Boy Through the Ages* (Edinburgh: Doran, 1927), pp. 31-53.

Swineburne, Irene and Laurence Swinburne. *Behind the Sealed Door* (New York: Snifen Court 1977).

Taylor, Alice. *Egypt* (New York: Holiday House, 1953).

Wallace, John A. *Getting to Know Egypt* (New York: Coward McCann, 1961).

White, Anne T. *Lost Worlds* (New York: Random House, 1941), pp. 93-165.

Fiction

McGraw, Eloise J. *Mara, Daughter of the Nile* (New York: Coward McCann, 1953).

GLOSSARY

Compiled by Runoko Rashidi
With the Collaboration of Regina L. Blackburn

Ba: One of several Kemetic words for various aspects of the personality, often translated as 'soul.'

Bas-relief: A carving or sculpture that projects slightly from the background on which it is carved.

Book of the Dead: A collection of Kemetic religious texts mostly written on papyrus and placed with the mummy in a burial, attested from the new Kingdom to the Graeco-Roman Period. The Kemetic *Book of the Dead*, also known as the *Book of Coming Forth by Day*, preserves the early religious traditions documented in the *Pyramid Texts* and *Coffin Texts*.

Cartouche/Shenu: An oblong figure containing the name of a Kemetic monarch.

Cataract: The stretch of powerful rapids interrupting the flow of the river Nile, caused by areas of granite interspersed in the Nubian sandstone belt. There are six numbered and several minor cataracts between Aswan and Khartoum.

Cenotaph: A symbolic tomb additional to the owner's actual burial place.

Coffin Texts: The prominent Kemetic religious texts written inside Kemetic coffins beginning about 2100 B.C.E.

Colossus: An enormous statue, usually of a king and typically set up outside a temple.

Crook: A major Kemetic symbol denoting royal or divine authority.

Demotic: A Kemetic script generally used on business documents from about 700 B.C.E.

Dynasty: A line of rulers belonging to the same family; also the period during which a certain family reigns.

Early Dynastic Period: The major phase in Kemetic history encompassing Dynasties I and II. The Early Dynastic Period is also known as the Archaic Period.

First Intermediate Period: The obscure phase in Kemetic history encompassing Dynasties VII through X.

Flail: A major Kemetic symbol denoting royal or divine authority.

Heb Sed: An ancient Kemetic festival connected with both physical and spiritual rejuvenation and renewal.

Hieratic: A cursive Kemetic script derived from hieroglyphs.

Hieroglyphs: 'Sacred Signs'; the name associated by the early Greeks with the ancient Kemetic system of 'picture writing.'

Hyksos: Translated both as 'Shepherd Kings' and 'Rulers of Foreign Lands,' the Hyksos were the Asiatic invaders of Africa who occupied Kmt and formed Dynasties XV and XVI.

Ka: The individual essence, life force or personality.

Maat: Truth, justice, order and righteousness.

Mastaba: An Arabic word meaning 'bench,' because of its shape. Applied to early Kemetic brick or stone tombs.

Megalithic: Constructed of large stones.

Middle Kingdom: The major phase of Kemetic history encompassing Dynasties XI through XIII. The Middle Kingdom is also known as the Feudal Age.

Monolith: A single gigantic stone or similarly huge object, often in the form of an obelisk or column.

Mortuary Temple: A temple dedicated to the worship of a deceased monarch.

Necropolis: A Greek term for a cemetery marked by its size and importance.

Neter: The personification of a divine principle.

New Kingdom: the major phase of Kemetic history encompassing Dynasties XVIII through XX. The New Kingdom is also known as the Age of Empire.

Nilometor: An instrument used for measuring the height of the river Nile.

Nomarch: The chief official of a Kemetic nome.

Nome: A major administrative district of Kmt. There were 42 Kemetic nomes.

Obelisk: A monolithic tapering shaft, usually of granite,with a pyramidion on top; a solar symbol.

Old Kingdom: The major phase of Kemetic history encompassing Dynasties III through VI. The Old Kingdom is also known as the Pyramid Age.

Papyrus: A plant once grown prolifically in Kmt's Eastern Delta. From an exceptionally early period papyrus became the major Kemetic writing material. Papyrus was also extensively used in the manufacture of boats, ropes, sandals, baskets, etc.

Peristyle court: A monumental court supported by massive rows of columns with an open space in the center.

Pharaonic: Pertaining to or resembling the pharaohs or kings of ancient Kmt.

Pyramidion: The decorated capstone of a pyramid or obelisk.

Pyramid Texts: Early Kemetic religious texts inscribed on the walls of pyramids from the end of Dynasty V to Dynasty VIII.

The Rosetta Stone: A bilingual decree of Ptolemy IV inscribed in 196 B.C.E. and translated by Jean Francois Champollion in 1822.

Sarcophagus: An ornate stone coffin.

Sea Peoples: The Indo-European invaders of Kmt in Dynasties IXX and XX.

Second Intermediate Period: The obscure phase in Kemetic history encompassing Kemetic Dynasties XIV through XVII.

Serekh: Image of a brick facade to a palace or enclosure with a rectangular space above.

Stela: A stone column or upright slab decorated with carvings or inscriptions.

The Two Lands: The union of Upper Kmt (South) and Lower Kmt (North).

Third Intermediate Period: The obscure phase in Kemetic history encompassing Dynasties XXI through XXIV.

Uraeus: The most characteristic Kemetic symbol of royalty or divinity. A Uraeus usually took the form of a rearing cobra and a vulture, and was worn on the monarch's forehead or crown.

Vizier: The highest official in the Kemetic administration.

Wadi: An Arabic word meaning dried-up river-bed.

BIOGRAPHICAL NOTES ON CONTRIBUTORS

BLACKBURN, Regina L.

Dr. Regina L. Blackburn is an educator and writer. During the past ten years she has taught at several major colleges and universities, including Scripp's College in Pomona, California; California State University at Northridge; California State University at Long Beach; and Lemoyne-Owen College in Memphis, Tennessee. In 1987 she completed an extended research and educational tour of Kmt (Egypt).

She has written a series of biographies entitled *Outstanding African Women: Ancient and Modern*, and was a significant contributor to *The Black Seeds of World Civilizations: Researches and Essays*, edited by Runoko Rashidi and scheduled for publication in 1989. She is currently working on a contemporary novel focusing on the ongoing struggles of African-American women.

BRUNSON, James E.

Art Historian James E. Brunson is employed at Northern Illinois University in DeKalb, Illinois. He has taught part-time in the N.I.U. Art Department, and received his Master of Fine Arts Degree in Painting and Drawing from the same institution. He has exhibited his work throughout the Midwest and Southern United States. He recently completed a lithographic series on the African presence in Egyptian mythology (Osiris, Isis, Horus). He is currently completing documentation for an educational course on the Black image in World Art, and was a major contributor to *The Black Seeds of World Civilizations: Researches and Essays*, edited by Runoko Rashidi, and scheduled for publication in 1989.

In 1985 Brunson wrote and published *Black Jade: The African Presence in the Ancient East and Other Essays*. Now in its second printing, *Black Jade* is the first comprehensive work to focus on the African presence in Chinese and Southeast Asian antiquity. For information write to: James E. Brunson, Grant Towers North #202 C, Dekalb, IL 60115.

CHANDLER, Wayne B.

Wayne B. Chandler is an Anthrophotojournalist and Co-Chairman of What's

A Face Inc. He has done extensive research into the origins of race and ancient civilizations and is co-producer and writer of A People's History To Date-4000 B.C. to 1985 and 365 Days of Black History, parts I and II. Through the photo archives of What's A Face Inc. Mr. Chandler and his associate Mr. Gaynell Catherine have been instrumental in unearthing key photographs relating to the African presence in the Olmec civilization, as well as the civilizations of ancient India, Southeast Asia, Egypt, and China. He is a committee member of the Historian Roundtable and has lectured in various locations in the U.S. He was visiting lecturer at the University of D.C. from 1978-1983 and instructor at the prestigious Ananda Institute from 1982-1986. In 1984 he helped implement the program Genius Transformation which proved that when under-privileged children are exposed to proper historical information, along with diet and exercise, their psychological perspectives undergo a radical change for the better. From 1987 through 1989, he is working with archaeologist Dr. Edward Otter on various excavations of pre-historic Indian sites in the southeast and midwest. He has been involved with the Journal of African Civilizations since 1985 and his contributions include "Jewel in the Lotus: The Ethiopian Presence in the Indus Valley Civilization" (1985); "The Moors: Light of Europe's Dark Age" (1986); "Trait-Influences in Meso-America: the African-Asian connection" (1987); "Hannibal: Nemesis of Rome" (1988); and "Of Gods and Men: Egypt's Old Kingdom" (1989). Current project is a collaboration with Creative Fox Associates in the production of "Strangers in Their Own Land", a five part documentary involving Drs. Van Sertima, Runoko Rashidi, Asa Hillard III, and Alexander Von Wuthenau. Any comments regarding chapters published or unpublished are gladly welcome. He may be reached at P.O. Box 928, Adelphi, Maryland 20783.

CLEGG II, Legrand

Legrand Clegg II is a member of the Board of Trustees at Compton Community College in Compton, California. He is also Chief Deputy City Attorney for the City of Compton. He has engaged in research on black history and culture since 1963 and his work has appeared in a number of national journals and magazines since 1969. He has lectured on university campuses across the U.S. and has co-produced a filmstrip entitled "The Black Roots of Civilization."

CLEMENT, Elizabeth

Certified interpreter, translator and teacher of French in the Atlanta area.

D'ALMEIDA, Irene

Irene d'Almeida was born in Senegal and raised in Benin. She is a doctoral candidate at Emory University in Atlanta. Her field study is Comparative Literature, with an emphasis on African literary criticism. She is presently Assistant Professor of French at the University of North Florida in Jacksonville. She translated Chinua Achebe's *Arrow of God* into French.

DAVIDSON, Basil

Basil Davidson is a noted anti-imperialist scholar and writer who has vigorously campaigned for African liberation for many years. His works on African history include: *The Lost Cities of Africa; Africa in History: Themes and Outlines; A History of East and Central Africa to the Late Nineteenth Century;* and *A History of West Africa to the Nineteenth Century*. Among his more recent books are *Africa in Modern History* (London, Allen Lane, 1978) and *No Fist is Big Enough to Hide the Sky: The Liberation of Guine and Cape Verde* (London, Ze, 1981).

Basil Davidson is an active and significant contributor to numerous journals and periodicals in both England and America.

DIOP, Chiekh Anta

Cheikh Anta Diop was born in Diourbel, Senegal on December 29, 1923. He died in his sleep in Dakar on February 7, 1986. At age 23, he went to Paris to continue advanced studies in physics. Within a very short time, however, he was drawn deeper and deeper into studies of the origin of civilization in Africa. Becoming increasingly active in the African student movements agitating for independence of French colonial possessions, he became convinced that only by re-evaluating and restoring Africa's place in the history of the world could the physical and mental shackles of colonialism be lifted from Africa. His first doctoral dissertation submitted at the University of Paris in 1951—based on the premise that Egypt was a Black African civilization—was rejected. This dissertation was published nevertheless under the title *Nations Negres et Culture* in 1955 and won him wide acclaim. Two additional attempts to have his doctorate granted were turned back until 1960 when he entered his defense session with an array of sociologists, anthropologists, and historians and successfully carried his argument. After nearly a decade, Diop had his 'Docteur es Lettres.' In that same year were published his *L'Unite Culturelle d'Afrique Noire (The Culture Unity of Black Africa)* and *L'Afrique Noire Pre-Coloniale (Precolonial Black Africa)*.

During his student days, Diop was an avid political activist. From 1950 to 1953, he was the Secretary-General of the Rassemblement Democratique Africain (RDA) and helped launch the first Pan-African Student Congress in Paris in 1951. He also participated in the 1st World Congress of Black Writers and Artists held in Paris in 1956 and the 2nd such congress held in Rome in 1959.

Upon returning to Senegal in 1960, Dr. Diop continued his research. In 1966, the 1st World Black Festival of Arts and Culture held in Dakar, Senegal honored Dr. Diop and Dr. W.E.B. DuBois as the scholars who exerted the greatest influence on Negro thought in the 20th century. In 1974, a breakthrough occurred in the English-speaking world when *The African Origin of Civilization*, a translation and compilation of the first 10 chapters of *Nations Negres* . . . and three chapters from *Anteriorite des Civilizations Noires*, was published. Subsequently, Dr. Diop published two additional books still in French, including his last, *Civilization ou Barbarie (Civilization or Barbarism)*.

Dr. Diop was Director of the Radiocarbon laboratory at the Fundamental Institute of Black Africa (IFAN) at the University of Dakar. He sat on numerous international scientific committees and achieved recognition as one of the leading historians, Egyptologists, linguists, and anthropologists in the world. He travelled incessantly, lectured widely, and was cited and quoted voluminously. He was the 'pharoah' of African studies. The book *Great African Thinkers* (1986) edited by Ivan Van Sertima and Larry Williams, is based on his life and work.

FINCH, Charles S.

Charles S. Finch, M.D. is a board-certified family physician who is currently Assistant Professor of Community Medicine and Family Practice at the Morehouse School of Medicine. Dr. Finch completed his undergraduate training at Yale College, his medical training at Jefferson Medical College, and his Family Medicine Residency at the University of California, Irvine Medical Center. He has worked as an epidemiologist for the Center for Disease Control and was formerly a clinical preceptor at the Duke-Watts Family Medicine Clinic in Durham, North Carolina. He was the founder and chairman of the Raleigh Afro-American Life Focus Project between 1981 and 1982 and is a co-founder and Co-Convener of Bennu, Inc. of Atlanta. He is currently the Associate Editor of the *Journal of African Civilizations* and author of "The African Background of Medical Science." "The Works of Gerald Massey: Studies in Kamite Origins," and—with Mr. Larry Williams of Bennu, Inc.—the co-author of "The Great Queens of Ethiopia," all published in the *Journal of African Civilizations*. In addition Dr. Finch has visited Senegal, West Africa where he has begun studies on the empirical basis of traditional West African medicine. On his most recent visit, he interviewed Dr. Cheikh Anta Diop.

GOLDMAN, Phaon (Tarharka)

Phaon Goldman is a former Professor of African and Afro-American Studies. He has travelled extensively in Africa, Europe and the Far East and attended graduate school at Howard University and The American University. As part of his required studies he made a widely-heralded content analysis of speeches and articles by Marcus Garvey, leader of the largest black national organization ever to exist in America, and by the Honorable Elijah Muhammad, patriarch of the Nation of Islam or the Black Muslims. The aim of this treatise was to highlight the organizational parallels and tactics of these two mass-based, highly successful, urban black movements. Because of his reputation as a writer and as a scholar of African as well as Afro-American history, the late Dr. William Leo Hansberry employed him as a research assistant while preparing several proposed volumes on African history.

Mr. Goldman has contributed articles on a regular basis to *The Afro-American Newspapers, The Pittsburgh Courier, Muhammad Speaks* and Johnson Publications. His articles have also appeared in the *Negro History Bulletin* and *Black Scholar*. After completing the U.S.Department of Archive's Institute for Genealogical Research, Mr. Goldman developed and successfully marketed the *Family History Starter Kit* to aid Americans trace their families' histories. He has written under the pen names of "Sundiata" and "Tarharka" as an expression of his African heritage.

HILLIARD, Asa G., III

Asa G. Hilliard is the Fuller E. Calloway Professor of Urban Education at Georgia State University, Atlanta, Georgia. He holds a joint appointment in the Department of Educational Foundations and the Department of Counseling and Psychological Services. Dr. Hilliard served previously as a department chairman and as dean of the School of Education at San Francisco State University. He is a graduate of the University of Denver with a bachelor's degree in psychology, a masters in counseling and guidance and a doctor of education degree in educational psychology. He has had experience as a teacher, administrator, researcher and lecturer throughout the United States and in several foreign countries, including a six-year period of professional service in Liberia, West Africa.

KARENGA, Maulana

Dr. Maulana Karenga is currently a visiting lecturer in Ethnic Studies at the University of California, Riverside, He also is the executive Director of the Institute of Pan-African Studies and the African American Cultural Center, Los Angeles, and national chairman of Us Organization, a cultural and social change organization. Moreover, he is initiating co-founder and board member of the Association for the Study of Classical African Civilizations (ASCAC); and board member of the National Council of Black Studies (NCBS) and African Heritage Studies Association (AHSA). Dr. Karenga is the creator of Kwanzaa and the

Nguzo Saba. He has also authored numerous scholarly articles and books. His latest works include: *Introduction to Black Studies, Selections From The Husia: Sacred Wisdom of Ancient Egypt, The African American Holiday of Kwanzaa: A Celebration of Family, Community and Culture,* and *The Book of Coming Forth By Day: The Ethics of the Declarations of Innocence.*

LUMPKIN, Beatrice

An associate professor of mathematics at Malcolm X College in Chicago, Professor Lumpkin has written on the Afro-Asian foundations of mathematics for *Freedomways*, the *Mathematics Teacher, Science and Society* and *Historia Mathematica*. She has also written two major articles for the *Journal of African Civilizations*—"The Pyramids—Ancient Showcase of Science and Technology" and "Africa in the Mainstream of Science and Technology" She is author of a children's book, *Young Genius in Old Egypt*.

OBENGA, Theophile

Theophile Obenga was born in Congo, Equatorial Africa. He was educated in Belgium, France and the United States. He is considered as one of the foremost students and followers of the late Cheikh Anta Diop. In the preface to Obenga's most renowned book *Africa in Antiquity*, Diop introduced him as follows: "Obenga is a polyvalent scholar with a threefold training as a philosopher, historian and linguist and knowing Greek, Latin, French, English, Italian, and practicing Arabic and Syriac. More importantly, he is the first Black African of his generation able to read the pharaonic language in the texts: he holds a degree in Egyptology and is a member of the *Societe Francaise d'Egyptologie*". During the UNESCO Colloquium on "The Peopling of Ancient Egypt and the Decipherment of Meroitic Writing" held in Cairo (January 28-February 3, 1974), Diop and Obenga's brilliant and eloquent demonstration on the African essence of Black pharaonic Egypt's culture and civilization was a major landmark in African studies and sanctioned the death of cultural imperialism's long lasting attempt to whiten ancient Egypt. Under Marien NGouabi's government in the Congo, Obenga was Director of the *Ecole Normale Superieure* where he created an outstanding method for teaching African historiography and later became Minister for Foreign Affairs. He is presently Director General of the International Center for Bantu Studies, the only high-tech African-oriented data base and cultural center of its kind focussing on the Egypto-Bantu world and headquartered in Libreville, Gabon. Obenga is the author of a massive scientific production partly published by *Presence Africaine* and including, in particular, *Precolonial Central Africa, Zaire: Traditional Civilizations and Modern Culture, Stele for the Future* (poetry), *For A New History, Traditional Literature of the MBochi*, and *The Bantu: Languages, Peoples and Civilizations.* He just completed a major study on *The African Philosophy in Pharaonic Times, 2780-330 Before the Christian Era*, excerpts from which are published for the first time in English in this issue.

PATTEN-VAN SERTIMA, Jacqueline

Jacqueline Patten-Van Sertima is photographic consultant, art director and cover designer for the *Journal of African Civilizations.* Mrs. Van Sertima has also recently established the Journal's new audio arm, Legacies, Inc. As director, she produces companion audio cassettes to each volume of the *Journal of African Civilizations* as well as of various presentations made by Dr. Van Sertima and colleagues.

As a photographer, Mrs. Van Sertima has won international distinction for her hand-painted photography and its significant contribution to social awareness. Listed in the Cambridge *World Who's Who of Women* for "distinguished achievement," their *International Register of Profiles* and their *International Who's Who of Intellectuals*, she is given equal acclaim in the United States in *Who's Who in America* and *Personalities of America* for "oustanding artistic achievement and contributions to society." Mrs. Van Sertima received her B.S. degree in Psychology/Sociology and M.S. in Education from Hunter College, New York.

RASHIDI, Runoko

Runoko Rashidi is a cultural historian with a special interest in the Black foundations of world civilizations. He has actively researched the Black presence in Asia, particularly India. From 1981 to 1984 he was African History Research Specialist at Compton Community College in Compton, California. Among the major programs he developed and coordinated during this period were: The African's People's Conference, An Evening for *The Journal of African Civilizations*, The Black Presence in Early America, The Black Presence in Early Europe and The Significance of the Pyramid in Black History. From 1985 to 1987 Rashidi served as History Editor for the National Black Computer Network, based in Los Angeles, California.

Rashidi was a founding member of Amenta in 1979, the Southern Cradle Research Organization in 1980, the Egyptian Civilization Monitoring Committee in 1984 and the Africans/Ali Mazuri Monitoring Committee in 1985. His written works have appeared in *Afro-Am, The Challenger, Dalit Voice, Habari Gani?, Return to the Source, Royal Afreeka Society, The U.C.L.A. African Studies Center Quarterly Magazine, UFAHAMU, Works Magazine* and *ZAMANI!* Rashidi has been a major contributor to *The Journal of African Civilizations.* His

J.A.C. articles include: "The African Presence in Sumer and Elam" in 1982; "African Goddesses: Mothers of Civilizations" in 1983; "The Nile Valley Presence in Asian Antiquity" in 1984; "The African Presence in Early Asian Civilizations" in 1985; "Ancient and Modern Britons" in 1986; "Dr. Diop on Asia: Highlights and Insights" in 1986 (noted and reviewed in *Presence Africaine*, 2nd Qtr. 1987); "Men out of Asia: The Black Presence in Prehistoric America" in 1987; and "Ramses the Great: The Life and Times of a Bold, Black Egyptian King" in 1988. In 1988 Rashidi co-edited with Dr. Ivan Van Sertima *The African Presence in Early Asia*.

In October 1987 Rashidi formally inaugurated the First All-India Dalit Writers Conference in Hyderabad, India, and delivered a major address on "The Global Unity of African People." On October 19, 1987 he made extended presentations before militant Black organizations in the South Indian capital cities of Madras, Tamil Nadu and Bangalore, Karnataka. He is currently working on a major book entitled *The Black Presence in Ancient and Modern India*

Rashidi is the Founder (1987) and National Coordinator of the Africans/Dalits Support Group. For information write to: R. Rashidi, 4140 Buckingham Road Suite D, Los Angeles, CA 90008; or call 213 (293-5807).

SY, Jacques Habib

Jacques Habib Sy was born in Dakar, Senegal. He was educated at the Sorbonne (Paris) and Howard University (Washington, D.C.) and received a training both in communications and history.

He is the author of several publications on African commuunications systems and history. He recently completed a study on the *Contribution of Black Africa to the History of Communications* (forthcoming: New Jersey: Ablex, 1989) and is co-editing a two-volume book on *The Life and Works of Cheikh Anta Diop*.

As a journalist Habib Sy has been involved in communications policies in Africa with the Pan-African News Agency and UNESCO. Member of the National Democratic Union created by Cheikh Anta Diop in 1976, he was one of the leading members of this political party's press apparatus.

Dr. Sy has taught in several universities (Dakar, Howard University, Temple University and Texas Southern University) and is currently Associate Professor in the Department of Communication, Bowie State University.

VAN SERTIMA, Ivan

Ivan Van Sertima was born in Guyana, South America. He was educated at the School of Oriental and African Studies, London University and the Rutgers Graduate School and holds degrees in African Studies, Linguistics and Anthropology.

He is a literary critic, a linguist, and an anthropologist and has made a name in all three fields.

As a literary critic, he is the author of *Caribbean Writers*, a collection of critical essays on the Caribbean novel. He is also the author of several major literary reviews published in Denmark, India, Britain and the United States. He was honored for his work in this field by being asked by the Nobel Committee of the Swedish Academy to nominate candidates for the Nobel Prize in Literature from 1976-1980. He has also been honored, as an historian of world repute, by being appointed by *UNESCO* to the *International Commission for Rewriting the Scientific and Cultural History of Mankind*.

As a linguist, he has published essays on the dialect of the Sea Islands off the Georgia Coast. He is also the compiler of the *Swahili Dictionary of Legal Terms*, based on his field work in Tanzania, East Africa, in 1967.

He is the author of *They Came Before Columbus: The African Presence in Ancient America*, which was published by Random House in 1977 and is now in its eleventh printing. It was published in French in 1981 and in the same year was awarded the Clarence L. Holte Prize, a prize awarded every two years "for a work of excellence in literature and the humanities relating to the cultural heritage of Africa and the African diaspora".

Associate Professor of African Studies at Rutgers University, Van Sertima is also Visiting Professor at Princeton University. He is the Editor of the Journal of African Civilizations which he founded in 1979. Professor Van Sertima has lectured to more than 100 universities in the United States and has also lectured in Canada, the Caribbean, South America and Europe. He appeared before Congress on July 7, 1987 to challenge the Columbus myth.

WILLIAMS, Bruce

Bruce Williams received his Ph.D. in Near East Archaeology from the University of Chicago. Since 1976 he has been responsible for publishing the excavations of the Oriental Institute Nubian Expedition between Abu Simbel and the Sudan frontier, and is presently engaged in preparing the volume on New Kingdom remains. His interests include the archaeological and historical relations of the Second Intermediate Period, the origins of pharaonic culture, and the development of Kushite civilization.

WILLIAMS, Larry

Historian and Research Specialist, Larry Williams is the Chairman of the Bennu Study Group of Atlanta, Georgia. His articles have appeared in *History, The Bible and the Black Man, The Atlanta Voice, Return to the Source, The Journal of African Civilizations*, and *Afrika Must Unite: A Journal of Pan-*

Afrikan Affairs.

In 1986, with Ivan Van Sertima he co-edited *Great African Thinkers (Vol. 1) Cheikh Anta Diop*. With Asa G. Hilliard III and Nia Damali, Williams co-edited *The Teachings of Ptahhotep: The Oldest Book in the World* (1987). Williams was a major contributor to *the Black Seeds of World Civilizations: Researches and Essays*, edited by Runoko Rashidi, and scheduled for publication in 1989.

APPENDIX

KEMETIC (ANCIENT EGYPTIAN) PLACE NAMES

COMPILED BY RUNOKO RASHIDI

Modern name	Graeco-Roman name	Kemetic name
Abu Simbel *		
Abusir	Busiris	Djedu
	Abydos	Aabdju
Akhmim	Panopolis	Khent-Min
Alexandria	Alexandria	
Armant	Hermonthis	Iuny
Aswan	Syene	
Asyut	Lykopolis	Zawty
Beni Hassan *		
Dahshur *		
Denderah	Tentyris	Iunet
Edfu	Apollinopolis Magna	Wetjeset-Hor
El-Amarna		Akhetaten
	Elephantine	Abu
El-Eshmunein	Hermopolis Magna	Khemenu
El-Kab	Eleithiapolis	Nekheb
Fayum Oasis	Moeris	She-resy/Mer-wer
Gebelein	Aphroditopolis	Per-Hathor
Girga	Thinis/This	Tjeny
Giza	Letopolis	Khem
Hawara *		
	Heliopolis	Iunu (On)
Ihnasya el-Medina	Herakleopolis	Henen-nesut
Kom el-Ahmar	Hierakonpolis	Nekhen
Kom Ombo	Ombos	Nebet
Lisht		It-Tawy

Luxor	Thebes	Waset
Meydum *		
Mit Rahina	Memphis	Ineb-hedj
	Philae	Pilak
Qift	Koptos	Gebtu
Qustul		
Rashid	Rosetta	
Sa el-Hagar	Sais	Sau
Sakkara *		
Samannud	Sebennytos	Tjebnutjer
San el-Hagar	Tanis	Dja´net
Tell Basta	Bubastis	Bast
Tell el-Dab´a	Avaris	Pi-Ramessu
Tell el-Fara´un	Buto	Pe
Tell el-Yahudiya	Leontopolis	Nay-ta-hut
Tod	Tuphium	Djerty

*** Major Pyramid or Temple site**

THE KEMETIC NOMES (PROVINCES)

COMPILED BY RUNOKO RASHIDI

Upper Kmt (Southern Egypt)

1. Ta-Seti (The Land of the Bow)
2. The Throne of Horus
3. The Double Plume
4. The Plumed Scepter
5. The Two Falcons
6. The Crocodile
7. The Bat
8. The Great Land
9. Min
10. The Cobra
11. Set
12. The Viper Mountain
13. Upper Tree of the Serpent
14. Lower Tree of the Serpent
15. The Hare
16. The Oryx
17. The Black Dog
18. The Falcon
19. The Double Scepter
20. The Upper Palm Tree
21. The Lower Palm Tree
22. The Flint Knife

Lower Kmt (Northern Egypt)

Anzti
The Black Bull
The Bull Calf
The Dolphin
The Eastern Harpoon
The Hearty Sovereign
The Heseb Bull
The Ibis
The Lower Royal Child
The Mountain
Neit
The Point of the East
Soped
The Thigh
The Upper Royal Child
The Western Harpoon
The White Wall

SOURCES CONSULTED

Butzer, Karl W. Early Hydraulic Civilization in Egypt: A Study in Cultural Ecology. Chicago and London: University of Chicago Press, 1976.

Montet, Pierre. Eternal Egypt. Translated from the French by Doreen Weightman. New York and Toronto: New American Library, 1964.